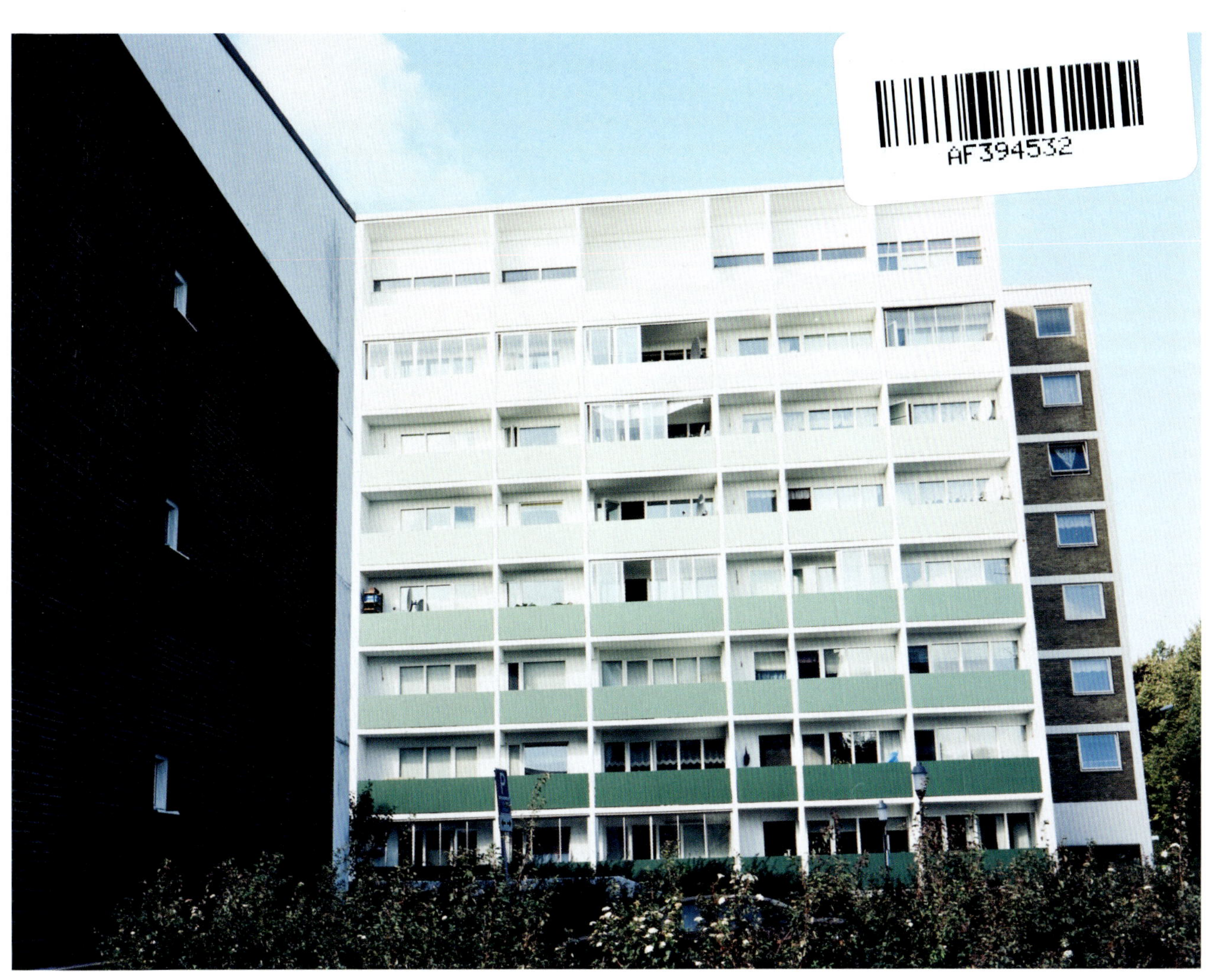

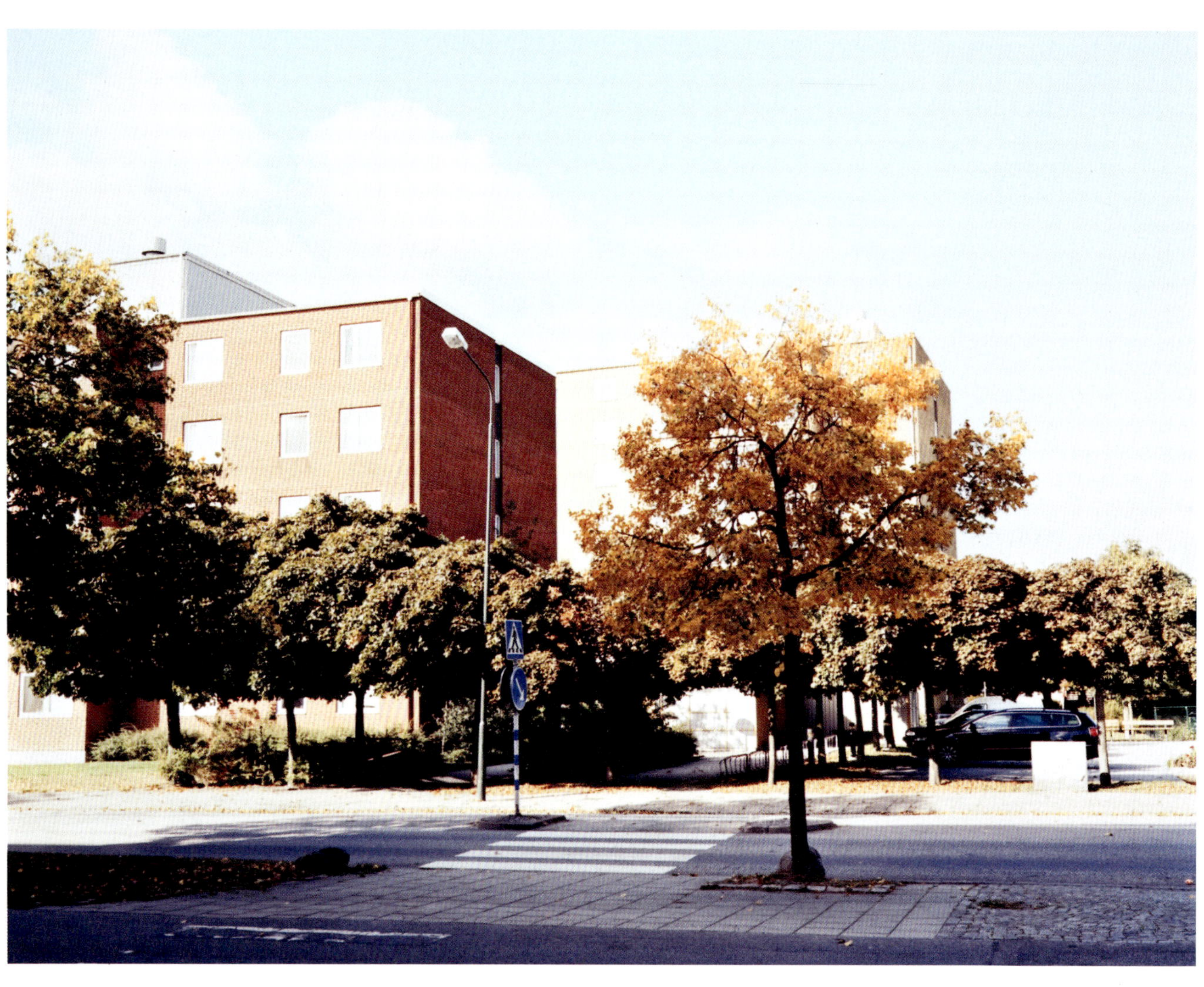

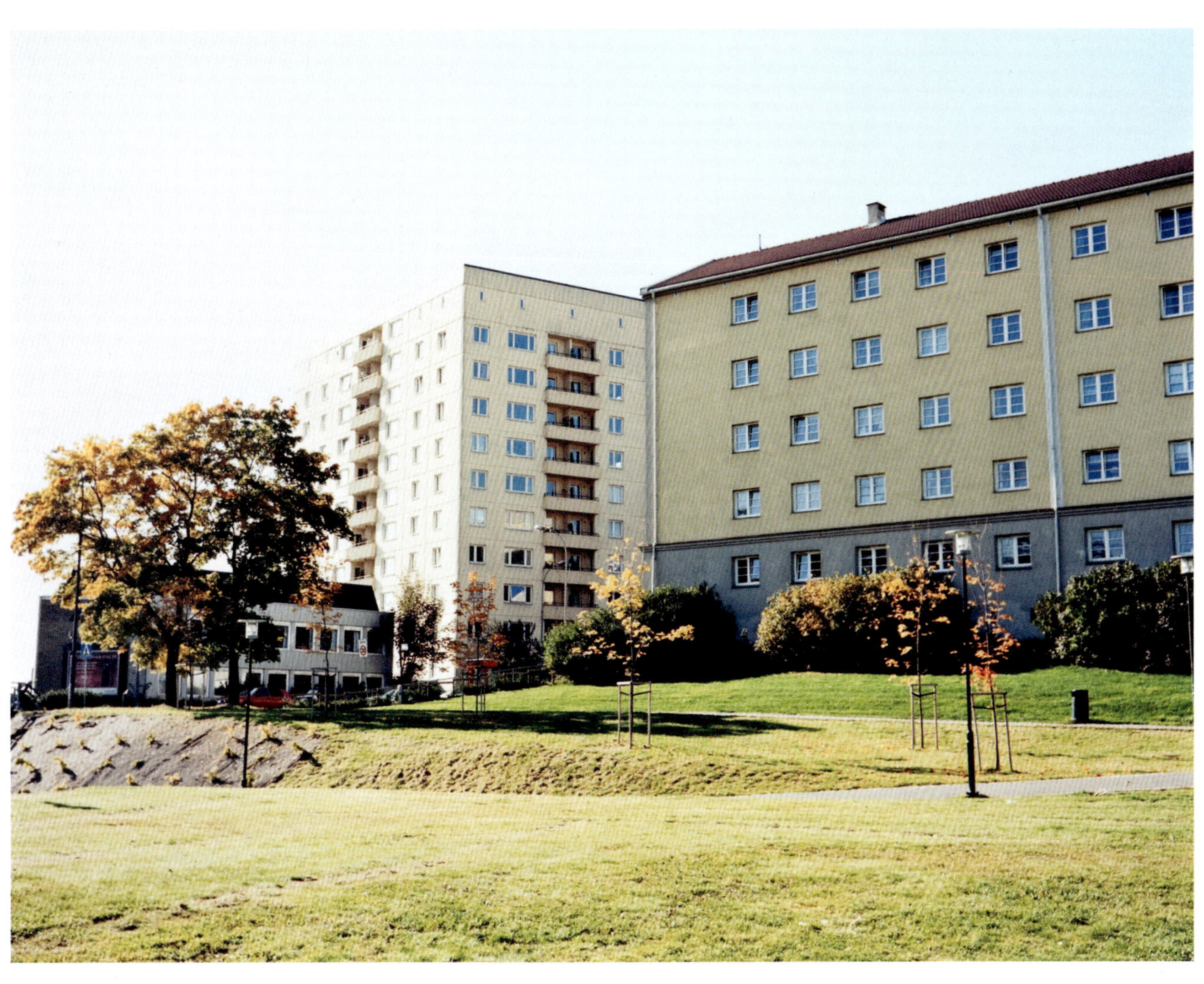

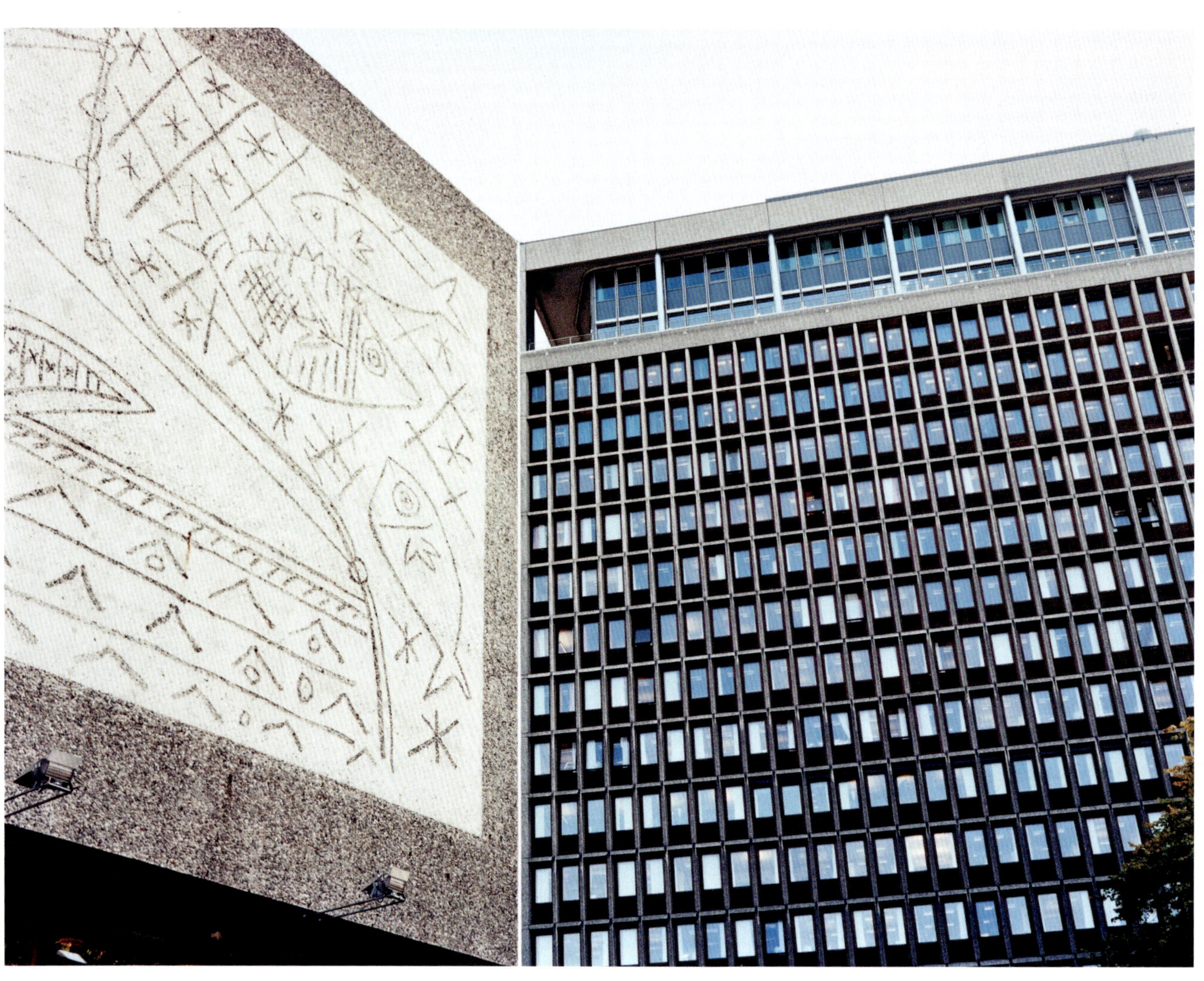

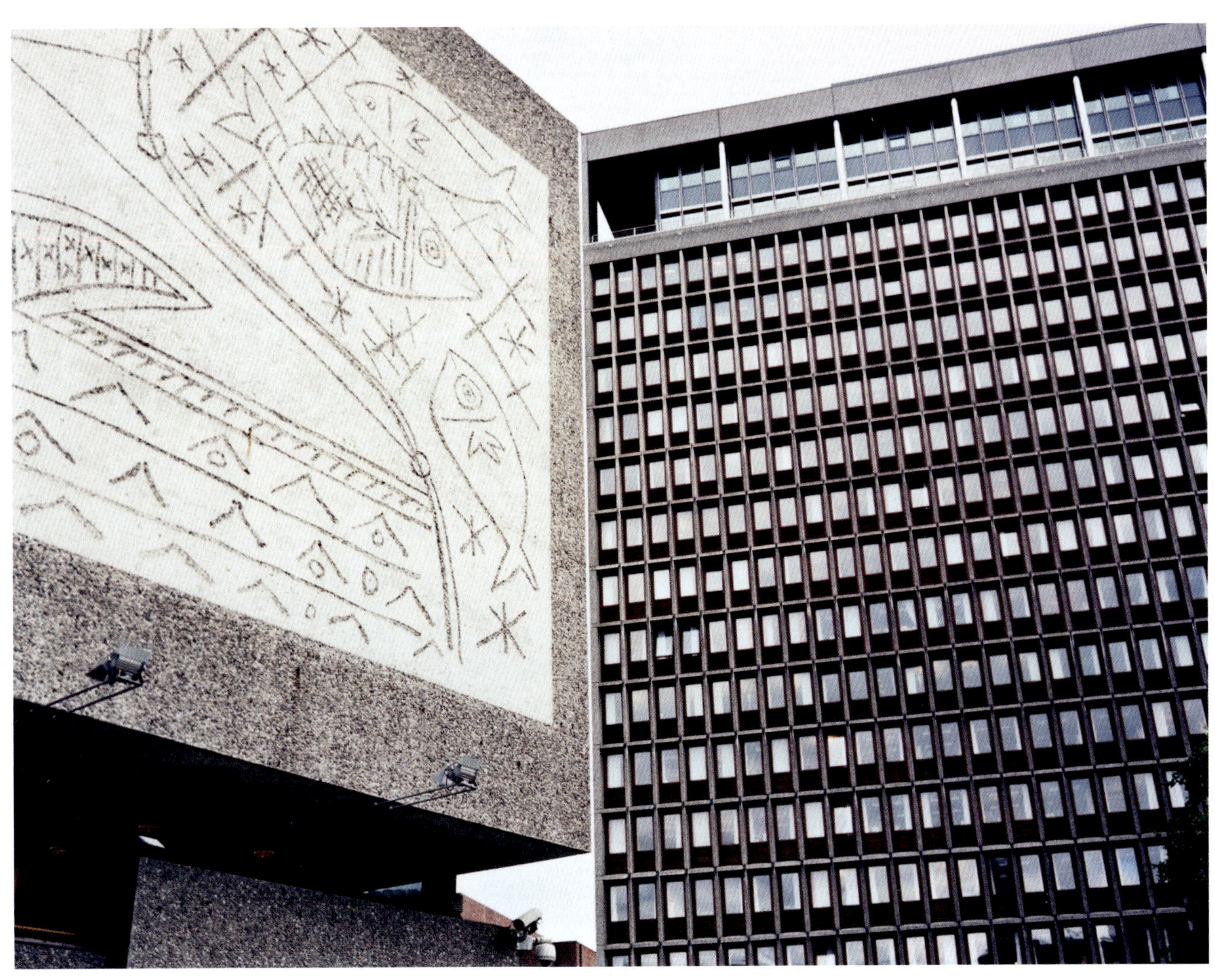

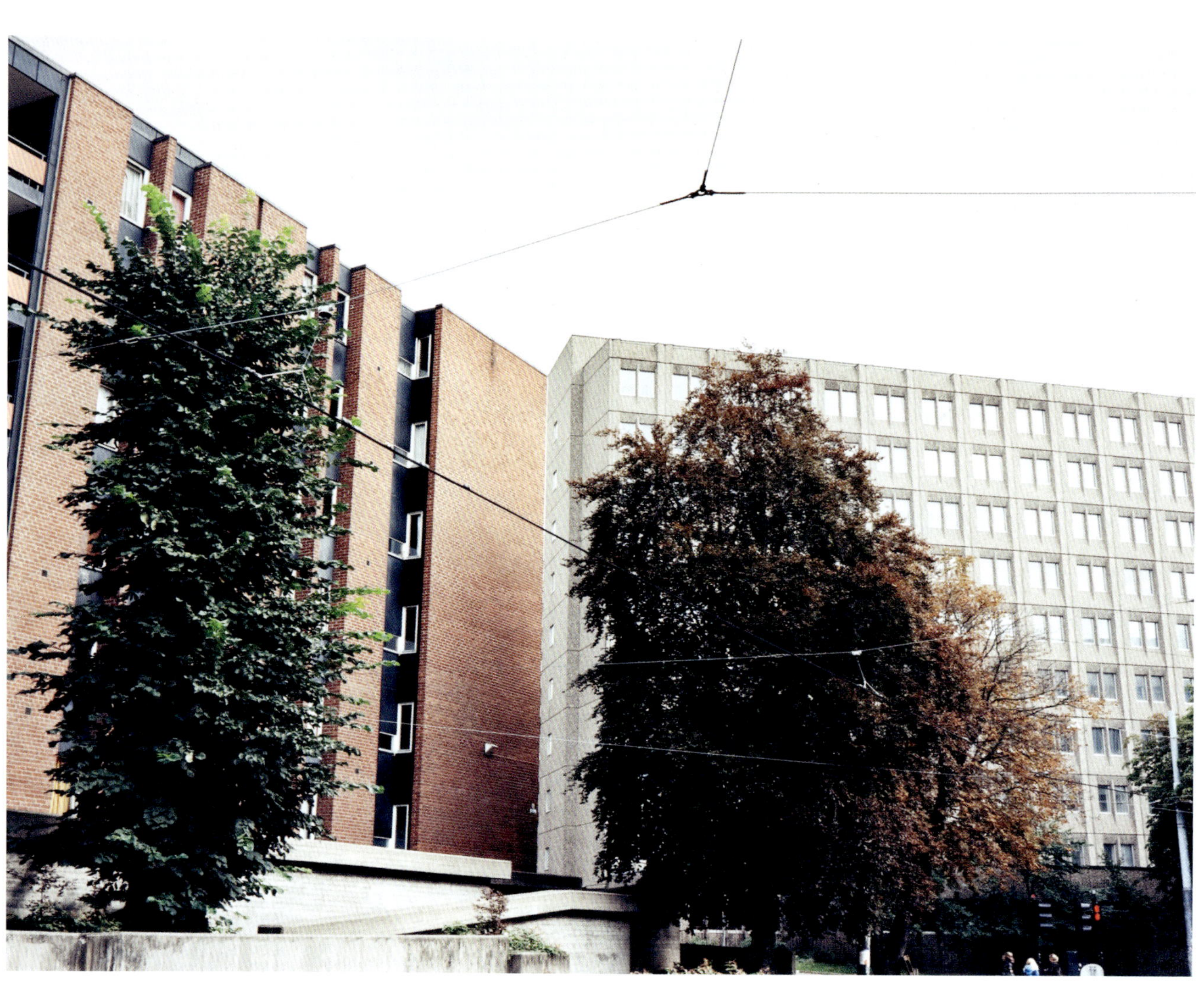

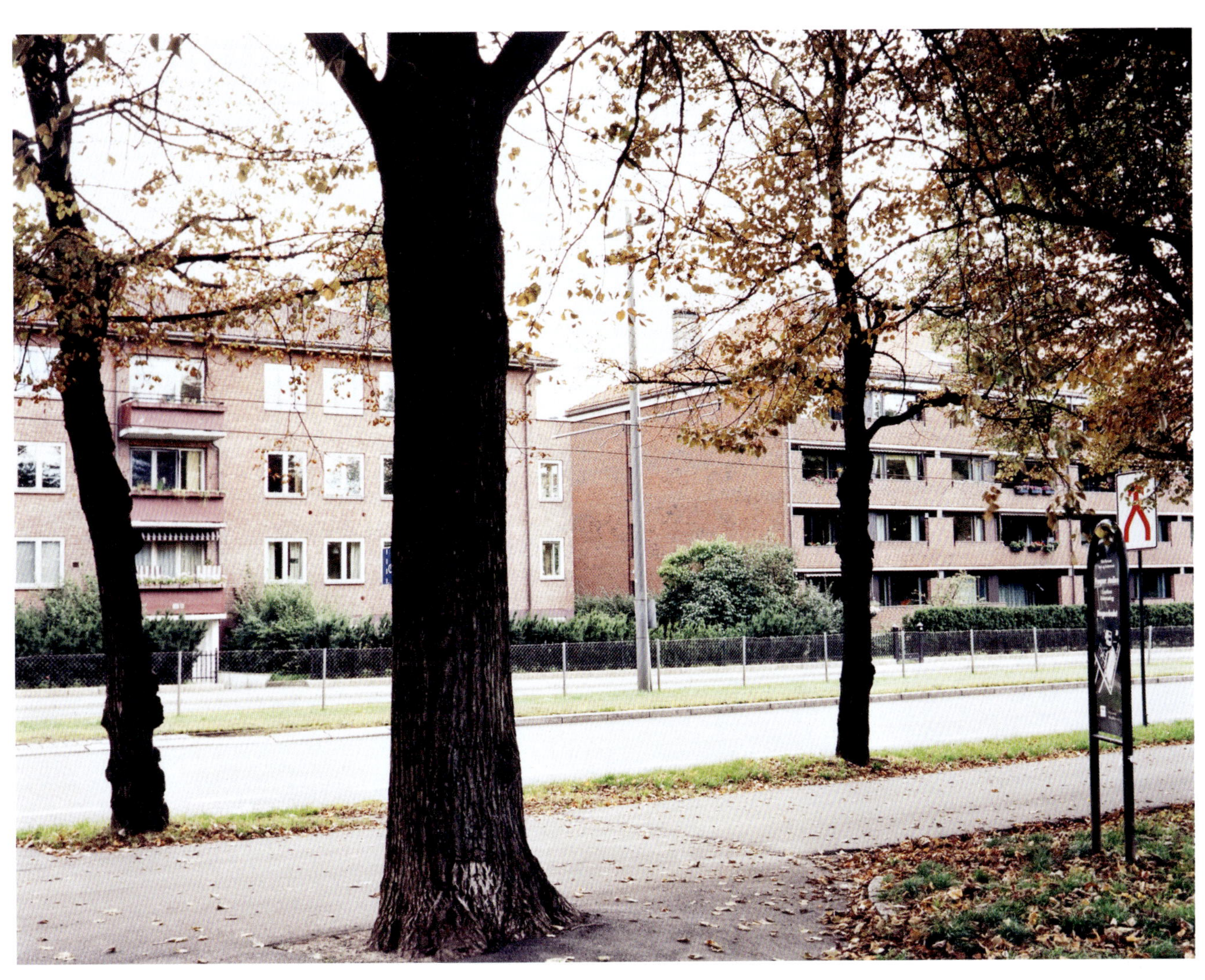

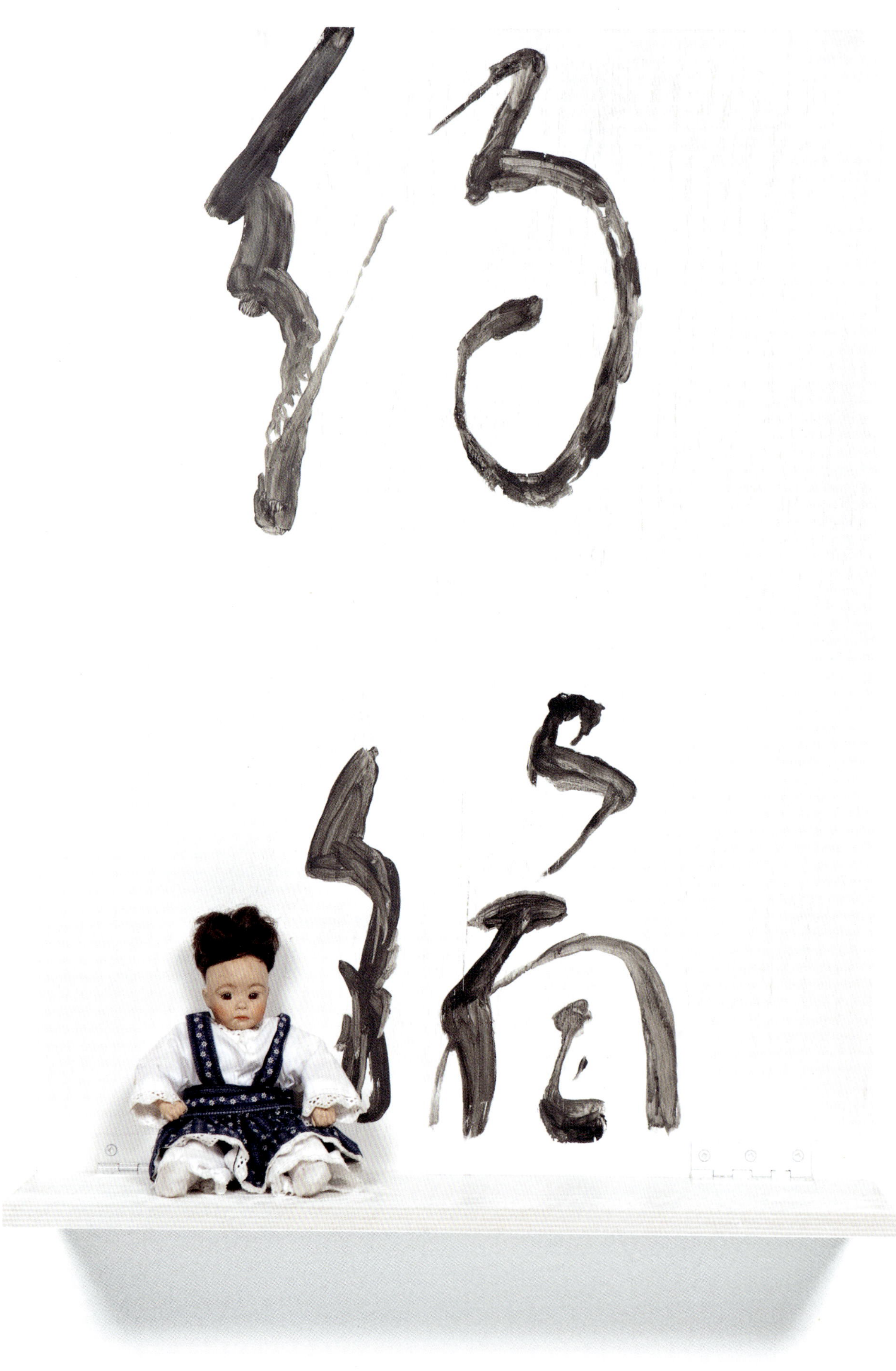

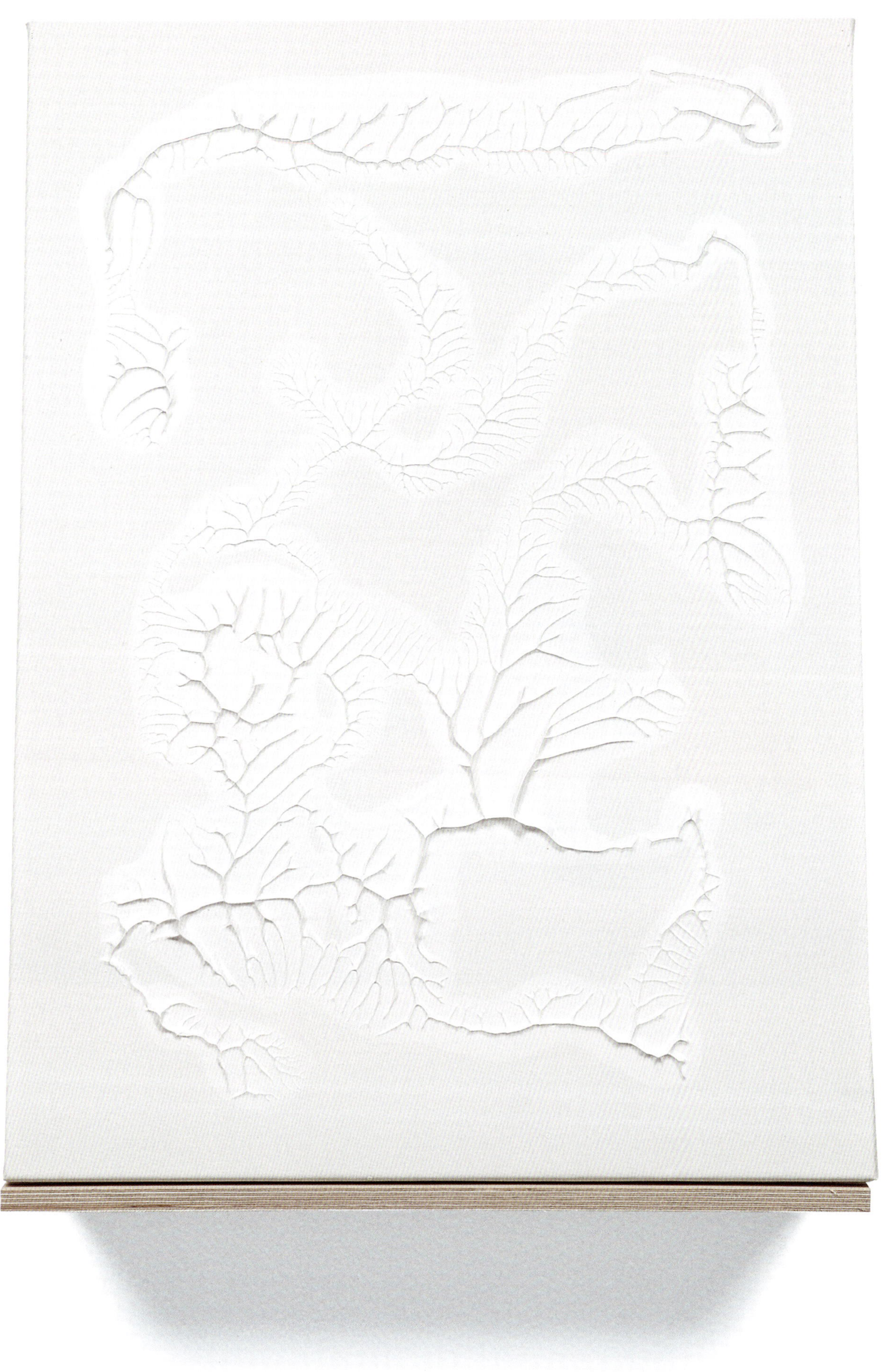

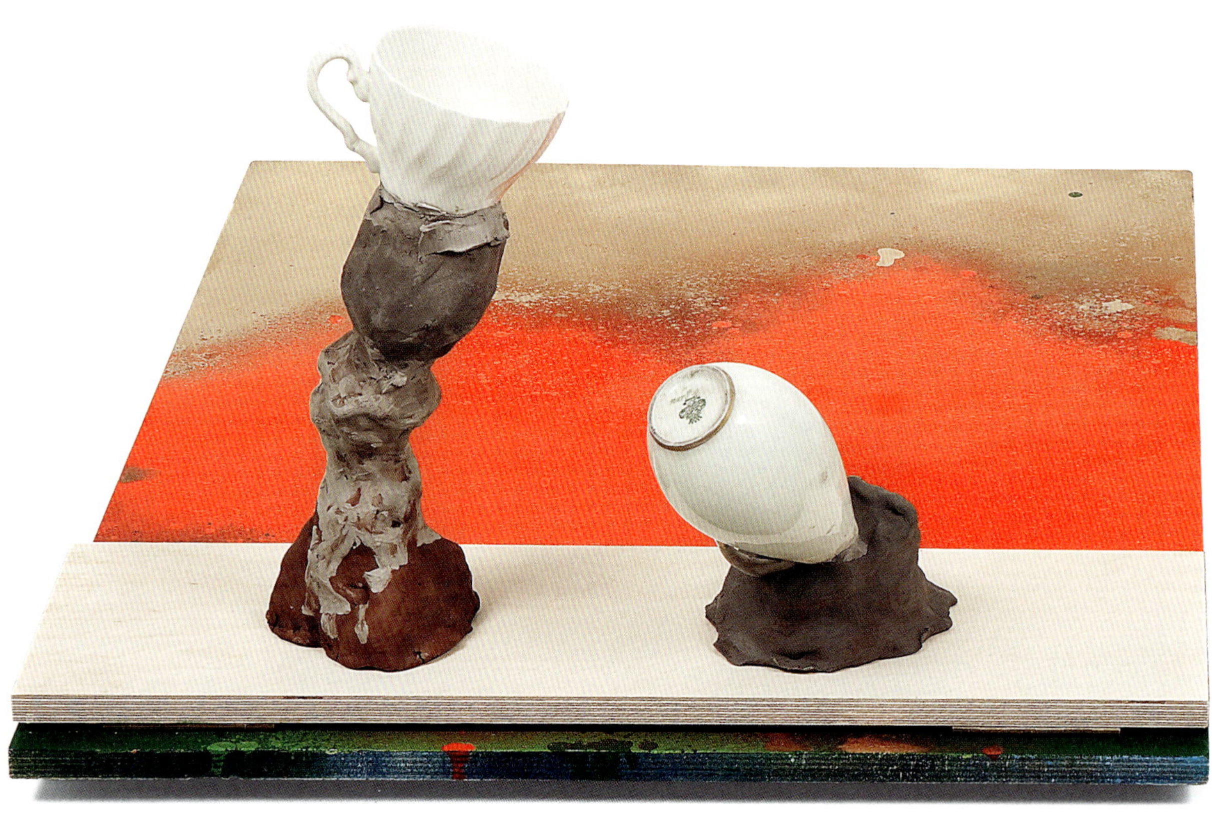

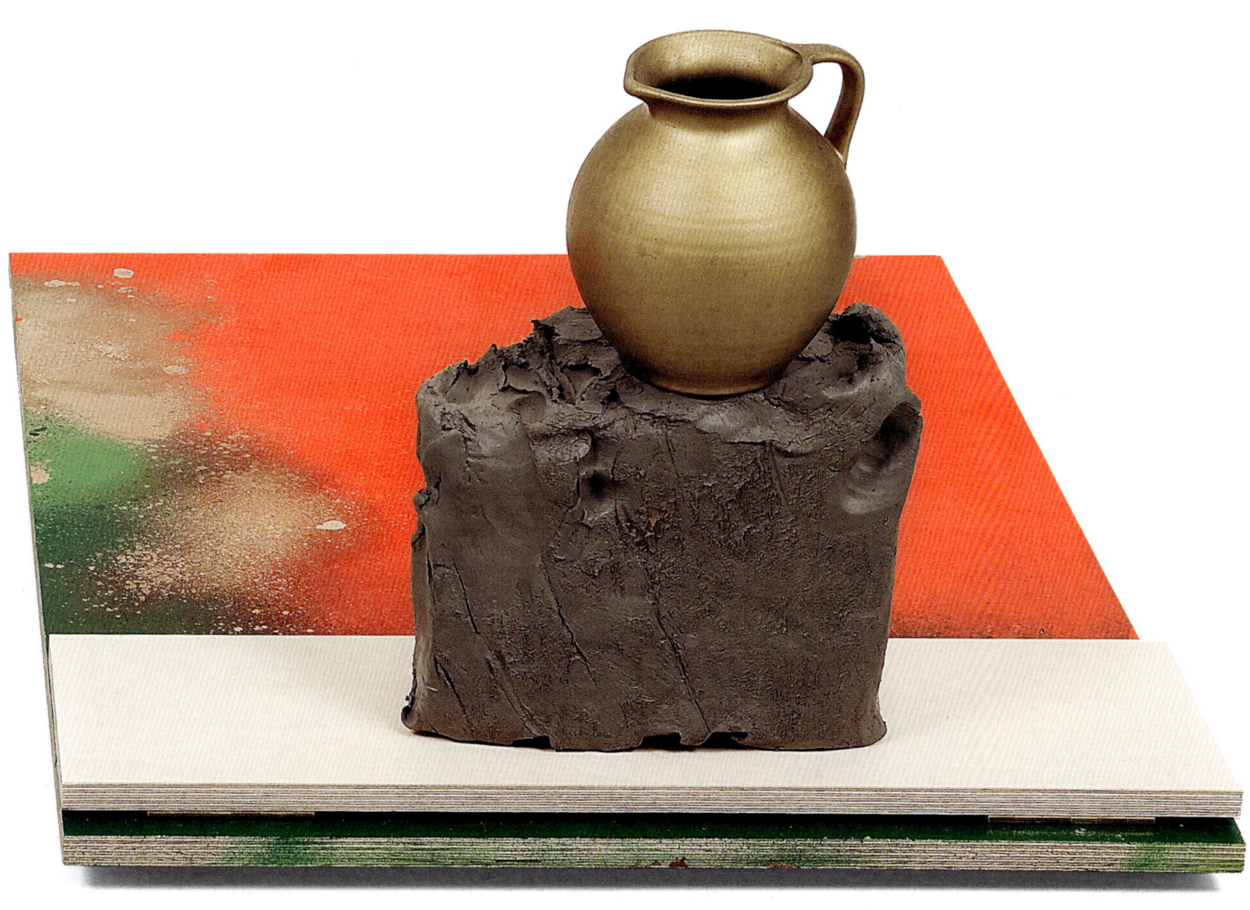

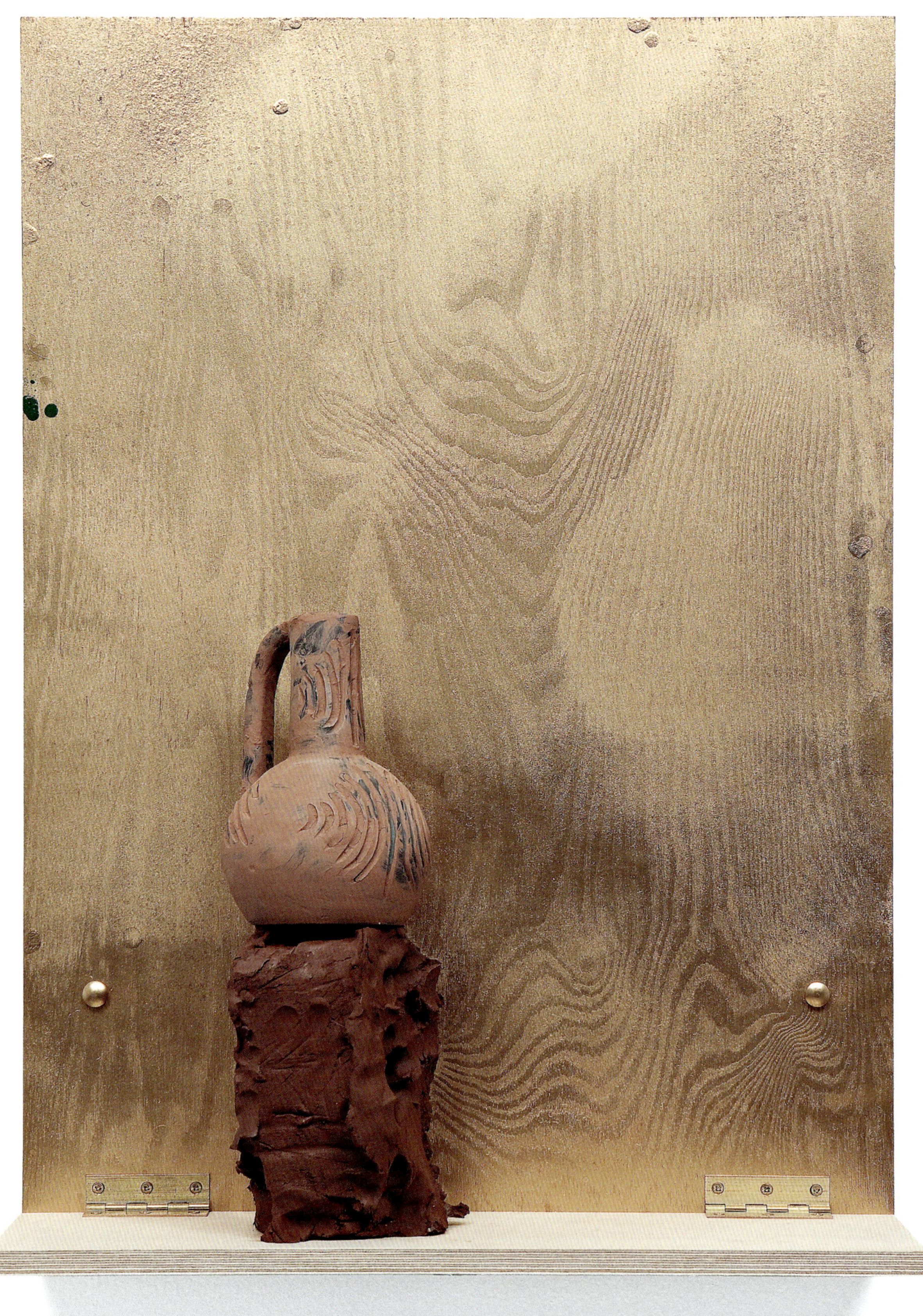

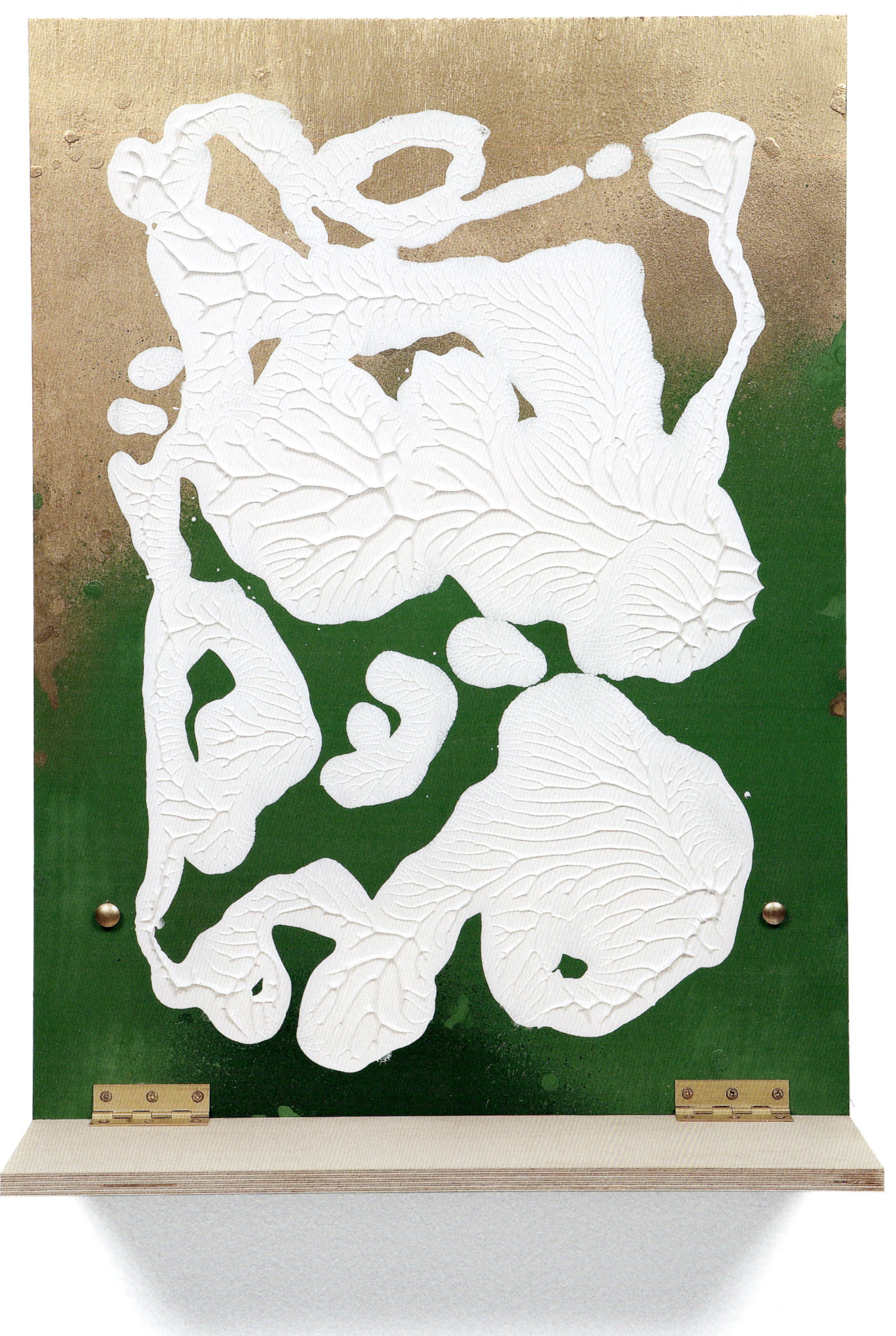

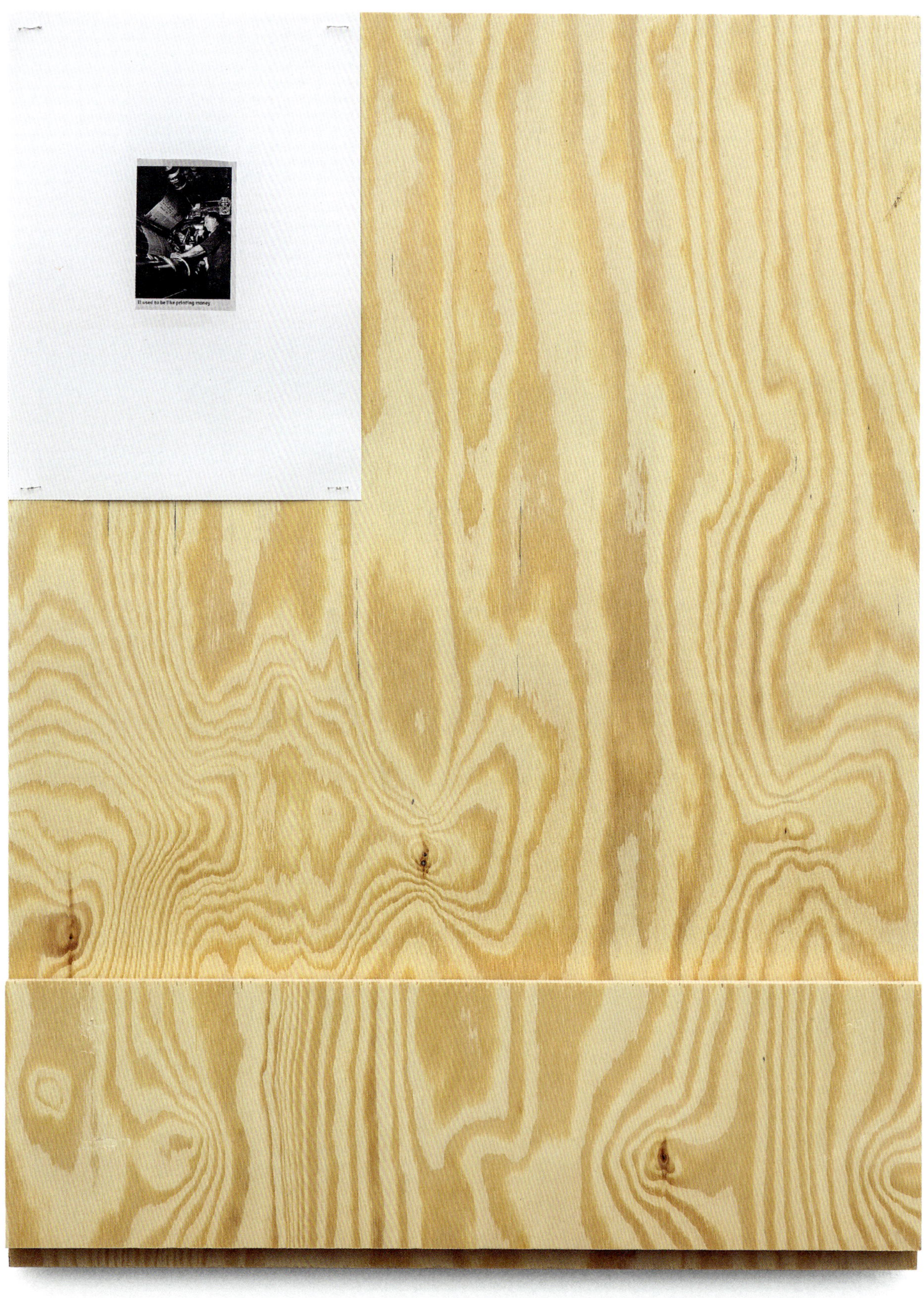
It used to be like printing money

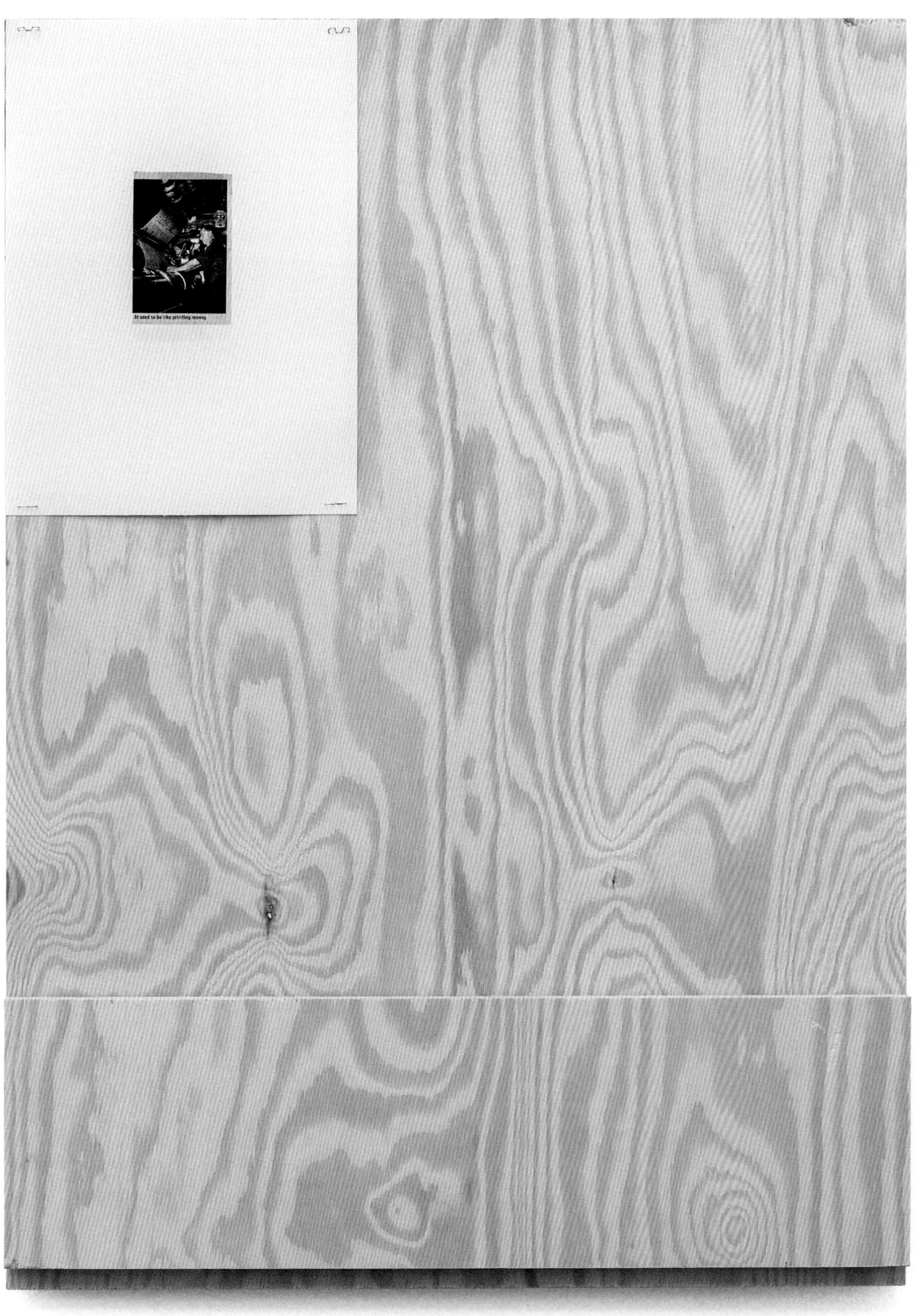
It used to be like printing money

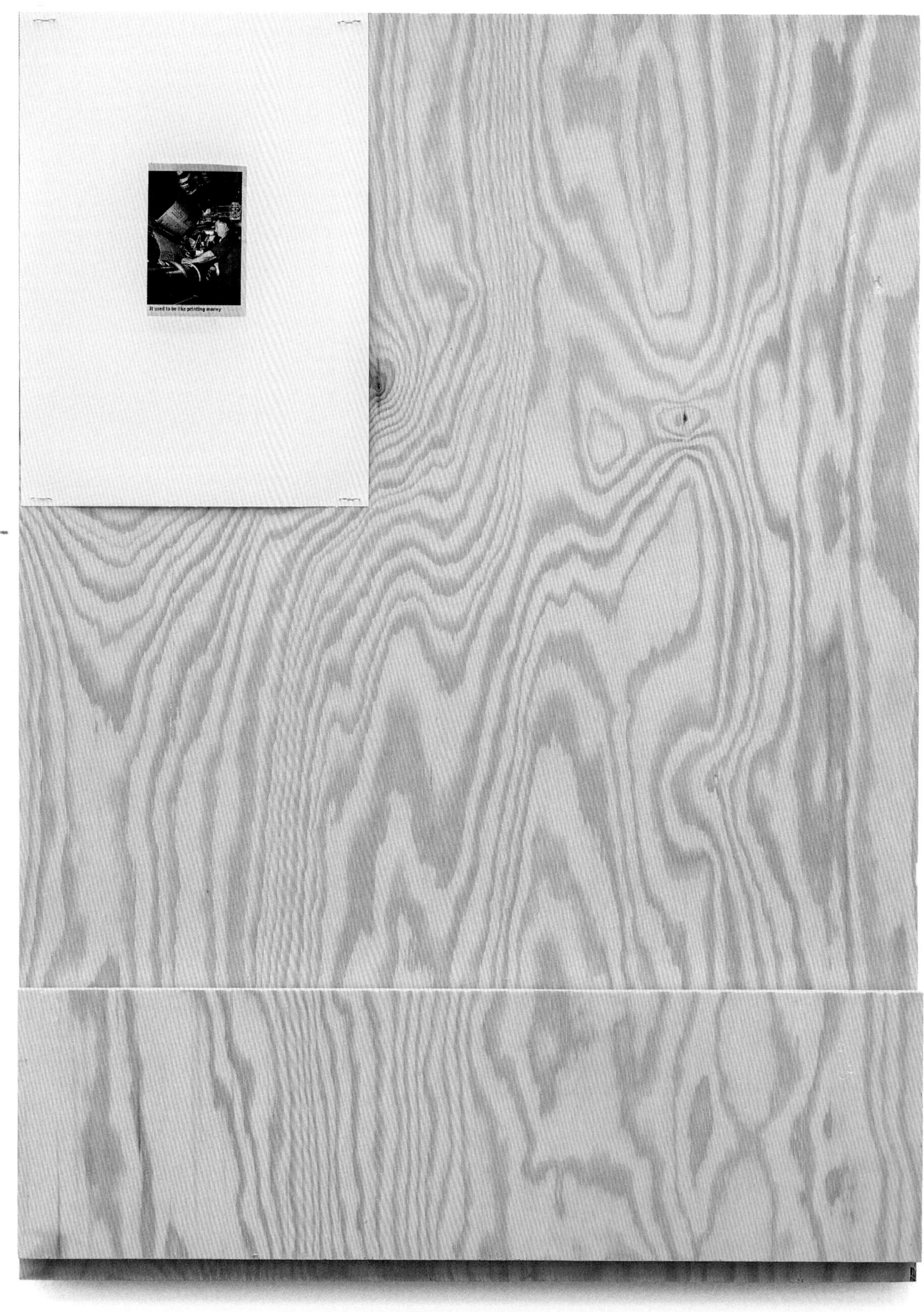
It used to be like printing money

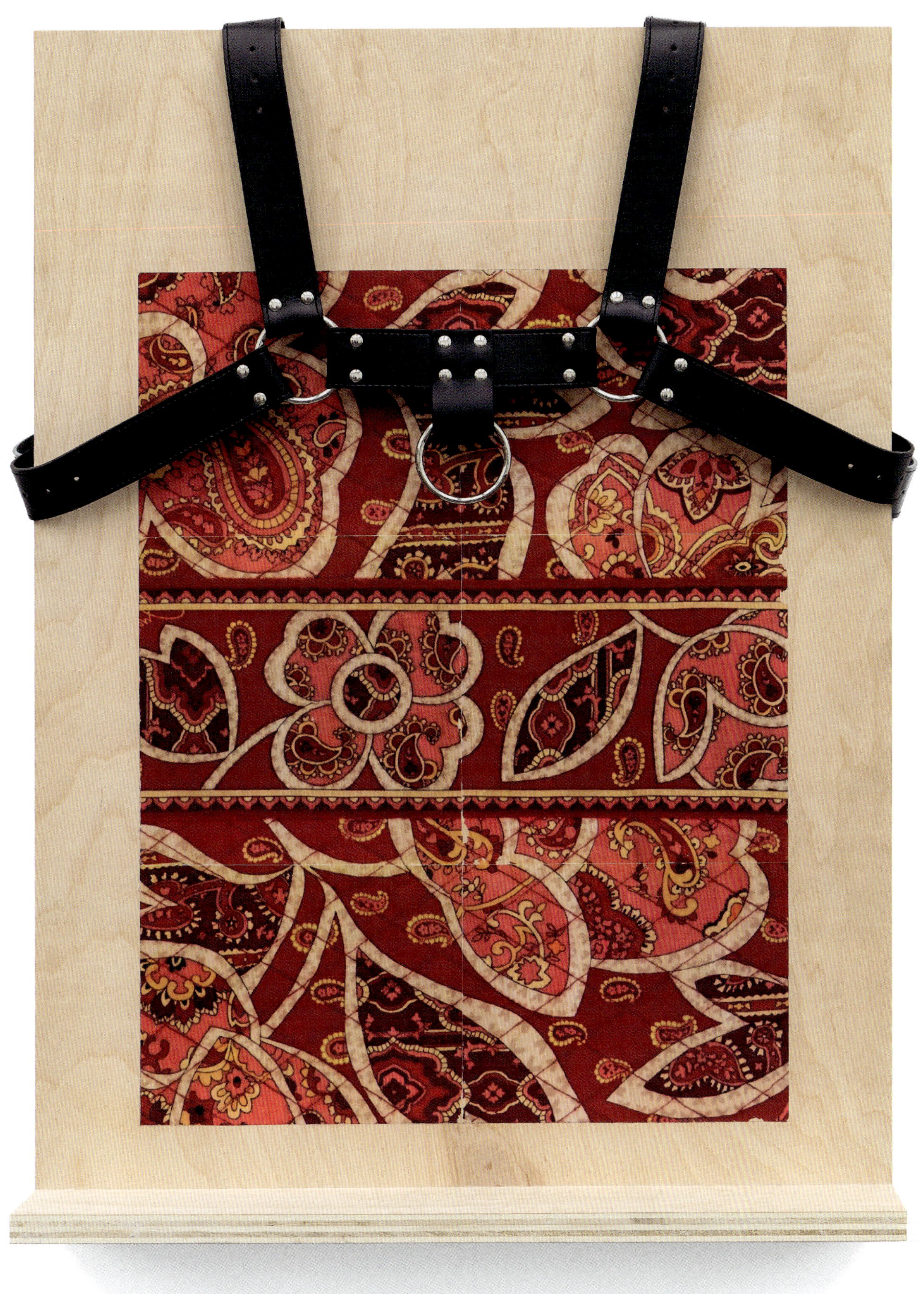

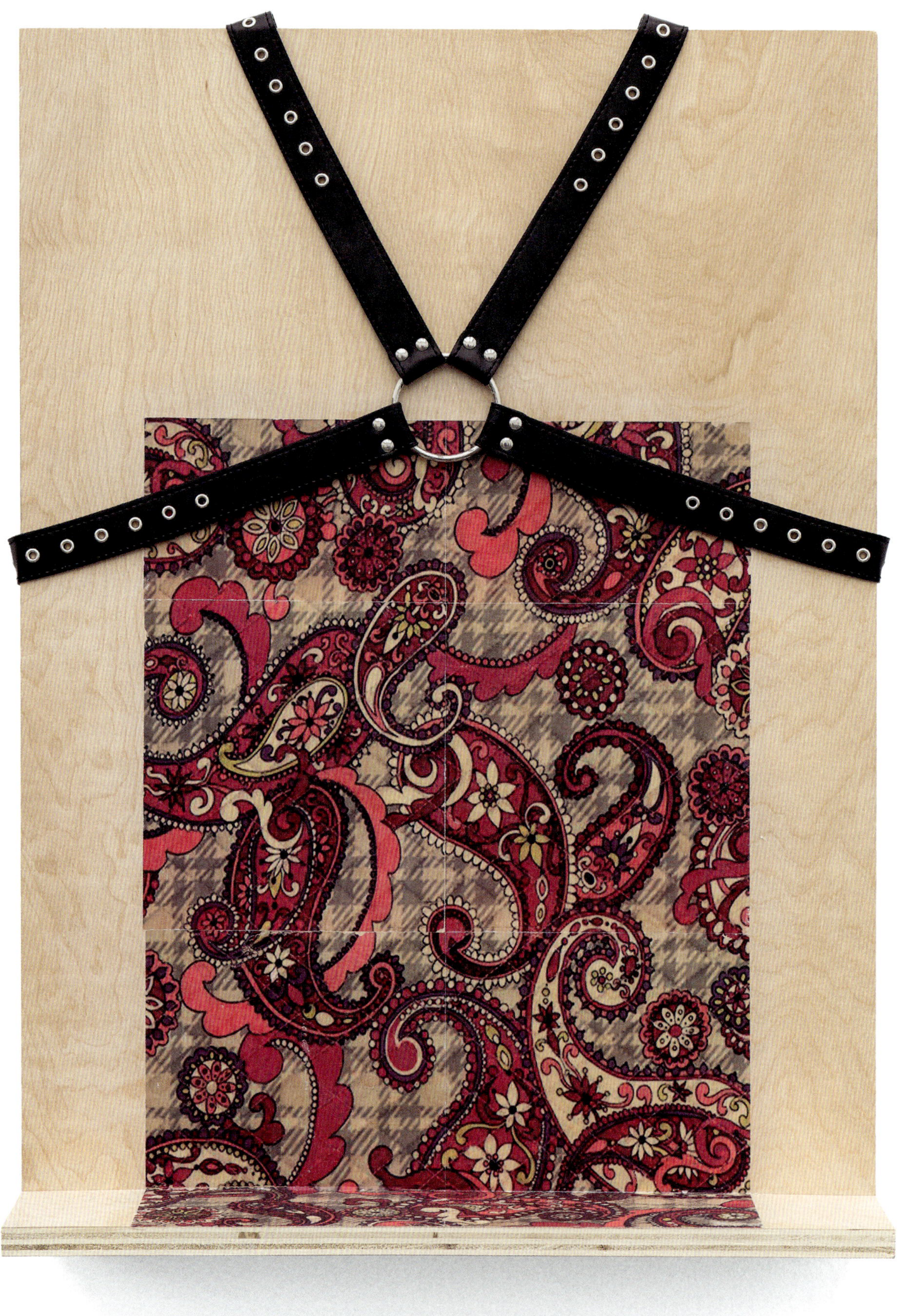

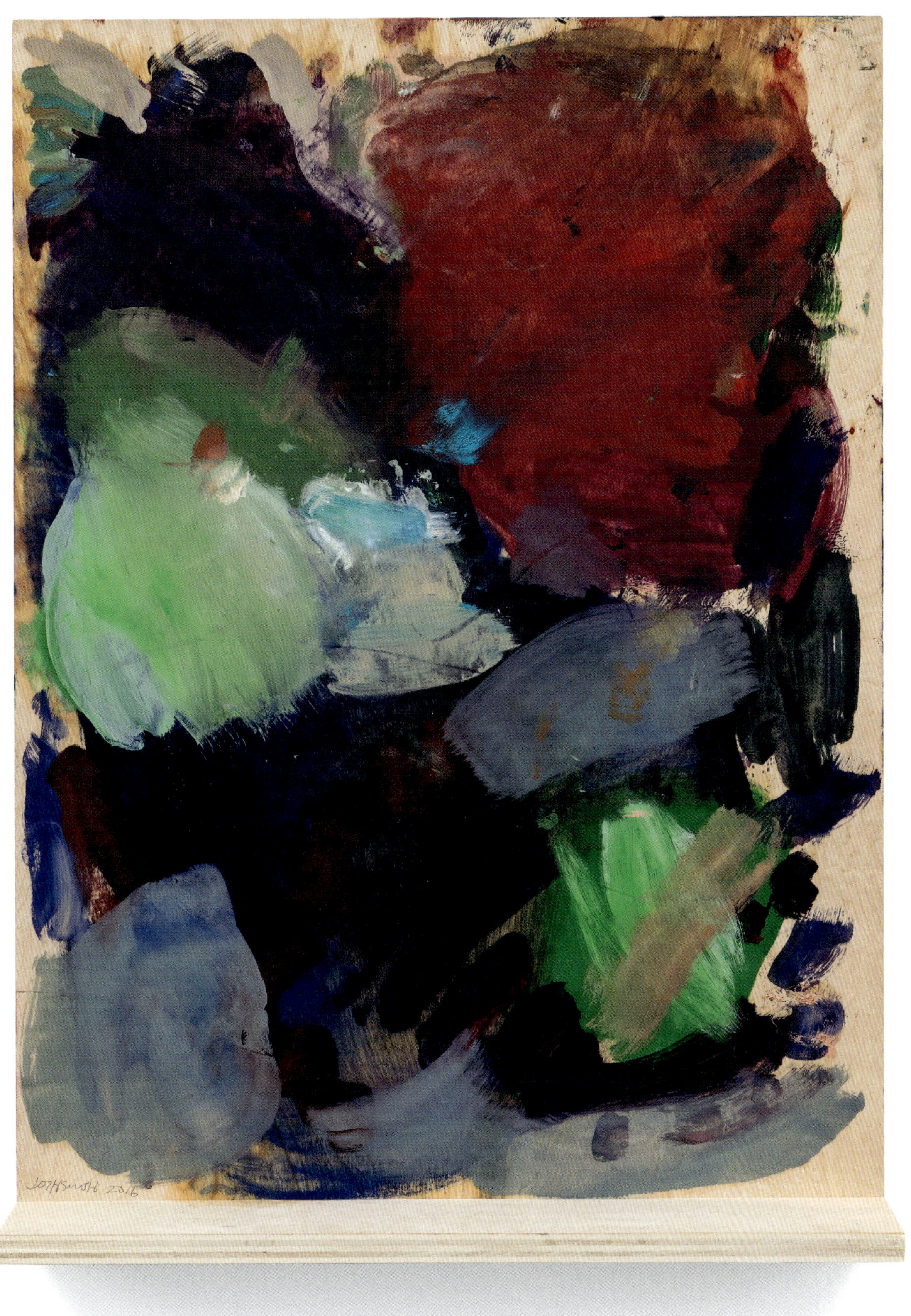

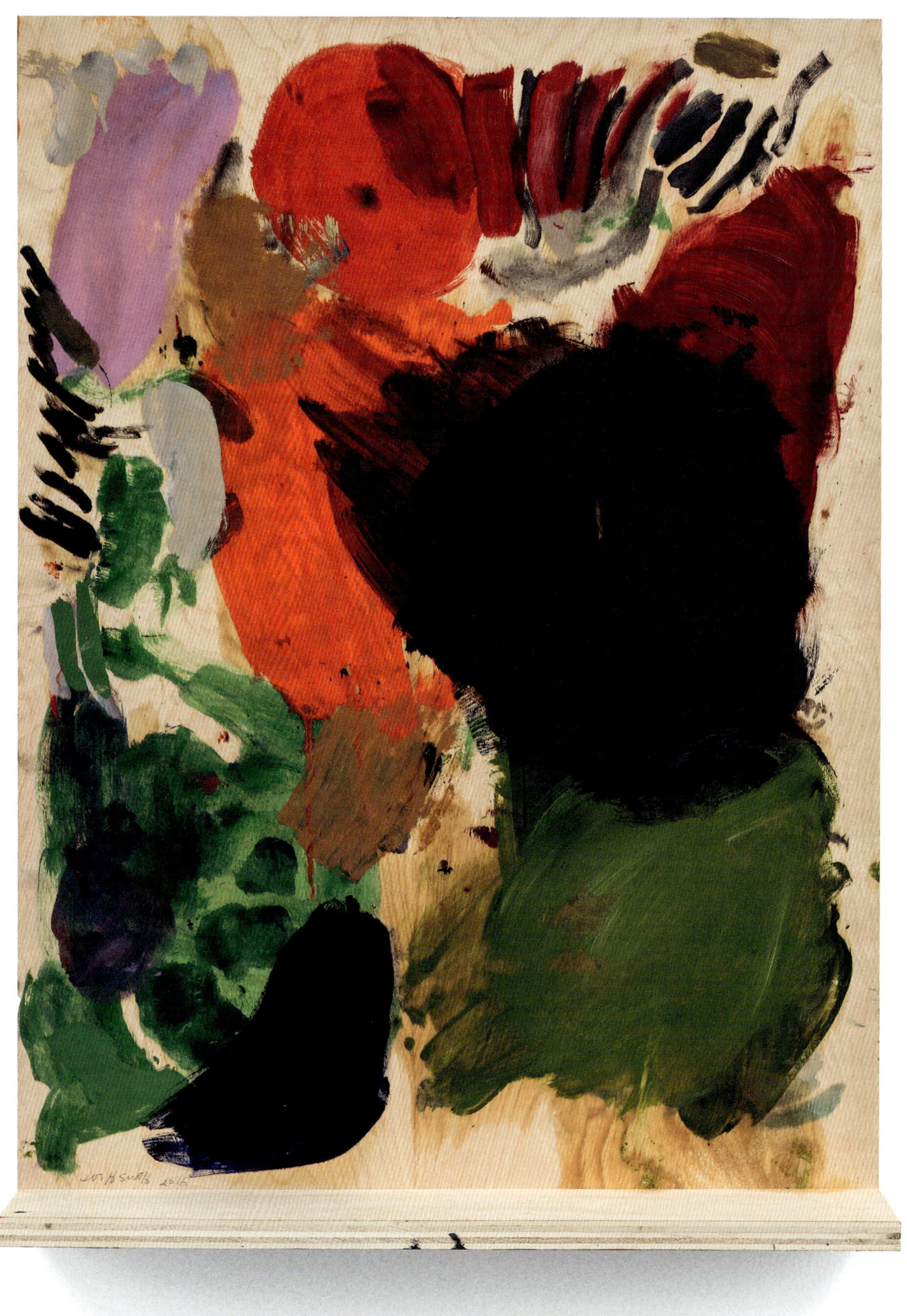

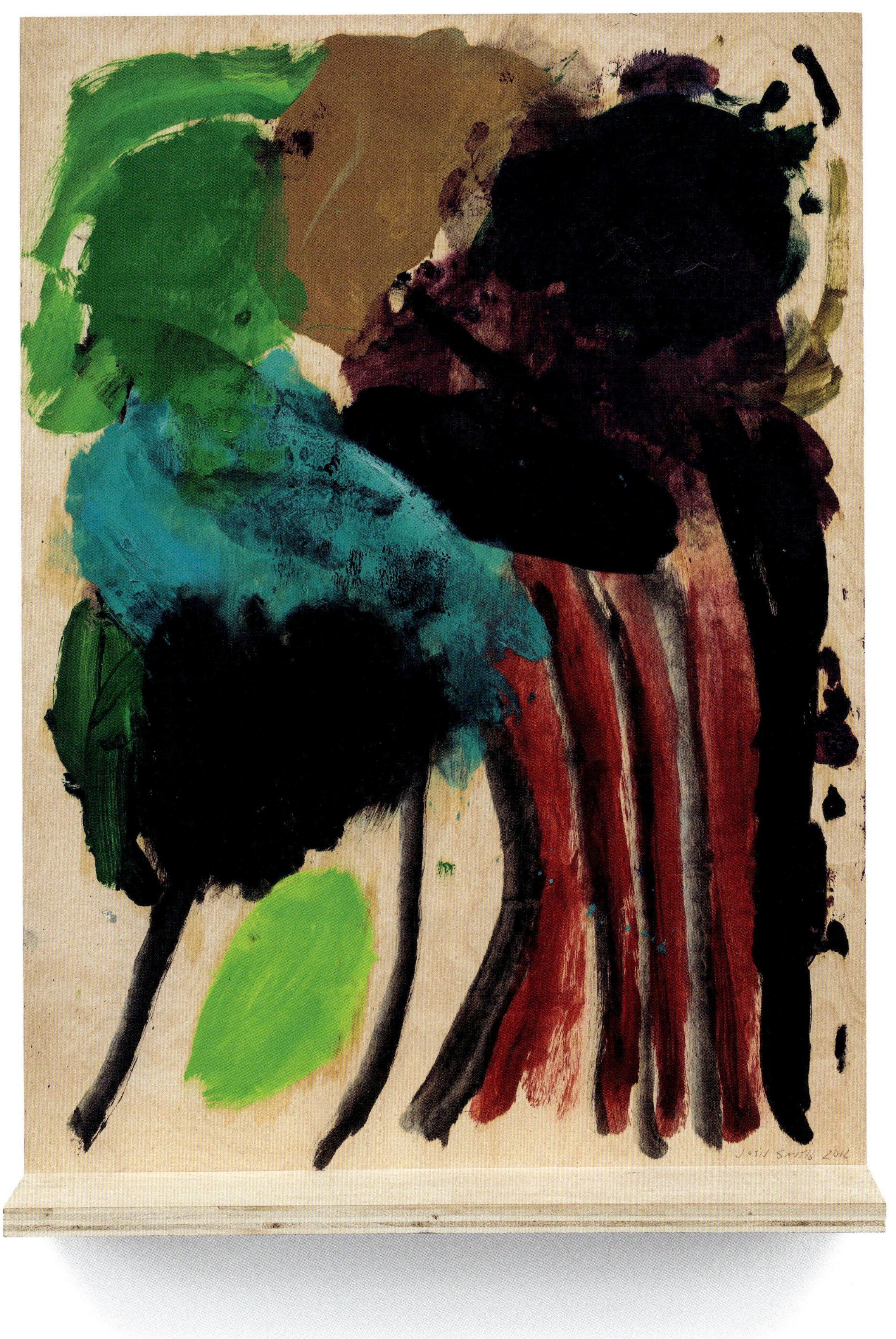
Josh Smith 2016

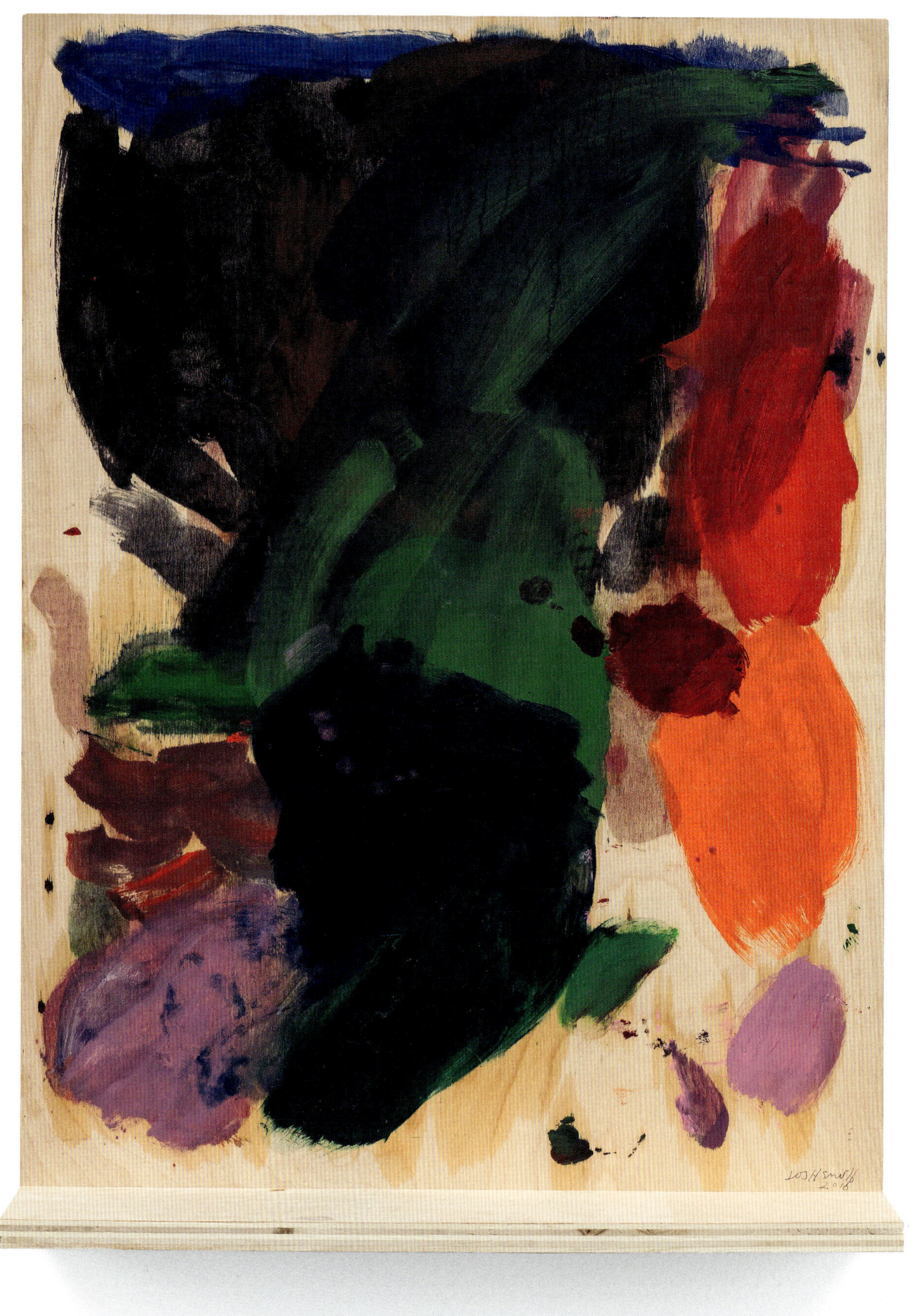

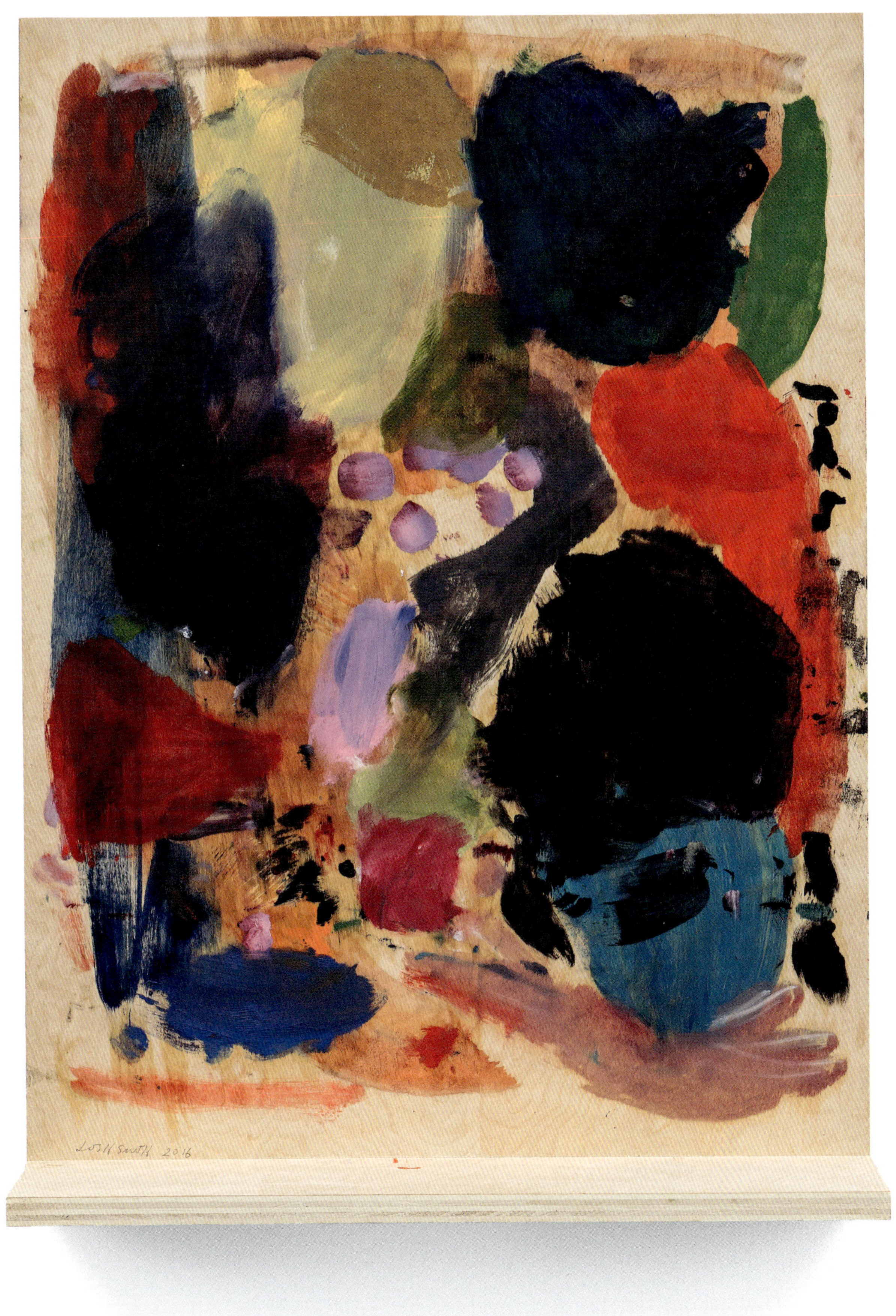

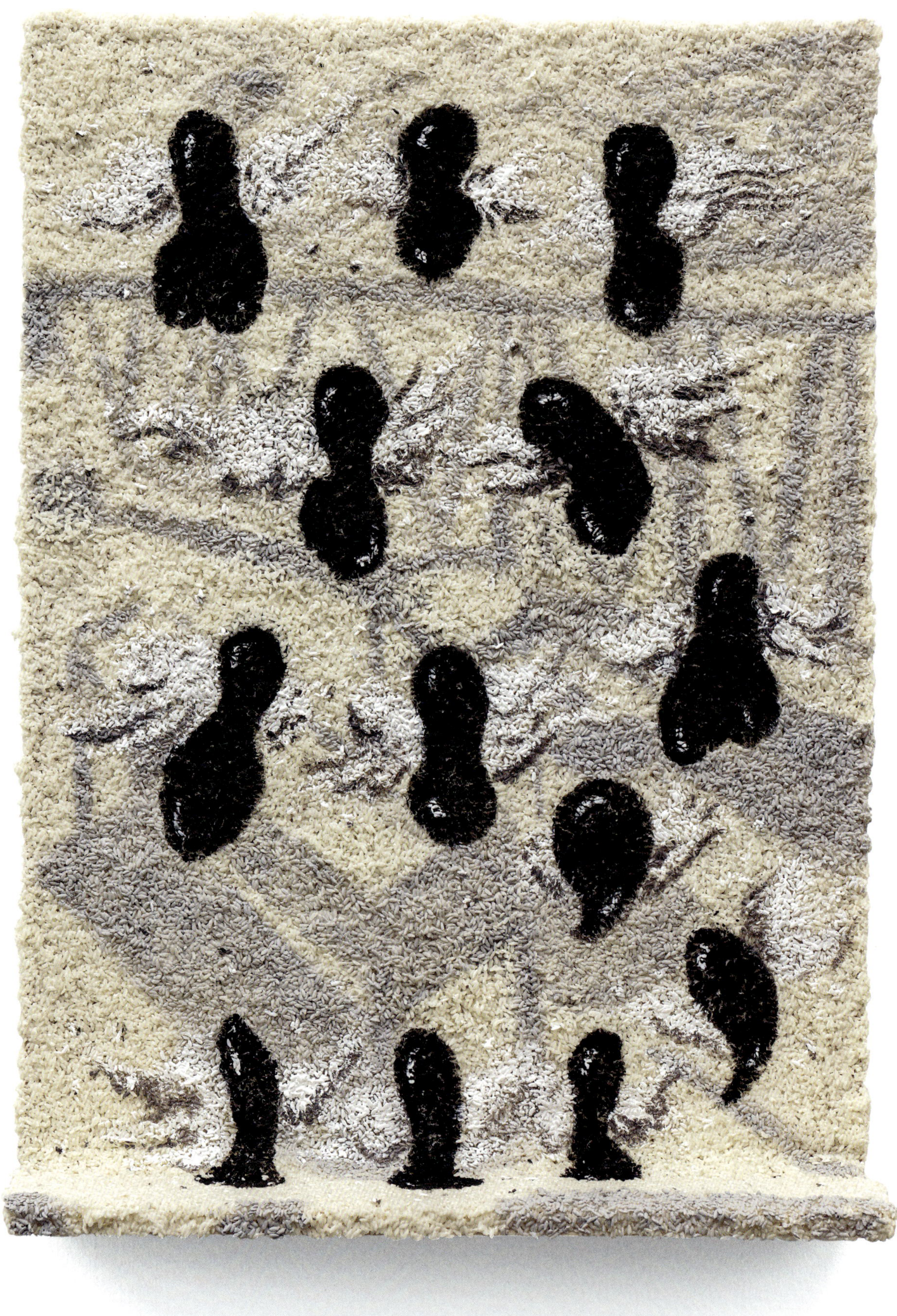

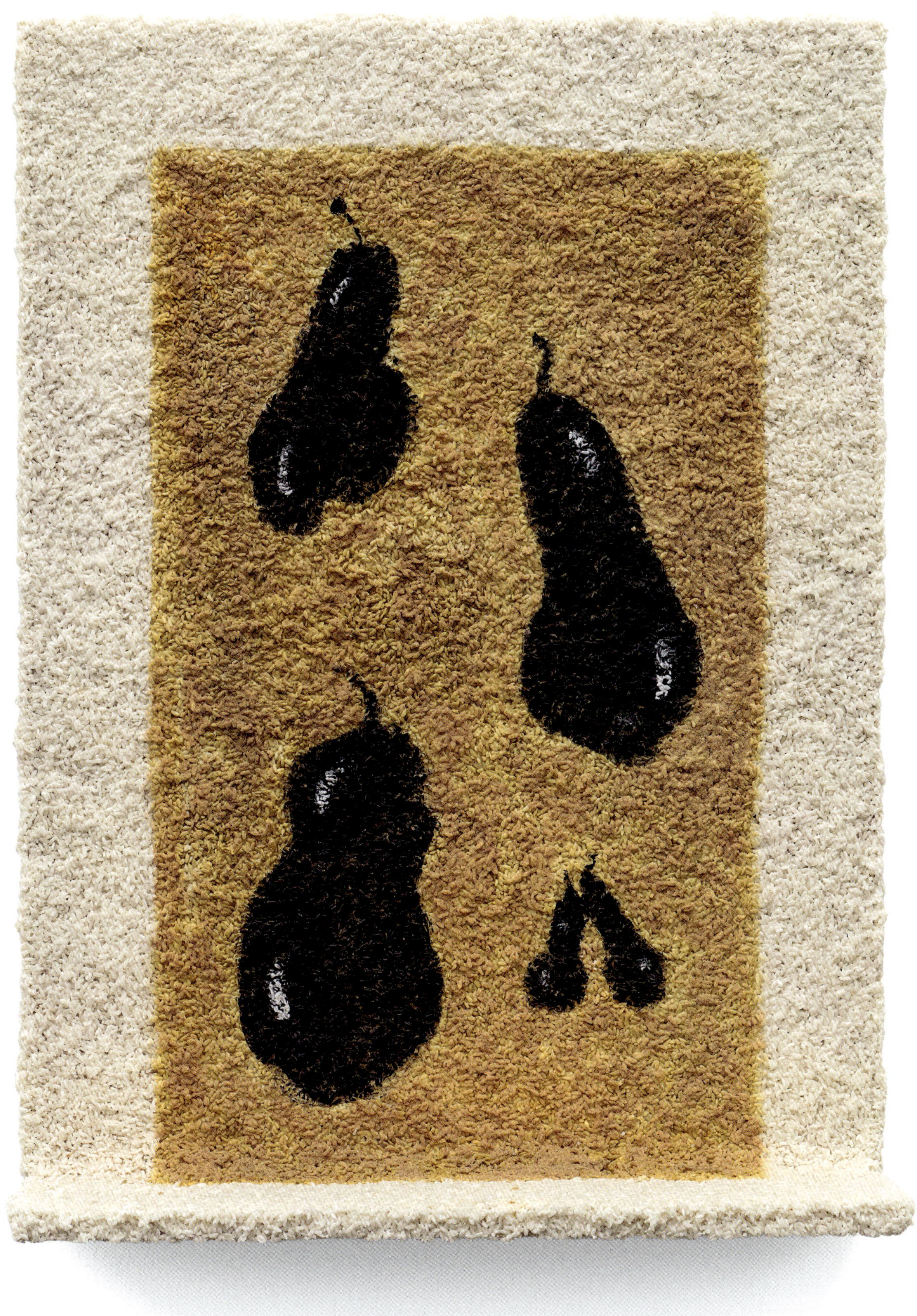

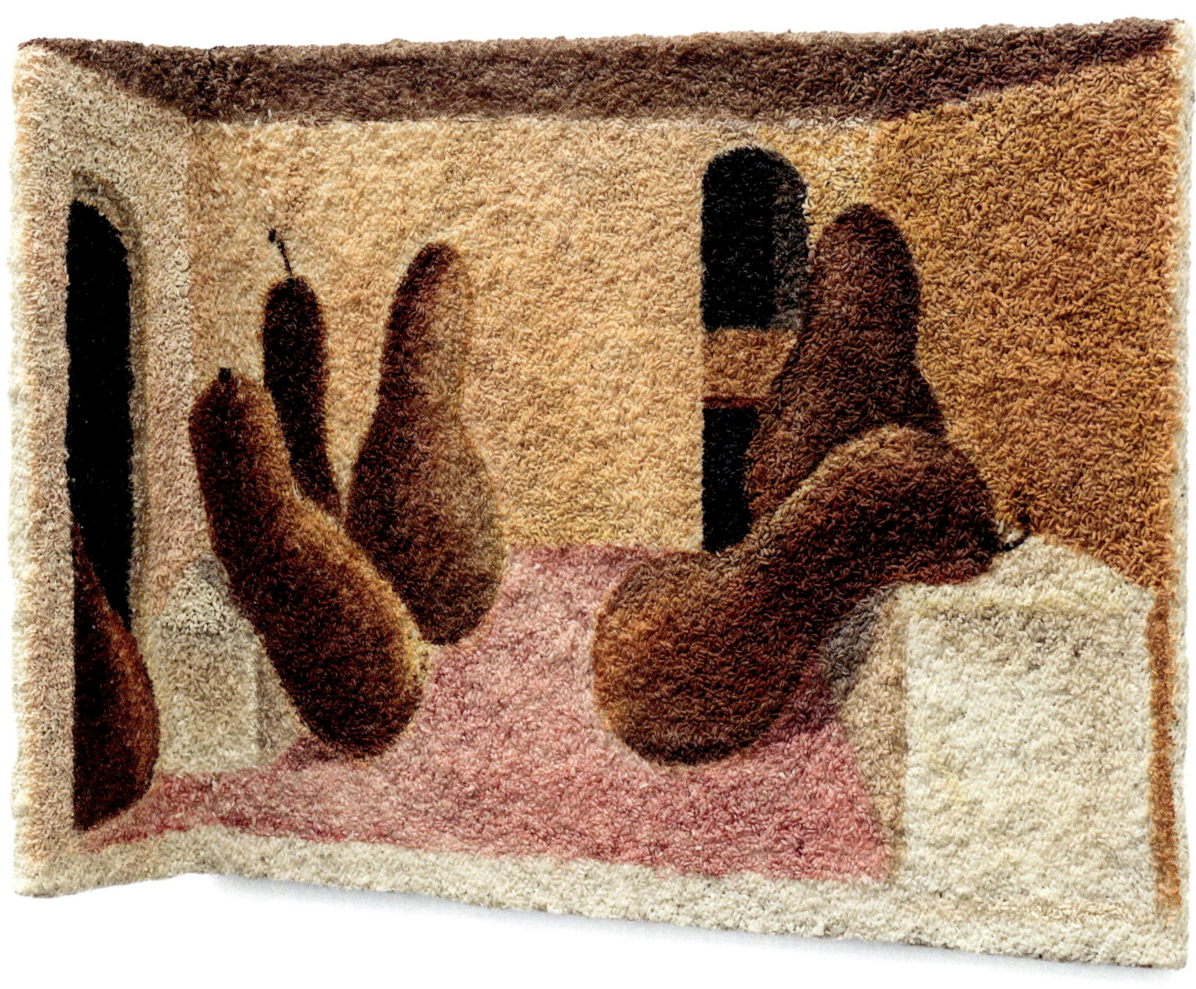

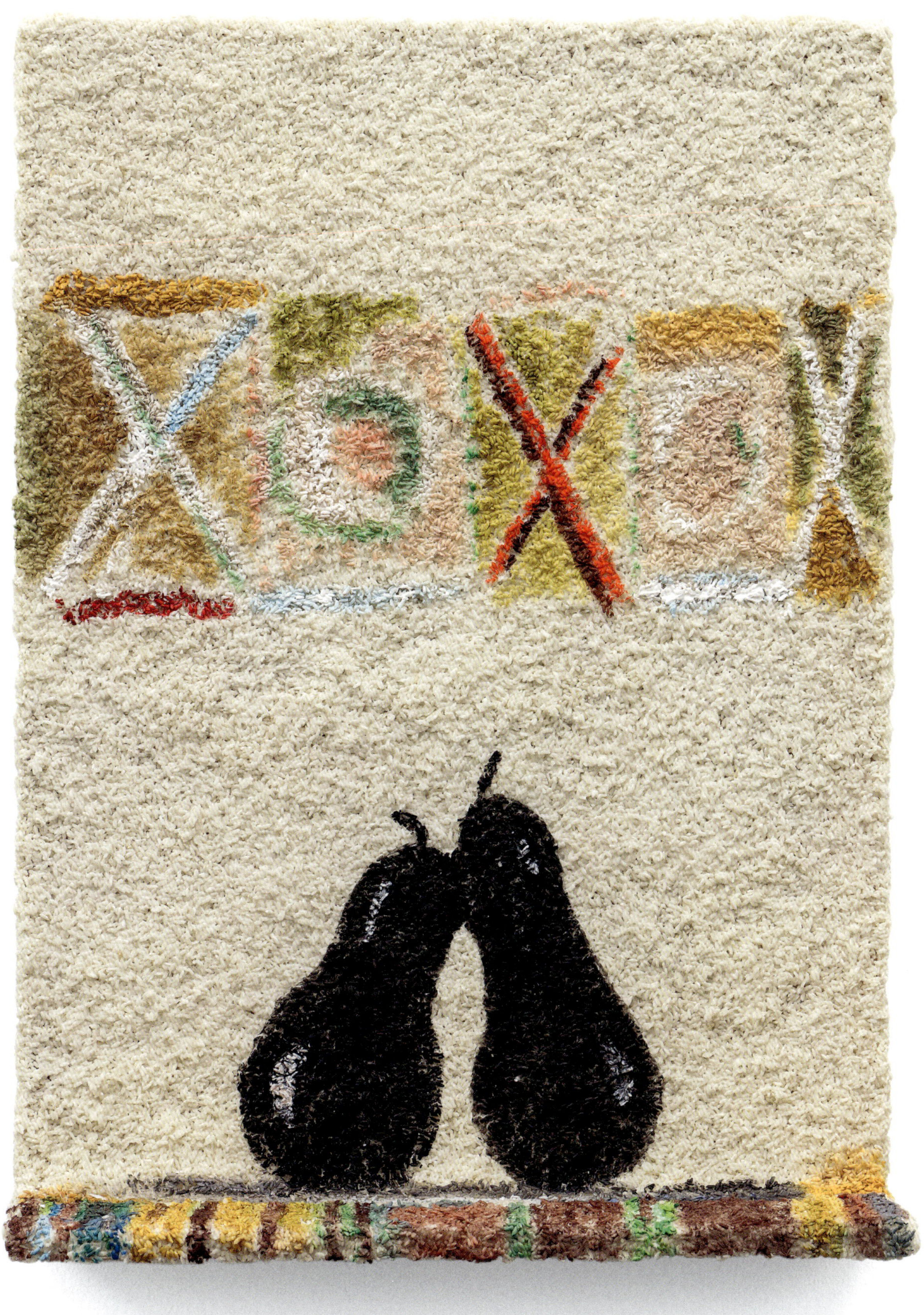

XOXOX

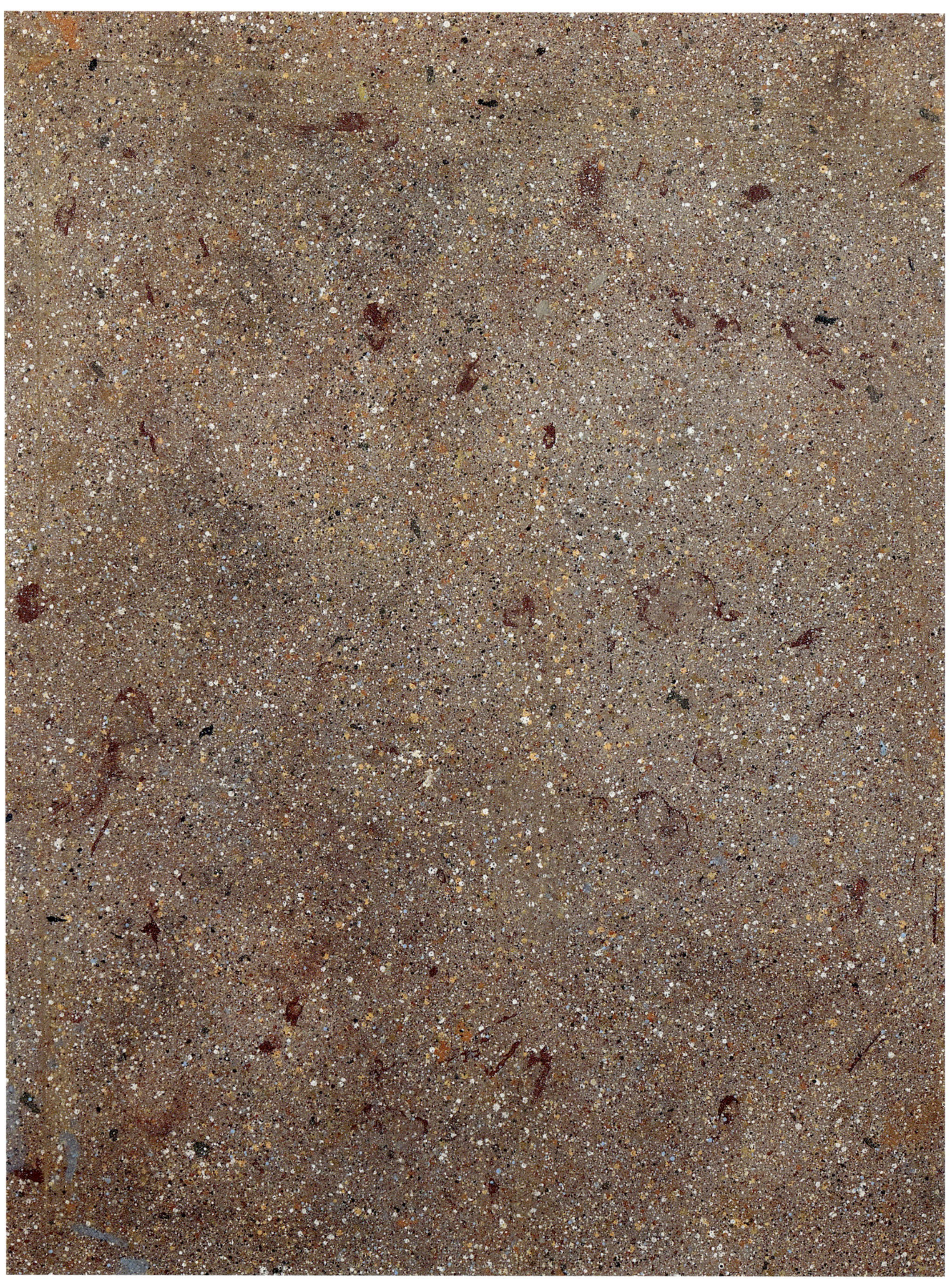

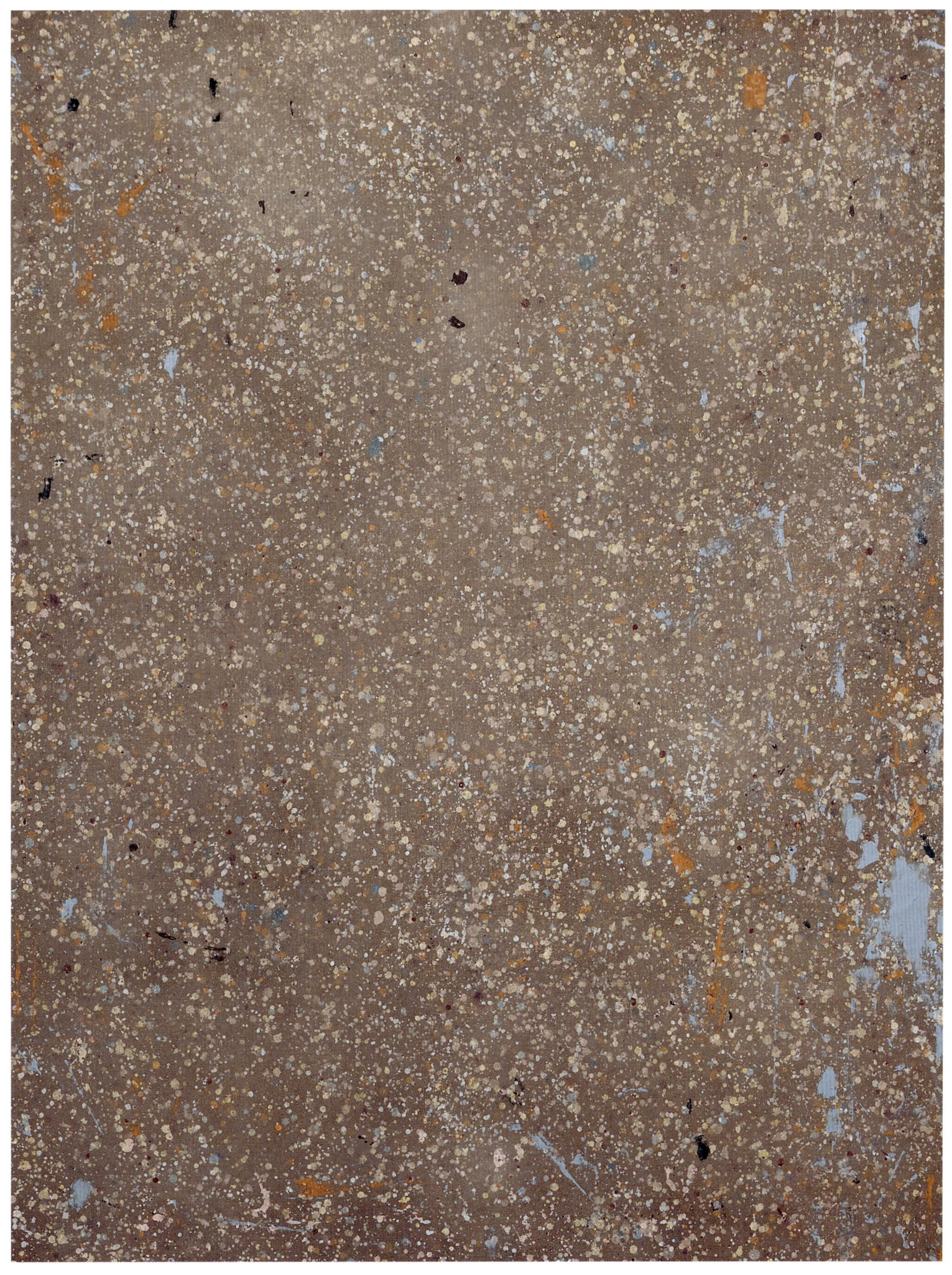

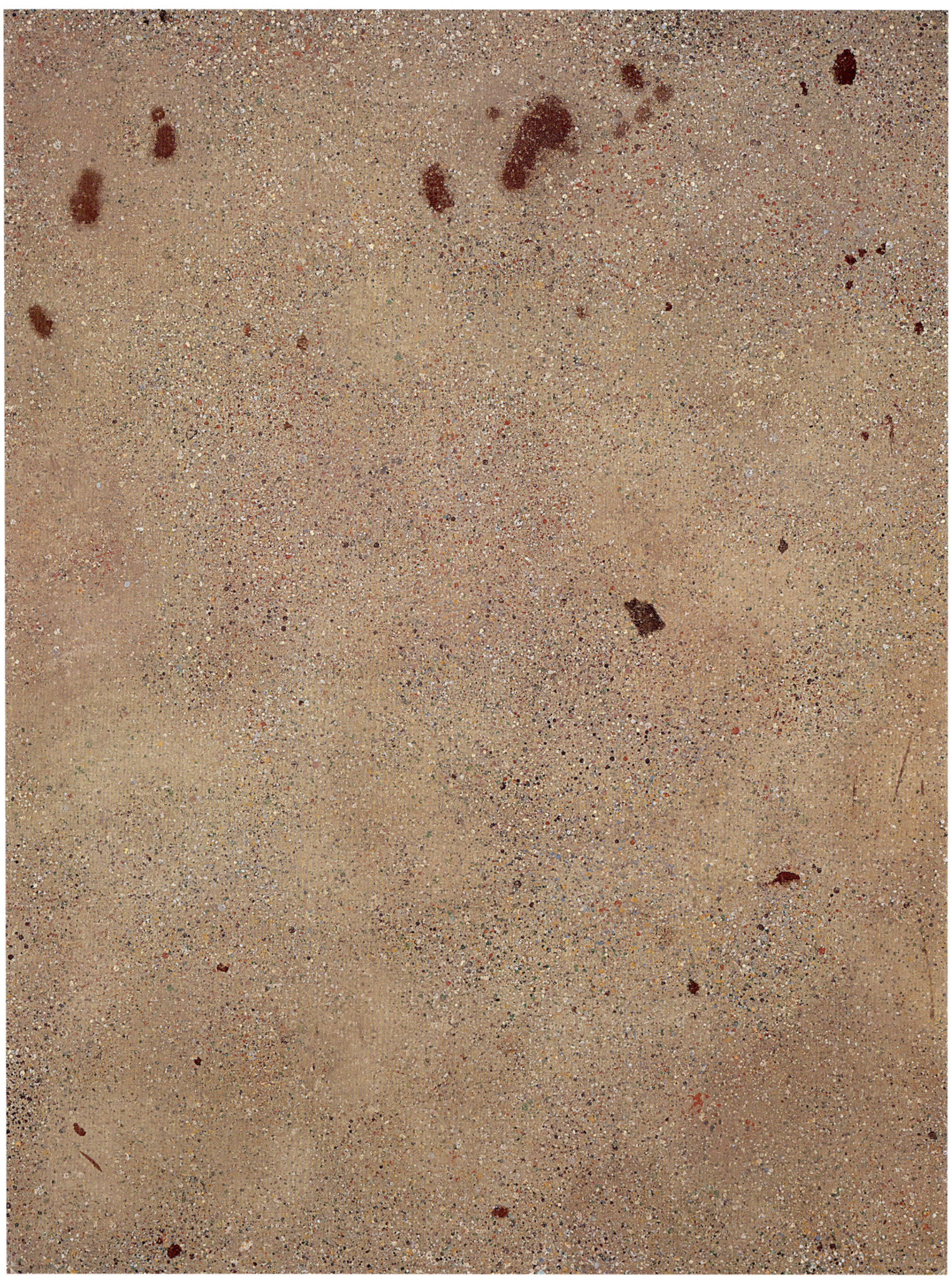

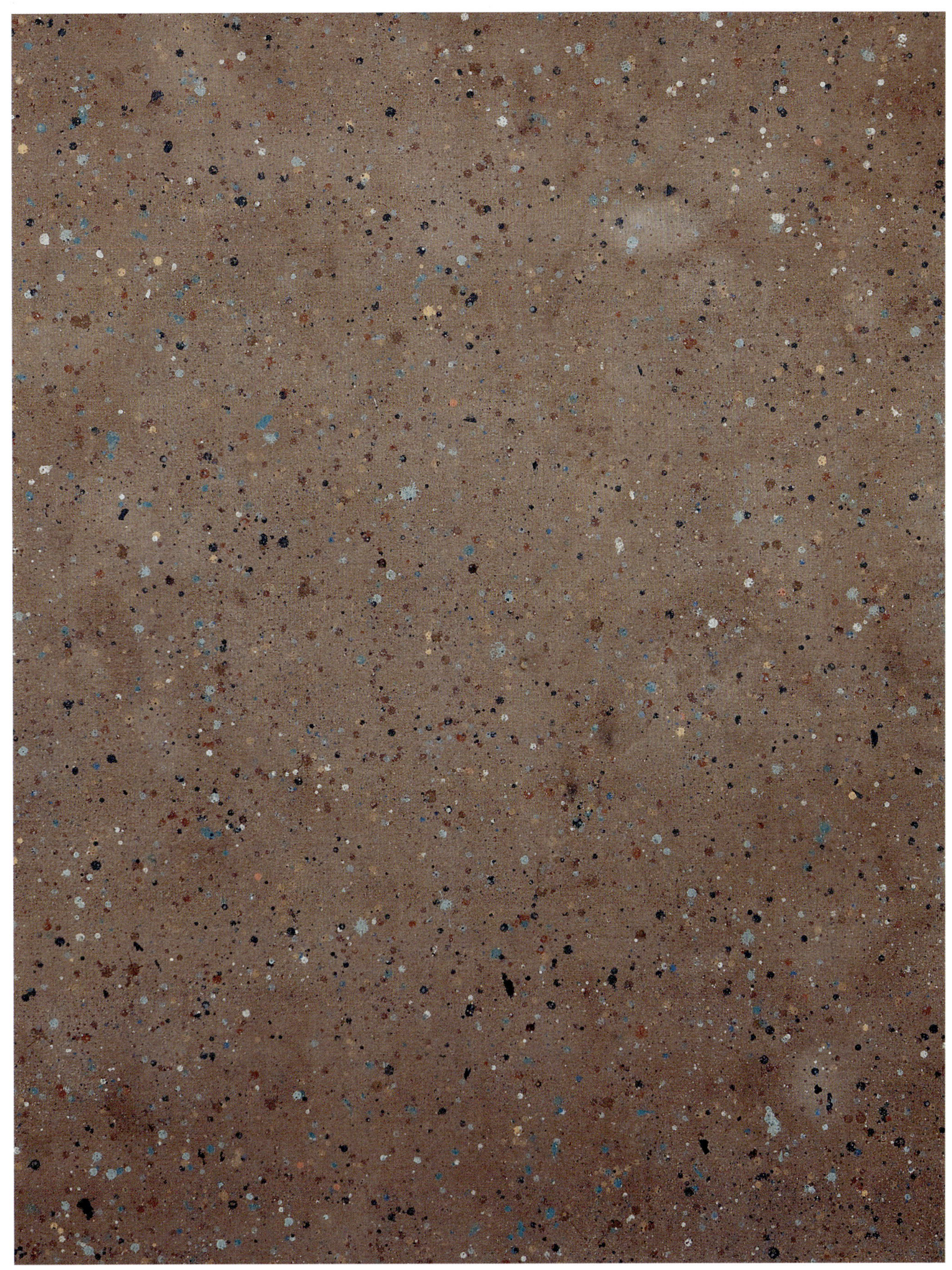

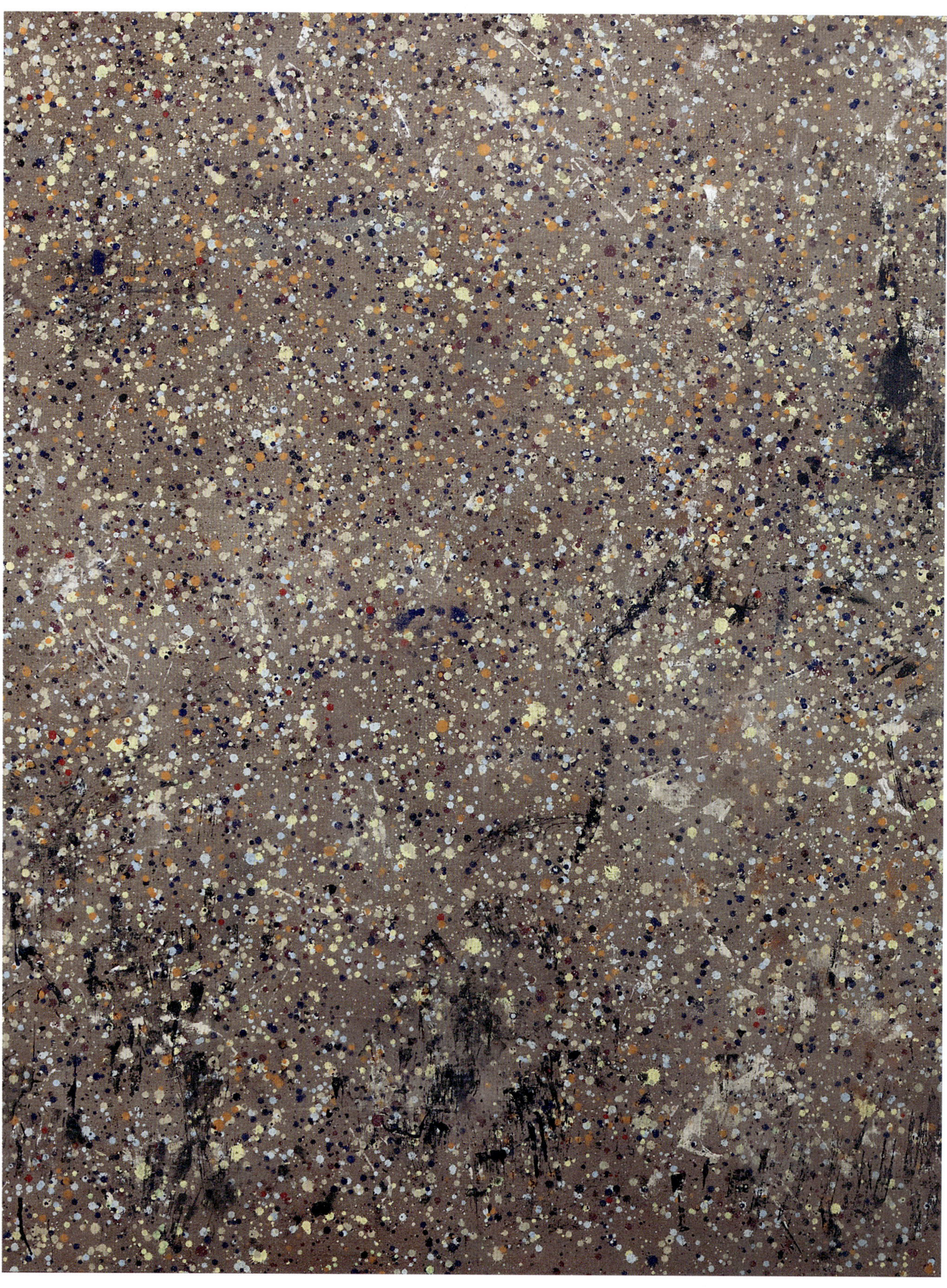

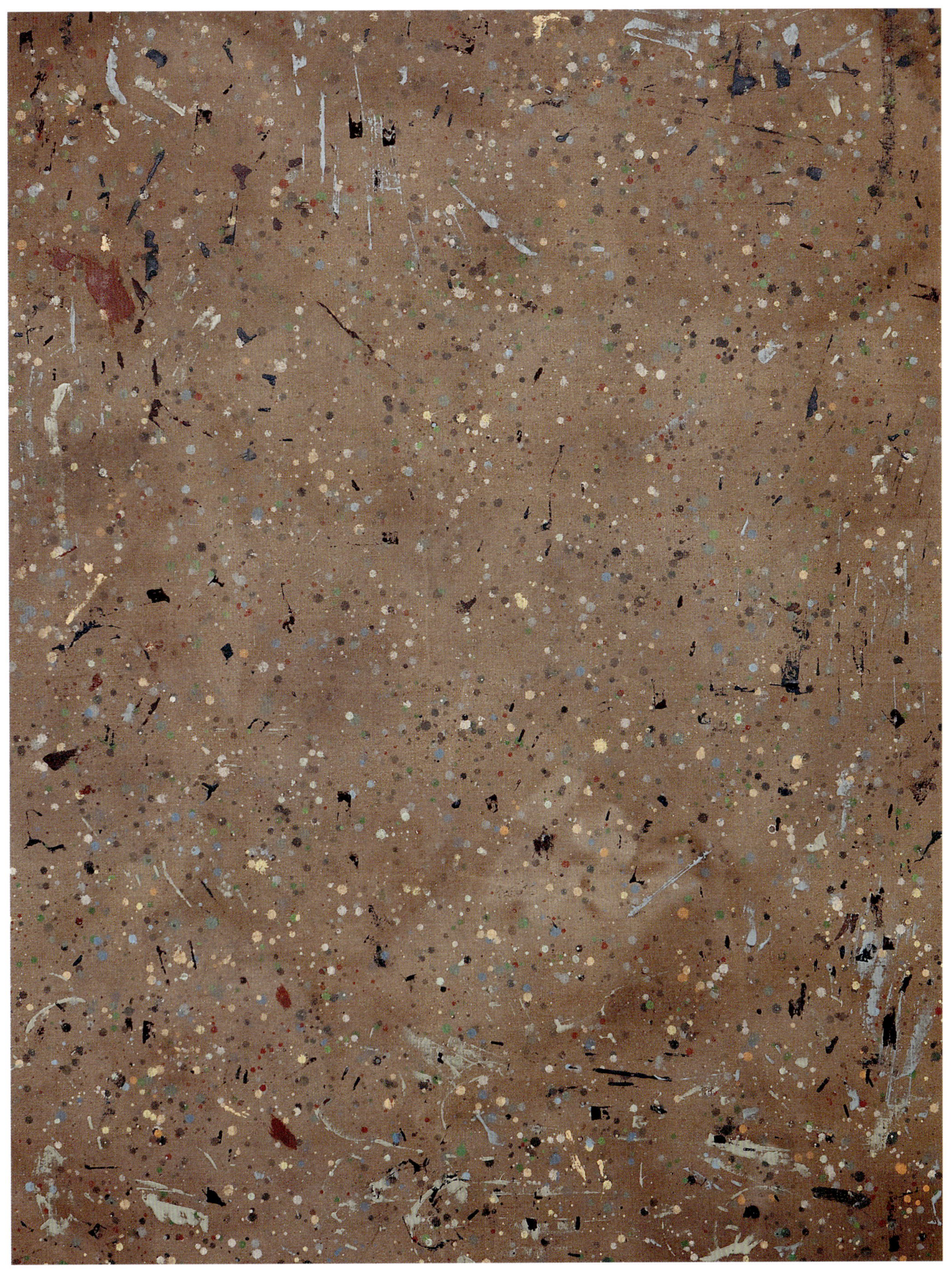

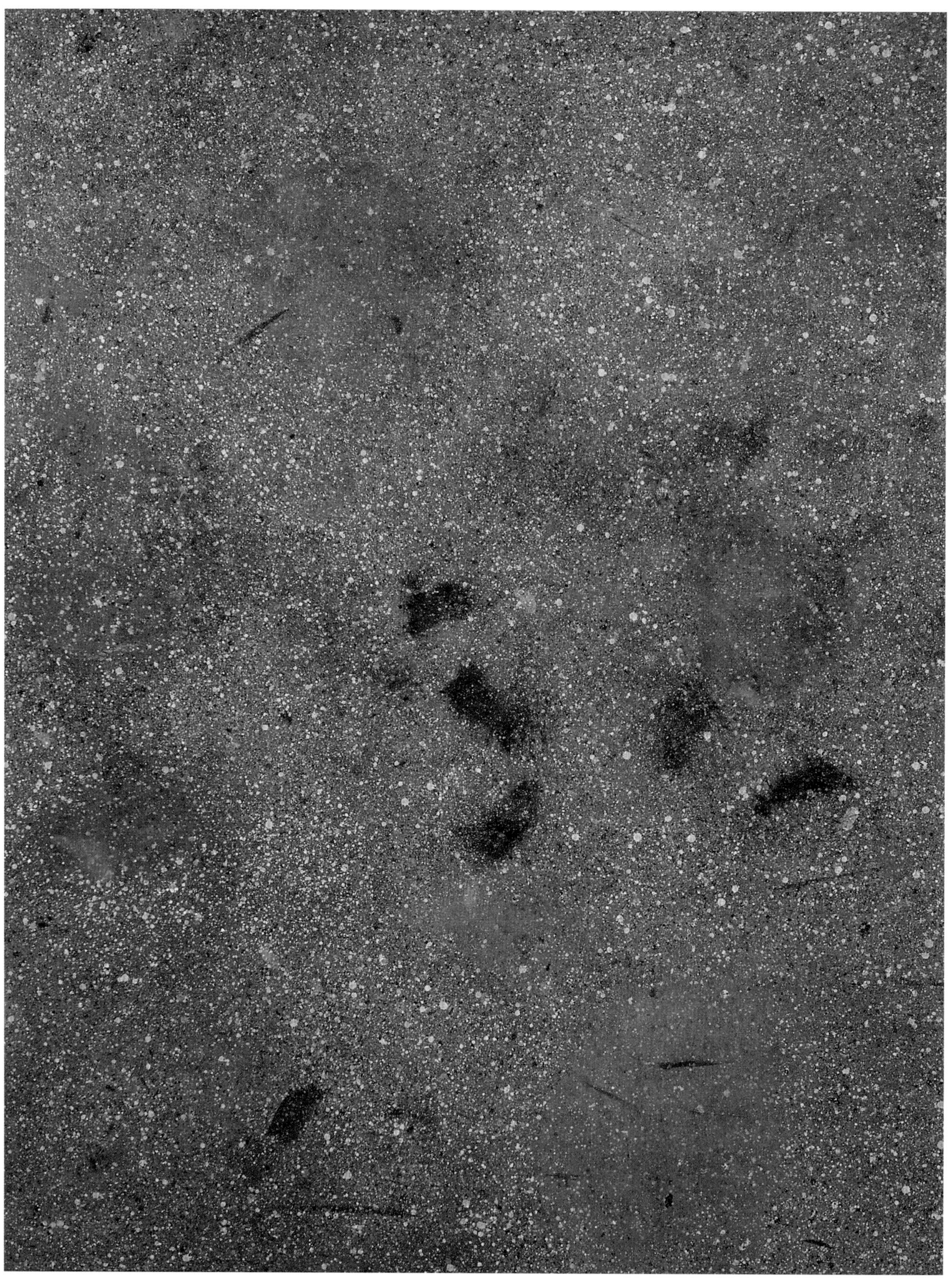

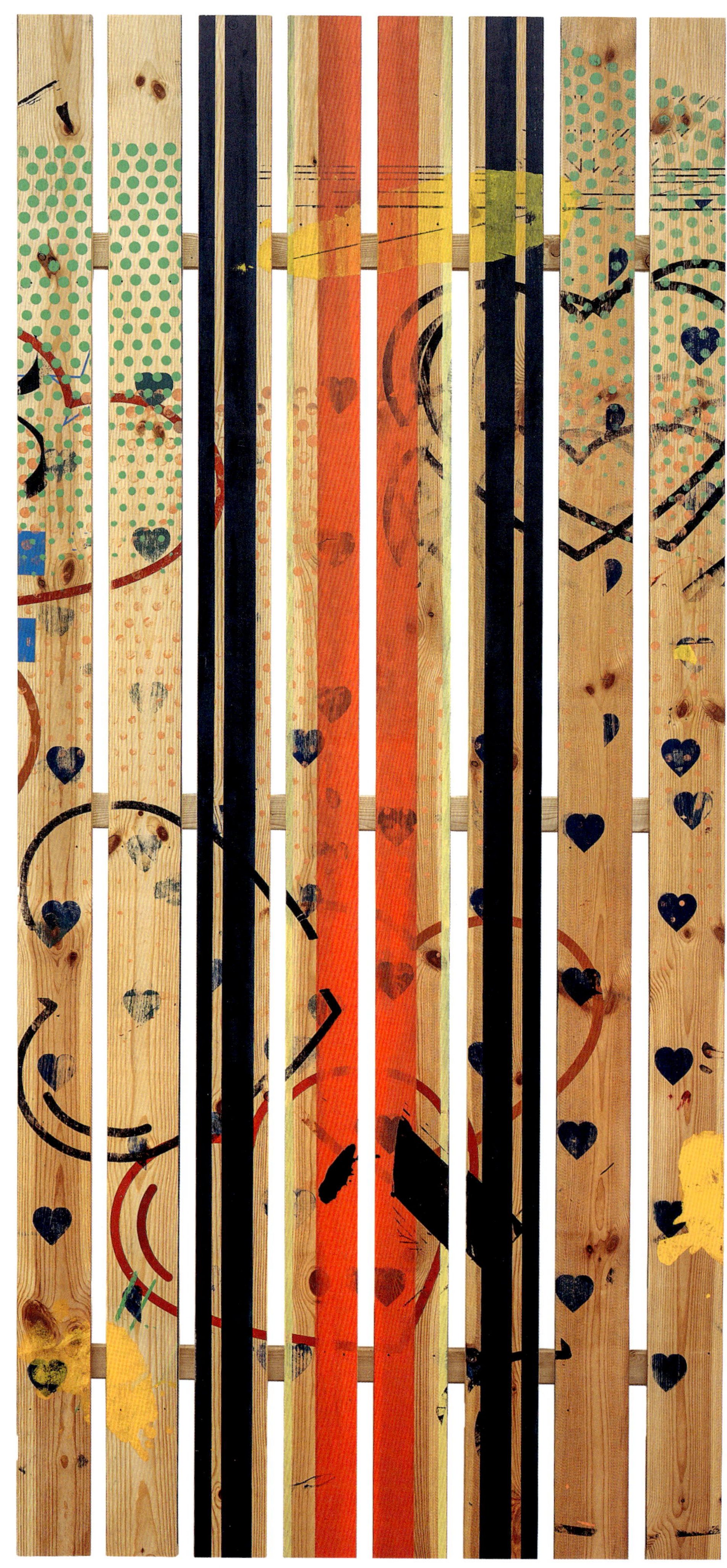

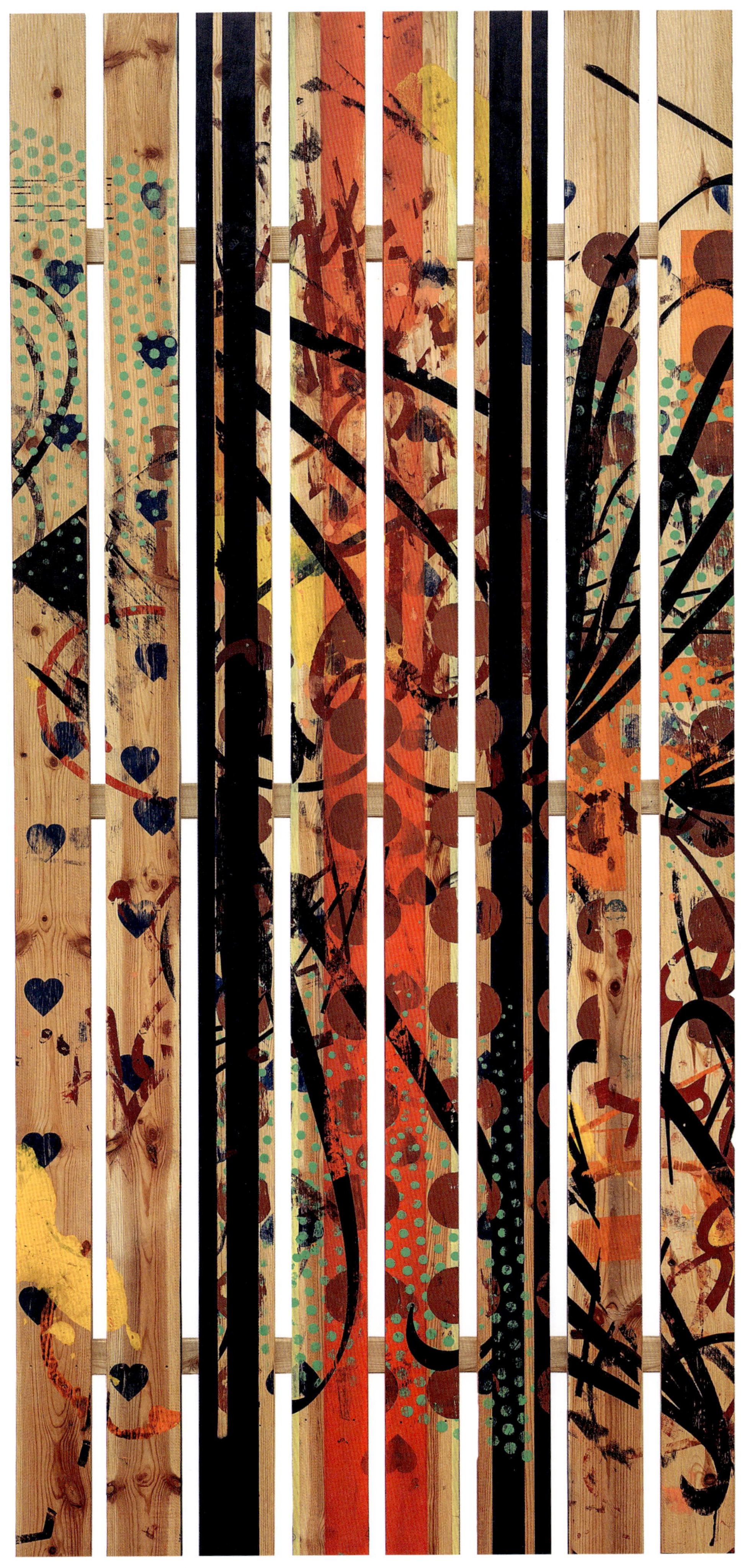

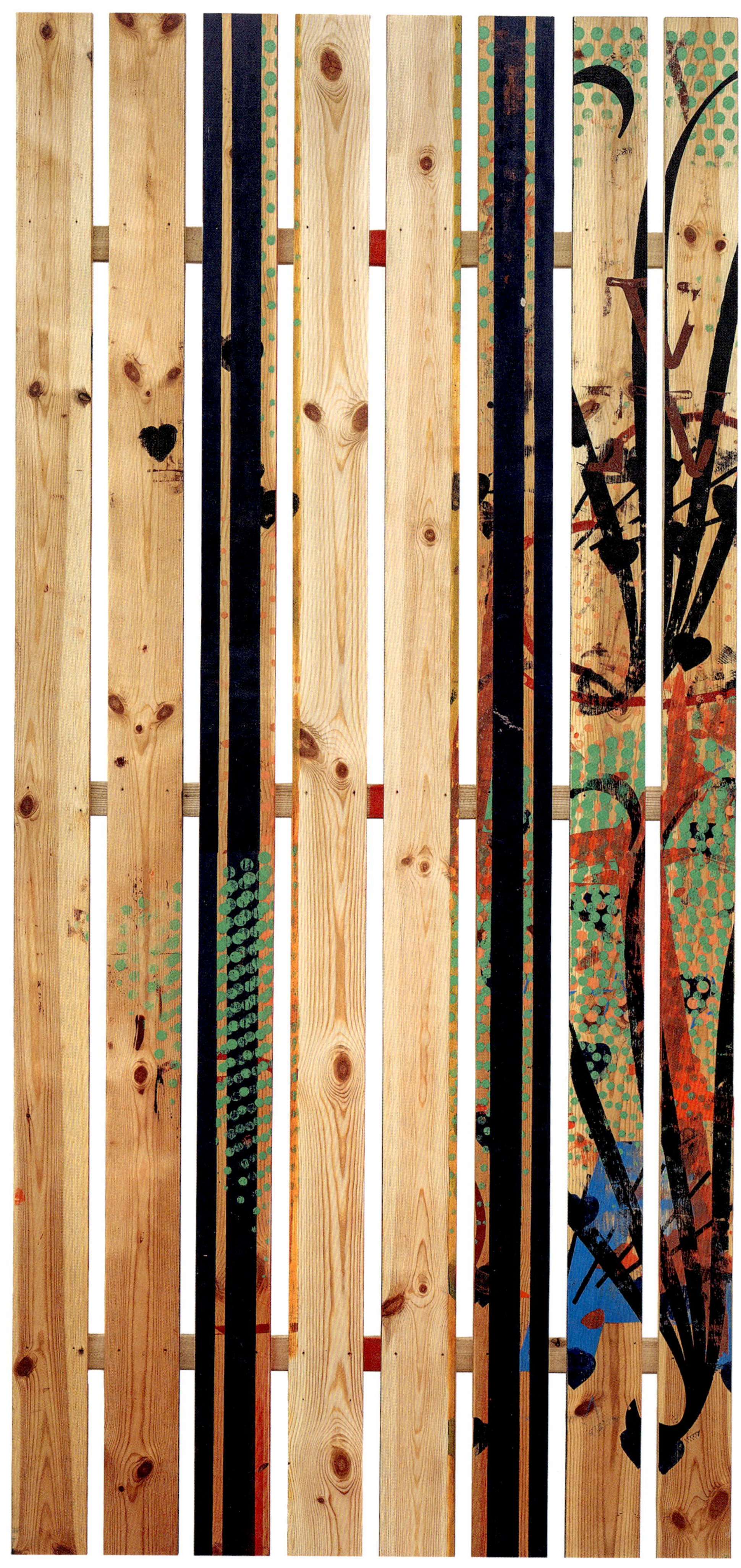

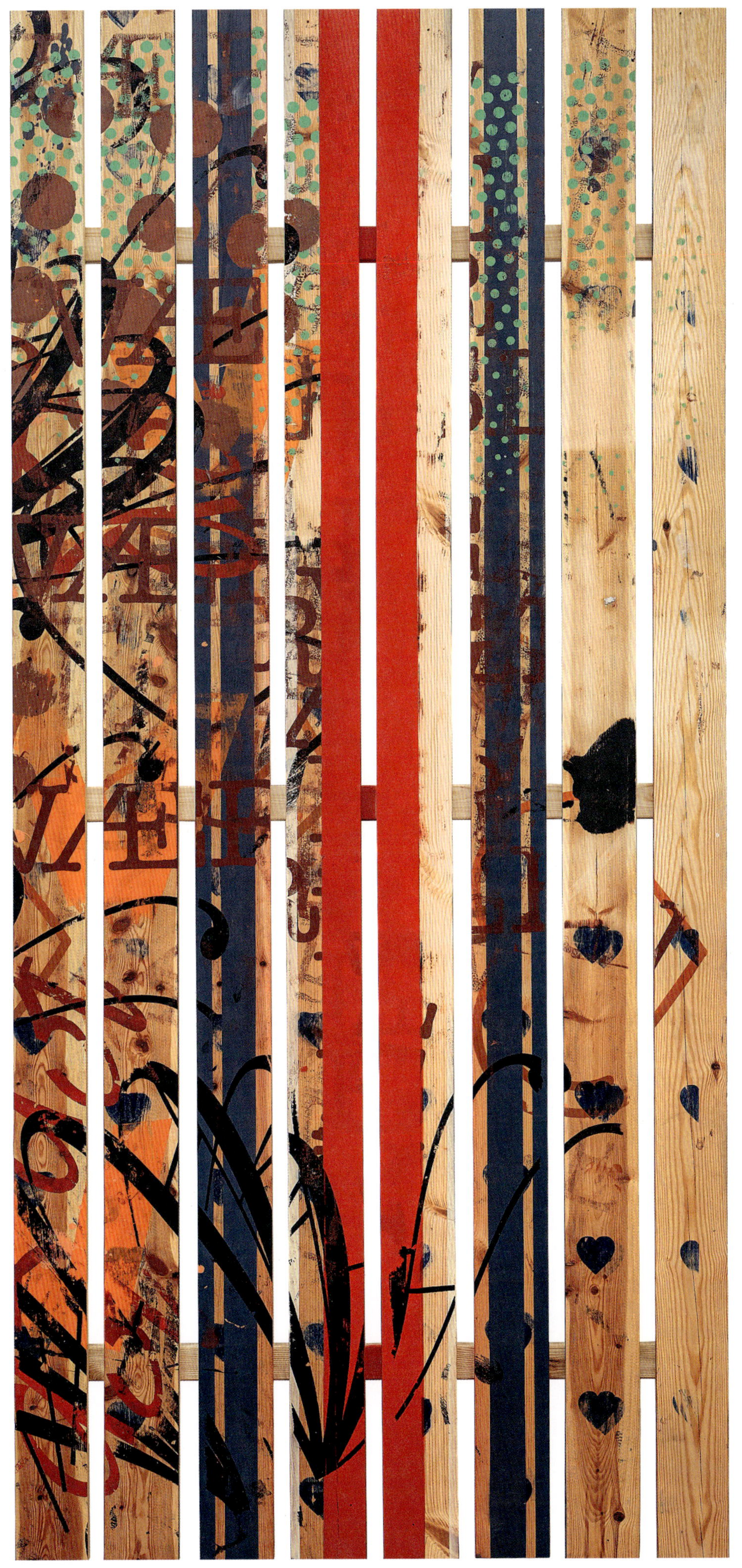

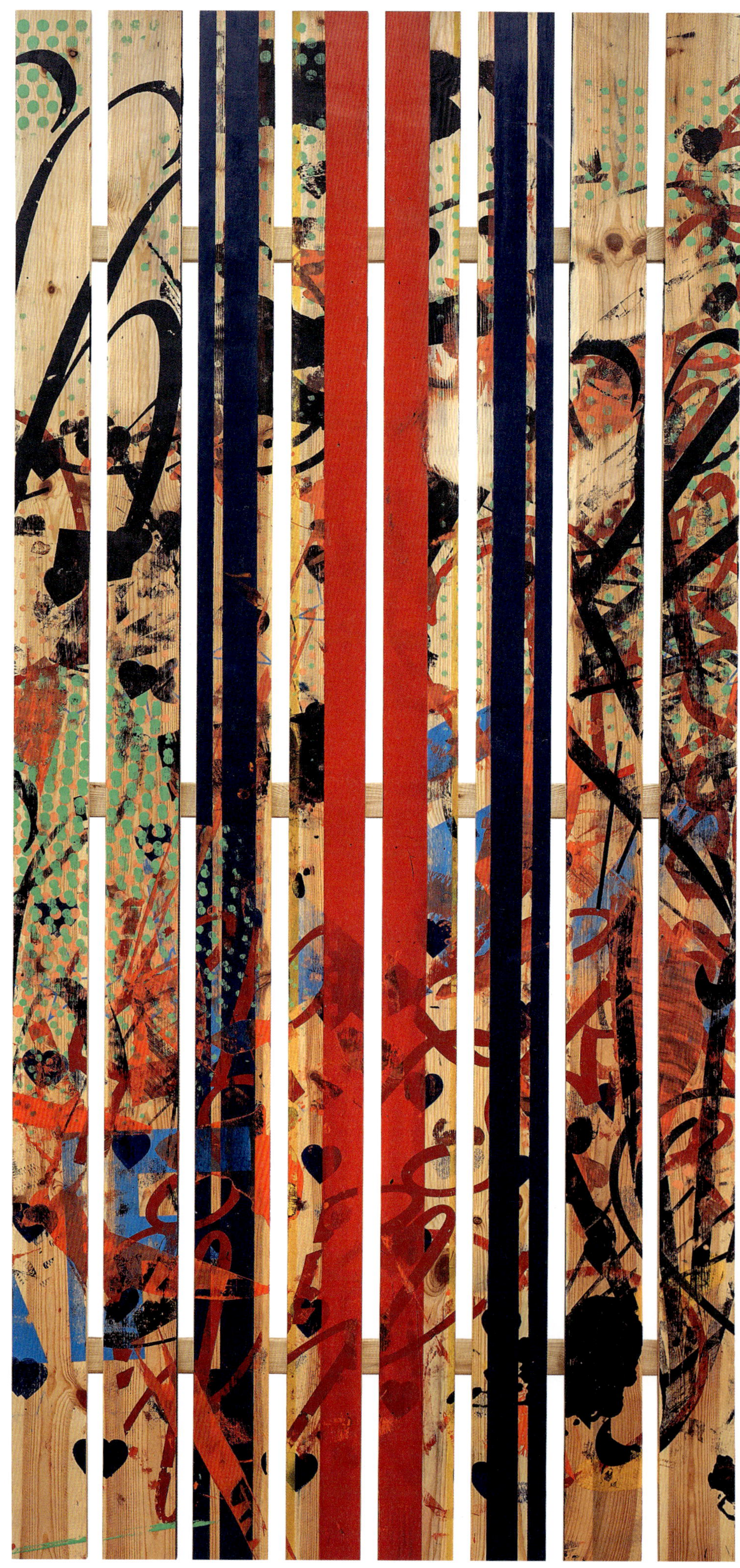

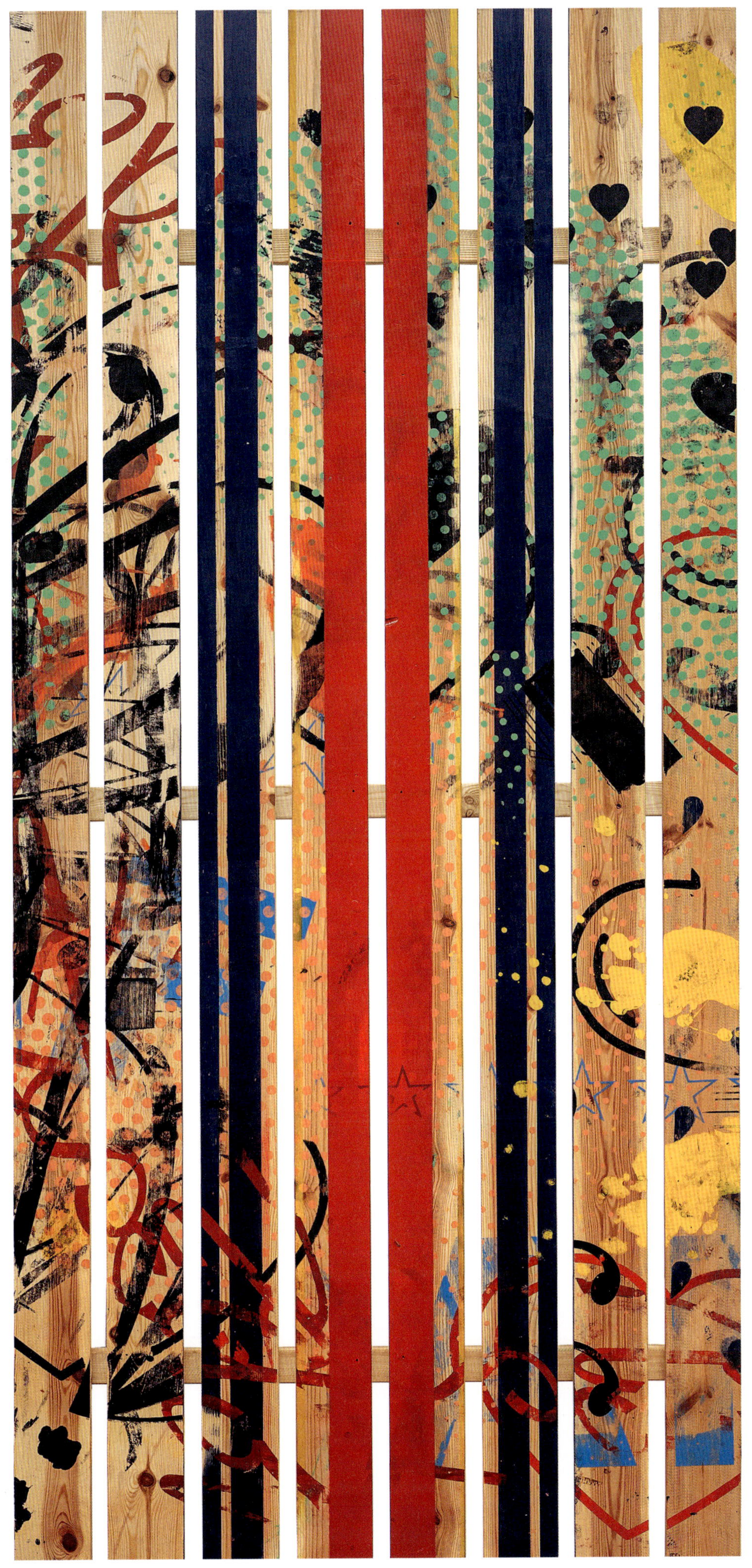

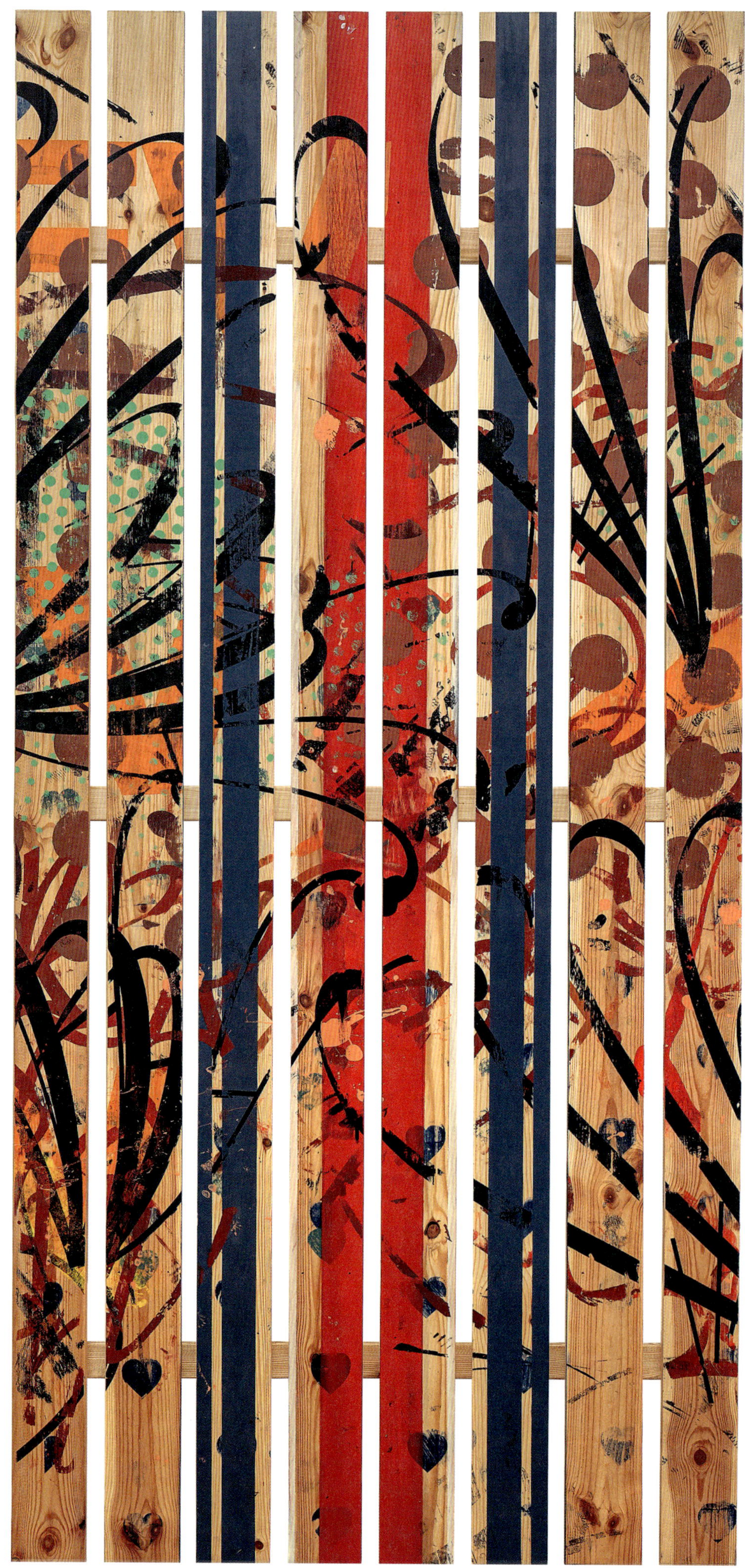

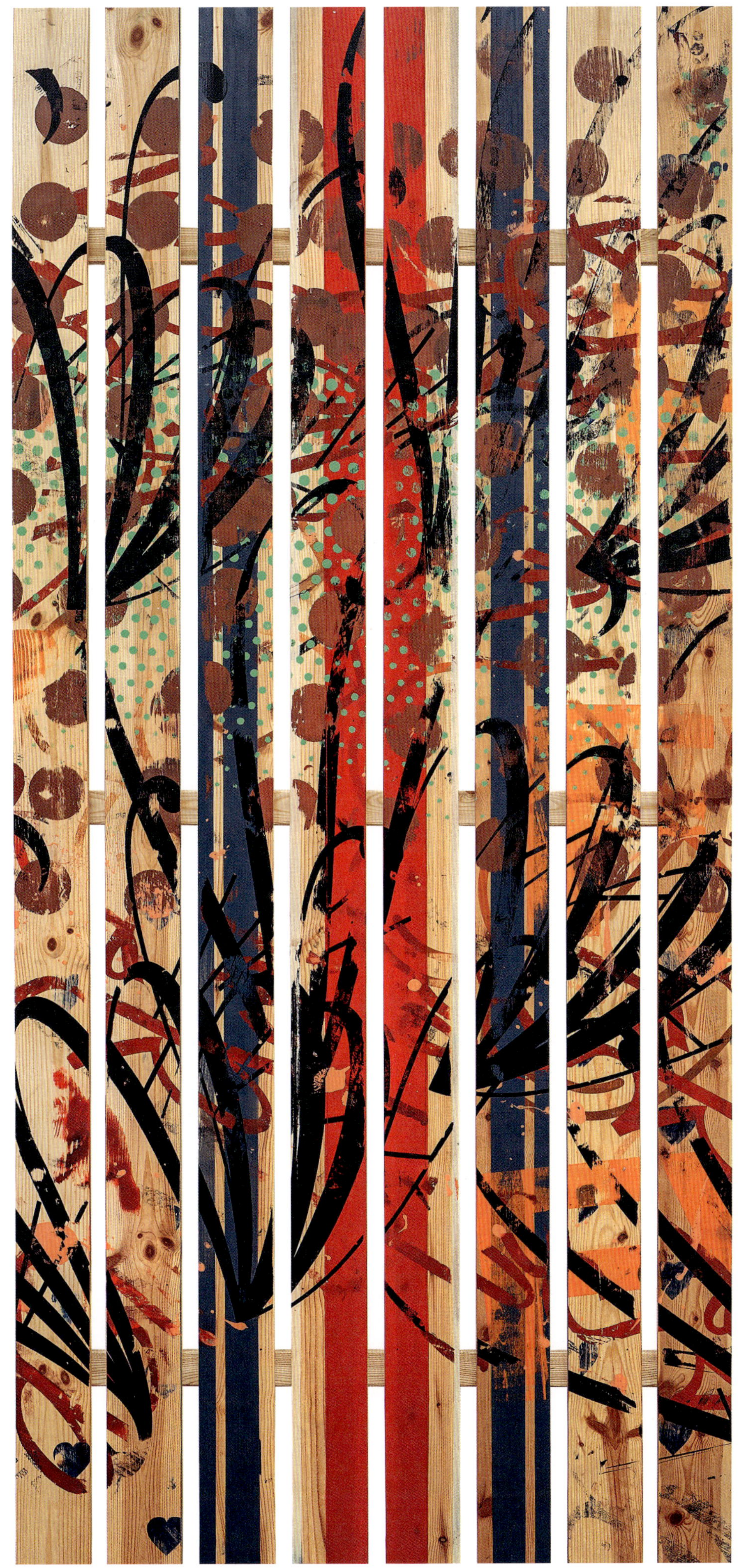

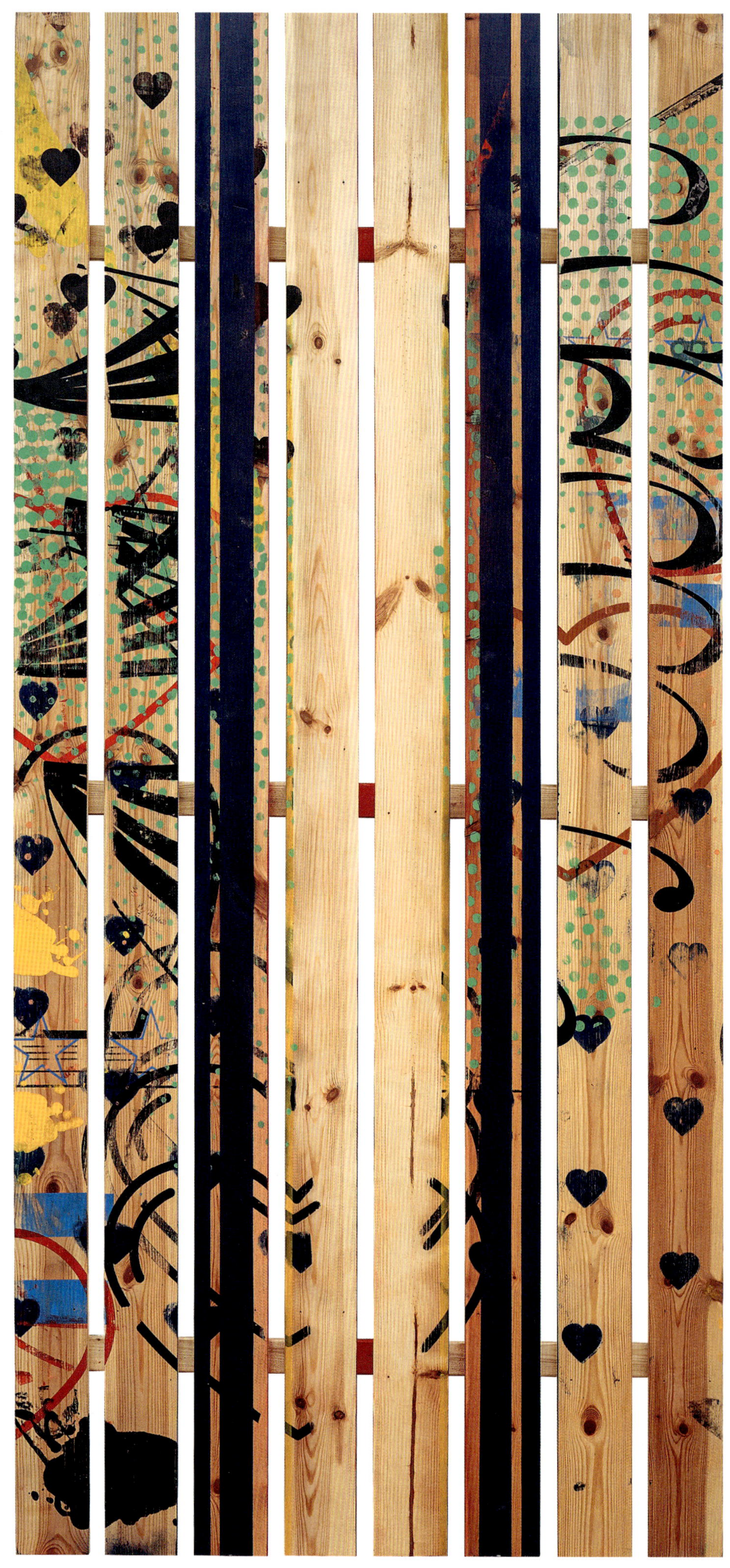

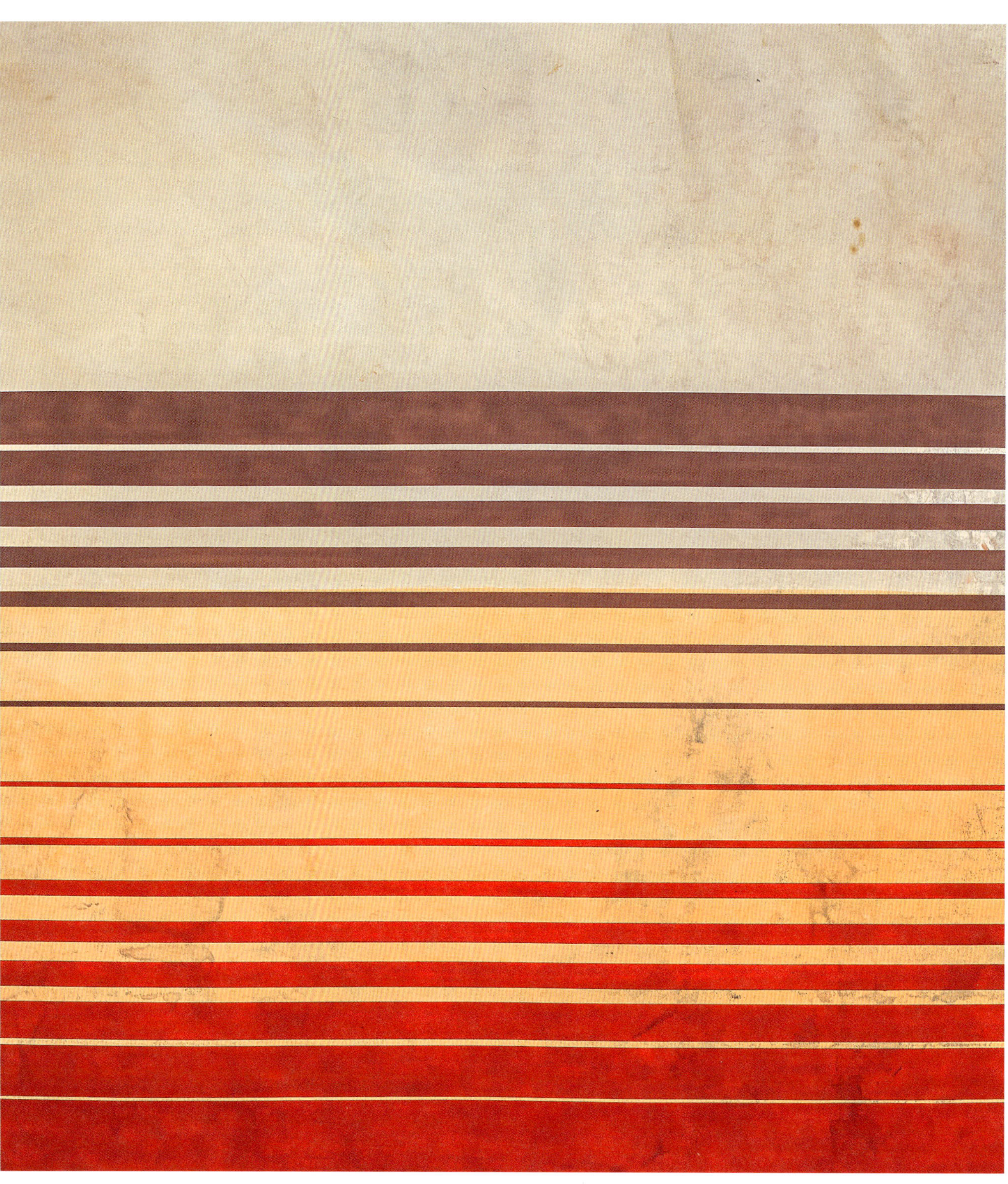

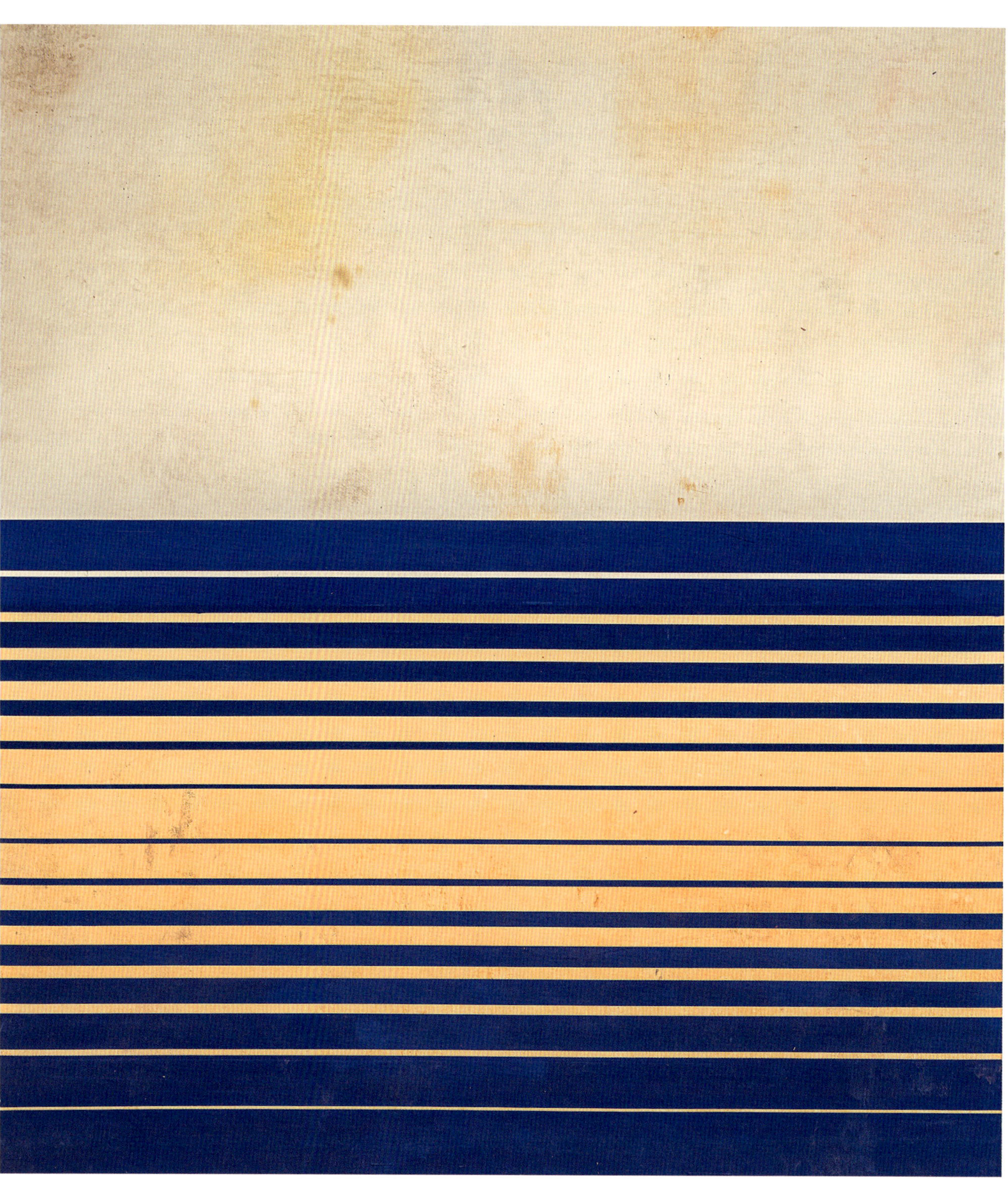

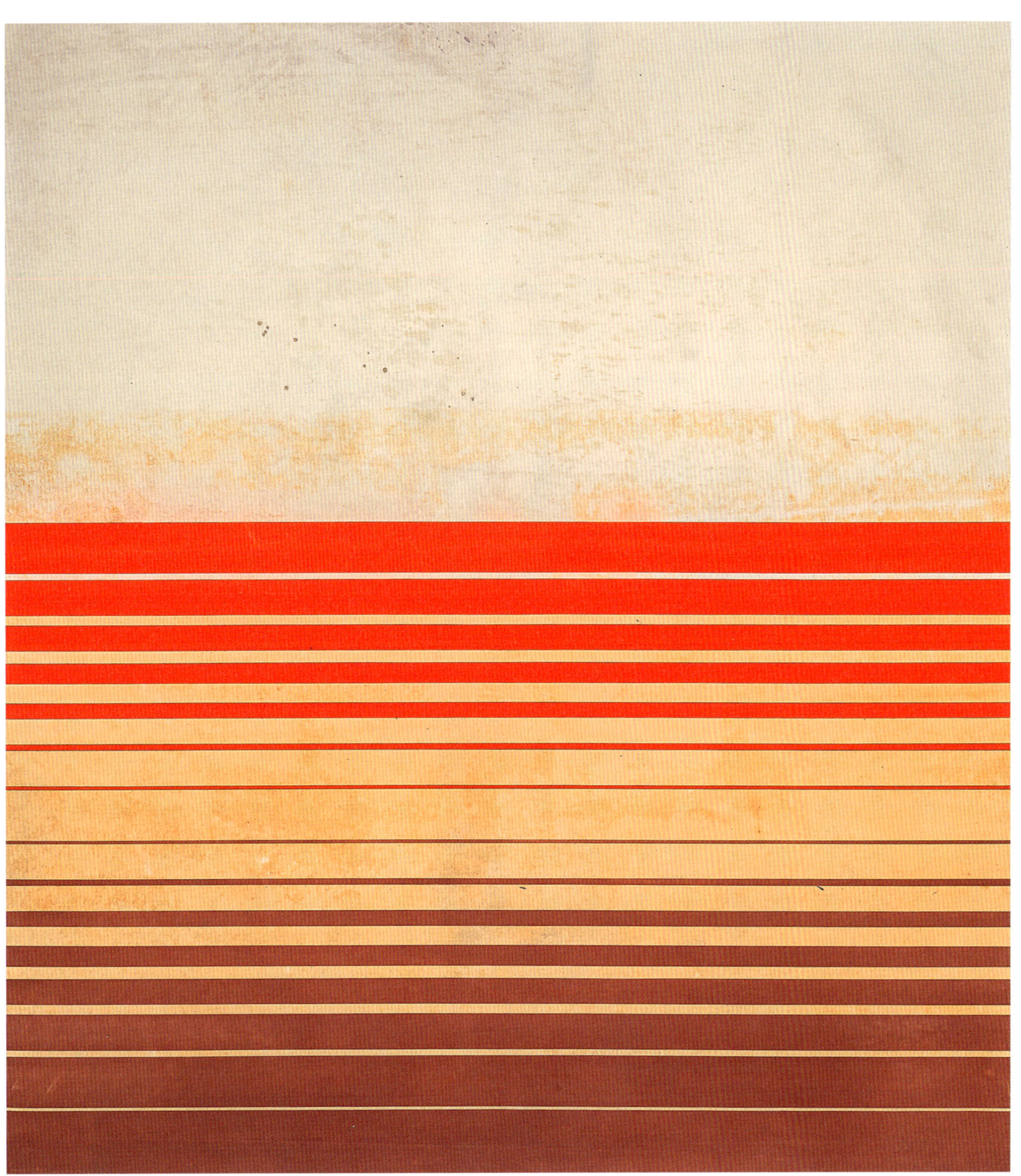

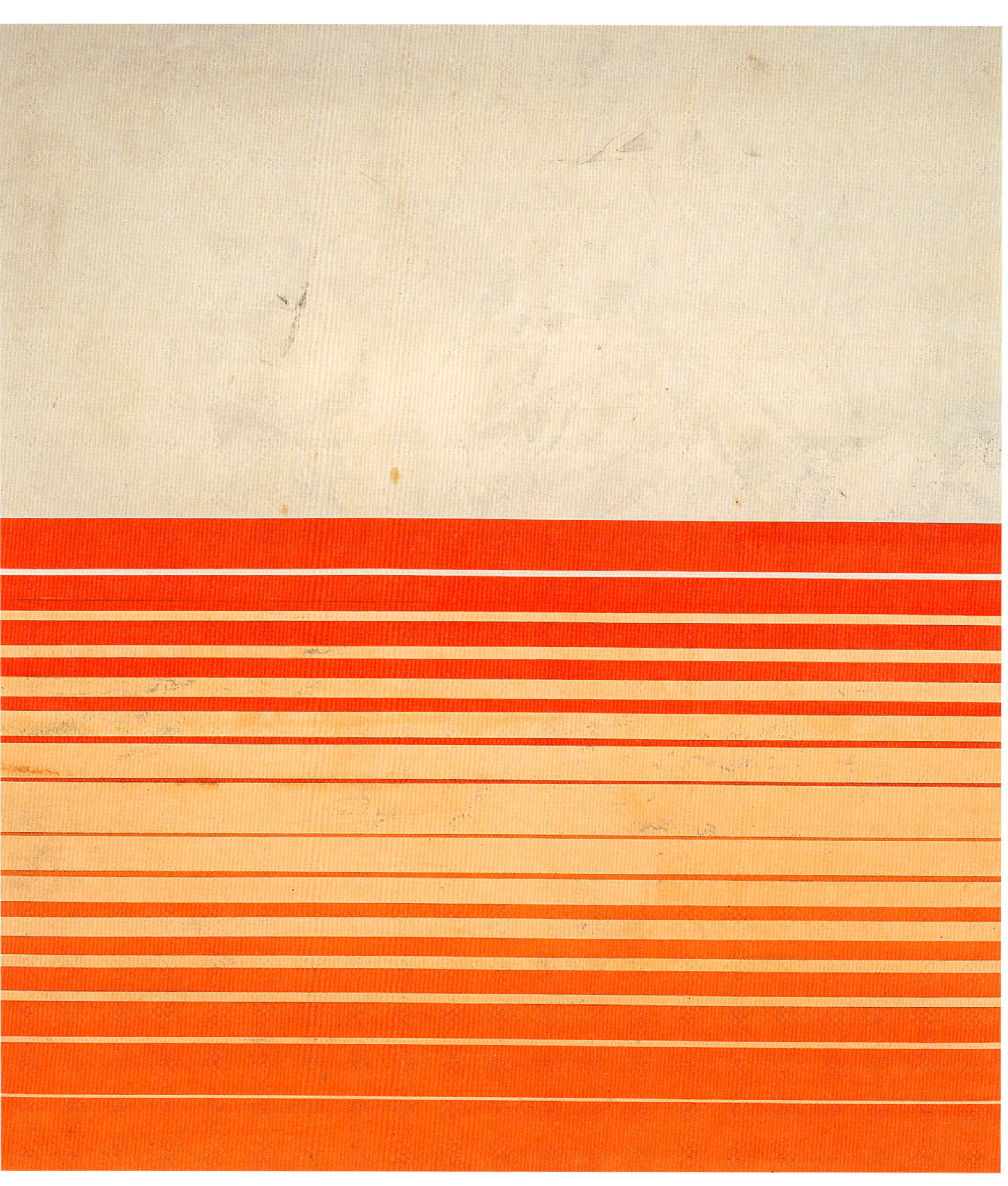

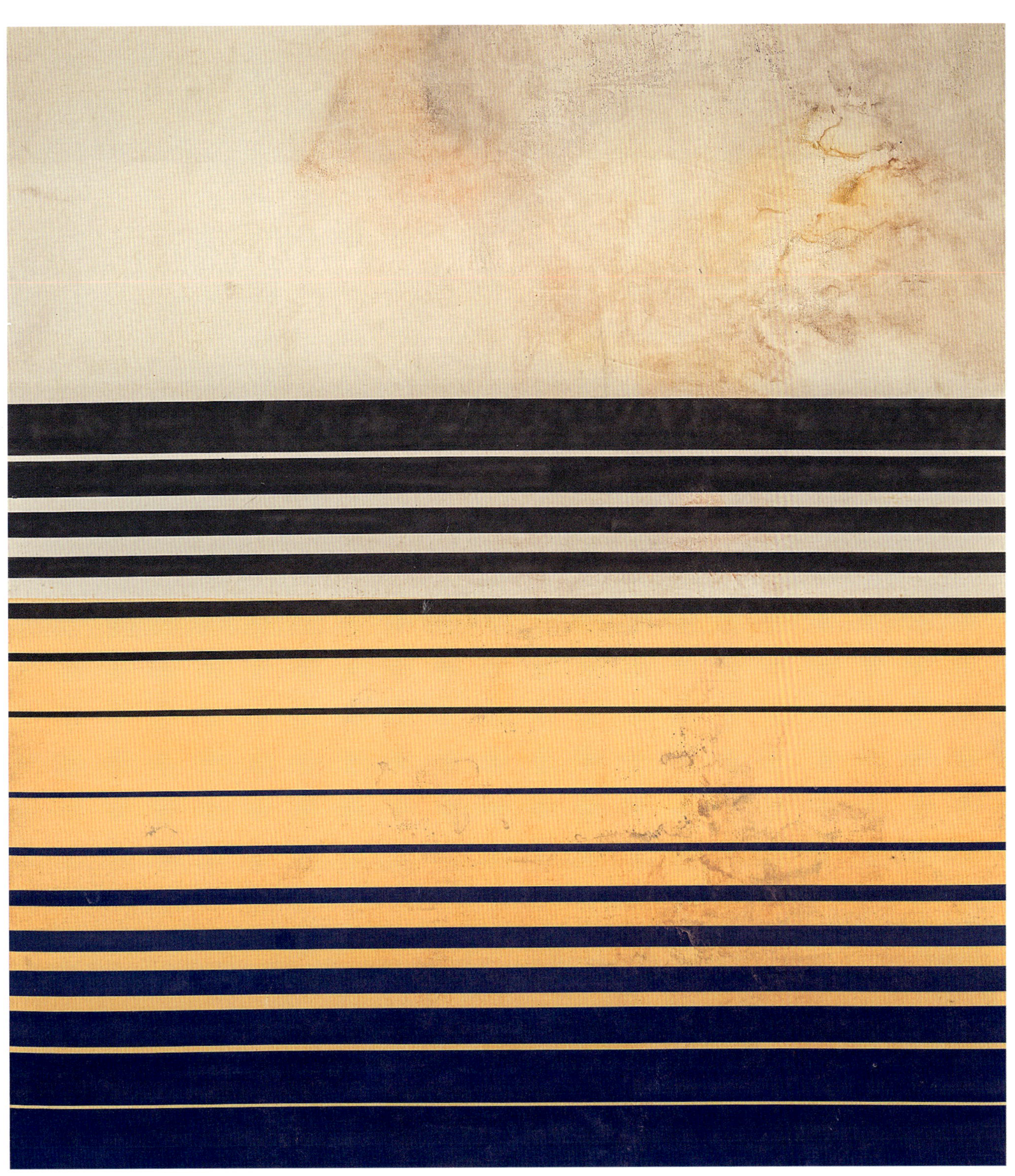

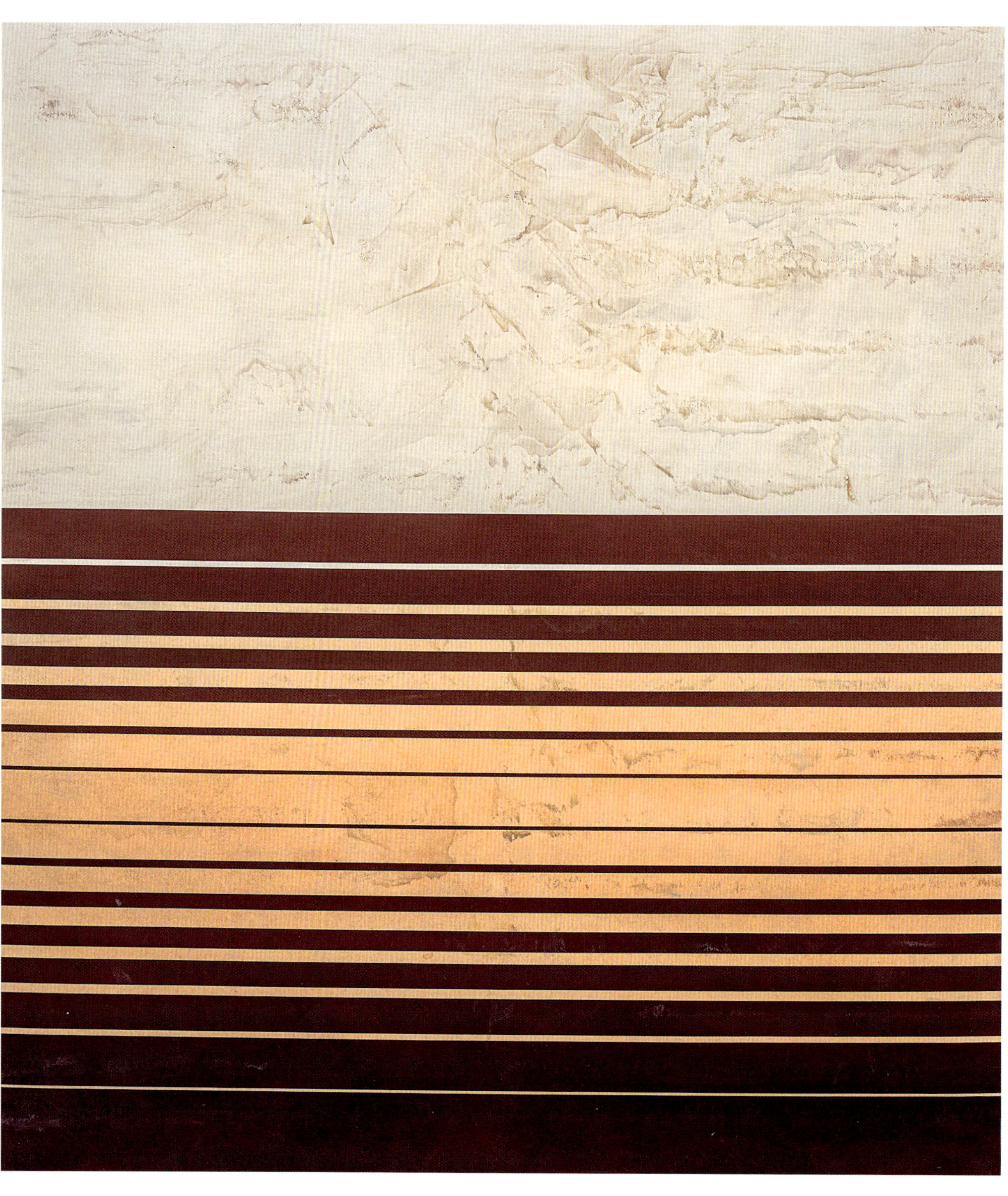

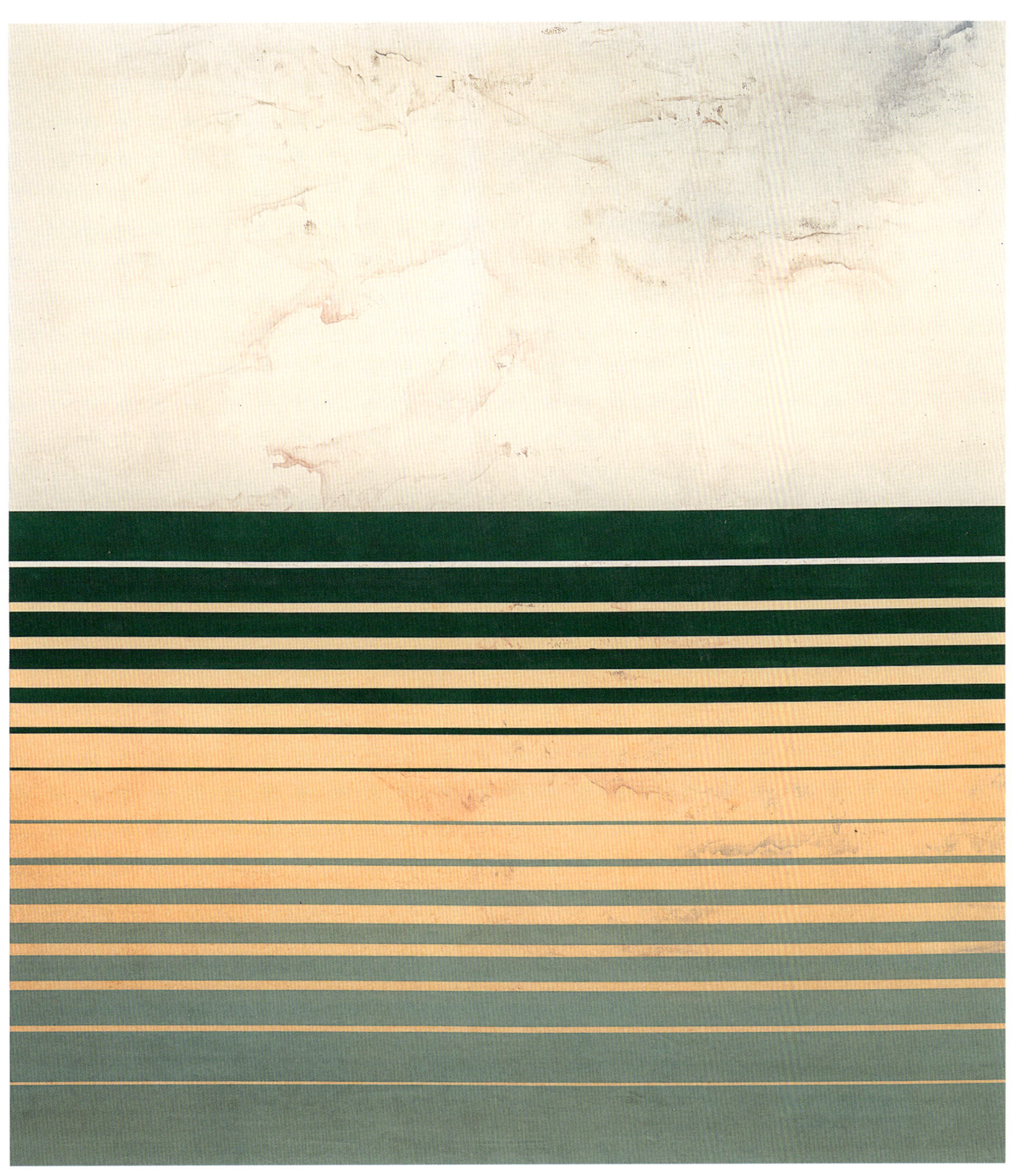

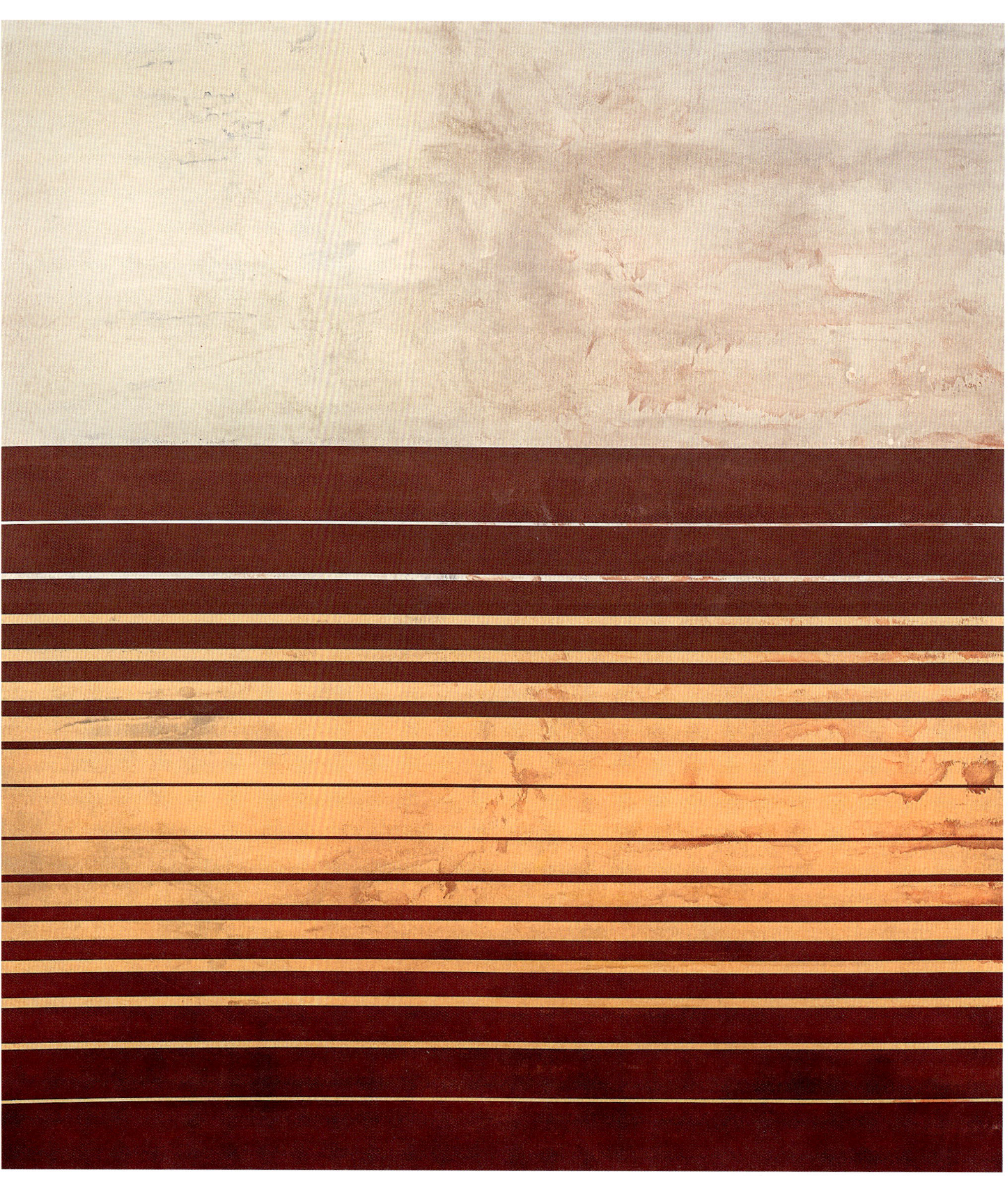

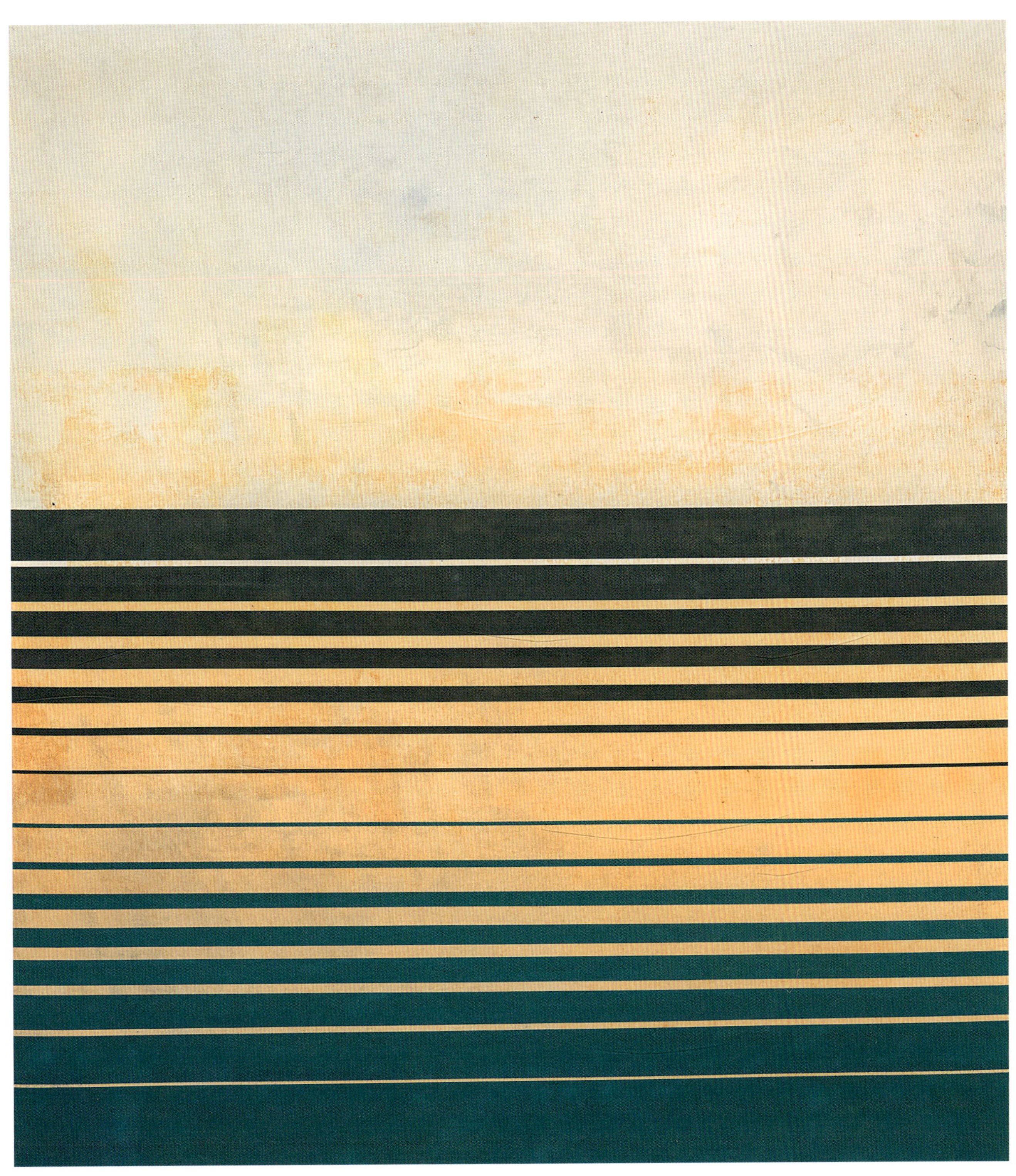

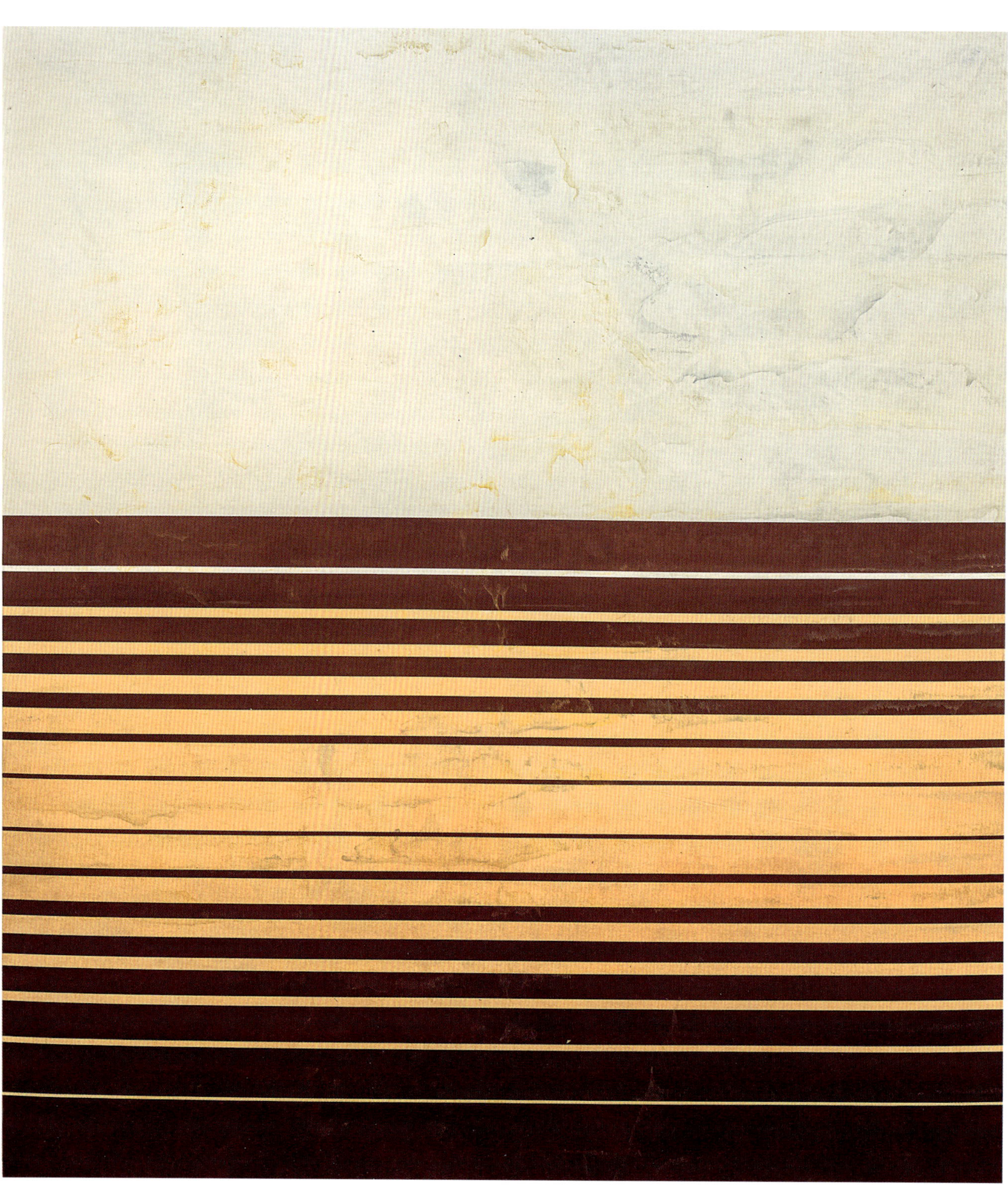

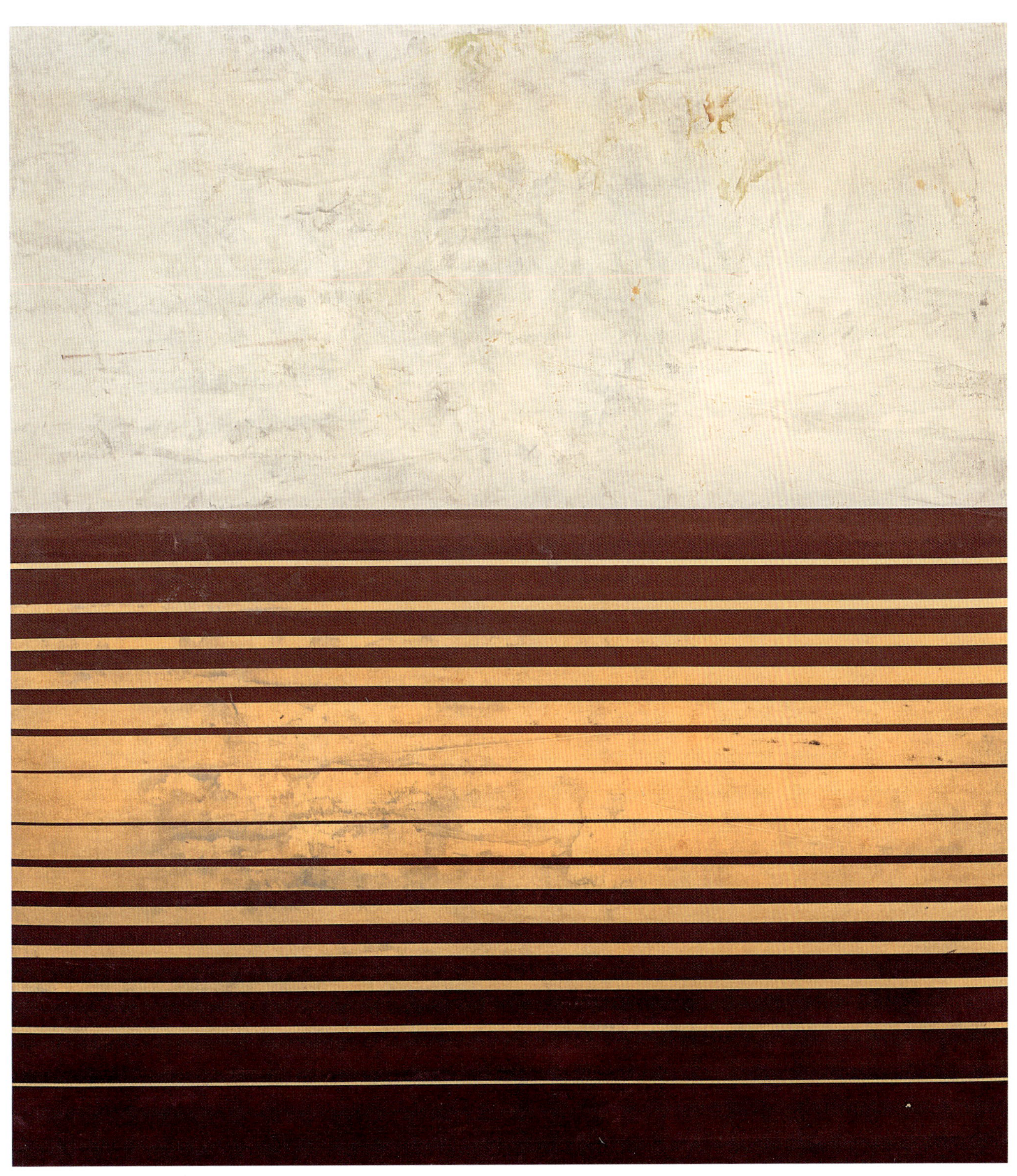

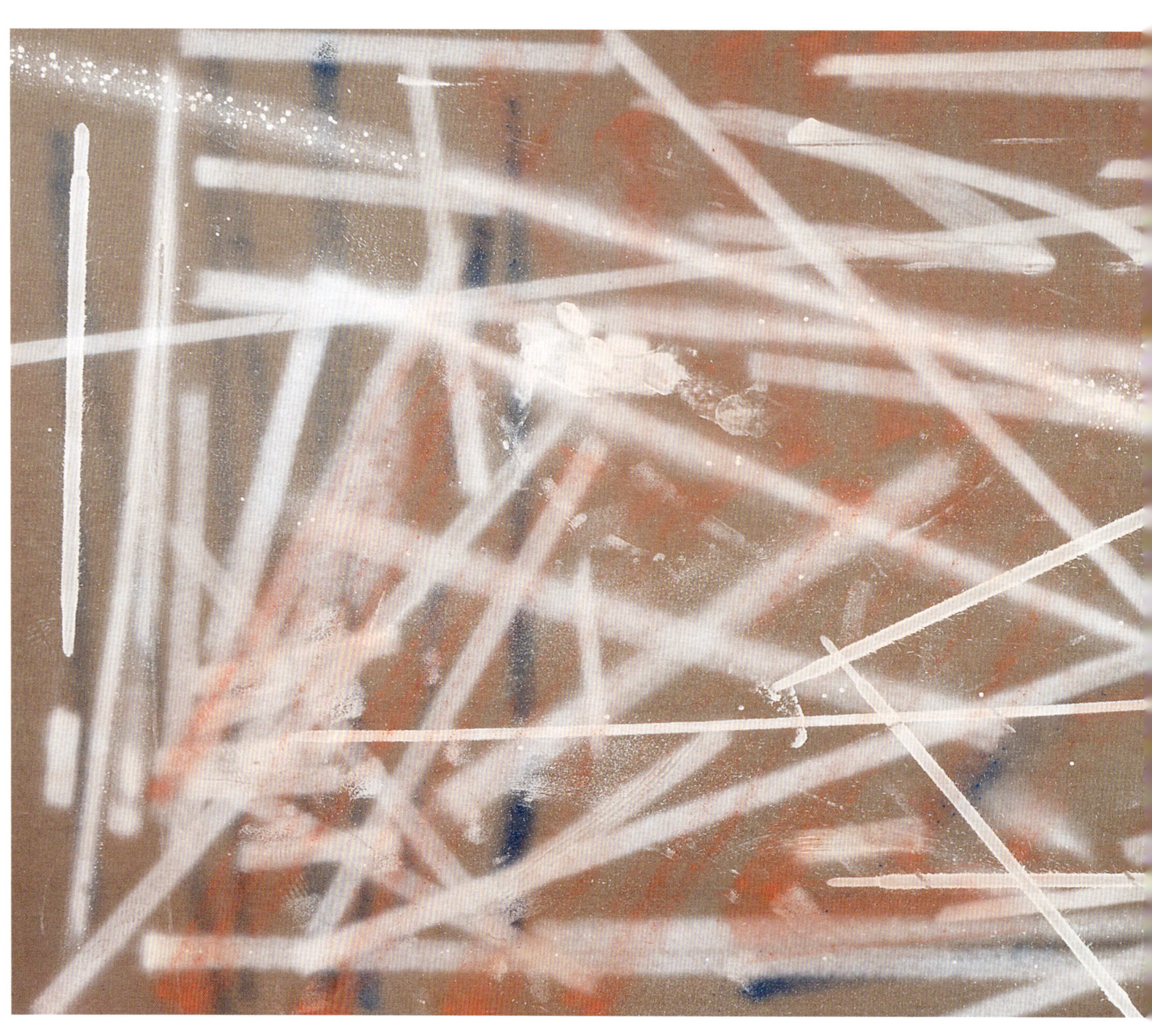

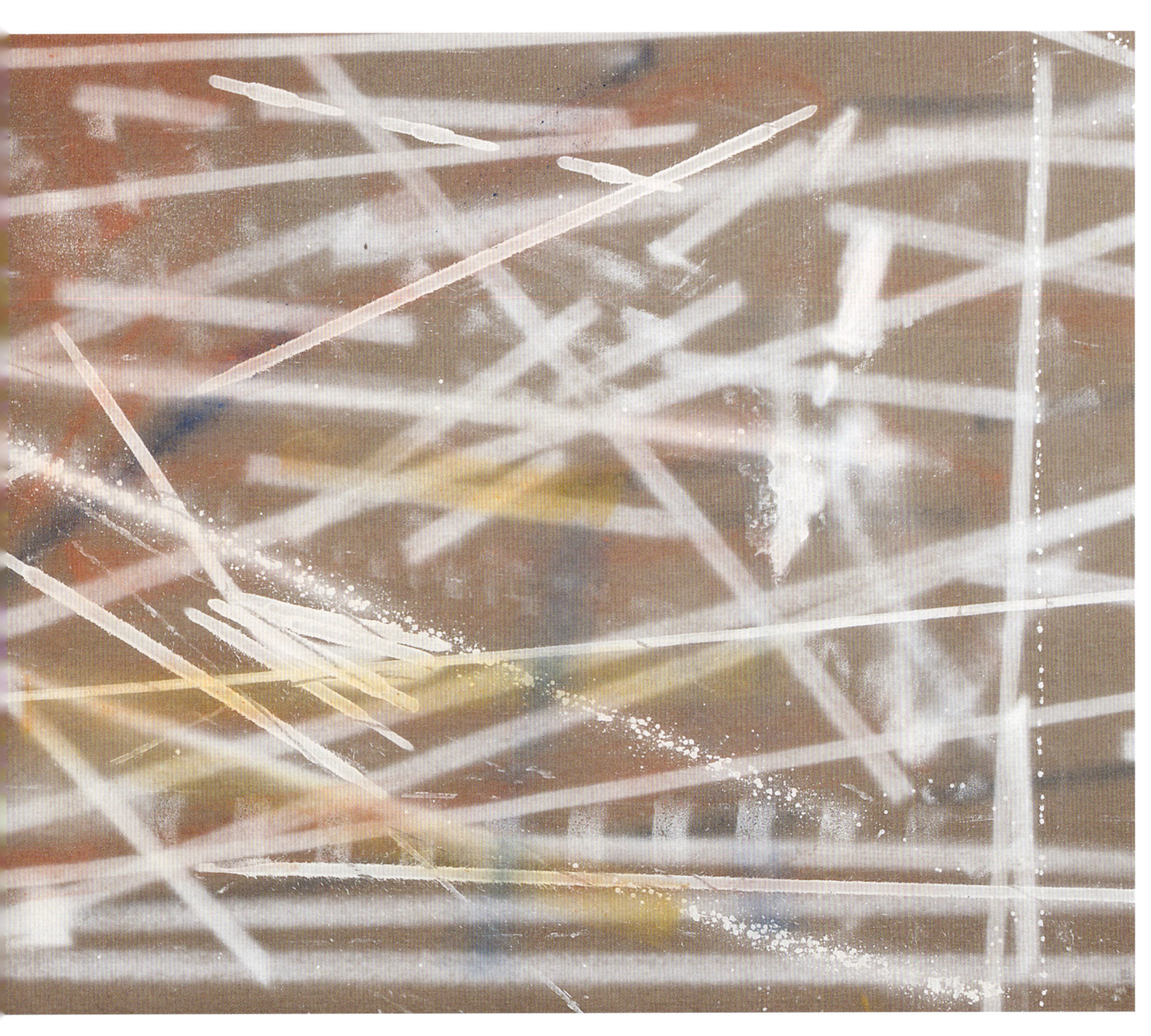

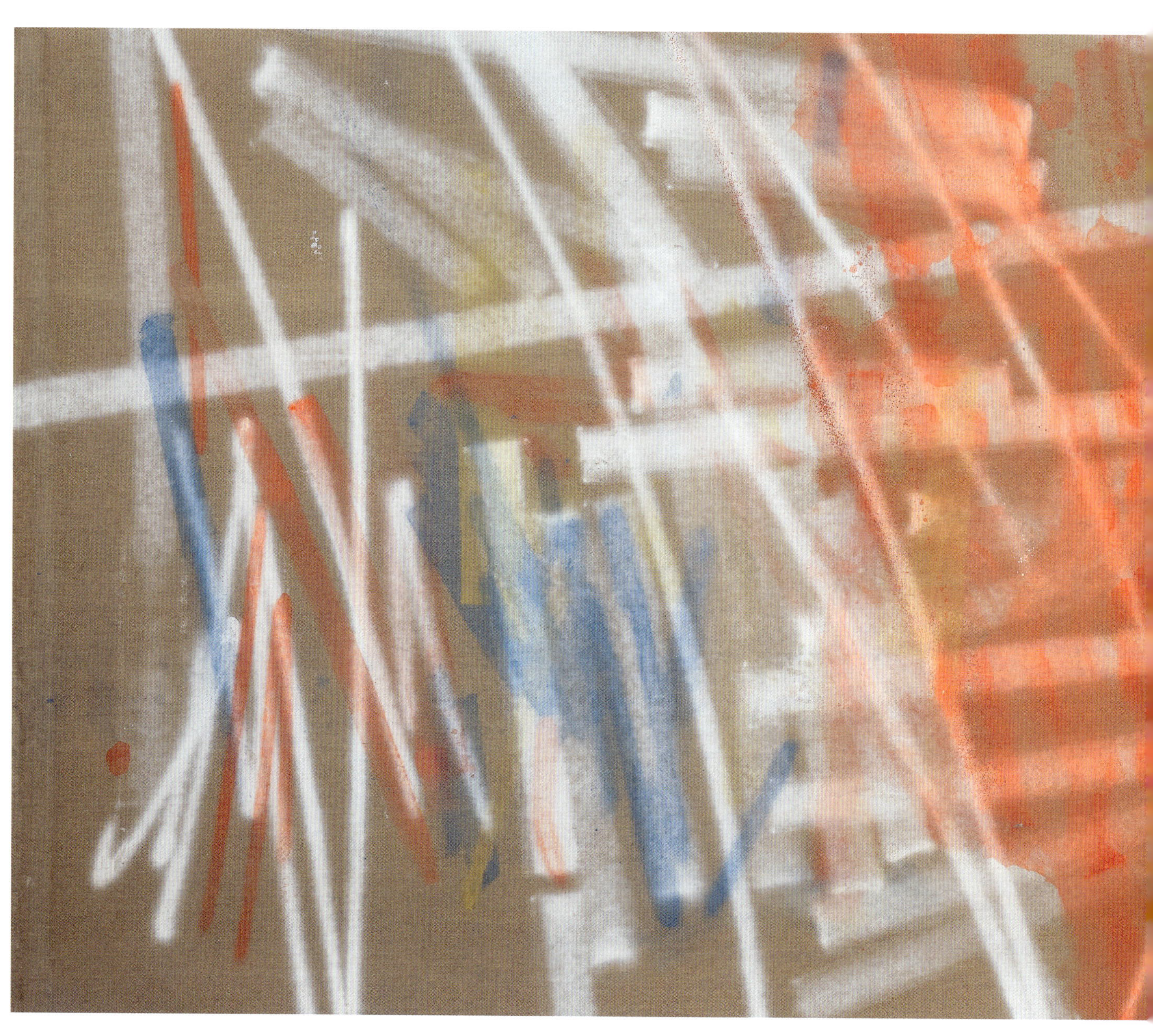

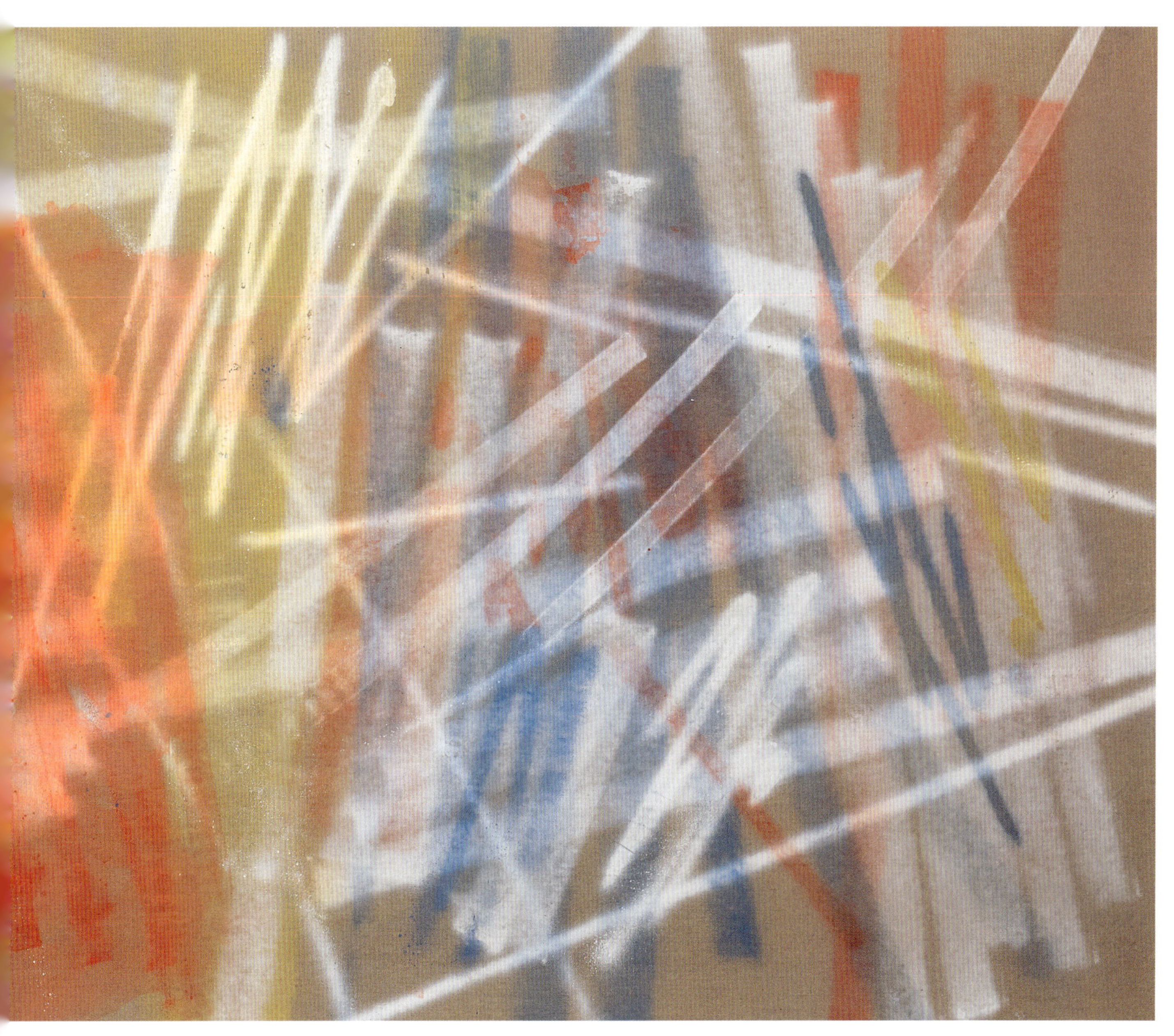

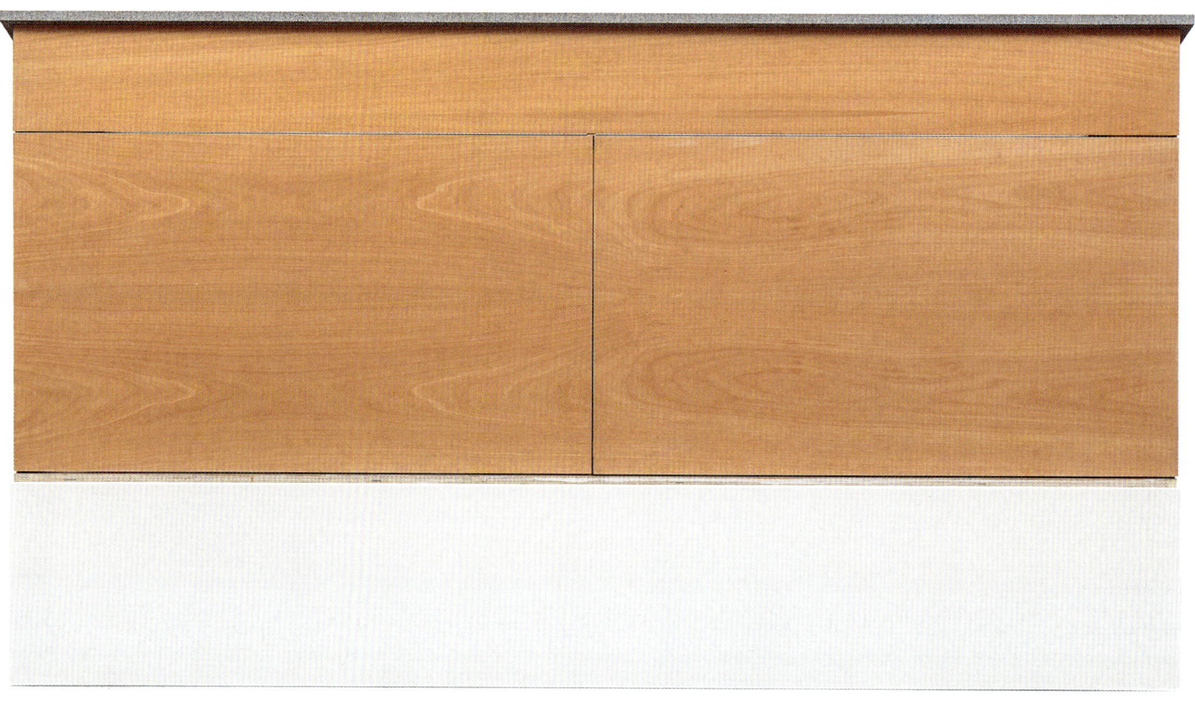

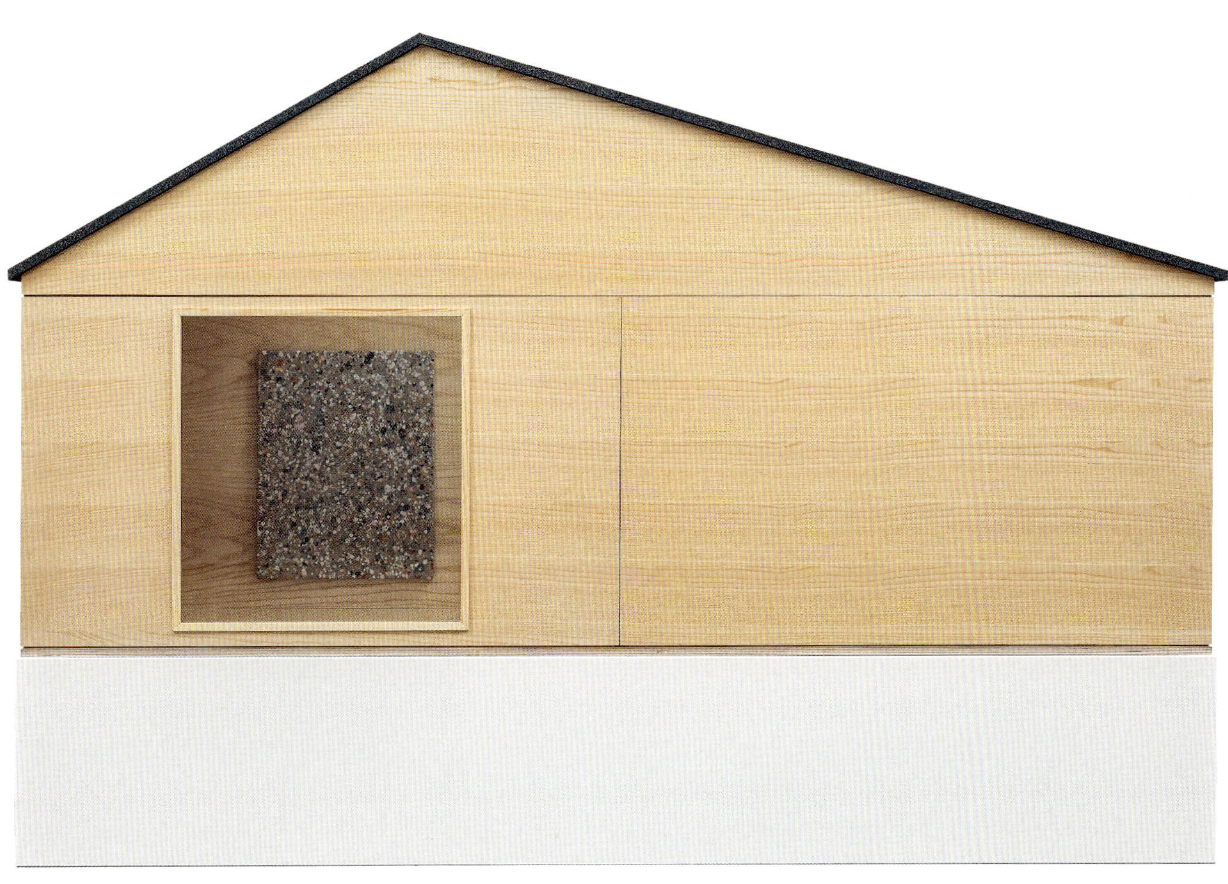

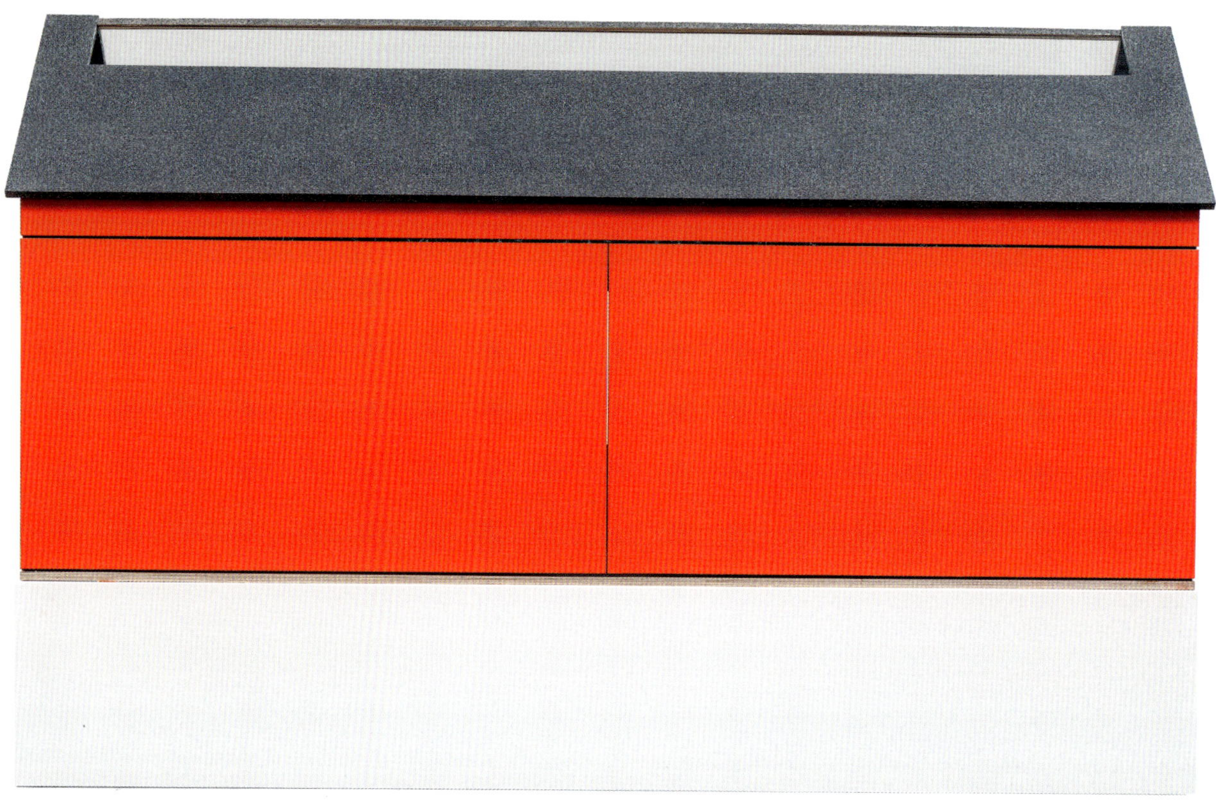

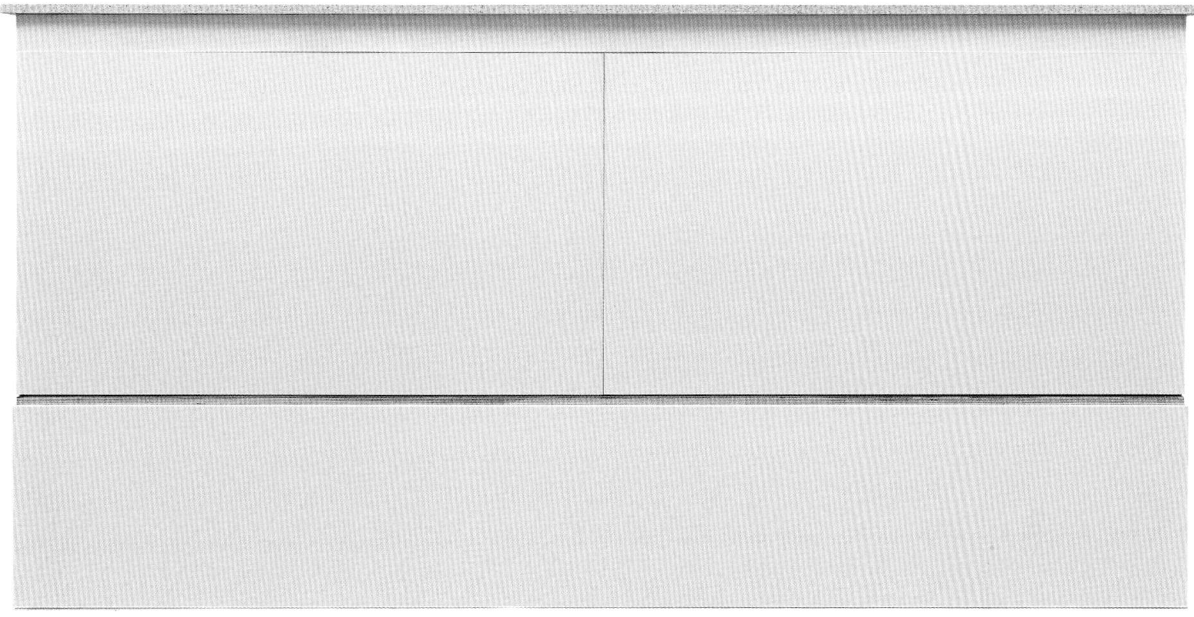

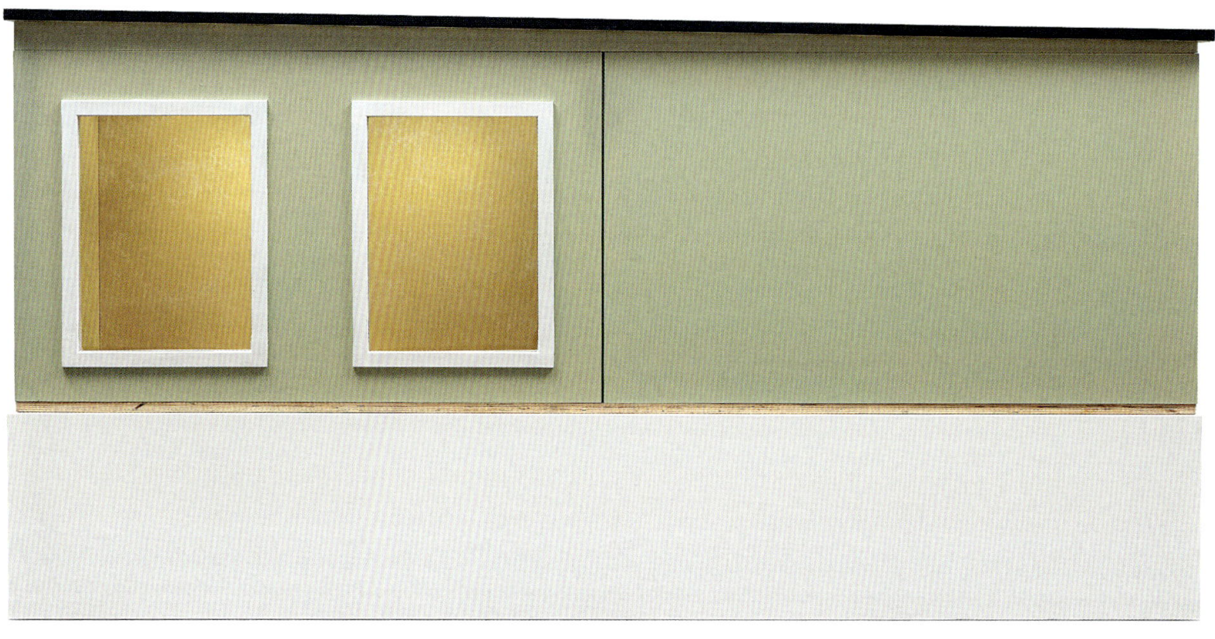

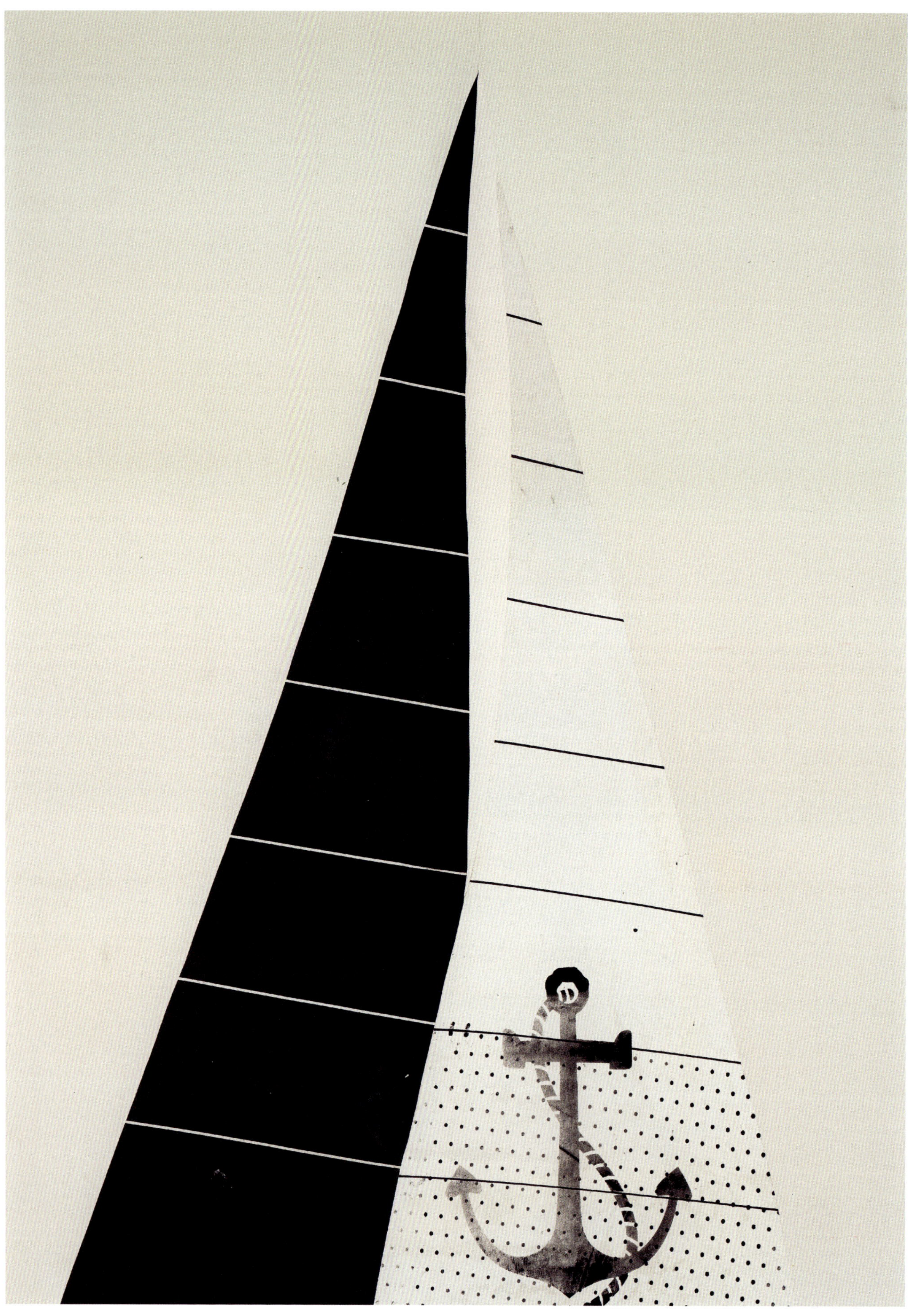

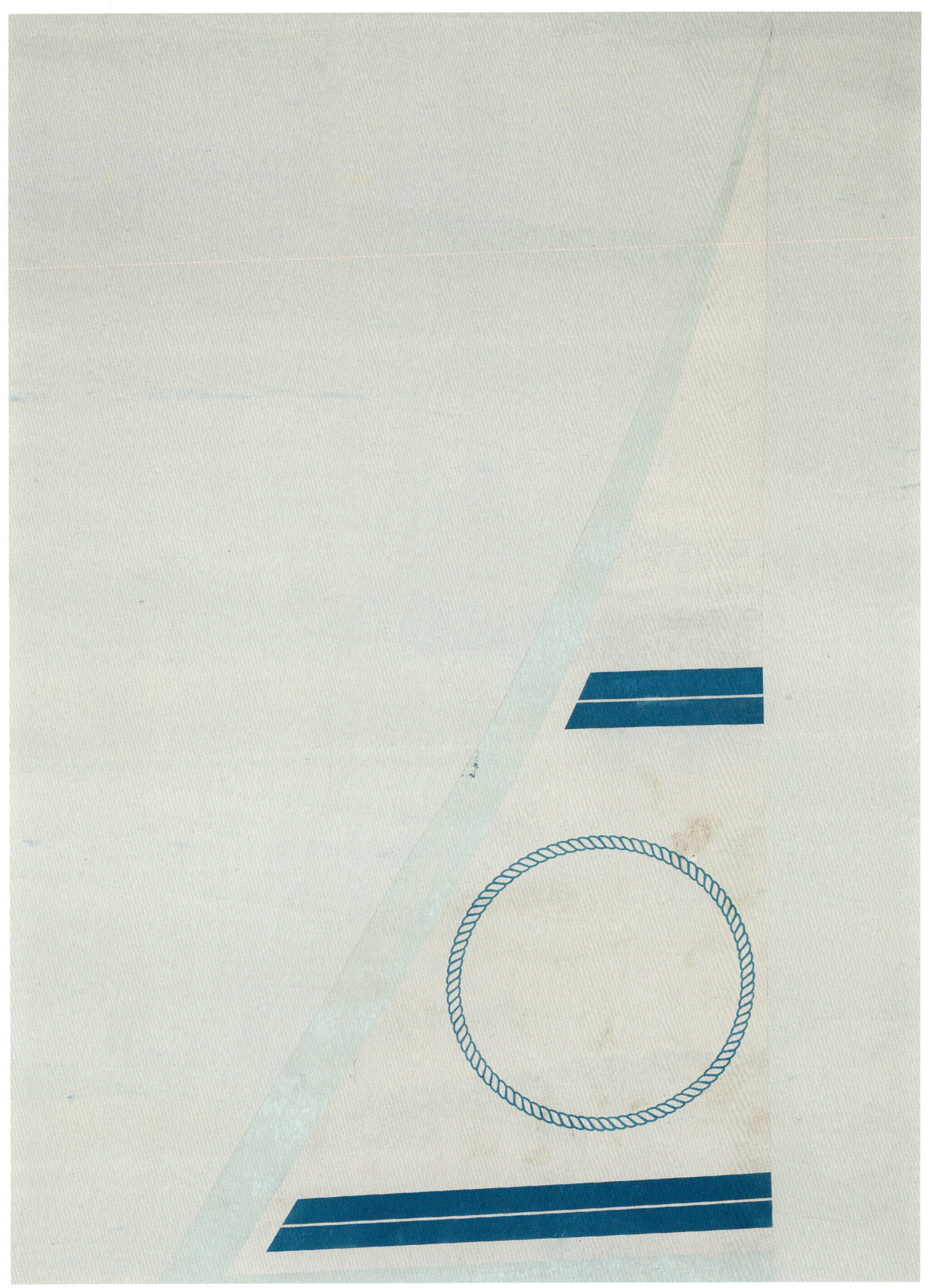

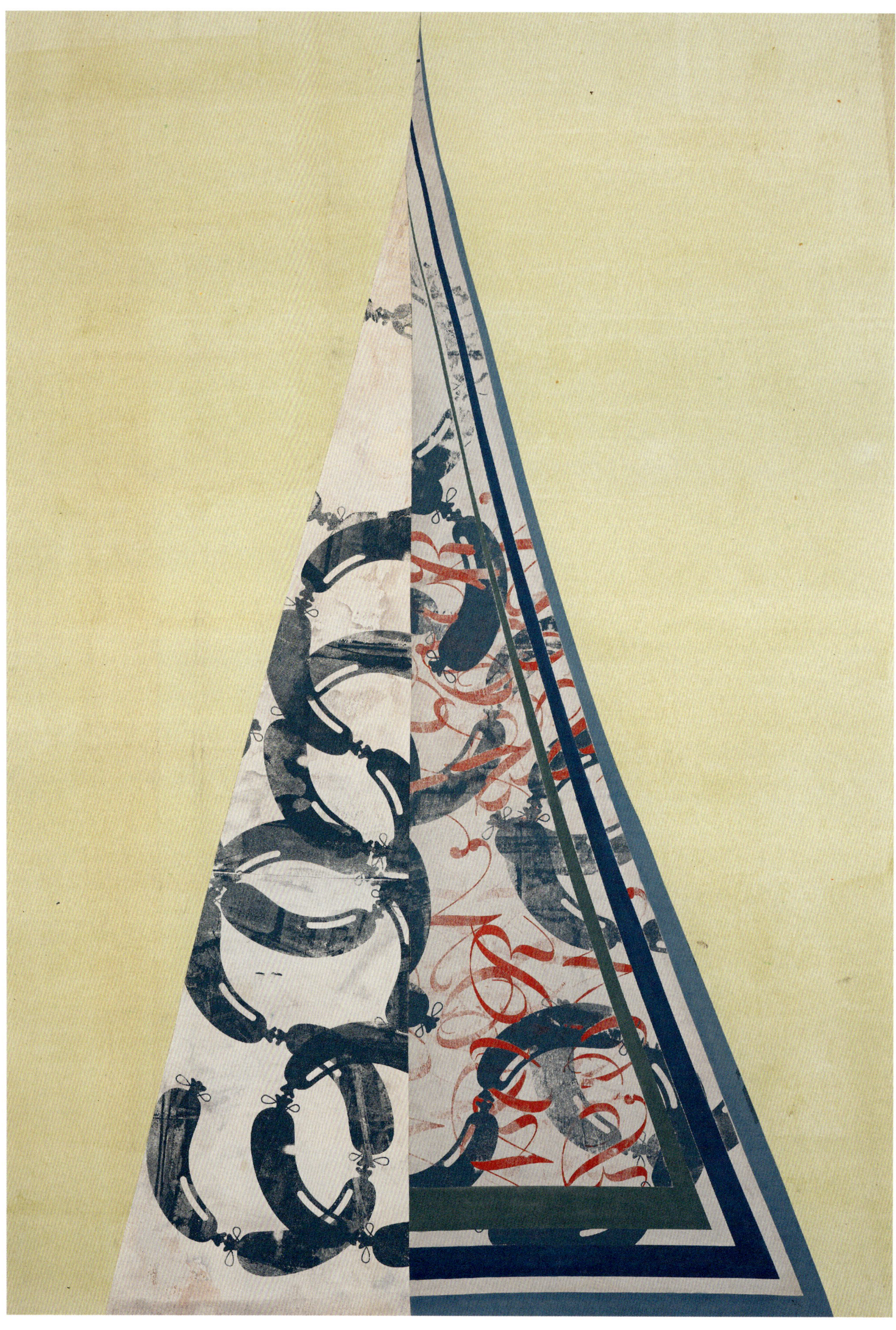

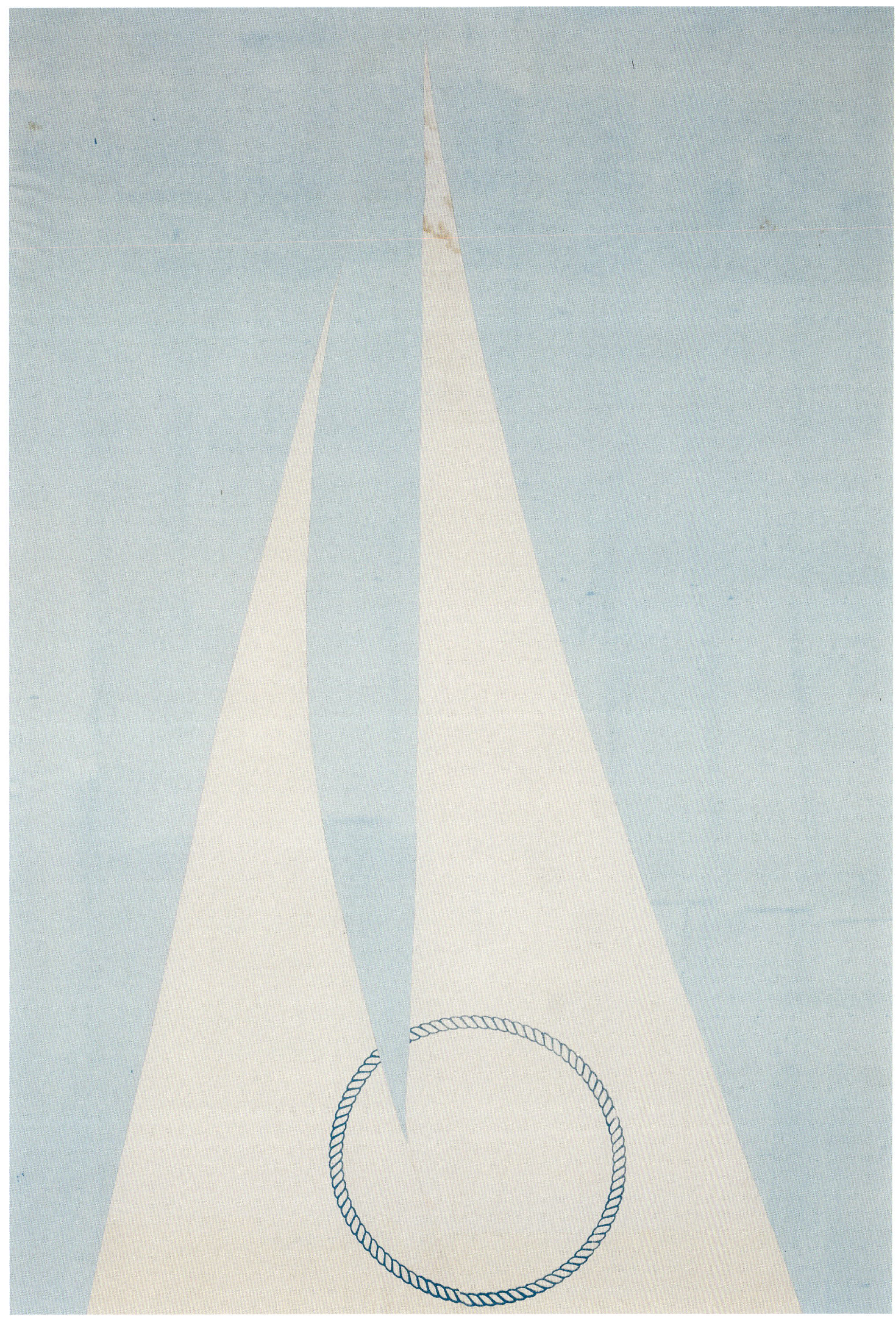

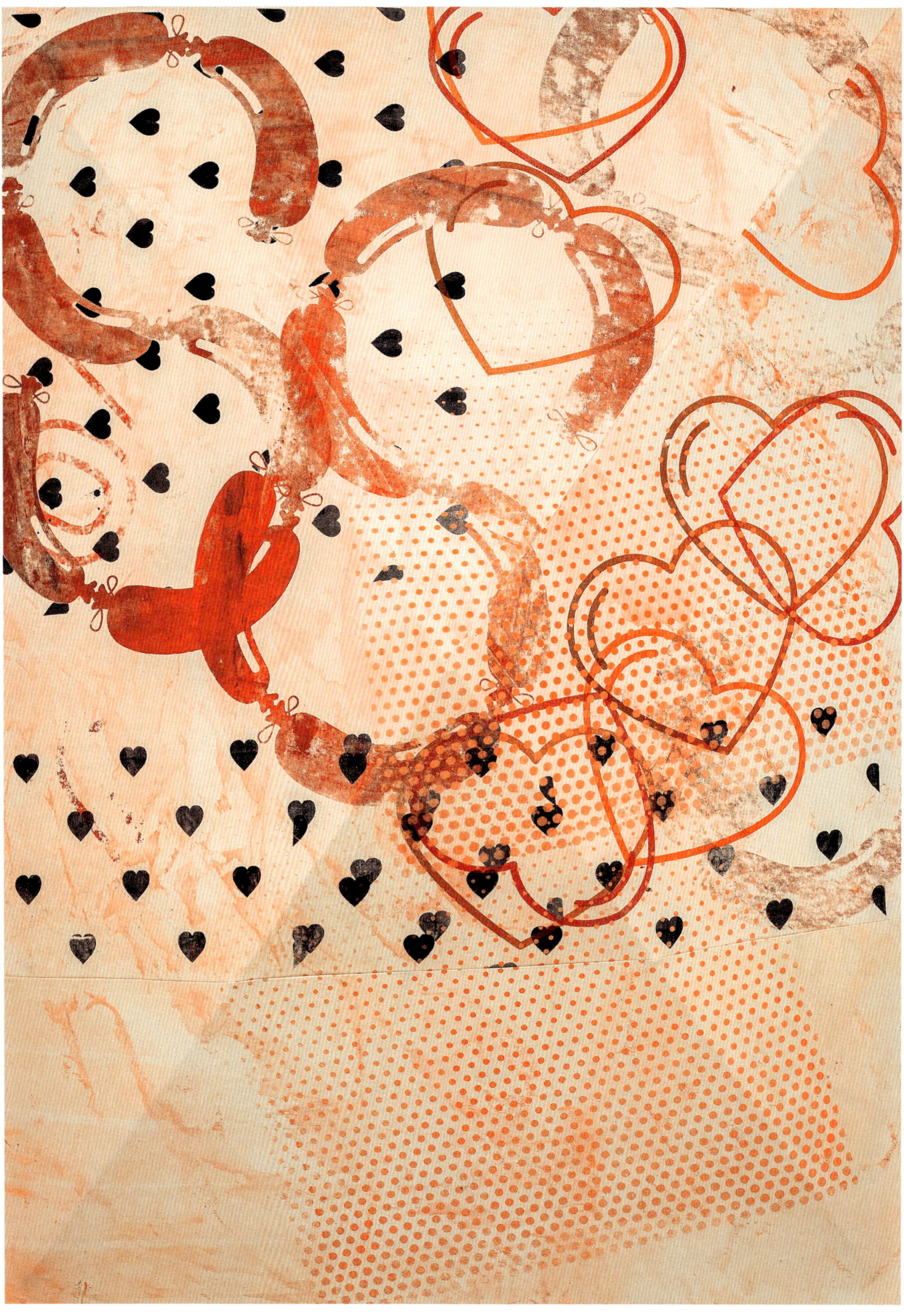

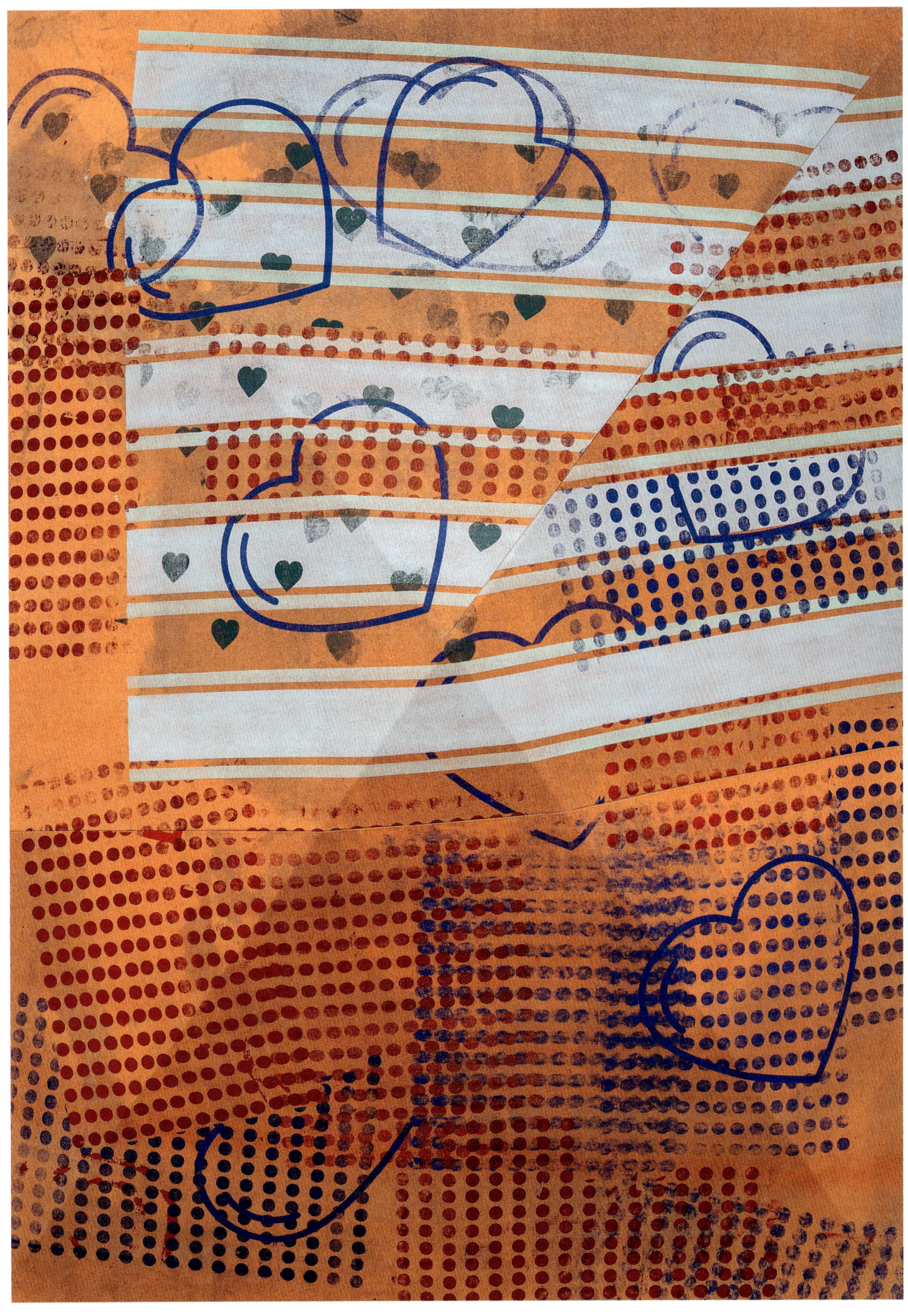

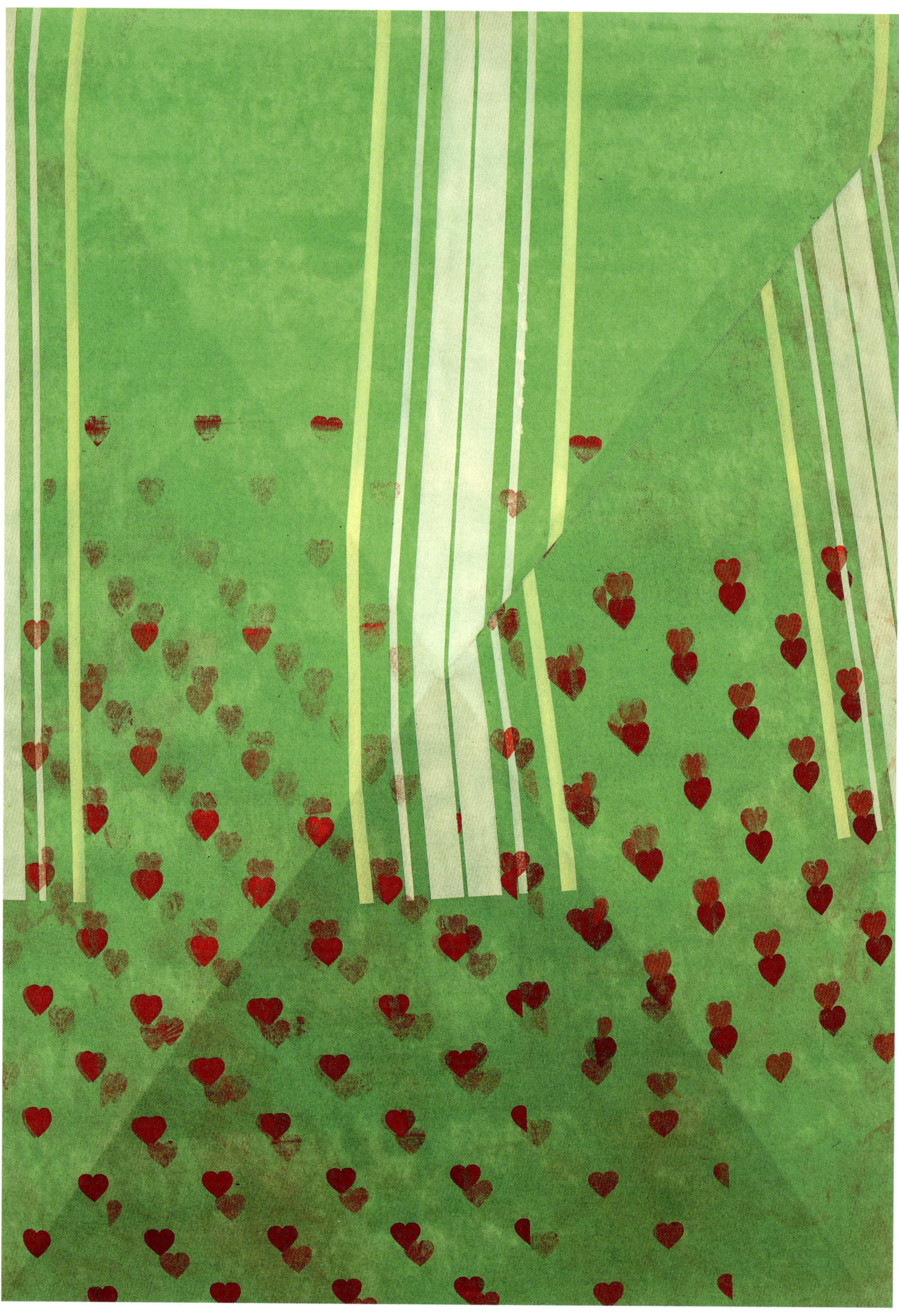

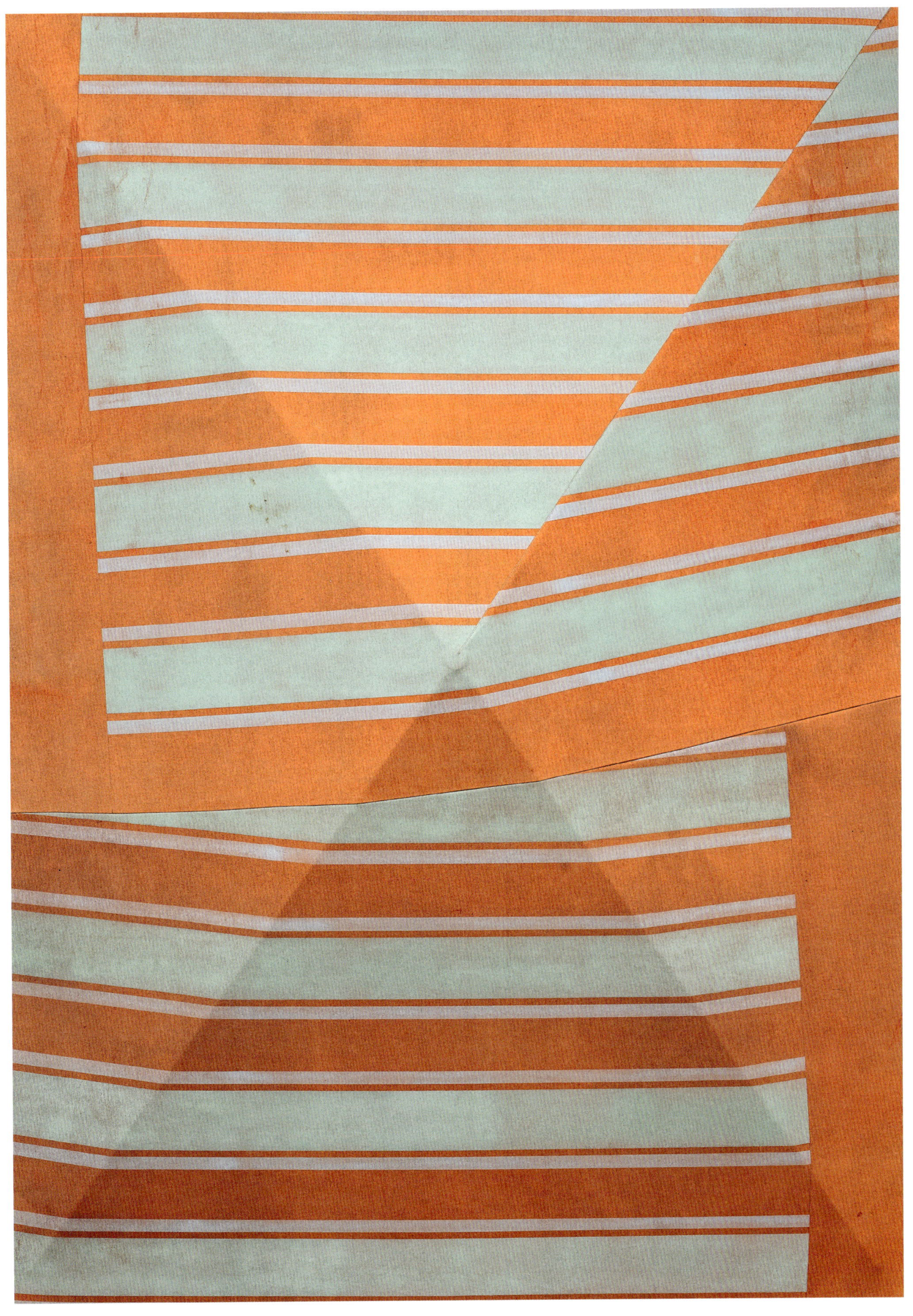

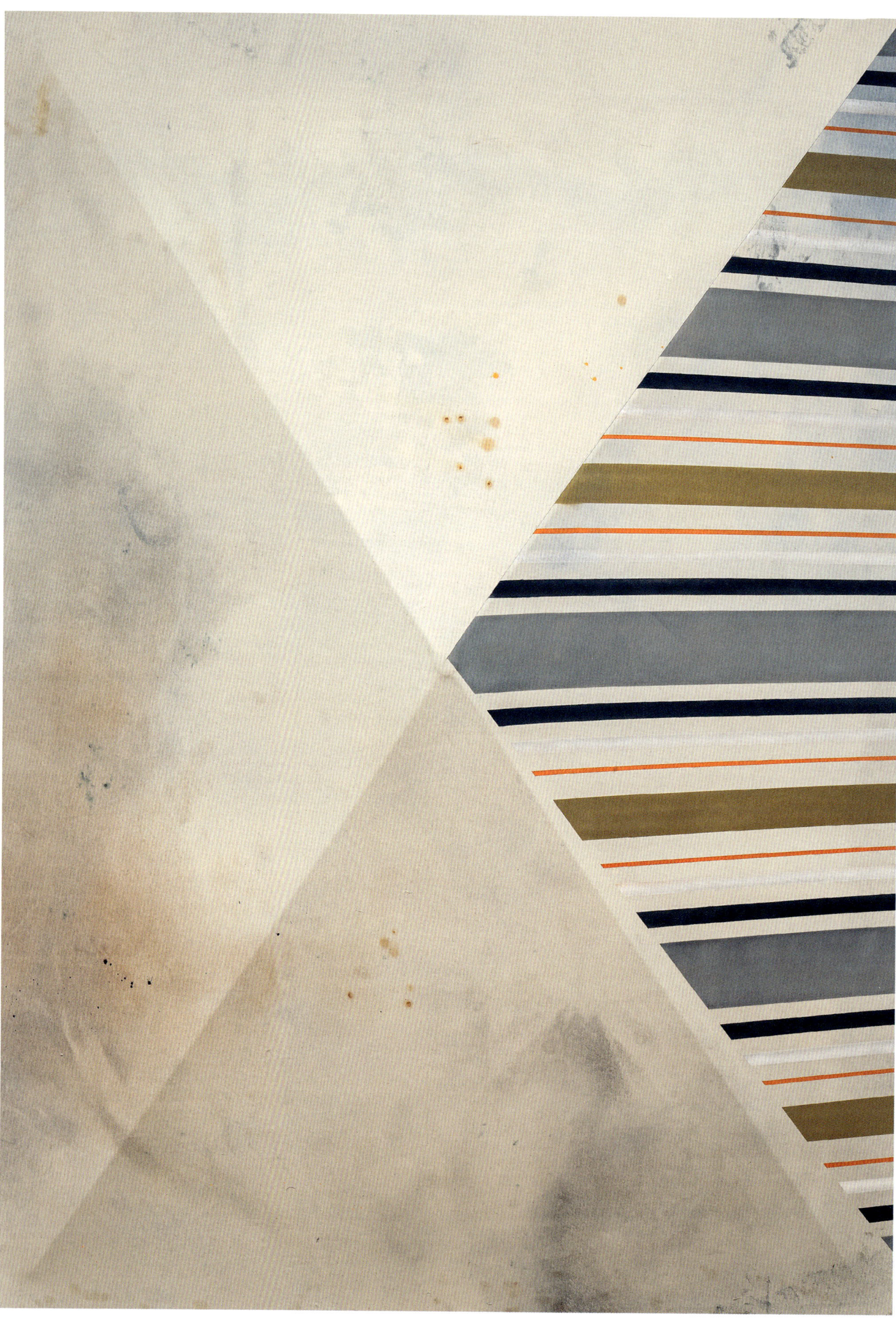

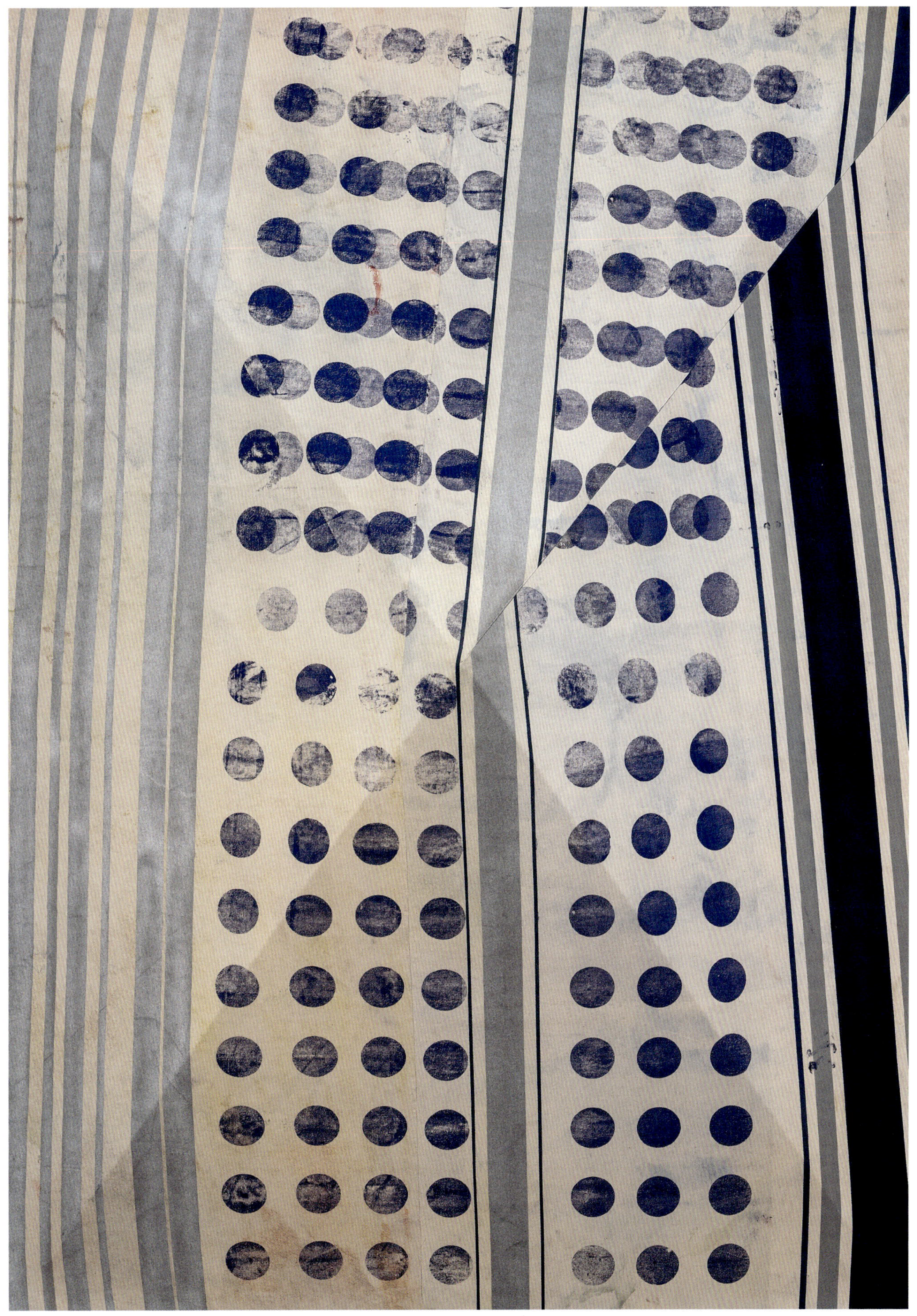

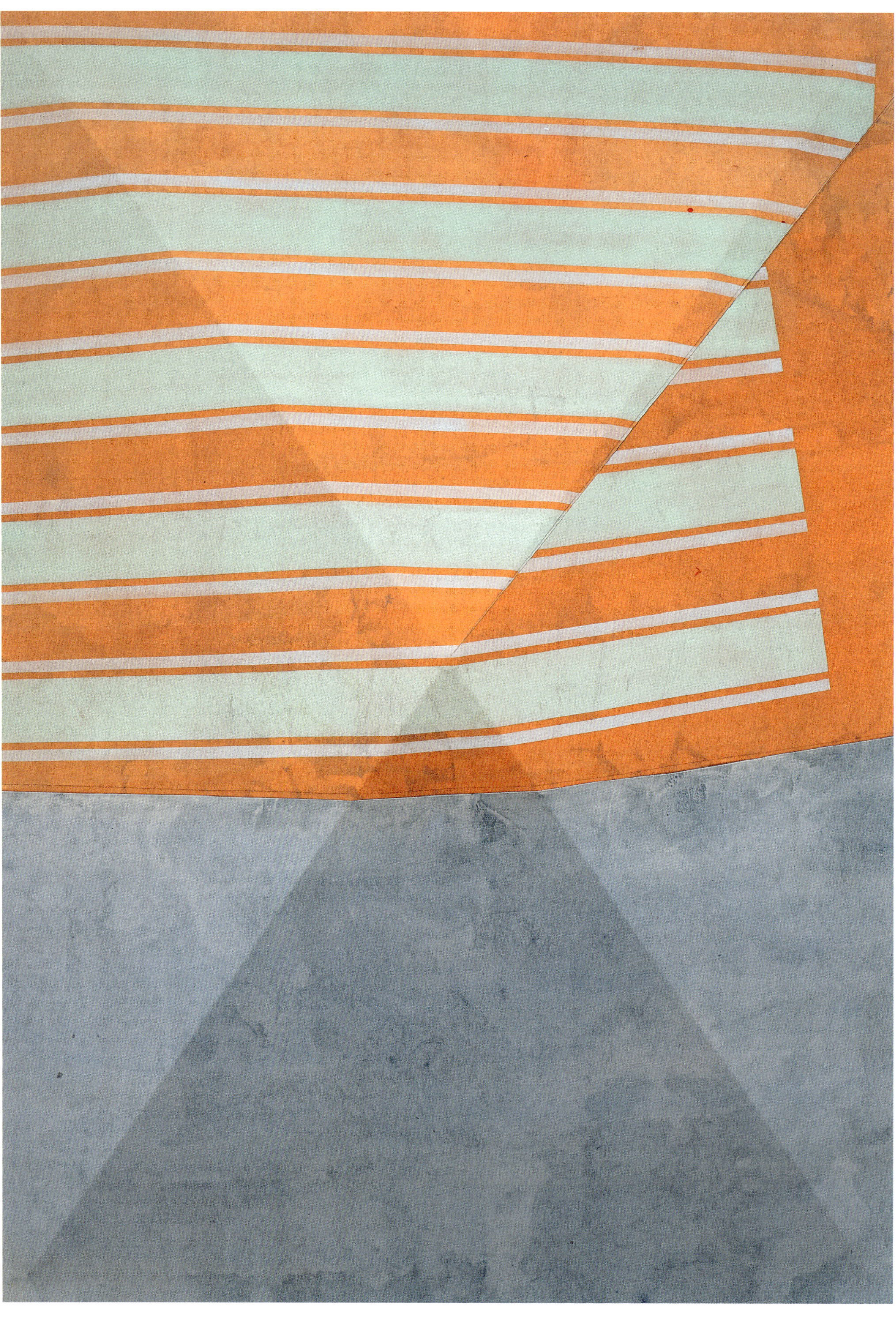

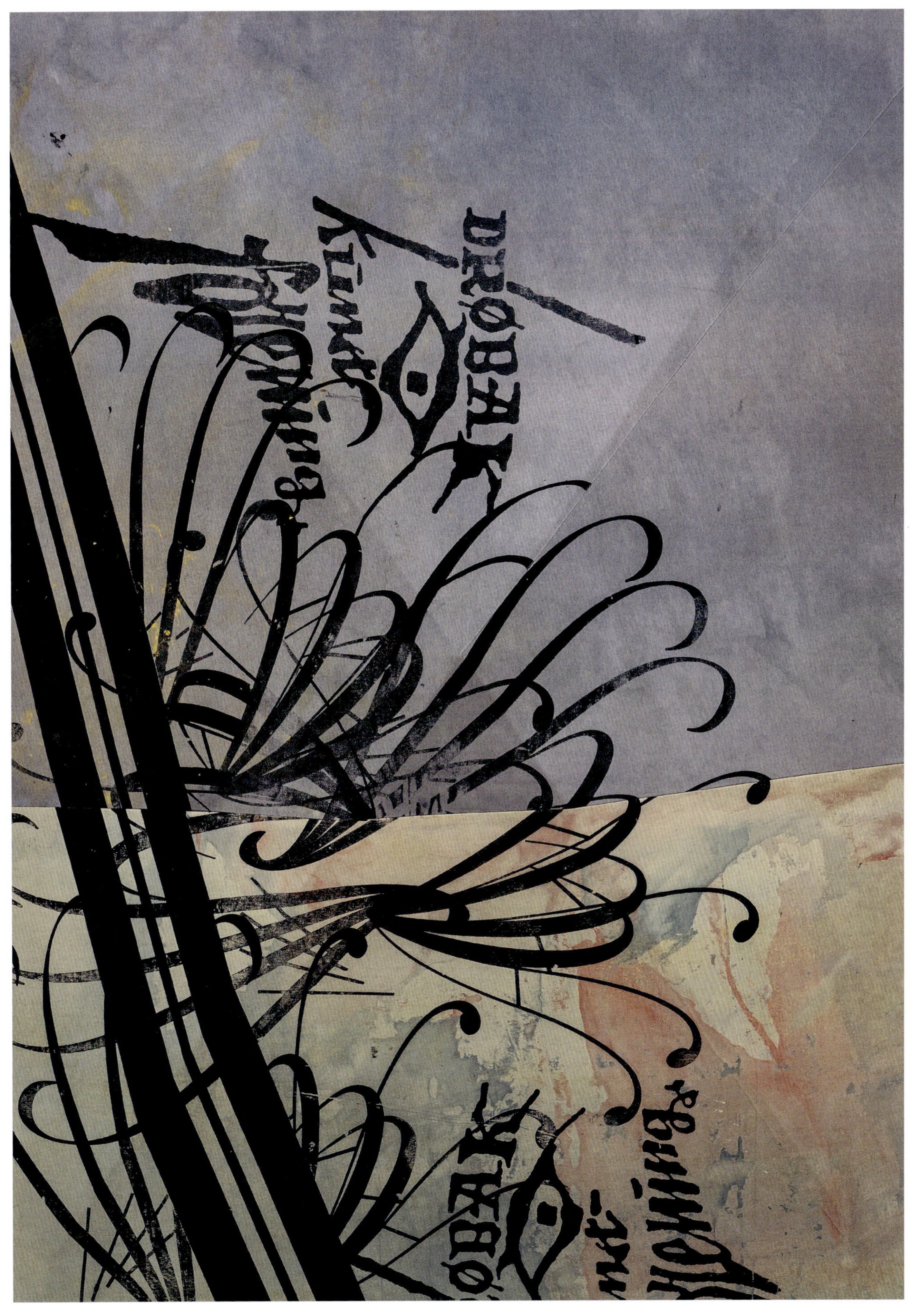

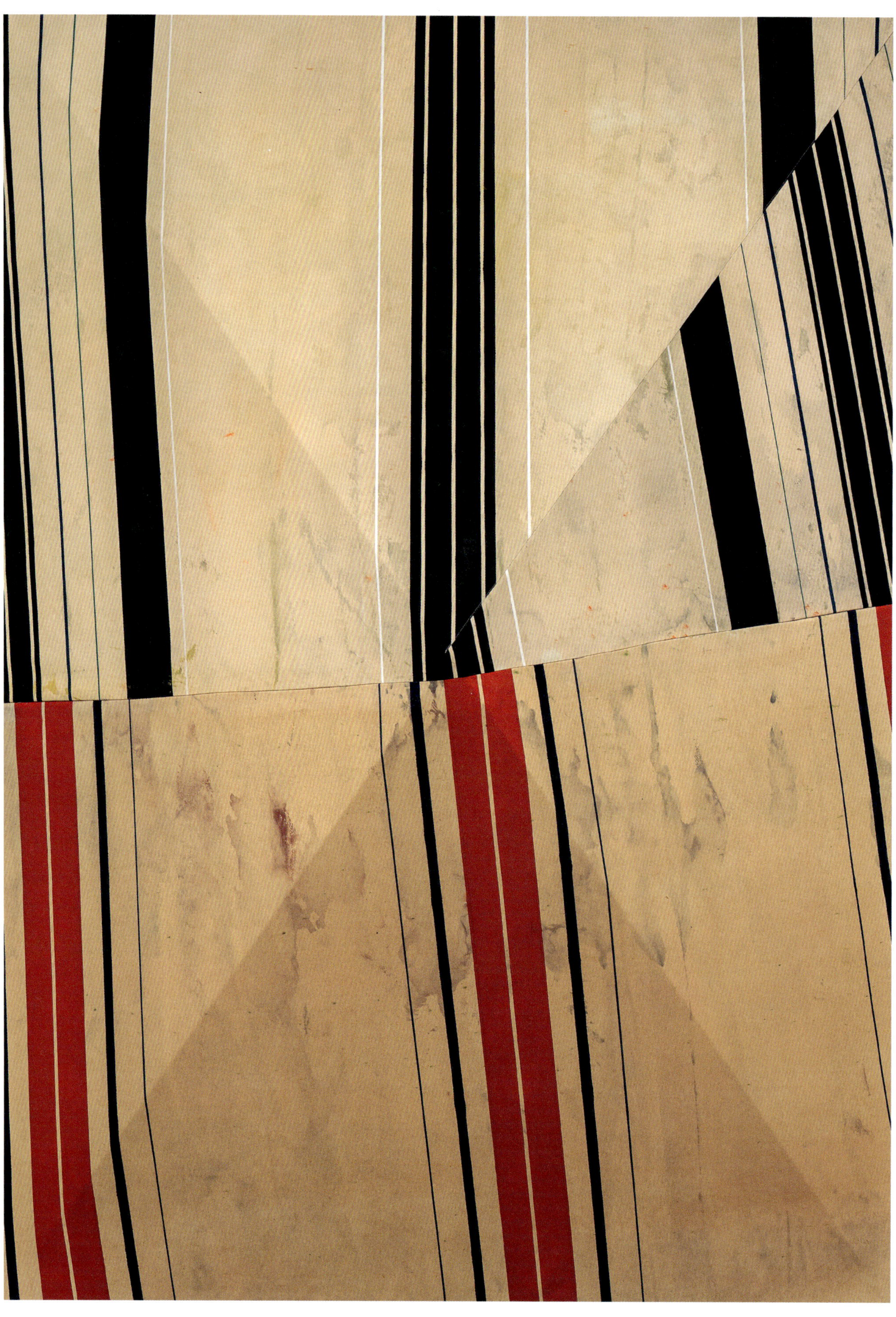

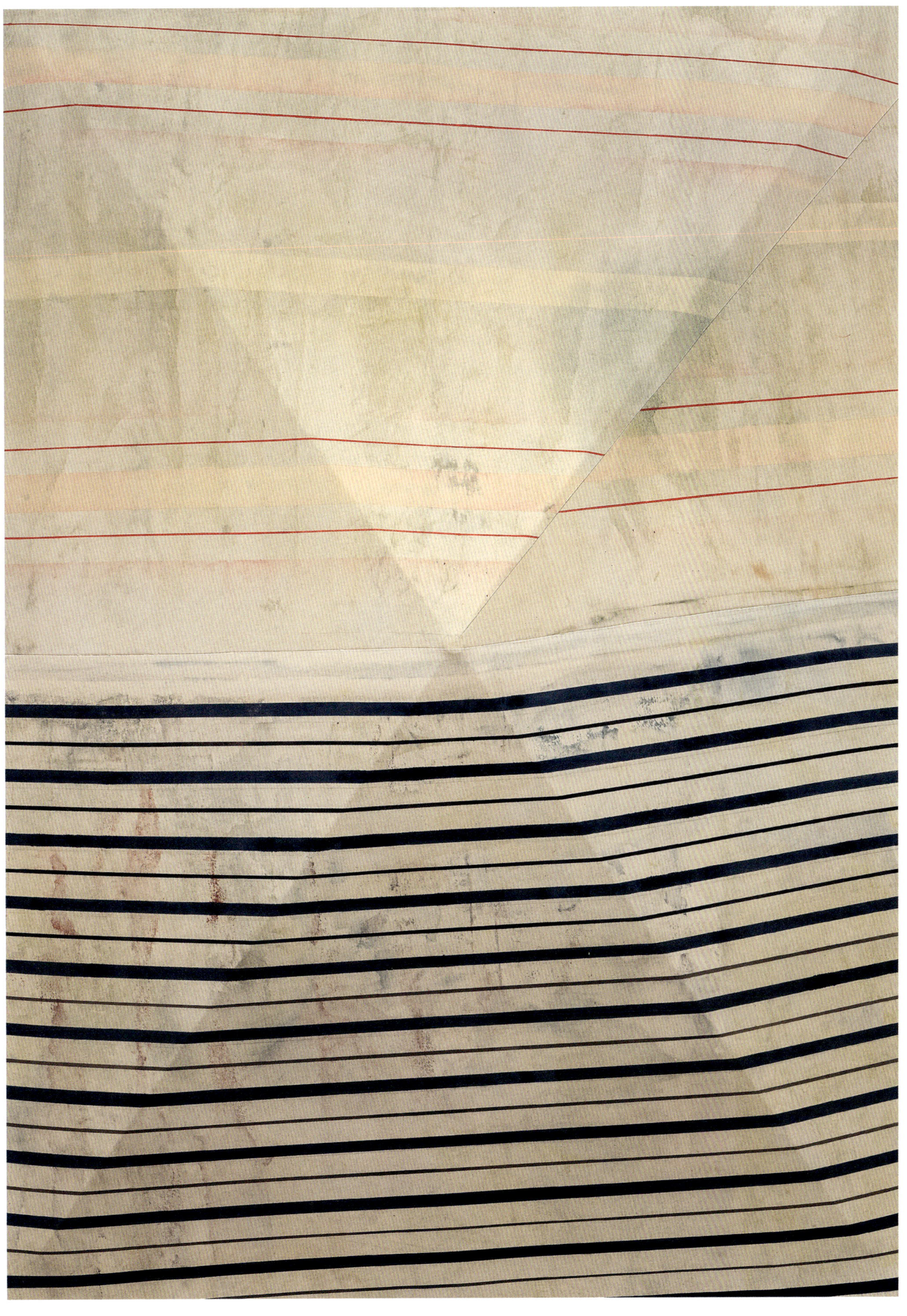

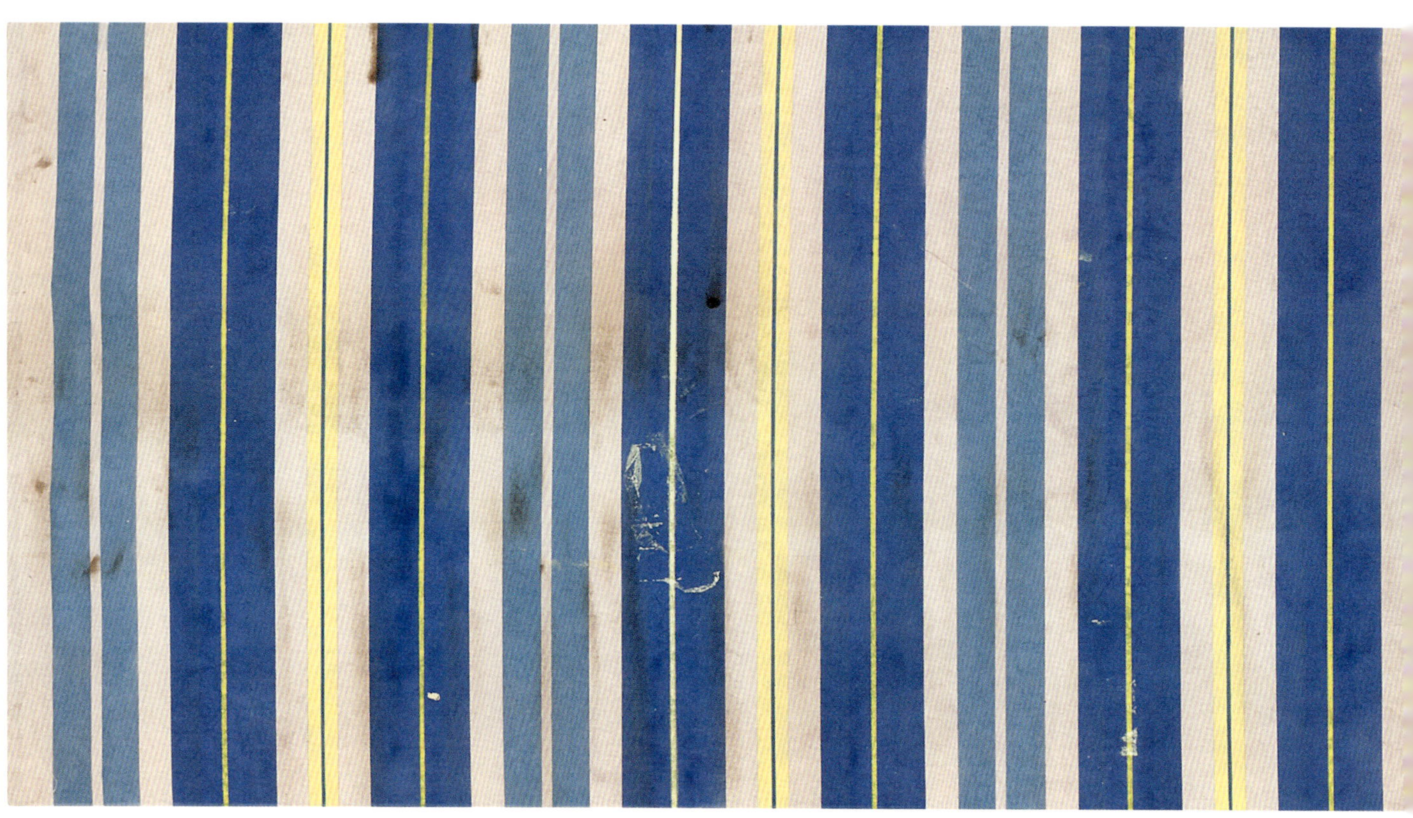

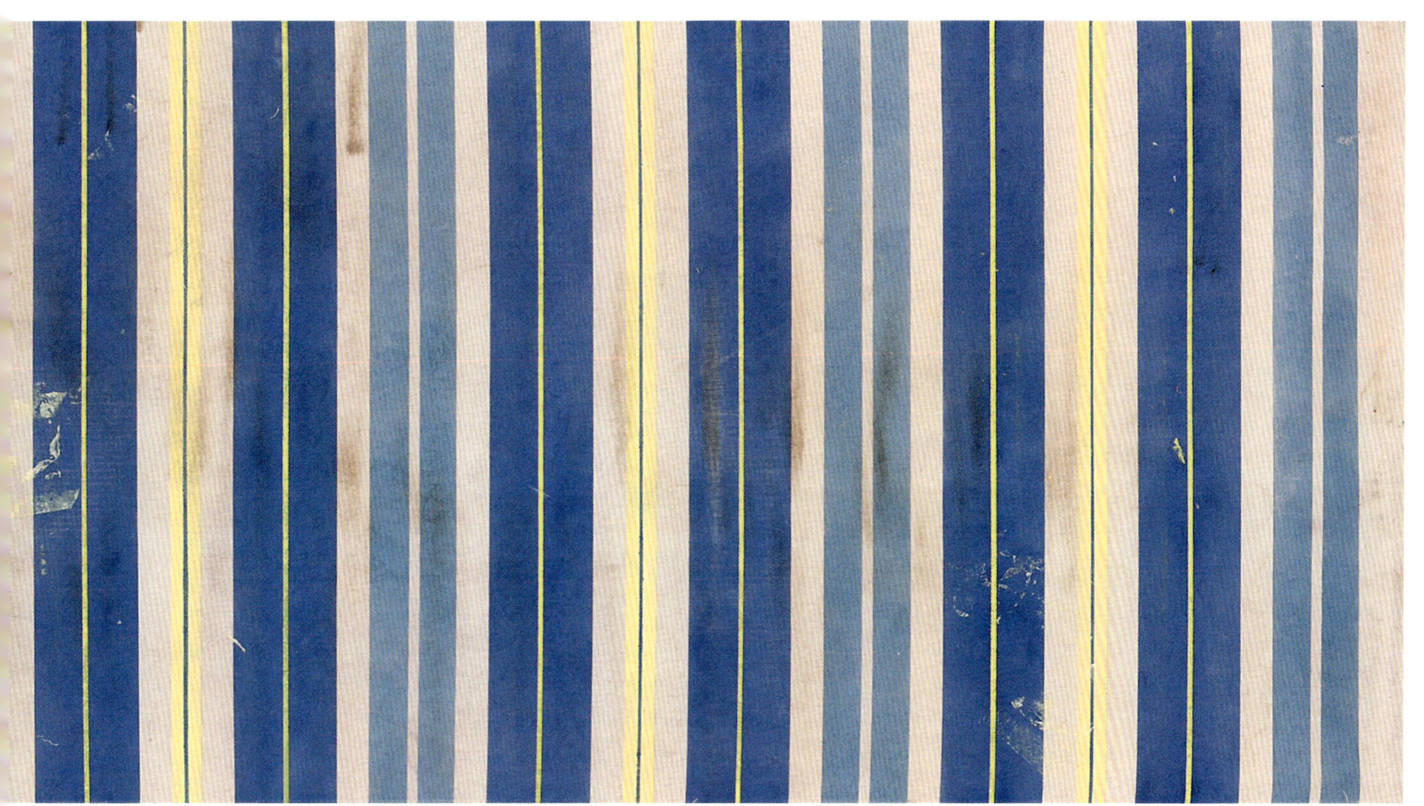

The exhibition is dedicated in loving memory to my friend Peter J. Amdam
—Fredrik Værslev

FREDRIK VÆRSLEV – FREDRIK VÆRSLEV AS
I IMAGINE HIM
Gunnar B. Kvaran

The medium of painting has a discontinuous and turbulent history. After centuries of development based on different views regarding representation in terms of perspective, line and colour, painting eventually evolved in the early twentieth century into abstractions of form and colours. Within this emerged certain internal logics of form and formlessness, as well as various approaches to colour, from expressionistic to monochrome. The behaviour of the materials also became an important factor. Until the mid-twentieth century, art and aesthetics were more or less limited to painting and sculpture.

Later, in the era of the ready-made, mechanical reproduction such as photography and video, and conceptual approaches to art-making, painting became more and more challenging. The traditional values, perpetual invention and reinvention of painting, as well as modernist ideas of 'progression', were declared to have come to an end. However, after the 'death of painting', artists are still engaging with forms and colours to create new types of paintings. This is what preoccupies the Norwegian artist Fredrik Værslev, who has been developing various different series of paintings over the last ten years.

When Værslev came out of art school in 2010, at the beginning of twenty-first century, he emerged into an art world that was radically different from that of the previous century, characterised by the fact that there was no longer any one ruling denominator. There were no geographically or stylistically related artistic movements or groups like those that had dominated the international art scene in the 1950s (geometrical and informal abstraction, Abstract Expressionism), 1960s (Pop art, Minimal art) and 1970s (Conceptual art). Artists of his generation emerged into a fragmented art world, with a horizontal structure and blurred boundaries between art and philosophy, ecology, science and political activism. Even the frontiers between geographically and culturally defined zones were becoming obsolete. If one can simplify, the art world was broadly characterised by a vaguely defined post-conceptualism and neo-modernism. Artists entered a world where everything seemed to have been done before, but where there also appeared to be endless freedom and possibilities relating to the notion of art. The studio became like a laboratory with conceptual and visual archives. In this kind of general context, the work of the artists became a form of isolated 'personal research', since there were fewer possibilities for connecting to others with a shared approach. For the post-conceptual artists, the focus was not on the development of a new and exciting language, nor on the possibilities of materials or techniques. The 'idea' that could take on diverse forms became the main principal.

Talking about this situation at the beginning of his artistic carreer, Værslev mentions the presence of artists like Ólafur Elíasson, Liam Gillick and Rirkrit Tiravanija and his special interest in the art of Dan Graham and Gordon Matta-Clark, but describes how he continued to pursue his own personal research. And than came the breakthrough. He often tells the story of how a gallerist from Venice who had invited him to do an exhibition sent him photographs of the exhibition space. Seeing that the floor of the space was its most visually arresting aspect, the artist decided to create paintings that made references to it. In this way, through the use of spray painting, with which he had worked for years as a graffiti artist, he created the Terrazzo paintings, an intelligent and ambiguous mix of a representation of terrazzo floor and a Pollock drip painting. This was the beginning of his 'method', which has grown into an original and increasingly complex conceptual/abstract representation, where his ideas and his personal sentiments are given form.

A similar operation and system of thinking characterises the series that followed, the Garden paintings, which were based on the terrace of his childhood home. The terrazzo and the terrace have in common the fact that they initially covered floors and have become paintings on the wall in the artist's process. Then came the Canopy paintings, based on furnishings from the same house. While close to appropriations, none of these works are copies of the objects to which the artist is referring. They are the representation of certain personal reminiscences, inspirations that carry memories, even nostalgia, relating to his childhood. In a way, they are semiotic paintings. They look like abstract paintings, and carry a clear reference to the works of certain abstract painters like Jackson Pollock, Barnett Newman and Daniel Buren, but his paintings have an intentional meaning, suggested by a model or a reference (terrazzo, terrace, canopys), which is a fragment of a more complex and vast personal story. The motifs functions as metonyms – a part (taken) for the whole.

It is important to note that the artist always works in series. Each series deals with one idea or subject matter, and each painting in that series has its own individual characteristics. There is no inherent logic relating to forms and colours from one series to another, since their drive and mechanics lie outside of the paintings – banal, low key, or deeply personal observations of the artist's social and personal environment. We can thus refer to his works as conceptual paintings.

In the earlier series, there is a remarkable balance, a certain kind of tautology, between the ideas and the objects. The variation of colours and finishes gives each of the paintings a certain degree of autonomy. However, in the series that followed, there is more emphasis on inherent logical developments of the forms and colours, materials and motifs. The Mildew paintings were transformers in a double sense: they were literally transformed by mildew, and they transformed the nature of Værslev's work. This is manifest in the series that came later, such as the Trolley paintings, where he abandons the objective references to terrazzo and striped canopys, for marks and traces made by the machine used for drawing lines on football fields or other sport facilities. These lines and traces are conditioned by the limited flexibility of the machine, but despite this, with the Trolley paintings Værslev enters the world of paintings in the first person, where invention takes over from the less spontaneous earlier representations. At Bergen Kunsthall in 2016, for example, Værslev used the machine to create a huge installation representing a sunset. These paintings retain the nostalgic aspect, since in his youth Værslev was a football enthusiast.

However, it is the Sail paintings, begun in early 2017, that are the first real compositions. Once again, the artist finds a motif from his personal iconography and mythology: the sail relates to the sailboats in Drøbak, his home city. In the Sail paintings, he mixes together the Mildew paintings and the sail references to invent a new form that allows him to develop a narrative structure through a variety of signs and symbols, often taken from the exhibition site, together with abstract forms and decorative elements that make references to the recent history of abstract painting (Frank Stella, Sigmar Polke, Philip Guston). In this way, Værslev has come up with new formats and images, like in the recent Pyramid paintings, that give more autonomy to the formal aspects of his works, letting go of the nostalgic memories.

It is important to mention Værslev's continuous dialogue with his close friends and collaborators. He has said that his mother Anne Britt Værslev has been an important figure for many of his projects.

For the Property paintings, 2007–2010, a number of his friends were invited to decide the format of canvases that were executed by another friend, Shwan Dler Qaradaki. The Swap paintings were also collective paintings by Værslev and his friends. For the Shelf paintings, on which he first collaborated with his mother, he makes a support for a painting or an artwork and invites other artists like Allison Katz, Josh Smith, Stewart Uoo and Matias Faldbakken to add to the work. Then we have the ongoing collaboration and dialogue with Per Christian Brath, his co-worker and best friend, whose skill as a tailor, amongst other talents, has been important in the creative process with the artist.

Another form of collaboration is his integration of a sign or aesthetic reference from the site or the location in which an exhibition takes place, and his intense dialogue with the architecture, such as that in the present show with Renzo Piano, the architect of Astrup Fearnley Museet.

Even though we see virtuoso painterly qualities and perfectionism in the execution of his works, Værslev is not attempting to evolve or take abstract painting further in the modernist sense of progression. His project, as a conceptual painter, is to create narratives that include memories of his social environment with its flavour of middle-class existence and aesthetics. Such narratives can in a way be seen as an auto-fiction. The artist is open and generous in communicating information relating to the geneses of his works – as we can see from many of the catalogue texts and interviews with him – to the point of, subconsciously or consciously, creating a mythology surrounding himself and his work.

However, what is remarkable is how these narratives are communicated; how they are organised within a layout that takes unexpected forms in the exhibitions. From the very beginning, Værslev has been interested in the physical context of the artwork and its relationship with the architecture of the exhibition space. One of his first experiments with painting as a medium and a format during art school, prior to the art academy, was to cut out parts of the canvas to show the wall and the architecture behind. Experimenting with the notion of exhibition layout and installation has been an important part of his creative process ever since. In fact, in his work with the exhibition format we can see more daring experiments and solutions than in the paintings themselves, and this is where his real originality lies. In exhibition spaces whose architecture is seen as difficult for the exhibition of paintings,

Gunnar B. Kvaran

he rarely tries to fit his works into the space by making compromises. On the contrary, he uses the difficulties as possibilities offered by the space to reinvent formal layouts that give an added value to his paintings and in that way, imbue them with a new meaning, as we have seen in his exhibitions at Standard Gallery, Oslo, 2012; Drøbak Kunstforening, Drøbak, 2013; The Power Station, Dallas, 2014; Lumiar Cité, Lisbon, 2014; Centre d'Art Contemporain Passerelle, Brest, 2015 and Kunsthal Aarhus, 2016. If the architecture is less challenging, more neutral, the series and the repetition of the paintings/motifs becomes more overwhelming, as we saw in Bergen Kunstall in 2017.

Thus it makes less sense to talk about Værslev's works based on single, isolated paintings than to talk about the series and above all the exhibition as a total installation and experience, which each time becomes a different work. His shows are meta-exhibitions that address the issue of exhibition-making or curating as such, and which carry a certain memory of earlier shows in terms of exhibited works, the use of architecture and the narratives. In a certain way, each of the paintings is an element or a raw material for an installation, a part of a new narrative structure, which aims to give the spectator an original existential experience.

The exhibition here at Astrup Feranley Museet is no exception, even though it is a survey-like presentation, showcasing Værslev's production over the last ten years through works from ten series. The artist has chosen to create a special installation, making the exhibition itself a new work. The layout does everything to avoid obvious and traditional solutions. Without any extra constructions of walls or interference with the existing architecture, the artist hangs the works to create parallel structures that match the architecture of the building but in an unconventional way. Alternatively, in other rooms he confronts the architecture by 'masking' a corner with a large painting or playing with scale, up or down, as is clearly seen with his Dollhouses and their relationship with the works in the surrounding exhibition space. More than confronting each and every painting individually, the spectator is taken on a journey leading to a pure aesthetic involvement. At the same time, the exhibition reveals the ongoing development and the mechanisms of Værslev's art.

The wonderful title *Fredrik Værslev as I Imagine Him* is borrowed from Peter J. Amdam, an artist, musician, curator, art critic and a very close friend of Værslev, who died in 2016 at only 45 years old. The title draws attention to the persona of the artist, who adopts and appropriates motifs, objects and images from his near and intimate surroundings, as well as from the recent history of American and European abstract art, without any kind of hierarchy, to produce his own mythology and narratives.

Let's take a ride
and run with the dogs tonight
in Suburbia
You can't hide
Run with the dogs tonight
in Suburbia

Break the window by the town hall
Listen! A siren screams
there in the distance, like a roll call
of all the suburban dreams

—Pet Shop Boys, *Suburbia*, 1986

Levittown, Long Island City, America. A housing community erected between 1947 and 1951 to relocate veterans coming back from World War II, Levittown was the first mass-produced housing project and emerged as a prototype for post-war Western suburbs. It still stands as a monument to the glory, or perhaps the bland conformity, of the American dream. Levittown's original development consisted of more than 8,000 detached kit houses made as stick-built boxes, which came in twelve-packs of parts, ready to be erected over the concrete-cellared foundations. Since then, this stick-frame construction has been considered the definition of suburban architecture, involving nailing together precut dimensional lumber to form the walls of low-rise buildings, still today the most common way to develop residential buildings in the US and many other countries.

The suburban architecture of the 1980s is ingrained in Fredrik Værslev's past and present living and working environments, from the place in which he grew up, Drøbak, a middle-class medium-sized city nestled in the southern fjords and surrounded by forests and farms, to Vestfossen, a town located one hour west of Oslo where his studio is established in a former cellulose factory. Elements taken from middle-class architecture, such as blinds and awnings punctuate most of his series, and traces of suburbia – the garden, the garage and the wooden balcony – appear as the common ground of his oeuvre. Indeed, Værslev's practice seems to refer more explicitly to banal and mundane suburban architecture than to the history of conceptual painting. His attachment to unspectacular colours and materials enhances his interest in modest, quotidian motifs and processes.

In his Garden Paintings for instance, Værslev produces standard wooden slats hung on the wall with metal supports, evoking the material language of architecture within urban environments, and reminiscent of a backyard fence or a picnic table. The slats he uses are readily available in hardware stores and can be observed on the streets of suburban towns in a variety of outdoor projects – sun decks, fences, storage boxes. His Canopy paintings are shaped like awnings, and recall those one would see while driving past suburban houses outside Western cities in the 1970s and 80s, with shades of blue, brown or orange. The familiar domesticity conveyed by these particular works is magnified by the seriality of their making; Værslev often uses industrial machines like those employed to make lines on sports fields or roads, leaving irregular traces on his canvases.

In his Dollhouses series, Værslev refers to the toys commonly given to young girls growing up in Scandinavia, but his Dollhouses materialise as a mid-size replica of suburban post-war Scandinavian multi-storey buildings, made of cheap industrial materials such as plywood and MDF. At Astrup Fearnley Museet, the houses measure approximately 1.50 m wide by 1.20 m high and 40 cm deep, and are spray-painted in dull colours, mainly different shades of grey – ash charcoal, iron, slate – all blending into a representation of middle-class reality. The Dollhouses also recall the ground-breaking play written in 1878 by Norwegian dramatist Henrik Ibsen, *A Doll's House*, in which he staged the progressive awakening of house-wife Nora Helmer. Few plays have had a similar impact on social norms and conditions, and few characters can claim an equivalent importance as a role model as Nora. Perhaps the tragic middle-class housewife realising that her life is a facade is the perfect character to inhabit Værslev's houses.

The materials used in the artist's compositions also reflect his attention to the banal and the mundane. His Dollhouses are a tool to frame and present his Terrazzo paintings, made of the eponymous composite material used for floor and wall treatments. Terrazzo consists of chips of marble, quartz, granite, glass, or other materials, mixed with cement and used to decorate Venetian palaces, Art Deco houses and even the Hollywood Walk of Fame, but most commonly the staircases of post-war Scandinavian buildings. Terrazzo floors would become an omnipresent element in the steps and the outdoor spaces of middle-class flats and blocks during the 1950s and 60s.

Seeing the sheets of sleet untouched on
the wide streets,
I think of the many comfortable homes
stretching for miles,
Two and three stories, solid, with polished
floors,
With white curtains in the upstairs bedrooms,
And small perfume flagons of black glass
on the window sills,
And warm bathrooms with guest towels,
and electric lights—
What a magnificent place for a child to grow up!
And yet the children end in the river of
price-fixing,
Or in the snowy field of the insane asylum.

—Robert Bly, *Sleet Storm on the Merritt
Parkway*, 1962

Studying the youth of East London in the 1970s,
sociologist Phil Cohen, a prominent researcher
on subcultural and youth theories, argued that
young people develop a cultural style as a means
of coping with their particular circumstances
and of resisting the dominant values of society.
They reject the norms of mainstream society and
turn instead to the values of a delinquent subculture. As kids growing up in the countryside,
Værslev and his friends would play football, listen
to hip-hop, break dance and, above all, spray
graffiti on neighboring walls—all typical activities
associated with 1980s and 1990s middle-class
suburban subculture. Since Drøbak had no train
tracks to decorate, the artist and his friends would
find alternative places, such as water towers
in the woods, back alleys behind grocery stores,
or bus stops. They would build walls from any
material they could find and hang it between trees
in the forest. As a fundamental expression of the
underground and DIY culture of this time, graffiti
is a vernacular language, a rejection of conven-
tional modern beauty and a transgression of legal
restrictions of public space.

Painting graffiti on public spaces and buildings
formed Værslev's do-it-yourself approach to art
making. Throughout his practice, he pairs the
visual language of graffiti with the vocabulary of
branding through his method of filling canvases
with stenciled logos. In his pyramidal Canopy
paintings, the influence of graphic design can be
observed through a lexicon of symbols, text motifs
and logos, which the artist labels 'bad graphic
design'. Using silk-screen and stencil techniques,
Værslev overlays these images on top of
one another, with different colours and sizes,
combining them with various coloured stripes and
motifs from earlier series of works. His Pyramid
paintings presented at La Passerelle in Brest in
2015, for example, featured two stamped letters,
'FR' for France, while those newly produced
for Astrup Fearnley Museet display 'AF', possibly
a provocative fictional logo for the institution.

Værslev's oeuvre revolves around notions of
collaborative processes, perhaps due to the influence of his former professor at the Städelschule
in Frankfurt, Michael Krebber. Before becoming
a renowned artist and teacher, Krebber was
one of Martin Kippenberger's last assistants in
the 1990s. We can extend the comparison of
this working relationship to the one that Værslev
has been developing over the years with his
assistant Per Christian Brath. The importance
of exchanges with other artist friends and even
family members—particularly his mother—are
also an inherent part of Værslev's pratice. Anne
Britt Værslev asked her son for some works to
adorn her house, but struggling to accommo-
date the pieces in her domestic realm, asked him
instead to make a wall piece with a shelf so that
she could put a vase on it. This is how Værslev
produced his first Shelf painting, a wooden panel
with a hinged shelf at the bottom. Later, he invited
friends, such as fellow artists Mathias Faldbakken
or Josh Smith, to intervene on the shelves and
to propose new versions of it.

Not only interested in deconstructing the
notion of authorship though collaborations and
exchanges, Værslev also aims to redefine the
exhibition space. His powerful connection
to his immediate outdoor environment and the
Norwegian landscape is noticeable in his colour
palette: straightforward greys, greens, whites and
fading yellows, ivory, silver and brownish black.
His Sunset paintings are based on photographs
of sunsets that he took from airplane windows
with his phone during his travels. Produced as
a series employing the mechanical tracing trolley,
they suggest horizons blending and vanishing
at the surface of the canvas. Originally painting
with the four colours in which graffiti spray paints
are available—white, blue, yellow and red—Værslev
has now added tones of beige and grey. In addition
to his relationship with landscape and nature,
Værslev also makes a connection with time
throughout his practice. For an exhibition entitled
La Constance du Jardinier (The Constant
Gardener) in 2015, the artist was invited to exhibit
outdoors, on the Île des Impressionistes in Chatou
outside of Paris, where Caillebotte and Renoir
used to live and paint. Værslev decided to hang his

Martha Kirszenbaum

canvases directly on trees, *en plein air*, inviting weather and time to alter their surfaces. Throughout the duration of the exhibition, the works would be damaged by air, soaked by water and bleached by the sun. This direct interaction with nature created an experiment not just for the artists, but also for the viewer, whose perception would vary depending on the season and the weather.

These weathered surfaces also appear in Værslev's Canopy paintings, which are rolled up and stacked outside the studio to acquire a specific patina. Similarly, his Terrazzo paintings are left for months outside of the studio and exposed to the weather, a possible evocation of Edvard Munch, whose paintings were forced to endure harsh Norwegian outdoor conditions. Traces of wear, dirt, stains and footsteps can be seen on all of Værslev's compositions. For his Trolley paintings, he uses the tracing machine randomly and intuitively, embracing any malfunctioning, the results recalling an overlapping collage. The Terrazzo paintings also bear spots of dripped paint, reminiscent of Jackson Pollock's techniques. Værslev's approach certainly suggests processes and appearances related to post-war American abstractionists, but are closer to the practice of 'bad painting' that predominated in Cologne in the 1980s with artists such as Martin Kippenberger. Accidents, mistakes and uncontrolled gestures are precisely the parameters that hold together a practice enhanced by experimentation but also by failure and intentional deception.

MY ARCHITECTURE – ENCOUNTERING FREDRIK VÆRSLEV IN PHOTOGRAPHY
Therese Möllenhoff

Fredrik Værslev is a painter! it has been declared.[1] And there is no doubt that painting has been the hallmark of his artistic practice, which has been described as an "insistent focus on the painting process itself".[2] All the same, at a Walker Evans exhibition at Centre Pompidou in the summer of 2017 I unexpectedly encountered photographs reminiscent of Fredrik Værslev's works. And later I also met the photographer Værslev in the earlier series *My Architecture* (2008–2011).

In the 1930s photographer Walker Evans (1903–1975) travelled around the USA, documenting everyday urban motifs such as shop windows, signs, crossroads and public buildings – a practice that would prove to have a decisive impact on the history of photography and art. In a little-known photojournalism series published in the magazine *Architectural Forum* in 1958, Evans shifted his focus from the descriptive and serial images of buildings and began to zoom in, with obvious fascination, on the wear and tear and the patina that occur in architectural details during years of use: the surfaces of walls, floors and doors, some of which featured inscribed drawings and scribbles.[3] He remarked that a trained eye was necessary to uncover these distinctive details. Evans's close-ups of architectural details almost take the form of abstract artistic motifs. They immediately bring to mind the characteristic qualities of Fredrik Værslev's paintings. And Evans's own description of the distinctive visuality of the architectural surfaces – "This is the restless, cacophonic design created by time, the weather, neglect and the fine hand of delinquent youth" – could be applied almost wholly to Værslev's works, whether referring to the Terrazzo paintings, the Canopy paintings or the Garden paintings, which were also created through the interaction of a precise hand, the weather, and the random effects of time.

In *Architectural Forum* the photographs are accompanied by Evans's own texts: brief reflections on the motifs and their artistic qualities. In a detailed study of a faded wall or a worn-out floor Evans finds images that he feels could have been devised by an artist like Jackson Pollock. But while Pollock's paintings did not derive from observations of everyday architectural surfaces, those of Fredrik Værslev do precisely that. Værslev possessed the eye Evans had described as necessary for recognising the painterly potential inherent in commonplace architectural forms that have developed a patina through time, weather and chance, and it seems almost as though it was Fredrik Værslev himself that Evans was foreseeing when he wrote in the photo essay "Color Accidents" that someday a "bright young stylist" would emerge who would deliberately borrow these motifs.

Evans's correlation of photography of architectural surfaces and abstract painting brings to mind the story behind Værslev's breakthrough series, the Terrazzo paintings, which were also based on a kind of detailed photographic study. In 2009, when Værslev was invited to hold his first solo exhibition, he requested photographic documentation of the exhibition gallery. The response he received was an email that, instead of including the usual photos of the room's layout and walls, consisted of a number of pictures focusing on the floor space. In the almost absurdly distorted photographs, the images were dominated by a characteristically speckled terrazzo floor, which appeared as an architectural equivalent of Jackson Pollock's drip paintings. These photographs inspired Værslev to create a series of paintings in which he would imitate the floors of the exhibition space. Using a spray-box technique he had learnt during his period as a graffiti painter in the late 1990s, he created the illusion of both terrazzo floors and a kind of modernist drip painting. The Terrazzo paintings would become the first in a long list of works that make use of the interaction between an ostensibly neo-modern abstract painting and a trompe l'oeil-like representation of architectural elements.[4]

When, more than 50 years earlier, Evans associated his photographs of worn architectural surfaces with Pollock's paintings, he also wrote that "[s]uch a specimen may serve as a reminder that it does require authority to bring off a painting with something new in it; for a perfect painting, immense authority".[5] This quote reminds me of something Fredrik Værslev said in an impassioned explanation (which could only have come from someone who truly believes in painting) that his evaluation of the Terrazzo paintings is an evaluation of each tiny detail, all the way down to the individual spots. That he feels that he has ventured into perilous painterly territory simply by adding one extra drop, and even a single spot could entail that he had gone too far and had to discard the work. "What are you looking for within this process?" I asked Fredrik. The answer: "A perfect painting."[6]

MY ARCHITECTURE

Like Walker Evans, Værslev has moved around the city with a camera and an eye for architecture. During the preparations for this exhibition, the early series My Architecture turned up, providing a new encounter with Værslev as a photographer.

My Architecture (2008–2011) is a series of analogue photographs taken with a medium-format camera. The series was begun in the spring of 2008, while Værslev was still a student at the Malmö Art Academy.[7] In the small photographs, 32 x 40 cm, we see a variety of urban motifs from Malmö and Oslo. At first glance they appear to be ordinary, modest building motifs. Upon closer inspection the distinctive compositional features of the images emerge; they all stage a perspective-related encounter between various independent building types, where the artist has discovered the perfect point where the buildings meet the viewer's gaze and merge with each other. These are far from neutral, documentary architectural photographs. Rather, the motifs have been sought out and selected with a meticulously compositional eye, originating in a personal narrative. *My Architecture* is based on the search for a pattern, or a kind of game, which Værslev says he has been playing since he was a child. On his way to and from school, football training or visits with friends he searched for points in his surroundings where two buildings or two forms of different kinds could be combined visually and merged into one – without any other objective than to make things add up: "This search for possibilities in my surroundings produced a sort of calmness and satisfaction, and a sense of creating my own spaces within the public space – not unlike the possibilities that later attracted me to both graffiti and art production."[8]

The interest in discovering these potential meeting points, searching visually for "secret" compositional encounters, was something that Værslev developed further when, as an art student in Malmö, he tried to find a method of working with his interest in architecture. In his search for architectural encounters, now with the camera, he discovered places where, for example, a seven-storey building could merge with a two-storey building despite the fact that they were separated by 50 metres. The photographs document this perceptual fusion and flattening. They immortalise a perspective on the artist's architectural surroundings that he compels his gaze to encompass, where the flattening effect

of the photograph and the merging of the buildings cancel out the depth perspective of the topography of the buildings. This tactic eliminates both the space between the buildings and the size ratio between them, although a certain degree of scale and perspective is maintained through the shapes that are adjacent to the buildings, such as trees and people. In this way Værslev activates the abstracted view of architecture that the photograph anticipates, and uses the dislocations of perspective and the play on lines that professional architectural photographers often manipulate after the fact. Værslev's analogue photographs are far from being digitally manipulated; on the contrary, they are extremely low-tech, making use of a perspective that is first discovered and enforced through the eyes and then through the lens.

A number of "painterly effects" are also produced in *My Architecture*. In the photographs architectural shapes are abstracted into formal surfaces in the same way as in Værslev's paintings. The building motifs assume flattened formal qualities, and exist simultaneously in the sphere between abstraction and representation – real architecture and an abstract surface. The photographs reinforce the formal qualities of the façades of the buildings, which in several instances acquire a nearly modernist form of expression. The façades of the high-rise building in *My Architecture (Oslo #11)* and *My Architecture (Oslo #15)* almost take on the appearance of a modernist grid, and the block of flats in a picture such as *My Architecture (Malmoe #01)* brings to mind a colour field painting with graduated hues.

In the same way as Værslev's paintings activate references to the history of twentieth-century painting, the photographs in *My Architecture* evoke references to the history of photography. Lines can be drawn from both vernacular photography and the new topographics movement's documentation of urban spaces to the conceptual building photography of the American West Coast – without any evidence that the series relates to any of them. The Oxford English Dictionary defines "vernacular architecture" as architecture that is "concerned with ordinary domestic and functional buildings rather than the essentially monumental". For a number of artists in the previous century, it was precisely this subject that would form the point of departure for the development of an innovative photographic view of reality. Artists such as Walker Evans or, later, Ed Ruscha documented for the future an ordinary, non-monumental architecture comprising simple buildings such as grocer's shops, petrol stations and blocks of flats – buildings

Therese Möllenhoff

that would eventually be demolished or altered. Just as they immortalised prosaic motifs from their contemporary architectural reality, Værslev's photos also produced fragments of an urban history, in this case from two Scandinavian cities in the early 2000s. Although these photographs were taken in the previous decade, they captured an urban cityscape that has already changed or is in the process of changing.

My Architecture (Oslo #13) presents a meeting between the old pathology building of the National Hospital of Norway at Pilestredet 32 and the student housing at Pilestredet 36. These two building still exist, but have undergone such extensive changes that the motif as shown in Værslev's photograph is already more or less unrecognisable. The photograph was taken before the pathology building was renovated in the period 2009 to 2013 to become part of the Oslo and Akershus University College. The old high-rise from 1970 has been stripped, clad in shiny aluminium sheets and supplemented with a glass structure connecting it to a new 7-storey building, in other words a total change from the sober, greyconcrete façade that can be seen in Værslev's picture. In the photograph the old high-rise is staged as being seamlessly connected to the building located diagonally across the street, the Pilestredet Student Residence Hall. The 7-storey brick building, constructed in 1978, is immortalised as a surface that converges completely with the 12-storey pathology building. The student hall, too, has been modernised with a new top storey and new window designs since Værslev took his picture. The concrete panels that led from the lower part of the building to street level, linking the bottom of this building visually with the concrete structure of the high-rise in the photograph, have, like Værslev's picture, also become history.

Even when Værslev directs his attention to more significant buildings, such as the those of the Government Quarter in Oslo in *My Architecture (Oslo #11)* and *My Architecture (Oslo #15)*, the impermanence of the urban landscape is suggested. These works document the encounter between one of the short ends of the "Y-block", decorated with Pablo Picasso's mural "The Fishermen", and the façade of the high-rise behind it. The motif and the compositional area between the two buildings are facing an uncertain future. At the time of writing, the summer of 2018, an application for demolition of the Y-block has been submitted despite a recommendation for con-servation by the Directorate for Cultural Heritage

and earnest efforts by various support groups to prevent the building from being torn down.

However, *My Architecture* does not seem to orient itself towards urban history or a reflection on the traditions of architectural photography. On the contrary, the series corresponds to the more personal narratives that often provide the point of departure for Værslev's artistic practice. As opposed to, for example, Evans's and Rus-cha's serial documentation of architectural types, in Værslev's early series we can recognise the artist's recurrent use of autobiographical elements, always based on an "I" perspective, where all the motifs seem to arise from personal experiences and observations from his own life–awnings and terrace flooring from his childhood home, sailcloth from growing up by the sea. In *My Architecture* the personal component derives from an artistic con-tinuation of a young man's game of finding angles where architectural surfaces merge in perfect juxtapositions. It is also connected with Værslev's background as a graffiti painter and this culture's specific way of approaching photographic docu-mentation of its interaction with urban spaces.

What makes *My Architecture* most interesting is, perhaps, that the series provides an under-standing of Værslev's eye. *My Architecture* could be described as a kind of perceptual exercise, demonstrating the premises for the artist's interest in *encounters within architecture*. The series can function as a link between his perceptual method as an artist and the motifs that we are familiar with from his later production as a painter. The search for patterns in his architectural surroundings can be recognised in the choice of various archi-tectural forms as "motifs" in his later paintings–whether this applies to stone floors, terrace planks or awnings. Viewed as a method, *My Architecture* reflects how Værslev relates to his surroundings, as can also be seen in his work with space and installation in exhibitions, where the paintings are often staged in encounters with the architecture. In these encounters one can recognise the vision that was evident in the photographs from *My Architecture*. When viewing Værslev's artistic practice through *My Architecture* it emerges that this small and relatively modest photo series demonstrates, in a variety of ways, significant principles of Værslev's practice: the accentuation of the visual potential of urban surfaces and the abstraction of architecture into ostensibly formal elements, which nonetheless constantly hover ambiguously between abstraction and representation, and not least his distinctive eye for encounters with architecture.

1   "Fredrik Værslev is a painter!" is the title of one of many
    essays addressing Værslev's artistic practice. Salvadori,
    Alberto: "Fredrik Værslev is a painter!" in *Reality Bites*,
    Alberto Salvadori and Caroline Soyez-Petithomme, eds.,
    8-15. Milan: Mousse Publishing, 2015.
2   Astrup Fearnley Museet's own description of Værslev's
    artistic practice at http://afmuseet.no/utstillinger/2018/fredrik-
    varslev (accessed 13 July 2018).
3   Evans, Walker. "Color Accidents". Architectural Forum.
    Vol. CVIII (no. 1), January 1958. As shown at the exhibition
    at Centre Pompidou, Musée national d'art moderne, Paris.
    See also Campany, David. *Walker Evans – The Magazine
    Work*. Göttingen: Steidl Publishers, 2014.
4   This type of duality is typical of Værslev's artistic production.
    An initial apparent abstraction and formalism, whether
    this entails spots of paint or geometric stripes, with strongly
    modernist references, has nevertheless always emerged
    from a personal narrative and materials that are perceived
    as being far from both the "contentlessness" of modernist
    visual art and an anti-narrative approach, and from the
    approach taken by Værslev's neo-modernist contemporaries
    in the 2010s, with their seemingly more distanced and
    process-oriented re-evaluation of the abstract painting.
5   Evans, Walker. "Color Accidents". *Architectural Forum*.
    Vol. CVIII (no. 1), January 1958.
6   Værslev, conversation with the author, 27 October 2017.
7   While Værslev was a student he worked on several photo-
    graphic series before beginning to paint. Some of these
    photographic works were shown at Johan Berggren Gallery
    in Malmö, Sweden, including the poster series "Modern
    Living" (2006), where Værslev documented a number
    of architectural surfaces in Malmö as potential sites where
    graffiti could be created, or where one could "bring the
    painting into architecture" (Værslev, conversation with the
    author, 13 July 2018).
8   Værslev, email to the author, 7 July 2018.

                                                    Therese Möllenhoff

Something is definitely holding me back from literary work. It is the need for style.
—Robert Musil, *Diaries 1899–1941*

Aesthetic intolerance can be terribly violent.
—Pierre Bourdieu, *Distinction: A Social Critique of the Judgment of Taste*, 1979

One of the joys of train travel, I have always felt, occurs when you find yourself riding into town at dusk or in the early evening hours, and see the lights go on in the apartments lining the tracks as the train chugs from station to station. During these mellow moments, I invariably keep an eye out for what people hang on their walls – and I am always struck by the fact that art, in fact, is everywhere, that even the most humble and modest-looking of dwellings and living quarters are invariably marked by moments, however fleeting or understated, of aesthetic consideration: a picture in a frame, a reproduction of a painting, a poster of an art exhibition, perhaps the kind of drawing bought as a souvenir on a city trip. Objects, mostly images, that simply state, whisper-like, that here too, or even here, the idea of art persists. In the undying shape of painting, of course.

In the flashpoint year 1967 – a date regularly given as the birth-year of Conceptual (that is to say, contemporary) art – four up-and-coming French artists who availed themselves primarily of paint, paintbrushes and canvas (that is to say, the stuff of modernity, not contemporaneity), founded an impromptu collective during the yearly Salon de la jeune peinture at the Musée d'art moderne de la ville de Paris, distributing the following manifesto among the exhibition's visitors on opening day:

Because painting is a game,
Because painting is the application
(consciously or otherwise) of the rules
of composition,
Because painting is the freezing of movement,
Because painting is the representation
(or interpretation or appropriation or disputation
or presentation) of objects,
Because painting is a springboard for
the imagination,
Because painting is spiritual illustration,
Because painting is justification,
Because painting serves an end,

Because to paint is to give aesthetic value to flowers, women, eroticism, the daily environment, art, dadaism, psychoanalysis and the war in Vietnam,
We are not painters.[1]

They were called Daniel Buren, Olivier Mosset, Michel Parmentier and Niele Toroni (BMPT for short), and by programmatically adopting one distinguishing painterly mark or signature 'style' each – circles, daubs and stripes, all manually applied to the canvas in a workmanlike manner, all equally bête, as only a painter's instinctual mannerisms could be[2] – they perfected the sardonic blueprint for Conceptual art's foundational antagonism towards painting as the embodiment of everything that was wrong with art in 1967. Simultaneously, they inaugurated the history of what came to be known as 'institutional critique', by turning, brush in hand, against the most hallowed of all of art's institutions: *la peinture*. For painting, in the age of the Vietnam war, was clearly a moral affront comparable to the barbarism of 'poetry after Auschwitz', in Theodor Adorno's deathless phrase.[3]

Around the same time, though tellingly far removed from the traditional power centres of Paris' left and right bank, another collective of French artists sought to interrogate painting's stranglehold over the canonical conception of art – the conflation of all art with painting, and of all painting with art – by resorting to a comparably reductive, back-to-basics approach – though they were ostensibly a lot less worried about being called, mistakenly or not, 'painters'. (This may have been a function of their operating in the relative anonymity of mid-sized French Mediterranean cities and towns – a fact to which we shall be returning shortly.) Stubbornly, indeed, almost myopically committed to grasping the medium's true 'material' conditions – these were the late 1960s after all, the high-water mark of historical materialism's popular appeal – the artists primarily focused on painting's underlying structural binary, the coupling of which gave the group its name: Support/Surface. The collective's glory years stretched from 1966 to 1974, during which time they appeared in numerous self-organised exhibitions (often in the most unlikely locales) and published a journal titled, rather grandiosely, *Peinture: Cahiers théoriques*, noted for its highly politicised, manifesto-style language and predilection for dour doctrine. Revisiting the work made under the Support/Surface banner today, it is hard to imagine the Maoist fervour and militancy that animated the making of so much of it, whether the surface-centric 'paintings' of Claude Viallat, Jean-Pierre Pincemin, Louis Cane and André-Pierre Arnal (all of whom worked, in one way or other, with unstretched canvas) or the support-focused 'paintings' of Daniel Dezeuze, Toni Grand or Bernard Pagés (all of whom worked, in one way or other, with wooden stretcher bars). True believers in the revolutionary cause – yet for all the reasons why Buren, Mosset, Parmentier and Toroni insisted on distancing themselves from the bourgeois stigma of painterdom – Dezeuze, Viallat and co. defiantly embraced the form's crudest clichés and limitations. To them, it was precisely because, in the popular imagination, painting equalled art and art equalled painting that any attempt at revolutionising art in their time (what else could they possibly have wanted?) was unthinkable without a fundamental, internal interrogation of art's most powerful shorthand and 'popular' expression, namely painting.

I have dwelt on the intertwining stories of BMPT and Support/Surface as a context for Fredrik Værslev's work for a number of reasons. Firstly, there is the matter of deep, but perhaps only half-conscious aesthetic affinity. There are evident shades, for instance, of Buren's work in the sequence of Canopy paintings ('shades') that Værslev exhibited on the so-called Ile des Impressionistes in the Parisian suburb of Chatou in 2015 and outside the Kunsthal Aarhus in 2016. Or consider the echoes of Dezeuze and co. in the series of spray-painted wooden pallets mounted on blank gallery walls, as well as the cotton-covered architectonic canvases that constituted the core of Værslev's *Querelle* de Brest installation from 2015. (Brest, Chatou, Dijon: there must be a reason why the Norwegian artist's work has been received so favourably in the French institutional sphere – something to do with deconstruction perhaps?[4]) Or take the traces of Toroni in the paintings that Værslev made using a line-painting trolley usually seen on a football pitch. Think, finally, of the resonance of André-Pierre Arnal or Claude Viallat's work in, say, the terrazzo floor paintings that first shot Værslev to art-world atten-tion, as well as the languid maritime imagery of the more recent 'sail paintings'. Here we must briefly pause to take note of the recurrent thematic of *plein air* painting as the art form's most cliché-laden avatar as well as an under-recognised subtext of much of Værslev's work. It is no coinci-dence that Værslev debuted his Canopy paintings on the 'Island of the Impressionists', named after its erstwhile patrons Gustave Caillebotte, Claude

Monet and Pierre-Auguste Renoir, and that Chatou is an important milestone in the history of landscape painting's steady degradation into the innocuous kitsch of cookie-cutter Impres-sionist imagery. This significant factor undergirds the reasoning behind Værslev's own take on the landscape tradition, realised most memorably on a monumental immersive scale at the Bergen Kunsthall in 2016, where the artist chose to depict a sunset, of all motifs.[5] Likewise, much of the 'imagery' of certain Support/Surface representatives derives from the movement's roots in Provençal seaports like Montpellier and Nice, endowed with a long history of modern art's association with open-air leisure, with the figure of the sailor and the sailboat. This is a curiously crucial element in Værslev's image-world (whose open-air roots could be said to reach back to his suburban graffiti period)[6] and acts as a particu-larly potent metaphor for certain free-wheeling, 'amateur' aspects of artistic pictorial practice.

Secondly, I wish to wrest the discussion of Værslev's work away from that of contemporaries such as Jacob Kassay, Oscar Murillo, David Ostrowski, Josh Smith, Lucien Smith and others – artists whose work I believe only very superficially relates to that of Værslev. In looking at his paintings, I am interested in charting another genealogy – one that is less invested in generational 'movements'.

Thirdly, and on a related note, in associating Værslev's practice with that of the aforementioned historical antecedents, we are able to reassess his work in the broader, much more illuminating context of the moment of institutional critique: the moment of Buren and his cohorts, certainly, that of Michael Asher – who, I was somehow not surprised to discover, during a conversation with the artist in a half-empty studio in Vestfossen in the fall of 2017, is in fact Værslev's 'favourite' artist. (Michael Asher: all the politics we'll ever need.) Granted, not the canonical Asher of mythologising *October* journal lore, but an older, more experiential Asher – an artist for whom the question of criticality was never decisively divorced from aesthetic concerns and pictorial considerations: a 'painterly' Asher for whom the alpha and omega of all so-called institutional critique was always 'the work of art as an aesthetic fact'. (See, for instance, his documenta 5 installa-tion from 1972, the Pomona College intervention from 1970, and various European gallery exhibi-tions organised in 1973: examples of *Kontextkunst* not so far removed from the seeming surface concerns and phenomenological inquiries of our

Dieter Roelstraete

French anti-painters.) I share Værslev's enthusiasm for this slightly less sanctimonious Asher, and have long ranked his *Installation Münster*, 1977 – the legendary tiny caravan that appeared in four consecutive Skulptur.Projekte Münster editions, from 1977 until 2007, changing places across town over the course of a fourteen-week period – among my favourite works of art. And there is clearly something of Asher's caravan in Værslev's nautical hang-ups.

Which leads me to the fourth, and most important reason for our looking back at French Conceptual painting from the late 1960s and early 1970s – the notion of class. For alongside, and opposite, the expanded notion of landscape, it is the correlating register of class – so crucial to grasping the cultural ferment and turbulence that spawned the 1960s Conceptual art revolution and conditioned the embattled position of painting within it – that allows for a more comprehensive understanding of Værslev's project. (This is precisely where, in my view, his work differs so substantially from that of his predominantly American peers.) The biographical ingredients of this particular narrative are well-known by now: growing up in a small town in suburban Norway in the 1980s and early 1990s in a single-parent household with limited access to what Pierre Bourdieu has termed the 'aristocracy of culture'; acknowledging the influence of his mother on his development as an artist (she appears to have been instrumental, for instance, in laying some of the conceptual groundwork for his Shelf paintings[7]), and negotiating the thorny issue of 'taste' that an uninitiated parental voice brought to bear on this very development (enter the spectre, inevitably, of kitsch); the banal teenage drama of having to choose between football (enter the mark-making trolley as painting device) and everything else (eventually narrowed down to a quasi-criminal graffiti career) in a macho society on the periphery, relatively speaking, of Europe (a machismo I understand so much better having devoured Karl Ove Knausgård's *My Struggle*). Such a biography expresses itself through the modest claims to privacy articulated in the muted, bleached-out colour palette of awnings, canopies and garage doors blinking in the watery summer sun; a microcosm conjured by snapshots of dogs, sweaters with dogs on them; a small motor-boat lazily docked in a yachting harbour. The resulting picture is one of a world (I am invoking – not describing – it here from the vantage point of recognition: the world of apartments lining the train tracks at dusk) in which art is simply painting, and painting simply

art – where the legitimacy of painting as the royal road to art was simply never in question, and probably never will be. Which is, in its way, a good thing, for critiques of painting as a compromised institution deserving de(con)struction are typically the privilege and province of the inhabitants of the larger institution of art – a function, ultimately, of access and entitlement, and a psycho-social variation on the dialectic of inside and outside, of insider and outsider. (Am I really calling Værslev an 'outsider' artist here? To the extent that his work, in the maelstrom of contemporary painting production, seems to represent the height of 'insider' art – 'zombie formalism' – yes, perhaps.[8]) If painting, of whatever stripe, continues to occupy the place of art proper in what I referred to earlier as the 'popular imagination' – a class-based concept if ever there was one, in the rarefied realm of the professional art world – then it is precisely from this perspective, quite literally 'on the fence', that Værslev paints, indeed works. As the very definition, in people's perception and the popular imagination – that of Værslev's mother as much as mine, for instance – of 'art', the work of painting is worth all the apologetic critical effort in the world.

Shelf paintings, Terrazzo paintings, Pallet paintings, Canopy paintings, Trolley paintings: they speak, methodically, of the everyday aesthetic injunction of interior design, of the shifting continuum of working-class to middlebrow taste, of the inconspicuous consumption of free time, of amateur and hobby culture – but above all, perhaps, of 'work', that most confounding of cornerstones in all discussions of class. They summon a world 'after work', both literally and metaphorically: the realm of rest and relaxation after a hard day's work, as well as the post-industrial economy in which service has supplanted labour – a paradigm shift prophesied long ago, we now know, in the very Conceptual art revolution inaugurated by Asher, Buren, Mosset, Parmentier, Toroni and the like. (Doesn't the concluding statement of the BMPT manifesto 'we are not painters' simply mean 'we are not artisans – we do not *work*'?) Værslev's pallet paintings invite a particularly meaningful reading in this regard, and this is nowhere more potently illustrated than in a press photograph I found online of the artist's gallerist 'explaining' one of these paintings to an interested party, possibly a prospective buyer, at an art fair. Both personages are clad in the art world's requisite black, standing five feet or so away from the object in question; the woman puts her hand on her necklace in a legible sign of focused attention, while the man's hand is caught in mid-flight, gesturing towards the work of art – something akin to a flat wooden transportation structure ('pallet') mounted on a wall by way of two slim steel brackets and judiciously splattered with household paint. Although easily condensed into a crude joke about art-world elitism or the vagaries of 'taste', the real subject of this painting, it seems to me, is *work* – in all its layered and scattered meanings, from the aesthetic to the social and back again. This is what has become of the world of work – and only painting, witness to it all, remains.

1   Quoted in Charles Harrison & Paul Wood (ed), *Art in Theory, 1900–1990: An Anthology of Changing Ideas* (Oxford: Basil Blackwell, 1991), 850.
2   'Bête comme un peintre', Marcel Duchamp – himself a gifted maker of pictures – was famously fond of saying: 'Stupid like a painter'. The true depth of Duchamp's appreciation for this nineteenth-century quip of uncertain origin is debatable, of course, given his lifelong commitment to the painting paradigm – as the posthumous unveiling of *Etant donnés* in 1969 would confirm. The cliché of painterly mark-making as the nadir of conceptual stupidity – of dumbness as the monomaniacal painter's province – ensures a lone comedic highlight in Terry Zwigoff's otherwise forgettable *Art School Confidential* (2006), in which the film's leading tormented-artist character, played by John Malkovich, appears as an amalgam of Buren, Mosset, Parmentier and Toroni, with all their signature marks rolled into one knowing spoof of 'Conceptual painting'. Malkovich's character limits himself to twenty-five mindless years of painting triangles, and only triangles.
3   It would take years before Conceptual artists began painting once again – and then only 'because they thought it was a good idea'.
4   It is worth noting, in this regard, that the glory years of Conceptual painting in France coincided seamlessly with the apogee of deconstruction in French philosophy (Louis Althusser, Gilles Deleuze, Jacques Derrida, Jean-François Lyotard): a book like Derrida's *The Truth in Painting* (1979), half of which is really concerned with the question of the frame – the painting's literal limit as well as the institutional context of art – must be read in part against the backdrop of the critical success of the Support/ Surface campaign for a relentlessly self-questioning painting practice. Derrida never came closer to defining deconstruction than by describing it, in terms that would have blended in exemplarily well with the language of *Peinture: Cahiers théoriques*, as an interference in 'solid structures, "material" institutions … not only discourses or signifying representations'. Jacques Derrida, *The Truth in Painting* (Chicago: The University of Chicago Press, 1987), 19. Furthermore, Derrida's entire aesthetic argument in this text revolves around the dialectic of the artwork's interior ('image') and exterior ('frame') in ways that both reflect Buren's theory of the artist's studio as the ultimate framing device and presage Fredrik Værslev's negotiation of the same schizoid dynamic
5   In the catalogue-cum-artist's book accompanying this exhibition, Martin Clark argues that 'much of Værslev's previous work already addresses an idea of landscape –
or perhaps environment would be a better word', while Steinar Sekkingstad points out this project's affinity with the work of Edvard Munch (of all artists), zeroing in on a shared interest in landscape as design in both painters' oeuvres: 'wallpaper', supremely self-conscious ornament. See *Fredrik Værslev: All Around Amateur* (Berlin: Sternberg Press, 2016), 322. Considerations of décor and ornamentalism aside, it is certainly intriguing to view Værslev's work in the expanded context of, say, contemporary Land Art, of both the urban and suburban variety (see note 6). Returning to the notion of the 'invention' of plein air painting by the French impressionists, it is worth noting how this particular paradigm shift was in fact facilitated in a major way by the gradual industrialisation of the paint-production business (eg the invention of portable paint tubes) – a mildly ironic circumstance that clearly resonates with Værslev's own interest in the industrial application of house paint, or in painting that poses as a quasi-industrial or easily mechanised operation typically undertaken in a post-industrial space.
6   It would admittedly be a bit of a stretch to situate graffiti, as a quintessential public-art form (anonymous, collective, formulaic), in the historical continuum of *plein-air* painting – an apocalyptic Impressionism for the post-industrial age, perhaps? But it is nonetheless worth pointing out, in the context of our present historical excursus, the emergence of certain strands of political graffiti in the febrile environment of mid-60s Paris and its indubitable influence on Buren's interest in 'street' art. Seen from this vantage point, Værslev's trajectory from the street to the gallery does not necessarily follow the well-trodden path of Jean-Michel Basquiat, Keith Haring, Kenny Scharf and the like – its arc once again appears altogether more Frenc'. Besides Buren, Mosset and other French painters from the 1960s and 1970s, *affichistes* like Raymond Hains and Jacques Villeglé, or proto-*nouveau réalistes* and *tachistes* like Alberto Burri, Jean Fautrier et al. come to mind in mapping a mental family tree of art-historical antecedents for Værslev's version.
7   'Shelf Paintings, 2009-ongoing, is a response to long discussions with the artist's mother, Anne-Britt Værslev, in which she maintained that an ideal painting should have the same effect as the color of a blouse: it should set off the surroundings without itself being seen.' Gertrud Sandqvist, 'Fredrik Værslev', in *Fredrik Værslev: The Rich Man's Breakfast, the Shopkeeper's Lunch, the Poor Man's Supper* (Oslo: Standard (Books), 2012), 12. Anne-Britt Værslev has no way of knowing, of course, how much her conviction would have pleased Michael Asher.
8   See Ina Blom, 'Sympathy for the Zombie', in *Fredrik Værslev: All Around Amateur*, 339–344.

                                                          Dieter Roelstraete

TAKE GOOD CARE OF YOURSELF,
DO SOME WALKING
Åsmund Thorkildsen

> As artists, we know more about the history of
> our field, the infinity of alternatives, than artists
> ever knew before. And all this is reflected in the
> array of styles with which we beckon other's
> attention. For the first time blissful ignorance
> hasn't a chance.
> — Allan Kaprow in "The Artist as a Man of the
> World", 1964[1]

When addressing the subject of contemporary and
modern art, the question of generation matters.
The reason for this is that well established – or,
as we might say, well seasoned – artists, critics and
art historians have lived through several decades
in which questions relating to the practice, theoretical demarcation and discursive scope of painting,
and to the perceptual apparatus it presupposes,
have been widely discussed. Many of this
generation have witnessed, and indeed actively
contributed to, the corresponding developments.
This has continued in parallel to the teaching of art
history, which seeks to impart an intellectual grasp
of artistic eras and their sequence. This situation
is relevant when seeking to understand the art
of Fredrik Værslev. In order to explain his critical
reception we also have to consider the relative
youth of the circles in which he first exhibited,
for this generational dimension is evident in the
references, and the types of concepts and
approaches, that get mentioned in interviews,
reviews and essays. The artist himself and his
commentators are of the kind that Kaprow
described as early as 1964. The opening quote
shows just how far back ideas of pluralism reach,
the postmodern acceptance of a broad range of
idioms, and the idea that no one style, medium,
approach or thematic focus has a privileged claim
on being the correct and primary way of doing art
in the modern age.

Arthur Danto was a philosopher-critic who,
in the 1980s and 90s, reshaped our ideas on how
to look at contemporary art following the demise
of modernism; modernist art had regarded itself
as a closed system of symbols that aspired
to purge painting of all extraneous conventions,
a project that ground to a halt in the mid-1960s
after stripping the medium down to the bare essen-
tials of a flat object and a visually flat image.[2] Born
in 1924, Danto published philosophical essays in
the 1950s and 1960s that reflected on what was
happening in New York in those decades. This was
precisely the period in which Jacques Derrida was
deconstructing the prioritisation of speech at the
expense of writing that is central to the phenom-
enology of Husserl; according to Derrida, a form
of writing preceded and was always a precondition
for speech.[3] Kaprow and many of the artists who
followed him responded by removing the painting
from its blind frame, allowing the canvas to curl,[4]
and sending it out into the world, where it had to
hold its own relative to many other visual objects.
For Derrida, language was evicted from consciousness and the oral cavity and forced out into the
world and history.

PAINTING AS PAINTING – AND SO MUCH MORE

And it is out here in the world in the midst of life
that Fredrik Værslev paints, exhibits and sells
his paintings. To encode this process, we could
follow Ad Reinhardt and the early conceptual
artists in saying that an artwork is best understood
as "art-as-art", in other words, as an analytical
statement that can be used to mark off a closed,
self-referential game. To quote Ad Reinhardt's
maxim in full: "Art is art and life is life."[5] This might
look like two tautologies joined by a conjunction.
But that reading assumes that there is a watertight
barrier between art and non-art ("life"/everything
else), or between painting and non-painting
("life"/everything else). After Kaprow and Derrida,
and many others, this reading is challenged by
a different one, namely that paintings qua paintings can also be many other things, an insight that
is captured in the sentence that also serves as the
heading for this section.

Seemingly analytical sentences, which allow
us to say that the subject and the predicate mean
essentially the same thing, can be picked apart.
In an essay about the abstract paintings of Arne
Malmedal entitled "Malerier som maleri" (Paintings
as Painting), I began by writing:

> One of the most frequently quoted statements
> about the meaning of modern abstract painting
> is Frank Stella's "What you see is what you
> see". This statement has the form of a tautology,
> of a type similar to the title of this article,
> "Paintings as Painting". Stella's statement has
> given rise to the common misunderstanding
> that his pictures do not mean anything – that
> they are silent and devoid of meaning (…) If this
> is a misunderstanding and the two occurrences
> of the word "painting" do not stand for the same
> thing, then we have to be able to explain where
> the difference lies. And the claim here is that

painting that presents itself as such offers something new. The difference is of course signalled by that tiny word "as".[6]

The 1960s were a decade of highly conspicuous upheavals, a period that witnessed the last serious attempts to rescue art from culture. In her essay "Against Interpretation" (1961), Susan Sontag sought to promote an erotic approach to art, as opposed to one that was linguistic or reflective. She writes: "What we decidedly do not need now is further to assimilate Art into Thought, or (worse yet) Art into Culture."[7] In 1962, the philosopher Nelson Goodman presented a series of lectures at Harvard that he would later turn into his 1968 book *Languages of Art. An Approach to a Theory of Symbols*. In this work he teases out some clear distinctions and the possibility of a simplified, almost exemplary system of notation in art. He distinguishes between, on the one hand, pictures and sketches, and on the other, e.g. linguistic art forms – and classical concert music in particular. The greatest possible distinction exists between the kind of music which, in Western culture, is based on a precise notation system – i.e. works that have *scores* – and pictures and sketches where it makes no sense to distinguish between formalised notation and performance, as one does in the case of art music. Pictures and sketches possess dense syntax and everything in them is rendered visible, whereas notation systems have a syntax that is separate and distinct. Pictures and sketches exemplify their own idiom and there is no distinction between them and their meaning – "what you see is what you see" – although Goodman acknowledges that pictures can be highly complex and dense/ continuous phenomena. Pictures and sketches show what they mean, whereas a sentence says what it means. Within Goodman's system, this all seems self-explanatory. What is striking is that he presented this analysis at the very point in the history of American art when artists themselves were choosing to dismantle or at least blur the distinctions between the various symbolic systems. One good example of this is Allan Kaprow's *Happenings*, while the unconventional notation systems of Morton Feldman and John Cage made it difficult to decide which of several performances was the artwork as rooted in and determined by the notation. The point for Goodman is that in art music it is the score that determines whether a performance is an instance of the artwork. For it to be such, it can diverge only in minimal ways from the notation.

During the late 1960s and early 1970s, late modern abstract painting and sculpture produced a plethora of complex artistic phenomena: minimalism, process art, happenings, performance, dance, video, post-minimalism, land art, body art, conceptual art and installation art. This gave rise to considerable confusion in the associated terms and concepts. The most notorious debate of relevance to our current discussion about abstract and "modern" painting today came in the form of two celebrated essays by Michael Fried and Rosalind Krauss respectively. The issue here was the relationship between art and life, between something inherent and organic and something separate and dialogical, i.e. social. Fried's essay "Art and Objecthood" (1967) was a head-on critique of minimalism; the objects that were presented for the viewer's contemplation in exhibitions constituted an obstacle in that they required the viewer to enter into a relationship with them which they dictated. Although a dialogue is constituted here, it is one that Fried regards as seriously flawed. Fried argues that this situation is comparable to that of theatre. He maintains that art and theatre are diametrical opposites, as were art and culture for Sontag, and art and life for Reinhardt. The alternative to this mode of perception – and the view of humanity and the worldview that Fried's critique seems to entail – finds succinct expression in Rosalind Krauss' equally well-known essay "The Double Negative. Towards a New Syntax for Sculpture," which appeared in *New Passages in Sculpture* (1977).

Krauss is a notable defender of the view of art – and of the human condition – that distances itself from the notion of a private, inner, integrated ego, a notion that lies implicit in the humanist tradition and in the phenomenological tradition of Husserl, which Fried seems to endorse. For Krauss, it is external encounters that make dialogue possible; personality is shaped by influences from outside and does not exist as a kind of preformed consciousness or soul. Krauss' essay takes its title from Michael Heizer's earthwork project, *Double Negative* (1969). Important for Krauss is that this is an artwork that lacks a formal centre and can only be experienced out in the desert where it exists. There is no central or privileged vantage point from which the work can be viewed in its entirety. Heizer's *Double Negative* can only be experienced in real time and real space; it presupposes what Fried refers to as a "situation", and one that is theatrical. The dominant characteristic of such a situation, according to Fried, is *presence* (as it is of life in general) as opposed to presentness (which is something we can only experience through art).

Åsmund Thorkildsen

Note that Fried uses here the term for an abstraction, "present*ness*", i.e. a phenomenon that is non-empirical. The final sentence of his essay is explicit: "Presentness is grace."[8] There is also a clear literary allusion here. Allan Kaprow, in his essay "The Artist as a Man of the World", describes the artist's descent in status from intellectual and genius to a mere labourer and ultimately a Beat, remarking: "What a fall from grace!"[9]

(Fried and Krauss are familiar references for the generation reviewing Værslev, which is not surprising, insofar as these authors have been regular items on reading lists at universities and art colleges since the 1980s. As a reference point, they do, however, tend to be overlooked.)

But let us now attempt to approach Værslev's paintings as repetitions of and variations on late modern abstract painting – a species of apparition which some critics have described as "zombie formalism". It is this perspective that Ina Blom discusses at length in her article about Værslev in the catalogue that accompanied his exhibition in Bergen Kunsthall in 2016, when he was the official artist at Bergen International Festival Exhibition. What is the significance of this regular recurrence of abstract painting? What status can such painting have if we measure it against the status achieved by modernist painting in the years prior to around 1965? And how do our attempts to understand this recurrence and to describe it through analysis and reflection contribute to that status? One thing we are not talking about here is some kind of resurrection from the dead. Instead, we are dealing with a particular symbolic system that has been exhausted and reached its logical cultural-historical conclusion, meaning that terms such as "dead" and "resurrection" can only be used metaphorically and with great care.

How many times has abstract painting been revisited, revived in new guises by a new generation of young artists? In this respect Værslev and his teachers can make no claim to be the first. For the phenomenon certainly occurred in a big way in the case of neo-geo painting, which appropriated abstraction and was accompanied by lashings of theory and plenty of tongue in cheek. The new abstraction of the 1980s was humorous, ironic, self-confident, audacious, decorative – impertinent. It was inspired by pop art, and was characterised by the appropriation of outer appearances, just as pop artists had appropriated imagery from the advertising and media world. Roy Lichtenstein even painted ironic versions of comic strips, imbuing them with the heroic sheen of abstract expressionism, like some de Kooning paintings we might expect to find in the Duckburg Museum of Modern Art.

Artists who achieved prominence in the 1980s with variations of abstraction include Sherrie Levin, Peter Schuyff, Peter Halley, David Diao, Stephen Westfall, Andrew Spence, Philip Taffee, Steven Parrino, and David Reed. As a group, these artists declared an end to the process of mourning, if indeed such a thing had ever been real. In the Norwegian context, we can point to an essay on precisely this subject that appeared in 1990, with the title "Abstraksjon – Enda en gang" (Abstraction – Yet Again). This is how the essay began:

"Abstraction has been around for eighty years. It's a rich tradition."
—Stephen Westfall

Abstraction is a term we are used to seeing in combination with concepts such as non-figuration, avant-garde, etc. Today abstraction is back again, but we have to forget the connection to the avant-garde and its dogmas. Which is not entirely easy. When we consider the avant-garde's claim to represent the new, the latter half of our title may well come across as a complaint. But the phrase "yet again" is not used here to express disappointment at some supposed failure of art to move forward. Instead it is intended optimistically and without irony, to refer to a new generation of artists and critics who emerged in the 1980s. The idea that abstraction can offer a valid field of activity following the demise of the avant-garde presupposes new conceptual insights and a new sensitivity. In short, abstract pictures are being painted like never before. For some of those who started working with abstraction in the 80s, the starting point was theoretical. For the neo-geo artists, abstraction frequently played a part in their critique of ideas about originality and authenticity, and of the belief in the new. But even in the case of painters who have simulated the work of the suprematists or the stripe paintings of the 1960s – artists such as Sherrie Levine and Philip Taffee – one senses a yearning for a new innocence despite the evident irony. On its own, irony has never been a sufficient motivation to create pictures. Like many of their contemporaries who work with abstraction, the attitude of these artists can be described as disrespectful love.[10]

Although Værslev's commentators generally fail to mention these artists, the tensions between irony and innocence, disrespect and love, that are highlighted in the above essay will prove useful in our attempts to interpret, understand and appreciate Værslev's work. Because I accept that – as Reinhardt wrote – the interpreter of art is a "philistine".

In Norway, this debate has focused in particular on new instances of abstract painting, in other words abstract pictures that have been produced since the conclusion of the game to identify the logical endpoint of the symbolic systems that defined modernist painting. It was a game that played out in parallel – and was closely interwoven – with the rise of neo-expressionism, neo-figuration and the various *assemblage* and mixed-media techniques that favoured the installation form. Thus in Norway, the relevant debate has been ongoing for almost thirty years, meaning the debate about new abstract painting and how we should relate to it, given that we can no longer claim the passionate intensity and innovative transgressions that characterised the game prior to its logical endpoint.

Before we move on, let me mention one last contrast to illustrate the kind of things from which autonomous modernist art needs to be distinguished, namely that between art and jazz. It is this kind of pairing that gives rise to modernist dogmas such as: art is not culture, art is not theatre, art is not life, and art is not jazz.

This latter contrast is addressed in the essay "Standardbilder – Om maleriets forsoning med det levende sproget" (Standard Pictures. On reconciling painting with the living language), which was written for an exhibition at Henie-Onstad Art Centre, Sal Haaken, in 2004. In this text, jazz is discussed as a potential paradigm for abstract painting following the historical abstraction that was practiced before 1965. The term "standard pictures" adapts the meaning of "standards" in the field of jazz improvisation to the world of painting, setting up a parallel between improvisations on standard songs and painted variations on familiar motifs from the history of painting, within a range of idioms and styles. I quote from the essay:

> There are at least three qualities that make jazz a suitable paradigm for an approach to contemporary painting. Firstly, it has undergone its entire stylistic development within the scope of just some fifty years, a historical evolution for which painting has required at least six centuries. Forty-plus years seem more manageable, because they encompass fewer

standards. Secondly, jazz has no entrenched association with the social elite; it has traditionally been a popular art form, whereas even the most advanced avant-garde idioms were implemented in arenas and social contexts that were fairly far removed from voluntarily chosen proletarian settings in which bohemian artists lived (aristocrats with limited funds). In other words, in jazz there is no class problem rooted in family romance, little false consciousness, and few pretences that need to be either sublimated or suppressed. Thirdly, jazz is an art that involves improvisation and interpretation, one which today represents a tradition of improvising on standard themes, whereby creativity and individual expression are essentially reconciled with existing models.[11]

THE SHADOW RIGHT BEHIND US

The above remarks are intended as a reminder about this discourse, which I exemplify here with a few of my own contributions, just to be on the safe side, although of course many others could be cited. The reminder seems necessary because, when considering the generational issue there is a tendency to become so preoccupied with the spatiality and light of our own near future that we overlook the shadow that stands right behind us, a shadow that is produced by standing upright in the present and looking towards a future from where the light emanates. And if we have learnt anything from the history of painting it is that shadows generally lie directly behind objects that obstruct the light. Not surprisingly, in the discussions associated with the reception of Værslev's work we find references to his own generation and that of the recent past. More specifically, what emerges is a generation of people with close associations: teachers, their students, and the teachers' teachers. In such a situation the light is bright on contemporary figures, with a little of it spilling over onto the teachers and the teachers' teachers who stand clustered around them. But when we turn around and adopt the historical gaze, we notice that the light also falls on things that lie a little further back in time, things that have already been codified in books, lectures, retrospective exhibitions, and museum collections.

As someone from the generation that falls between Danto and Værslev, I have lived through a period which at the time was brightly illuminated, but which for our younger contemporaries is now in shadow. And it is an analysis of what lies in that

Åsmund Thorkildsen

shadow which I offer in this essay as a contribution to the understanding and interpretation of Fredrik Værslev's paintings. Needless to say, this does not amount to a critique or an objection of anything or anyone, but rather merely an attempt to fill out the picture. Because if we consider it from the angle of art history, the picture is fairly continuous.

Thus it should come as no surprise that painters like Peter Halley, Stephen Westfall, Sherrie Levine and Andrew Spence are currently languishing in the shadow of Værslev's generation. Neither is it strange that the non-painterly artistic practices that emerge from the situation in which Kaprow, Fried and Krauss immersed themselves also now stand in the shade. I shall return to some of these names in due course, because I am convinced they can help us to find a valid approach to Værslev's art. For his paintings can best be understood as existing in an expanded field and within the tradition of avant-garde practices that developed in parallel with one another during the self-satisfied period of modernist painting. It is worth noting, however, that the most thorough – and important – analysis of the postmodern period, to which Værslev undoubtedly belongs, has passed under the radar of those who write about him. What I am referring to here is the allegorical aspect in Værslev's work, for although his art can be described as theatrical, performative, and conceptual, it is the allegorical impulse and the expanded field in which it operates that provides the clearest structure for his works. More particularly, I am alluding to Craig Owens' 1980 essay "The Allegorical Impulse. Toward a Theory of Postmodernism".[12] Owen's analysis shows how allegory serves as both a formal structure (which breaks free of the syntax Nelson Goodman defined for images and sketches) and an attitude. With Owens' help, let us attempt to get closer to a sensitive, generationally oriented and art-historical interpretation of some of what it is that motivates Værslev.

A GENERATIONAL QUESTION

Before reviewing some of the features in the reception of Værslev's work and pointing out the recurrent references, I will offer some reflections on the generational issue. For we can assert that the development of a clear symbolic system is now past and that its active period can be viewed not just historically, but also from a historicist angle.[13] Yet historicism is not the only approach we can apply to the passing of time and history; we can also look at things from a chronological perspective of the kind recorded in calendars and in terms of generations. Although we can reject a dialectic, diachronic and metaphysical model of history, it is a fact that seasons come and go, the sun rises and sets, people are born, grow and die. This remains true regardless of whether – from a historicist point of view – "history is over" or modernist painting is a thing of the past. Things do not stand still, even if one rejects a historicist view of the way human society develops.[14] In the postmodern circumstances we now live in, with plentiful help from the accumulation, circulation and proliferation of digitally decoded and recoded images, there is a tendency for the synchronous, or visually simultaneous perspective, where all things exist in parallel, to displace the diachronic form of understanding, whereby phenomena are compared on the basis of the meaningful passing of time, which is often interpreted dialectically (and/or metaphysically). This is one of the insights in Fredric Jameson's *Postmodernism, or, The Cultural Logic of Late Capitalism*, first published in 1991. This tendency is clearly evident in the references that Værslev's generation operate with. Older and recent events are considered in the same breath, while things that happened in between are overlooked. Omissions of this kind tend to be short-lived, and it is quite possible that in the course of time all relevant factors will become simultaneous, presented to the eye as a spectacle in the museum's state of eternal tranquillity.[15] One trend we can associate with so many of the artworks that are readily accessible on the internet is that they are rarely accompanied by information such as their titles, production dates, exhibition history, or the collections in which they are kept.

The reflections presented here on art historical inscriptions of relevance to the generational question and to periodisation, and the remarks on the fact that in chronological terms we are now living after the conclusion of a particular way of working with, creating, understanding and relating to paintings, are all of a provisional nature. The history of art in our era will be reinterpreted by future generations, and they will see things and uncover connections that we now ignore or place too little emphasis on. In my view, the story of painting to which Værslev seems to contribute is one that considers the varied ways of working with painted objects under a vast range of different circumstances. It is a story that has been unfolding more or less continuously since the 1950s, during which time we have seen numerous variations on familiar topics in the expanded field in which Værslev is such a conspicuous practitioner. One question I wish to ask, but am unable to answer, is whether this succession of artistic languages that have followed one another since the 1950s can be viewed as constituting a tradition, and whether a certain evolution can be read from the sequence in which works have been produced, exhibited and presented to the public more generally. It is by no means certain that they can, or that *ready-mades* exhibit a tradition, development or history. Undoubtedly, attempts will be made to inscribe such practices into one of the great historicist narratives, and we must read them with critical interest when they arrive.

In her contribution to the book that accompanied Værslev's Bergen International Festival Exhibition "Sympathy for the Zombie" at Bergen Kunsthall in 2016, Ina Blom considers the new wave of painting that arose at the turn of the millennium in terms of the cultural logic that Jameson attributes to late capitalism:

> Yet at this point the terms of its return were different, less dramatic. The hue and cry about "death" or "life" had subsided; paintings in the plural, were just *there*, doing their jobs on the walls, in the vaults and in the auction houses. They were more precisely undead – existing in that liminal zone where things just go on and on.[16]

Ina Blom's reading of Værslev can be set alongside that of Gertrud Sandqvist. Both are particularly interesting when it comes to the generational question, since both authors belong to the same "intermediate generation" as the present author, the generation that came before that of Værslev but after that which defined the historical paradigms and the reference points of late modernism. This is also of relevance to the issue of periodisation, to which we will return.

But first, here is a list of the references we find in the texts by younger art critics and curators: Rothko, Munch, Newman, Abstract Expressionism, Morris Louis, Klimt (his *Beethoven Frieze*), Pollock, William Turner, Kippenberger, Franz West, Daniel Buren, Olivier Mosset, Michael Parmentier, Nicole Toroni, Martin Barré, Simon Hantai, and the Support-Surface Group. These examples are taken from Martin Clark's in-depth text "The Persistence of Ground Across or As Its Own Remaking: Fredrik Værslev's Sunsets and Shelves".[17] These are older, well-rehearsed references – and of course all are highly relevant to the understanding of Værslev's art. Younger artists who are named include Cheyney Thompson, Blake Rayne, Scott Lyall, Sean Paul, and – from the intermediate generation – Moira Dryer. Others that could be of relevance to much of what Clark writes, especially with respect to Værslev's painting, but who remain in the shadows are Robert Morris, Isamu Noguchi, Brice Marden, David Reed and Jessica Stockholder. Morris and Noguchi are of course historically codified artists, and one of the reasons why they do not figure as references in Clark's discussion about theatricality, props on a stage, etc., is that they have featured little in the broader discourse about painting.[18] Rather more remarkable is the fact that none of those who write about the aspect of movement within the physical spaces where Værslev's paintings are shown – what Michael Fried calls their "situations" – makes any mention of Brice Marden. Of particular relevance given the themes of this essay is Marden's major painting installation *The Seasons* from 1975, which was shown in that year at Rice University, Houston, in rooms that also featured paintings by Mark Rothko and David Novros.[19] This was a milestone exhibition when it came to illustrating how the physical movements of the viewer relate to the visual organisation of forms on the canvas and their location in the space where they are displayed. The photographic documentation of that exhibition together with Nodelman's text are of immense relevance to an understanding of Værslev's exhibitions.

In "Sunset Surface", also in the 2016 International Festival Exhibition catalogue, the author Steinar Sekkingstad includes references to: Pollock, Munch, Asher, Greenberg, Buren, Ryman, Still, Newman, and Rothko. All of these derive from the triumphant post-war period of late modernist painting. Other references that Sekkingstad makes are the market for genre paintings among the Dutch bourgeoisie of the 17th century, "bedroom decor", the fact that Værslev's approach is site-specific, and that it is also sometimes "mechanistic" – an allusion to Værslev's occasional use of road-marking machines. Both Sekkingstad and Clark implicitly assume a number of phenomena which I have characterised as currently standing in the shadows; it is rather odd, for example, that neither of them should mention David Reed, especially when modern painting is considered from the angle of "bedroom decor". For Reed was not just the creator of this genre, but possibly also its most significant practitioner, an artist on a level here with Andy Warhol, who once described his own shadow paintings as "disco decor". As for the use of a motorised vehicle

Åsmund Thorkildsen

"as a brush", we need only remind ourselves of
Asger Jorn's use of a scooter to create patterns
in soft clay in conjunction with a monumental
ceramic work, or Roxy Paine's machine for the
assembly-line production of monochrome paintings. Among Værslev's younger contemporaries
one notable name is Ida Ekblad, who created paint
tracks with a shopping trolley she pushed around
using her hands and feet.

Also mentioned are the shaped canvas phenomenon and a number of other well-established,
historically codified artists, including Frank Stella,
Victor Pasmore, Robert Rauschenberg, Enrico
Castellani and Pino Pascali.[20] These are artists
who work free-form, sometimes using blind frames
and sometimes by seeking alternatives to the
usual orientation of the canvas parallel to the wall.
Not surprisingly, Vanessa Clairet mentions the
impressionists Monet, Renoir and Pissarro when
discussing the exhibition "The Constant Gardener"
that took place on the "impressionist island"
La Grenouillère, where Værslev hung stripe paintings in the trees,[21] whereas Kristian Skylstad refers
to Munch, Bridget Riley, arte povera and Michael
Bould, Damien Hirst and Wolfgang Tillmans.

Værslev himself is fascinated by various
contemporaries and immediate forerunners.
Some of the names he mentions from the period
after Newman and Rothko but before the
youngest generation are the non-painters Gordon
Matta-Clark and Dan Graham, and the allegorist
painter Sigmar Polke. This indicates that Værslev
draws on a broader, more expanded field than his
reviews and interviews would lead us to expect.

MODERNISM AND THE SERIOUSNESS OF ART

The texts of Gertrud Sandqvist and Ina Blom
stand out in that they address more general and
fundamental issues in relation to Værslev's art.
But their approaches differ. While Sandqvist
discusses linguistic psychoanalysis (Jacques
Lacan), Blom turns her attention to contemporary
financial speculation and capitalism, linking these
to the social anthropological theme of zombies
and its development at the hands of the entertain-
ment industry. The reason why these two stand
out is probably a consequence of their having
spent many years studying contemporary art and
its history. It has to do with periods.

Periodisation is the practice from the study
and analysis of history that involves dividing
the past into discrete stretches of time on the basis
of relatively stable characteristics. Of course,
this is not the unique and mysterious interweaving

of time and space, that experience of closeness
in the remote and remoteness in the close,
that Walter Benjamin describes in his analysis
of "aura".[22] The concept of aura is proposed
in conjunction with art in the age of mechanical
reproduction, which is also the title of Benjamin's
famous essay from 1935. Perspicuity, the
production of series, and minute discrepancies
in appearance, transitive objects whose visual
information is spread digitally and empirically
transformed … It is hard to imagine anything
further removed from the numinous experience
of perceiving the uniqueness in the here and
now of an auratic artwork. Benjamin–who is
also important for Craig Owens' analysis of the
allegorical impulse–is conspicuously absent
from the literature about Værslev's art, with the
exception of the contributions by Stian Grøgaard.

The periodisation which, in my view, might
be put forward in relation to the texts by Blom
and Sandqvist has to do, on the one hand, with the
generational question, and on the other, with the
reasons behind the respective interpretations–
which ideas and values it is that inform the reading
of Værslev's art. I would suggest that both writers,
in their different ways, associate Værslev with the
period of modernism. This reading of Sandqvist
and Blom is a response to what I perceive as the
profound seriousness of their texts, a seriousness
that is characteristic of modernism. For Blom, the
zombie paintings are a regrettable and superficial
expression of a civilization that has forgotten where
the myths of zombies originated–namely within
the culture of African magic among slaves on Haiti.
Blom's sympathy for the zombie painter can be
seen as a sympathetic response to those who no
longer believe that art can deliver a political message, who view the contemporary abstract painter
as a slave to the interests of financial speculation.
Instead, they opt for the frivolity of postmodernism
and become suppliers to the market. Blom picks
up on Værslev's frequently discussed materiality,
the fact that he paints on the floor, works with
very large formats, gets physically involved in the
production process, and that he exposes paintings
to the elements during the winter. Concerning
Værslev's materialism, Blom writes that it
"is so remote from contemporary materialisms
and their impact on our understanding of the
environment as well as emergent modes of sensing
and being…"[23]

By contrast, Gertrud Sandqvist certainly does
not regard Værslev as a zombie formalist. Instead
she associates him with a major tradition that sees
the artwork as the source of the sublime and as a

phenomenon capable of capturing and taming the gaze. She writes: "Fredrik Værslev offers us this reflection: to see greatness in the most neglected things."[24] This latter is in the spirit of Danto's reading of pop art, which he views as capable of transforming everyday life into something of higher value, a process he described as "the transfiguration of the commonplace", a phrase he also used as the title of a book in 1981.

Sandqvist reads Værslev's art as forms that tame the gaze of the other, as analysed by Jacques Lacan. She adduces heavyweight, historical references such as Plato, Kant, Merleau-Ponty and Hannah Arendt. For her, Værslev's paintings can be read in relation to the myth of the origins of painting, according to which the medium was given the role of taming the human gaze so as to protect it from its cruelty, from that primitive reality to which civilized people are only vulnerable when subjected to the incessant and unfiltered gaze of others, or when, during episodes of psychosis, the confrontation with the world loses all form.

I too am inclined to group this reading with the period of modernist painting, and not just because Sandqvist invokes an artist such as Munch. Another reason is that the passage just cited about the transformation of neglected things into something immensely grand and glorious carries an echo of "Ariel's Song" from Shakespeare's *Tempest* (1611), in which things are described as undergoing "… a sea change into something rich and strange".[25] It is perhaps not entirely surprising that Jackson Pollock turned to these verses when choosing titles for two modernist canvases that he painted in 1947, namely *Full Fathom Five* and *Sea Change*. But further support for viewing Sandqvist's reading as modernist is to be found in Lacan himself, notably in his discussion "What is a Picture?" in the book *The Four Fundamental Concepts of Psychoanalysis*:

> The social function, which was already emerging at the religious level, is now becoming clear. Who comes here? Those who form what Retz calls "les peuples", the audience. And what do the audience see in these vast compositions. They see the gaze of those persons who, when the audience is not there, deliberate in this hall. Behind the picture, it is their gaze that is there.
>
> You see, one can say that there are always lots of gazes behind. Nothing new is introduced in this respect by the epoch that André Malraux distinguished as the modern, that which comes to be dominated by what he calls the "incomparable monster", namely the gaze of the

painter, which claims to impose itself as being the only gaze. There always was a gaze behind.[26]

Both Lacan and Sandqvist seem to regard this as a permanent condition, something entailed by the myth of painting's origins, which is as such an inherent force in modern art. But I would argue that the modern period, as Malraux defined it, was the last in which painting was or could have been characterised in this way. And when we consider the periodisation relative to the generations which, historically, came before and after, we bear the influence of what immediately preceded our period, namely modernism in art. But when it encounters the light allegory, this gaze shatters; the "incomparable monster" withers in the glitter of the sharpened knives of the allegorical impulse, with all the humour, irony, joy of painting, and melancholy that ebb and flow through the improvisations on standard pictures, the nimble game with the forms and seriousness of modernism, that typified the free-style, designer abstractions of the 1980s and 90s.

A modernist impulse is evident in the readings of both Blom and Sandqvist. Both ascribe to painting a major, serious and solemn role, one that is made possible by the fact that painting and the other arts are seen as part of a broader narrative, regardless of whether it be the structuralist, the anthropological-psychoanalytic, the romantic-genial, the Hegelian-spiritual or the Marxist-sociological. According to these narratives, art can exert political force within society; it can save us from the impact of the gaze, and it can facilitate new encounters with the infinitely great, the awe-inspiring, the sublime.

Værslev and other alleged zombie painters choose to be passive rather than to make use of the opportunities inherent in Blom's seriousness, which would mean to use their position as artists for political ends. To my mind, this is what Blom is saying when she writes: "The question is whether or not your zombie painting contains the mythological memory of slave revolt, and thus also the seeds of collective organisation and uprising. To the extent that this is the case, this new 'asset class' might start to behave as a 'class' in the revolutionary sense of the word. (…) What is suppressed in zombie painting is precisely the potential for aesthetic collectivity and communality."[27] – A Norwegian contemporary artist is drawn into the vast political-activist complex that I wish to periodise as modernity; art is viewed as something of immense importance, so different from so many other things that it can serve a political function, fostering correct consciousness and

Åsmund Thorkildsen

social transformation by shortening the length of the birth pangs, as Marx put it. For Blom, the zombie painters are typically unwilling to shoulder this heavy responsibility, while for Sandqvist they can still help to erect a screen that pacifies the troll and holds "reification" at bay.

What does the agility of postmodernism have in common with the Popperian rejection of historicism and its totalitarian tendencies? Neither is passive or deterministic. Both imply a moral stance, which involves taking personal, individual responsibility either singly or collectively, and accepting that judgements are the outcome of communal assessments and meaningful analysis by posterity, rather than the outcome of prophecies or the predictions of theoretical models. The playfulness and flexibility that Værslev presents us with are things he takes responsibility for. He makes no secret of what he is doing. He does not claim special significance for his art by inscribing it into a narrative that is too broad. He makes no predictions about the future of others. The postmodern, allegorical impulse makes it possible to forget that the future is our destiny.

But is nothing lost in the period following modernism? It is: the belief in grand narratives, the belief in structures and prophecies that are inescapable but which simultaneously protect us from the fear associated with the terrible freedom of personal choice. The loss of these things can produce anxiety, just as for Benjamin the allegorist will be prone to melancholy. For many, the loss of the grand narratives – such as the autonomy of painting – amounts to a loss of meaning. Some are inclined to say that it is only the grand narratives that justify optimism, and for that reason they must be kept alive. But regardless of whether a few people think that the grand narratives and structures still apply, there is no reason for us to accept them as destiny or to expect that at some time in the distant future the relevant structures and prophecies will resolve all the problems of society or that they will result in enlightenment and self-awareness, albeit combined with permanent unhappiness. But what is lost is the possibility of artistic religiosity and the view of artists as clairvoyant and visionary. And what a relief that is – for many of us at least.

NOT TO PUT LIFE AND ART ON HOLD

The freedom that comes with the rejection of destiny and determinism represents an opportunity. One possibility is that we refuse to lower our gaze when encountering a picture, a painting, and instead look the painter and his work straight in the eye. A number of art historians and critics have done this, as indeed some artists have as well. The current essay is written by an art historian and critic who does not lower his gaze. And it is my impression that Værslev doesn't either. He is therefore open about whom he is inspired by and what aspects of late modernism and contemporary art he chooses to follow.

Some of those who have written about Værslev have touched on the performative and theatrical aspects of his work, the everyday, the ordinary, and the commonplace. Værslev even incorporates into his work objects, built structures and tastes that we associate with suburban life in a detached house in postmodern Norway. In other words, he alludes to the social group that is commonly referred to as the middle class or *petite bourgeoisie*. Largely overlooked in the grand narrative about the path to the classless society, the *petite bourgeoisie* has so far, yet provisionally,[28] outlived the industrial proletariat, as this was understood in the 19th and early 20th centuries. The survival of the *petite bourgeoisie* can be attributed to its participation in the as yet unfinished welfare state, its involvement in democratic discourse, peaceful transitions of government, economic growth in the industrialised countries, and its cooperation in labour policy.

So what happens if we refuse to lower our gaze when confronting modern painting and the world around us? We can join with Værslev in saying that we lift our gaze to the world and look beyond the ruins of the defunct behemoth, to a place where we find life, everyday life. The question is whether there ever could be anything other than everyday life for human beings. It would appear that modernist art, the neo-avant-garde and non-medium-specific late modern practices that came after the grand narrative and the conclusion of the symbolic system of painting and sculpture all have a place in the everyday life of a suburban home. The question we might ask here is: Does art need to be something greater than our actual lives? The answer will depend on the position we adopt with regard to the grand narratives of modernism. If we believe that they are finished and that we are now living with the loss, then the mature answer would be that art does not have to be greater than life, that art is merely a part of life. And to all appearances, this is a conclusion that Værslev's generation can happily live with.

Perhaps paintings could be experienced in much the same way as the dance of the graffiti artist, perhaps paintings could be part of a game, perhaps interpretations could be proposed and discussed without any need to accept them as answers. In my view, Værslev's art could function as having meaning in a conceptual framework of this kind – something we can participate in on the phenomenological level, but without the striving for transcendence or some ontological presence, viewing art as part of our culture, something we can enjoy like jazz, interpreting it as one aspect of our knowledge discourse, writing about it from a historical perspective, acknowledging that we are surrounded by the mundane at all times, and that if we look closely enough, this is all perfectly alright …

What kind of mood, situation, or view of life does this point towards? It would seem to foreshadow a pragmatic attitude to life, one where value is judged in terms of function and utility, one that admits the possibility of living well and meaningfully without having to refine it to the point that it promises to resolve every conceivable social problem, and put an end to all exploitation and abuse of other people. It points to a philosophy and a worldview of the kind I heard expressed by a disc jockey at the end of a late-night show at the Bay Area Jazz Station, KCSM, in the early hours of Saturday, 28th April, 2018: "I'm so happy for having been able to share this music with you. Take good care of yourself. Do some walking."

SOME SMALL STORIES

In her article "The Painter's Contract", published in conjunction with the exhibition *Fredrik Værslev: Querelle of Brest* in 2015, Caroline Soyez-Petithomme lists a number of elements in Værslev's art that are worth bearing in mind. But she does not attempt an explicitly allegorical interpretation of Værslev's paintings/exhibitions. She describes the theatrical aspect of the exhibition, the fact that he works in situ, or site-specifically, that he uses a kind of replay, whereby one picture is superimposed on another, which is already an appropriation, and displacement, whereby arbitrary features are taken as the basis for patterns or idioms etc. Soyez-Petithomme's text refers indirectly to major currents in the art that evolved after the demise of modernist painting and sculpture, although she does not reference the use by Fluxus artists of footprints as scores, or the structures of typical postmodern allegories. I share her interpretation of the paintings, that they are "infinitely compatible with everything that surrounds them".[29] This makes it difficult to understand an exhibition in terms of traditional alienation, as something that builds on a structure in the grip of change, but it is not incompatible with the use of changing contexts that are always site specific, and that – as in an allegory – the meaning changes depending on how it is constructed. Anyone who has noticed the linkage between such artistic practices and the digital networks of the internet will recognise that, in this kind of circulation, the works lack both permanent cultural anchorage in a social system and any kind of higher-order moral or social value system. Værslev's paintings are flexible and accommodating. As David Joselit has said, they are paintings for our time, meaning they are *transitive* paintings.[30] The most plausible anchorage for Værslev's paintings is to be found in his own private biography, on the walls of museums and private collectors – and as references to famous and not-so-famous artistic role models.

I wish to trace a few of these lines from Værslev's exhibitions back to the address where they originate. The reason for harping on about the artists who have landed in the shadow is that, for my own interpretation of Værslev's art, it is useful to consider artists who ceased to paint on flat rectangular surfaces, and who opted instead for an expanded performative field that involved the use of artistic processes that extend the concept of painting and sculpture – processes which Værslev has assimilated in the presentation of his own works. But there is a paradox here, because according to Caroline Soyez-Petithomme, Værslev claims, on the one hand that his paintings are unaffected by context, but on the other that they only become meaningful in consciously choreographed, allegorical and historically rooted contexts.[31]

In other words, in preparing for this contribution to the understanding of Værslev's paintings, I have toned down the exorbitant expectations that modernism brings to the field of painting. I myself do not regard Værslev as a zombie painter, because that description presupposes a narrative I do not use. It is, however, worth recalling the practices of painters such as Sam Gilliam, Steven Parrino and Fabian Marcaccio, building on the innovations of Fonata, Burri and Manzoni, practices such as cutting into, folding and stretching out the canvas and painting materials in rejection of the integral screen of modernism. It is worth remembering the revolting chewing-gum like substance that seems to ooze from a wound in a painting, like the green slime developed by the special effects department of some film studio. It is worth remembering Jasper Johns, who used a ruler fastened to the canvas with a thumb tack to draw a segment of a circle, and who attached the

Åsmund Thorkildsen

front of a drawer with a knob to one of his paintings. I would like to see artists using painting as a decorated textile again, as a kind of architectural understanding of a painting's function, a function that can be traced, via the 19th century studies of Gottfried Semper, all the way back to prehistoric architecture. I wish to remind you of Robert Ryman, who was more concerned with the light that fell on a white-painted canvas from outside–from the sun, reflection or lamps–than with the pictorial light evoked by the illusion of something spatial in traditional painting. I wish to remind you of the Ryman who made a visible feature of the bolts that secured the rusty foundations of a painting, and the assemblage artist Robert Rauschenberg who attached old bed linen, umbrellas, stuffed birds and hens to the picture surface. We should not forget Jessica Stockholder, who uses lamplight in her objects, and Jack Pierson who installed a fan and a red bar lamp together with a photograph of the Ronettes that was hung on the gallery wall behind a revolving record player. This in turn reminds us of the neon lights in the glass, metal and textile installations of Alan Sonfist and Mario Merz. Then there is Richard Artschwager, who drew and painted on Celotex, an industrial material much used in suburban interiors, and who made furniture sculptures from Respatex. When I look at Værslev's shelf paintings made for the home, I am reminded of Thomas Grunfeldt's 1980s shelf sculptures, which alluded to the aesthetic of office or lounge spaces with their potted plants and mirrors. And I wish to remind you of the painting *Andy Warhol's Cunt*. We should also remember Rudolf Stingel's silver-coloured paintings and the experience of strolling across the synthetic, Day-Glo orange, wall-to-wall carpet, which after the exhibition was cut into pieces and sold as pictures. There were also Stingel's *Carpet Paintings* and Franz West's chairs and sofas. There is nothing zombie about any of these. And I shall keep this in mind when looking at the wooden pallets that Værslev bolts to the walls, challenging us to see them as paintings. And isn't an empire window with its frame and muntins painted olive green and its glass painted black also a thing that can function as an artwork? New standards apply of what constitutes a picture, and they serve as common references.

Værslev makes little use of written text in his paintings, although it is not entirely absent from his work. Many of the figures he uses are almost like standard markers of late modern/ postmodern painting. Hand-painted stripes reminiscent of the fabrics used for awnings constitute an additional inscription, a kind of allegory, or marker. Not all inscriptions are in the form of alphabetic letters. The fact that he imitates/mimics/ appropriates the symbol of a manufacturing company makes it clear that we are dealing here with allegory. Daniel Buren, who explored the confusion that arises through the conscious use of urban and institutional displacement, painted a stripe–similar to the zips that Barnett Newman painted onto monochrome blue–over one that already existed in an off-the-shelf awning fabric. The tiny variations of zombie formalism are therefore already present in the work Buren was doing around 1970. Buren's status as an artist who works with allegory was evident in his major 2005 exhibition at the Guggenheim Museum in New York. For example, he took as his starting point the windows of Frank Lloyd Wright's building, both the one in the roof above the rotunda and those in the side rooms looking onto 5th Avenue and East 89th Street. Buren effectively created pictures by superimposing large circles of transparent coloured gels in Lloyd Wright's windows, slightly offset from the original circular muntins. This could be read as an allegory on the work of the celebrated architect over many decades and the considerable distances between the places where his buildings stand. Because his use of the balloon shape and the pure colours made it impossible not to think of the stained-glass windows in Wright's Coonley Playhouse in the Riverside suburb just outside Chicago, from 1911.

A similar process is hand-painting a picture of the pattern on a terrazzo floor and exhibiting it in a gallery hall that has just such a floor, one that Værslev first saw as a photographic reproduction. This too is a marker applied to something, one picture superimposed on another. Or cool abstractions hung on faded frescoes, where the painting becomes the wall and the wall a picture. These too are allegories. I have mentioned that pop art and concept art have received insufficient attention in conjunction with Værslev's paintings. But it was this kind of thing that was so liberating about the conceptual painting produced in the United States and England around 1970, the painting of a term–a marker, or guarantee–directly onto the canvas, on the monochrome field that was stipulated and declared to be a picture, a late modern painting. There is no need for a painting to be a picture or an icon in order to be a "picture"; its status can be determined "legalistically", as it were, which is what Nelson Goodman had in mind when he wrote that a painting's authenticity is not something that can be seen with the naked eye. If someone calls it a painting, then that's what it is – to give a twist to Donald Judd's dictum that if someone sees something as art, then art it is.

In 1969 Christine Kozlov painted the words "A Mostly Red Painting" on a red ground. Clear and unambiguous, no reasons for any doubt. Her artwork was not organic, but an allegory, with the structure of an analytical statement. And what about the series *100% Abstract* from 1967–68 by Art & Language? This artist group realised that, since pictures are bought and sold, not least as investments, their authenticity needs to be guaranteed. But it wasn't enough for them to supply this guarantee in written form, even though they did in fact do this in a number of "diptychs" entitled *Guaranteed Paintings*. It was not enough to include a written text somewhere within the visual field, either hidden away or contained in a small black square set within a larger black square, which guaranteed that the picture had genuine content. For who would buy a painting without a guarantee that it really was a painting? No, that was not enough. Pictures intended for circulation in the media and the market also need to be guaranteed in terms of type and genre. Thus they produced their 100% abstract pictures. In this case the conceptual and legal validity of the guarantee resided in the fact that each item was inscribed with a set of numbers that added up to 100, and in the sheer obviousness that anything with a monochrome background is abstract. Speculation, sale and resale depend on such legalistic certainty. Here we see an element of truth combined with humour and irony, a strategy that would also be used by the 1980s neo-abstractionists. Although these qualities are not an especially prominent aspect of Værslev's art, examples of this kind illustrate the embrace of the allegorical impulse. One late manifestation of this impulse, in which text is detached from drawing, are Richard Prince's monochromes from the late 1980s (also in the shadow), which feature the texts from cartoons as the only remaining element once the drawing has been removed.

The use of inscriptions or traces with external origins is a recurrent feature of Værslev's work. In this there lies an implicit critique of the interiority of the inner space, which Krauss attacked with such acuity in her essay "The Double Negative".[32] What we see in Værslev's work is something that comes from outside and references the empirical space in which the pictures are installed and the viewer moves, senses and reflects. This, together with his use of paratactic structures typical

of minimalism and pop art – a striped awning is a striped awning is a striped awning – complicates the task of interpreting the gaze that is always assumed to lie behind the picture or to be tamed *within* the picture. For how can the Lacanian gaze cope with allegory?

A further feature of Værslev's practice is that he works in distinct series. This is a concession to market forces. Just as in the supermarket one can choose between a range of similar soft-drink bottles or from a whole pile of Campbell's soup tins, a collector can choose one of several, almost identical stripe paintings, sail paintings, terrazzo paintings or shelf paintings.[33] This also demonstrates that Værslev understands the method used in happenings and certain conceptual artworks, which seek to ensure audience participation by issuing instructions on how audience should behave during the exhibition, or which distance practice from notions of genius and artistic originality by assigning written tasks. By approaching each exhibition as a task and the room as a space to be filled with material that is recognisable yet always slightly different, Værslev demonstrates that as an artist he acts as a man of the world. The fact that he actually paints pictures and does not use ready-mades amounts to a variation on the use of everyday forms in contemporary art.

In just these few lines we have seen that Værslev draws on artistic practices that lie in what I have called the shadow cast by his generation. Robert Gober works with handcrafted plywood, washbasins and ice-skates – handmade ready-mades. Then there is the artist Bertrand Lavier, who became known in the 1980s for hand-painting the surfaces of both flat and three-dimensional objects, such as windsurfing sails and grand pianos, so that they seem to become depictions of themselves. Lavier is such an obvious paradigm for Værslev's repainting and overpainting that is it is strange he has never been mentioned as such. Lavier is so rigorous in his approach that he even overpaints the small transparent window in the sail with a pastose but transparent paint that leaves the thick brushstrokes clearly visible.

TWO CASE STUDIES

Let us content ourselves here with taking a closer look at two of Værslev's series of paintings, namely those that use the form of a sail and those that use terrazzo patterns. We have just seen that Lavier painted the image of a sail on an actual sail, reproducing the colours and patterns of the

Åsmund Thorkildsen

original object as supplied by the manufacturer. Sails and awnings share the characteristic that they are always intended to be oriented towards something external, whether it be the sun, or the wind and the rain out on the sea, or the same out on the street, together with all the social and vehicular traffic that animates roadside bars and restaurants. Both phenomena have their own systems of signals – those of the regatta, of traffic, and social interaction.

The characteristic of a sail is that it captures the external force that drives the vessel forward – the wind that could be blowing from any direction. Værslev's sails are interesting as allegories because they exist as fragments; what we are not shown are the boats and the waves, and it is unclear where they have come from, where they are, and where they are going. They are situated in an exhibition, but the information they present is independent of the situation. And as references, the fragmentary markers in the form of colours, patterns and letters remain obscure. They give us no clues as to where they might be found – the rainbow from a San Francisco mural, or a flag hanging from a window, or numbers and stripes that belong to some kind of boat competing in some kind of race, or something completely different. Perhaps there's a reference hidden here somewhere. This is part of the melancholy of allegory, that it hints at meanings while at the same time denying us the possibility to follow through to something that might corroborate that meaning. The fact that we can only see the upper part of the sail and the direction it is blowing informs us that underlying this small segment is a physical, mechanical and mental reality. We can follow the artist's experience by imaging that this is what a sail looks like when seen through binoculars or when a film camera zooms in on it – two modern, mechanical devices that allow us to extend our visual range. At the same time, these physical devices carry the message of distance, the impression that, detached from its boat and any surrounding topography, this sail is merely a dream symbol for something indeterminate, something desirable that is far away yet seen here, at this very moment, an implication of the sail's direction.

In this sense we can say that these paintings, when studied one at a time, reveal the mysterious interweaving of time and space, that which is close as something remote and what is remote as something close. In other words, despite their technical structure, these hand-crafted paintings allow us to approach something auratically.

Thus they illustrate how Benjamin's structure can conflate with ritual and the religious. One way or another, they carry an aura, a rare experience elicited by the combination of sails, painting and nature. Can anything of this kind be said about the long frieze of a sunset that was shown in Bergen Kunsthall in 2016 and later in Dijon? These paintings were created by driving a road-marking machine along a length of canvas rolled out on the floor while consulting iPhone pictures of sunsets seen from an aircraft window. One aspect of this work that has been largely ignored in other texts is that it references the experience of viewing nature from a moving vehicle. Viewed from the window of a plane, the landscape changes only very slowly because it is so far away, but seen from the window of a car travelling at 90 kmph, it becomes a blur of horizontal stripes. Just imagine the result if you were to take a picture in this situation using a slow shutter speed. Road-marking machines generally follow the direction of the road, and by allowing some of the stripes to remain after attempting to wash them out, Værslev achieves a phenomenological analysis of what a sunset might look like when photographed with a slow shutter speed through a mass of tall pine trees from a moving car. The sunset becomes a sandwich of stratified lines that run parallel to the direction of travel. If there is one contribution here to the phenomenon of postmodern painting that does not derive either from the medium-specific minimum of modernist painting or from the many hybrids discussed above, it is Værslev's incorporation into his pictorial and exhibition practice of modes of experience that derive from photography and film and from the ways we perceive landscapes from aircraft and cars.

Both the artist and his commentators emphasise his interest in architecture. This relates, with regard to interiors, primarily to pictures, shelves, wallpaper and textiles, and where exteriors are concerned, to sun shades, installed at oblique angles and slightly away from the wall. This could be explored from the perspective of the house as a performative arena, where one moves between stations and positions, and everyday life can be seen as a dialogue with interiors. Thus, experiencing an exhibition with pictures in series, which is how Værslev often works, is like moving through an interior; the choreography is determined by the paintings and their figures, and relationships between the paintings. And it is here that the body's experience of movement can be relevant to our understanding of how Værslev's paintings and exhibitions have evolved in the way they have. We might well pause in front of the sail pictures, zoom in on and out from the canvas, and allow our minds, not to wander into the picture, but to follow the vector it suggests that points out towards a larger world.

In the case of the terrazzo pictures, the viewer is presented with a very different structure. The paradigm for the behaviour to be described here is provided by a famous video work, Bruce Nauman's *Slow Angle Walk*, *Beckett Walk*, from 1969. This work is meant to be presented on a small black-and-white TV monitor, with the tape playing in real time for one hour, which at the time it was created was the maximum length of a video tape. What we see in this video performance is a presentation of the human body's relation to the vertical, the horizontal, and to gravity, an exploration of balance and the interplay between the plumb line and the spirit level that determines our behaviour in the world. Nauman bends at the hip until his upper body and one of his legs form a line at 90 degrees to the other leg, which remains perpendicular to the floor. He then straightens up, swings his leg forward, takes a step, turns through 90 degrees relative to the direction of travel, and again stretches one leg out behind while leaning his upper body forward until both form a line parallel to the floor and at 90 degrees to the leg he is standing on. This he then repeats. The film is shot in real time and with the camera on its side relative to the subject, so that the floor is displayed vertically on the screen. This is a rigorous replay of some of the movements that Robert Morris makes in his video performance *Site* from 1964, movements that were photographed, then filmed for the retrospective exhibition at the Guggenheim Museum in New York in 1994.

What does Nauman's video have to do with Værslev's terrazzo patterns? In the current context, Værslev is closer to Nauman than to Pollock, even though it was the latter who became famous for painting on canvases laid out on the floor, a method Værslev also uses. We have seen the description of *Slow Angle Walk*, so what follows here is a description of how to approach a terrazzo painting that hangs on the wall. The line of sight to the painting is perceived as horizontal, given the viewer's upright position. This horizontal line is at 90 degrees to the pull of gravity, which was perpendicular to the canvas when it lay flat on the floor to be painted, in the same orientation as a terrazzo floor. A reflective experience of these paintings/allegories must involve an awareness of the body standing vertically on a floor in an exhibition space, looking at a picture of something that is usually on the floor – *as* a floor. In order to study the detailed ornamentation of a terrazzo floor *in situ*, one would have to lie flat on one's belly on the floor. By studying the painted, appropriated pattern as a painting on the wall, we can stand erect and look straight ahead at it instead of looking down. What happens when these pictures are shown in a gallery with terrazzo floors is that we alternate between looking straight ahead and looking down, and the best movement to facilitate this change is one whereby we bend at 90 degrees in the hip, a slow-angle standing-still performance choreographed by the artist and performed by the viewer.

The movement patterns – the dance of the painter and the viewer – during an exhibition of Værslev's paintings, where the main structure is paratactic, do not prevent us from relating to performance and dance. For what distinguishes this form of movement from the modernist, narrative, evolving type is the connection it shares with modern narrative dance like that of Martha Graham, a kind of dance and performance that is inspired by systematic primary structures and ordinary movements. Thus we have seen that both the sail and the terrazzo pictures show choreographies based on two movement structures. With the sail pictures we zoom in and out mentally, while moving sideways to the canvas – both mentally and physically – in the "wind direction", while in the case of the terrazzo pictures, the movement is determined by the alternating 90 degree bends. I believe it is something of this kind that Værslev has in mind when he talks about architecture, and it is something of this he has retained from his time as a graffiti artist – an awareness for the crucial importance of moving in front of and along the wall. These paintings are therefore inscribed in something different and more inclusive than an internal discourse – even if the insider trading of modern art is a necessary element of Værslev's project – something that is even detached from market logic, because these observations on possible ways of looking at Værslev's art can be difficult to administer and evaluate. Good architecture is a formalised and constructed outcome of people's freedom of movement. And perhaps it is this he wishes to convey – that we can see the dance while also being the dancer. In other words, there is no need to invoke the mourning of the melancholy allegorist, for we have already come to terms with what was, in the religion of art, a fall from grace.

Åsmund Thorkildsen

1   Allan Kaprow, *Essays on the Blurring of Art and Life*,
    edited by Jeff Kelley, University of California Press, 1993.
    Quoted from the first paperback edition of 1996, p. 46.

2   Stian Grøgaard took a detailed look at this "switch"
    and the changes it entailed in terms of types of space,
    physical presentation and experiential forms for critics and
    audiences in his essay "I Still Carry You Around", published
    in conjunction with the exhibition *East Bound and Down*,
    at the Power Station, Dallas, 2014.

3   Jacques Derrida, *Speech and Phenomena – and Other
    Essays on Husserl's Theory of Signs*, published in French
    in 1967 and in English in 1973. The American edition also
    included the 1968 essay "Differance", in which Derrida
    writes: "There is no purely and strictly phonetic writing.
    What is called phonetic writing can only function – in principle
    and *de jure*, and not due to some factual and technical
    inadequacy – by incorporating non-phonetic 'signs' (punctua-
    tion, spacing, etc.) …" Quoted from the edition published
    by Northwestern University Press, Evanston, 1973, p. 133.

4   In his discussion of this, Grøgaard makes the point that
    removing the canvas from the blind frame, allowing it to curl,
    either separate from or loosely attached to a blind frame,
    interferes with the autonomy of the picture or icon.

5   Ad Reinhardt in "Twelve Rules for a New Academy", Art News,
    May 1957, quoted from Ad Reinhardt, *Art as Art: The Selected
    Writings of Ad Reinhardt*, Viking Press, New York, 1975, p. 204.

6   Åsmund Thorkildsen, "Malerier som maleri", catalogue to the
    exhibition *Arne Malmedal – Paintings 1990–94*, Kunstnernes
    Hus, 1994, p. 7.

7   Quoted from Susan Feagin & Patrick Maynard, *Aesthetics*,
    Oxford Readers, Oxford & New York, p. 255. In the winter
    of 1966–67, Reinhardt wrote in his notebook: "Interpreters
    are philistines." Quoted from *Selected Writings*, p. 74.

8   Michael Fried, "Art and Objecthood". Quoted from the essay
    anthology *Art and Objecthood. Essays and Reviews*,
    University of Chicago Press, 1998, p. 168.

9   Kaprow, p. 47.

10 Åsmund Thorkildsen, "Abstraksjon – Enda en gang". Catalogue
    to the exhibition *Thomas Hestvold, Jakob Schmidt, Sverre
    Wyller*, Kunstnenres Hus, 1990, p. 3. In Note 1 in this essay,
    there is a quote from Stephen Westfall, "Geometric art can no
    longer feel utopian," taken from an article in *Vogue*, August 1989.

11 Åsmund Thorkildsen, "Standardbilder – Om maleriets
    forsoning med det levende sproget", catalogue to an exhibi-
    tion of painters from Galleri Haaken/Galleri K/Galleri Wang,
    at Henie Onstad Art Centre/Sal Haaken, 2004, pp. 4–5.

12 Published in the journal *October*, Vol. 12 (Spring, 1980),
    MIT Press, pp. 67–86.

13 The view here is that the development of modernist painting,
    as a rejection of obsolete conventions that strives for the
    essential, irreducible painting, follows a familiar historicist
    structure. It presupposes a familiar three-part progression,
    from a primeval social structure, consisting of various tribes
    with mythical worldviews that coexist in primitive equilibrium,
    followed by a dynamic era of competitive struggles, and
    finally a period characterised by the inevitable restoration
    of lost unity.

14 The historicism of Plato, Hegel and Marx was thoroughly
    debunked by Sir Karl Popper, especially in his essay
    "What is Dialectic?" (1937) and in the two books *The Open
    Society and Its Enemies* (1945) and *The Poverty of
    Historicism* (1957). Many of the academic responses to the
    avant-garde were inspired by Hegelian-Marxist thought and
    are consequently characterised by historicism. No doubt this
    helps to explain the dogmatic tendencies (art versus non-art)
    and the distaste for criticism that cannot easily be assimilated
    to the dialectic model. Popper's theory of science (falsification)
    rejects the Marxist-Leninist claim that Marxism constitutes
    a deterministic science that is capable of making valid
    predictions about the future of society.

15 Importantly, museums can of course present pictures
    chronologically and in art historical contexts. The various
    narratives we propose should never be presented as final,
    or as dogma, but rather should always be open to scrutiny
    and further research. Every system of hanging and every
    exhibition is ultimately an allegory, a time-limited experiment
    that explores one of many ways to understand pictures
    when their contexts change.

16 Ina Blom, "Sympathy with the Zombie", p. 341.

17 Published in the catalogue to the Bergen International
    Festival Exhibition, Bergen Kunsthall, Le Consortium and
    Sternberg Press, 2016.

18 By contrast, Michael Asher, a conceptual artist who works
    with the spaces of art institutions, is occasionally mentioned.
    He is one figure whom Værslev himself refers to in a
    number of interviews and texts.

19 This exhibition is discussed in Sheldon Nodelman's book
    Marden, Novros, Rothko – Painting in the Age of Actuality,
    University of Washington Press, Seattle and London, 1978.

20 See Alberto Salvadori in "Fredrik Værslev is a painter", in
    Fredrik Værslev: Reality Bites, Milan: Mousse Publishing, 2015.

21 The pictures in this exhibition produce a festive atmosphere,
    as if they were posters announcing a celebration, or some
    kind of Chinese lanterns hung up for a garden party.

22 Walter Benjamin defines an auratic experience of nature
    as "… the unique phenomenon of a distance, however
    close it may be." "The Work of Art in the Age of Mechanical
    Reproduction", in Walter Benjamin, *Illuminations*, edited
    by Hannah Arendt, translated by Harry Zohn, New York:
    Schocken Books, 1969.

23 Ina Blom, p. 342.

24 Gertrud Sandqvist, "Fredrik Værslev", in *Fredrik Værslev:
    The Rich Man's Breakfast, the Shopkeeper's Lunch,
    the Poor Man's Supper,* Standard (Books), Oslo, p. 14.

25 Ariel's song from Shakespeare's Tempest: "Full fathom
    five thy father lies;/Of his bones are coral made;/Those are
    pearls that were his eyes;/Nothing of him that doth
    fade,/But doth suffer a sea change/Into something rich
    and strange …", William Shakespeare *The Tempest*, Act I,
    Scene ii, lines 397–405.

26 Jacques Lacan, *The Four Fundamental Concepts of
    Psychoanalysis* [1973], first published in English in 1977.
    Cited from the 1991 Penguin edition, p. 113.

27 Blom, p. 344.

28 Provisionally, because in many of the forecasts about the
    future of society, the continued survival of the middle class
    calls for retrospective explanation. In the contemporary
    global community there are indications that in some of the
    major economies the middle class is struggling to understand
    its place in the world (to define its identity) and its economic
    potential. The final assessment of the position of the middle
    class has yet to be made.

29 Caroline Soyez-Petithomme, *Fredrik Værslev – Reality Bites*,
    Mousse Publishing, Milan, 2015, p. 31.

30 Joselit is quoted in Caroline Soyez-Petithomme, p. 33.

31 Might it be as simple as this: that in pragmatic terms,
    in order for a "painting" to satisfy the logic of the market it
    must be caught in the "reification trap" as an independent,
    unambiguously identifiable "thing"? Presumably, this is part
    of the context in which the art of Fredrik Værslev and every
    other painter exists, and which Ina Blom describes in critical
    terms in her analysis.

32 In this context we can overlook the fact that she has
    constructed a strawman, in that she misrepresents Harold
    Rosenberg's reflections on action painting.

33 The contrast between Værslev's type-similarity and the
    tiny individual differences that exist between Andy Warhol's
    paintings is merely superficial. For although Warhol works
    with identical reproductions, still he ended up making unique
    paintings, even when using mechanical means to reproduce
    the design, as in his *Shadows* series. Moreover, the tiny
    discrepancies we find in terms of the density of the printer's
    ink and in the mood colour means that they also vary
    as saleable units, just as the *Silver Elvis* was produced in
    versions with one, two or several Elvises.

FREDRIK VÆRSLEV AS I IMAGINE HIM
Peter J. Amdam

Fredrik Værslev as I imagine him. For a long time
I walked around and believed that my friend
Fredrik Værslev was a reformed hypochondriac.
Why on earth did I believe such a thing? He told
me so. He even added that they (I always imagined
"they" to be Norwegian national TV, NRK,
but that may very well be a function of my *own*
hypochondria) had made a documentary about
him before he became an artist and that they
had followed him around for over a year with
hand-held cameras. As if TV in general, and NRK
in particular, could vouch for the diagnostic truth
pertaining to the *Lehrjahre* of a romantic little
painter *in spe* obsessed with his own mythological
exotica of everyday life.

 I should have known better. Nobody has
seen the alleged hypochondriac docu, allegedly
there is a clause or stipulation about its unveiling
somewhere. Only to be opened after the death
of the painter. Something like that. The truth of
dead painting.

 It wasn't until Fredrik recited the same pastose
tale of hypochondriac glitz to Frog Magazine I
woke up and realized what that sunny side really
was up to. Buried in a myriad of stories about
gypsies, gold, mothers, hospitals, train rides
and flights there is this uncalled for and peculiar
confession: He reveals that, as a student
(and let me open a parenthesis here: is he still
not a student, especially now in his newfound
role as a "professor of painting" (or as a substitute
teacher for Dag Erik Elgin (and this semester
only), even more so given Fredrik's frantic
veneration of Michael Krebber, the older teacher
he never had at the *Städel*, a professor who
himself has a one or two things to say about
teaching painting, a post-dandy version of
Rancière's ignorant schoolmaster?) he kept on
reading Judith Butler's *Giving an Account of
Oneself*. Over and over again. But he still only
"understands" one tenth of it, he tells the Frog.

 As if the performativity of "giving account,"
psychoanalyzing, telling or indeed teaching
painting has anything to do with *understanding*.
Insert: seriality, surreptitious repetition.

 In any event, Fredrik is a man always not
on the move, always not alone, but secretive
and non-secretive, and because of that,
distrusts the marvels of interiority (although
he revels in them,) refuses the traps of subjectivity,
entirely surface and shimmering, but bereft
of miragy images. Imagine Fredrik Værslev
the *teacher*?

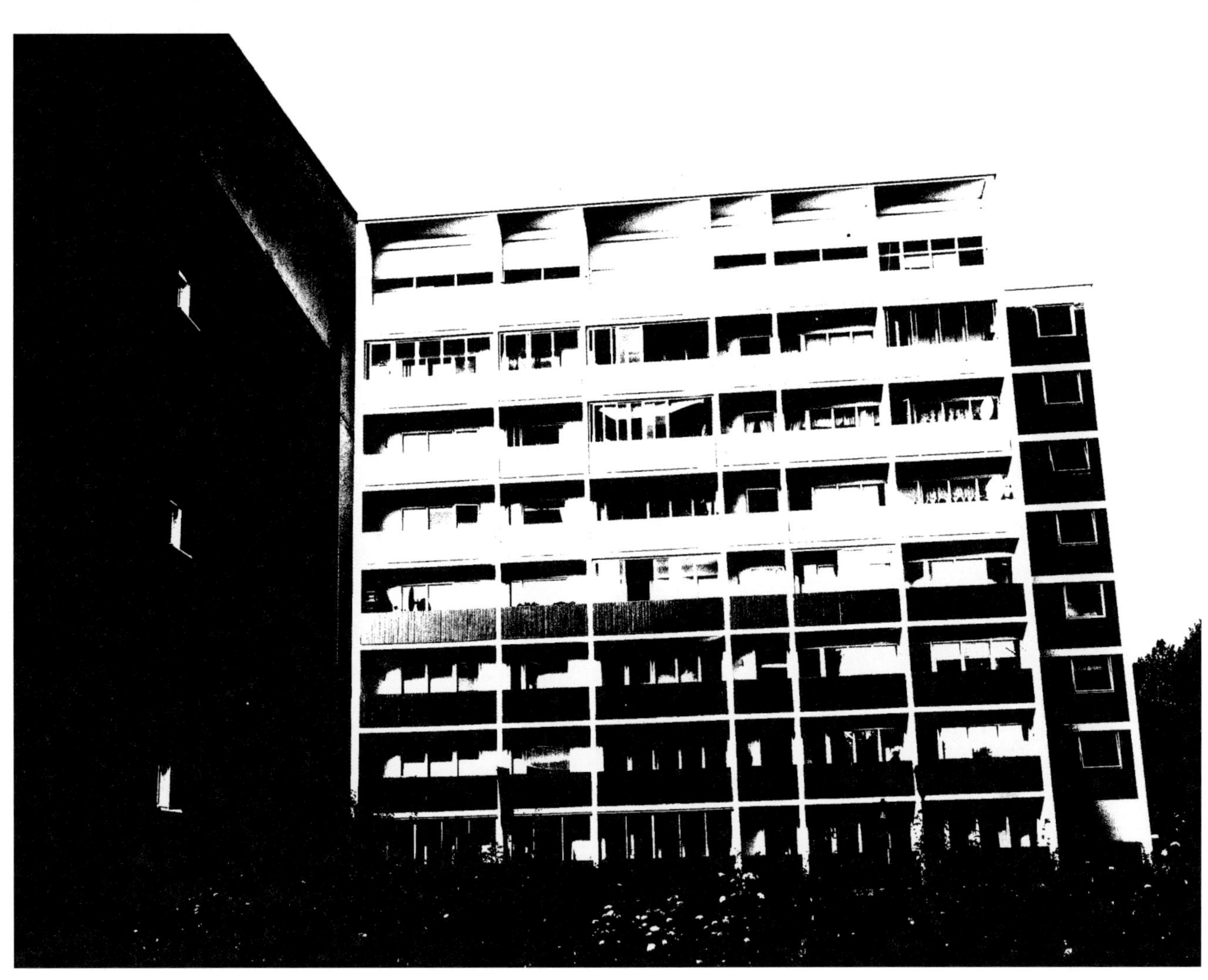

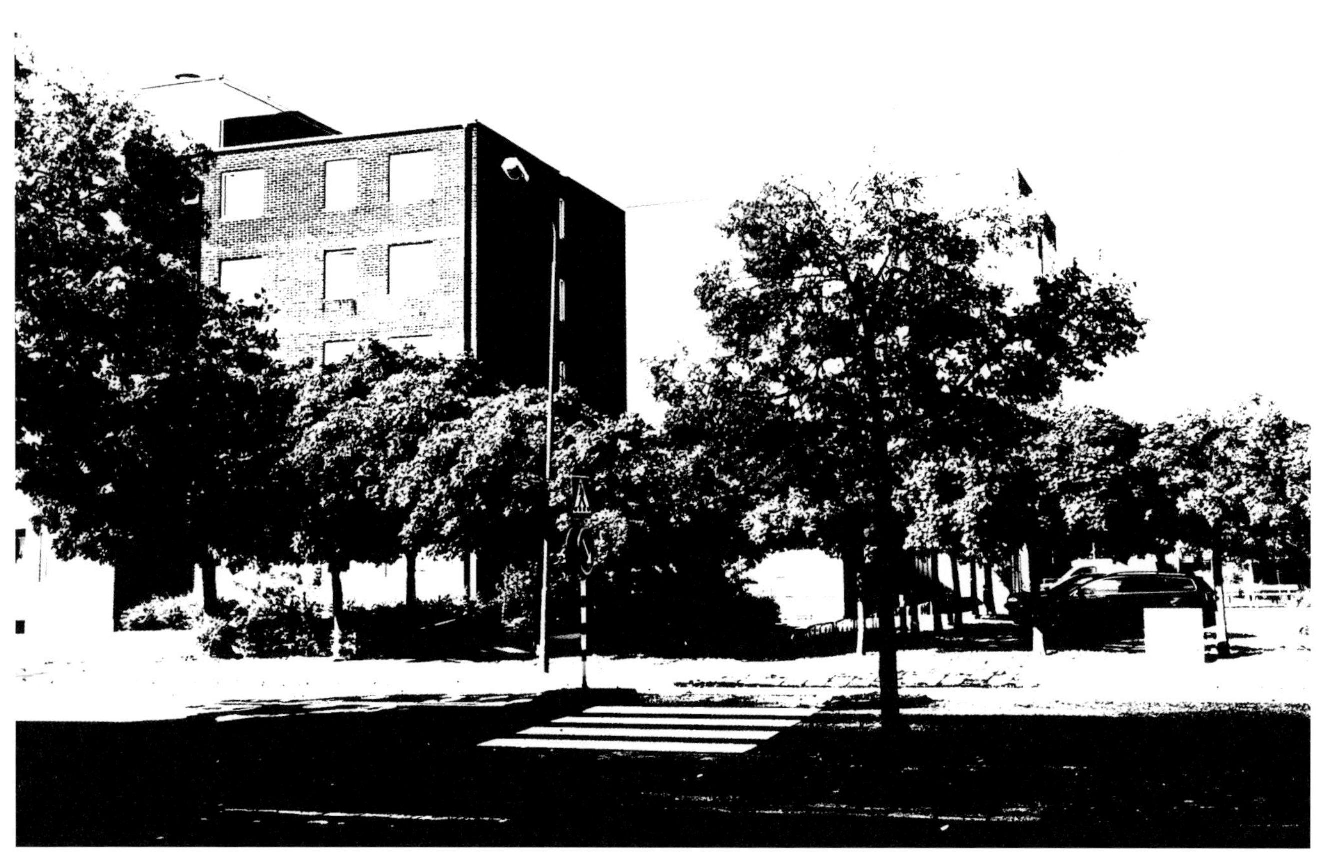

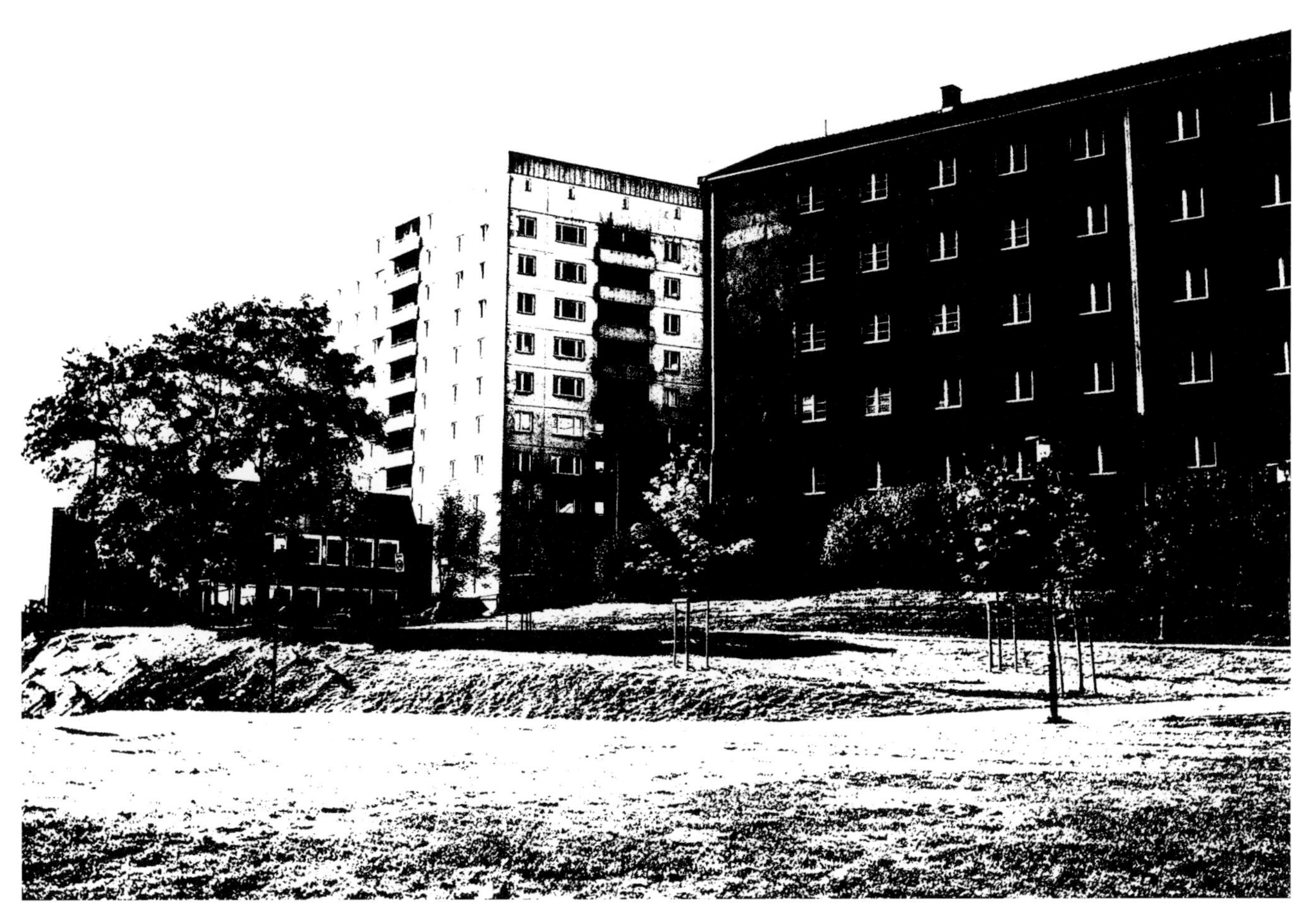

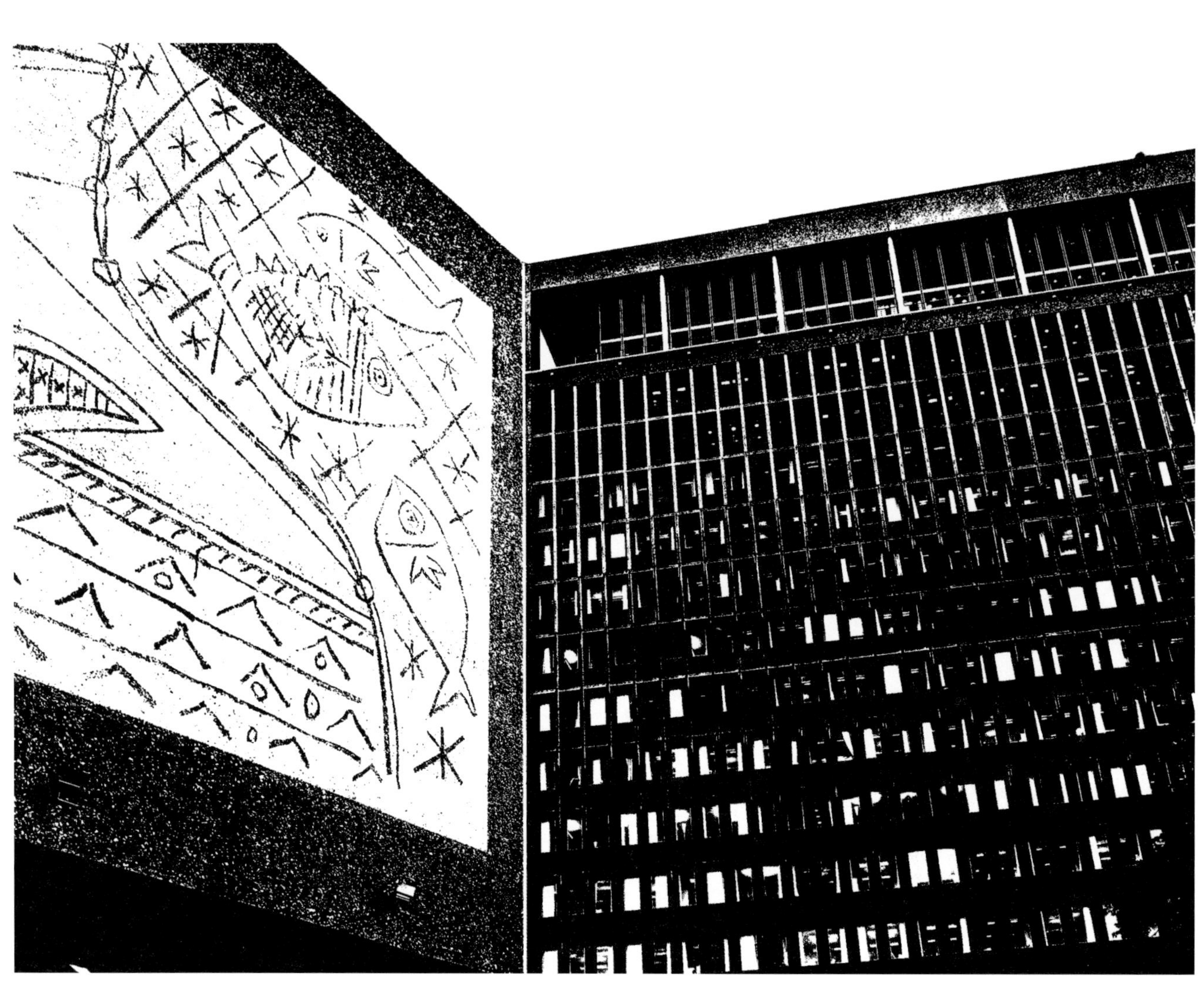

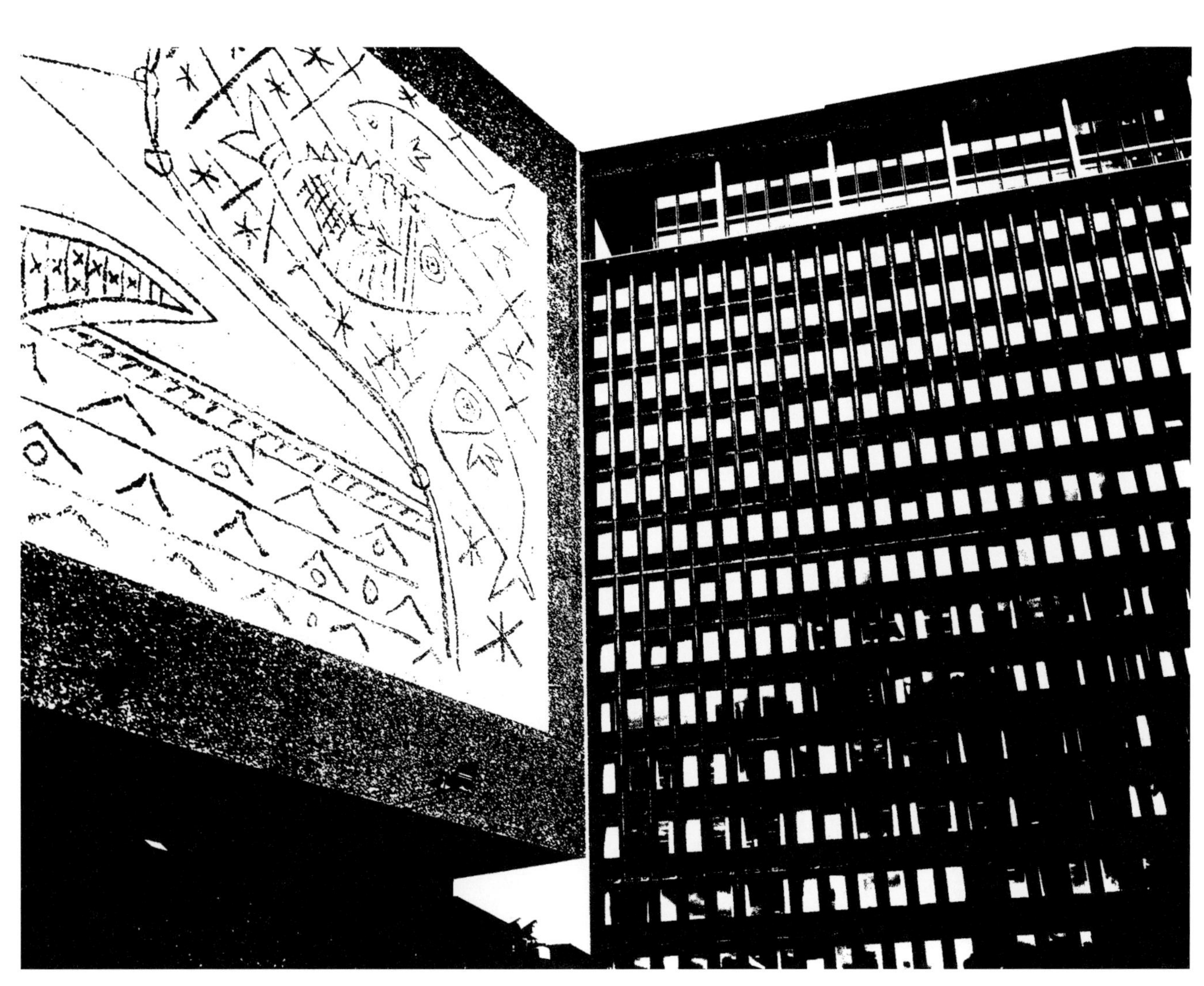

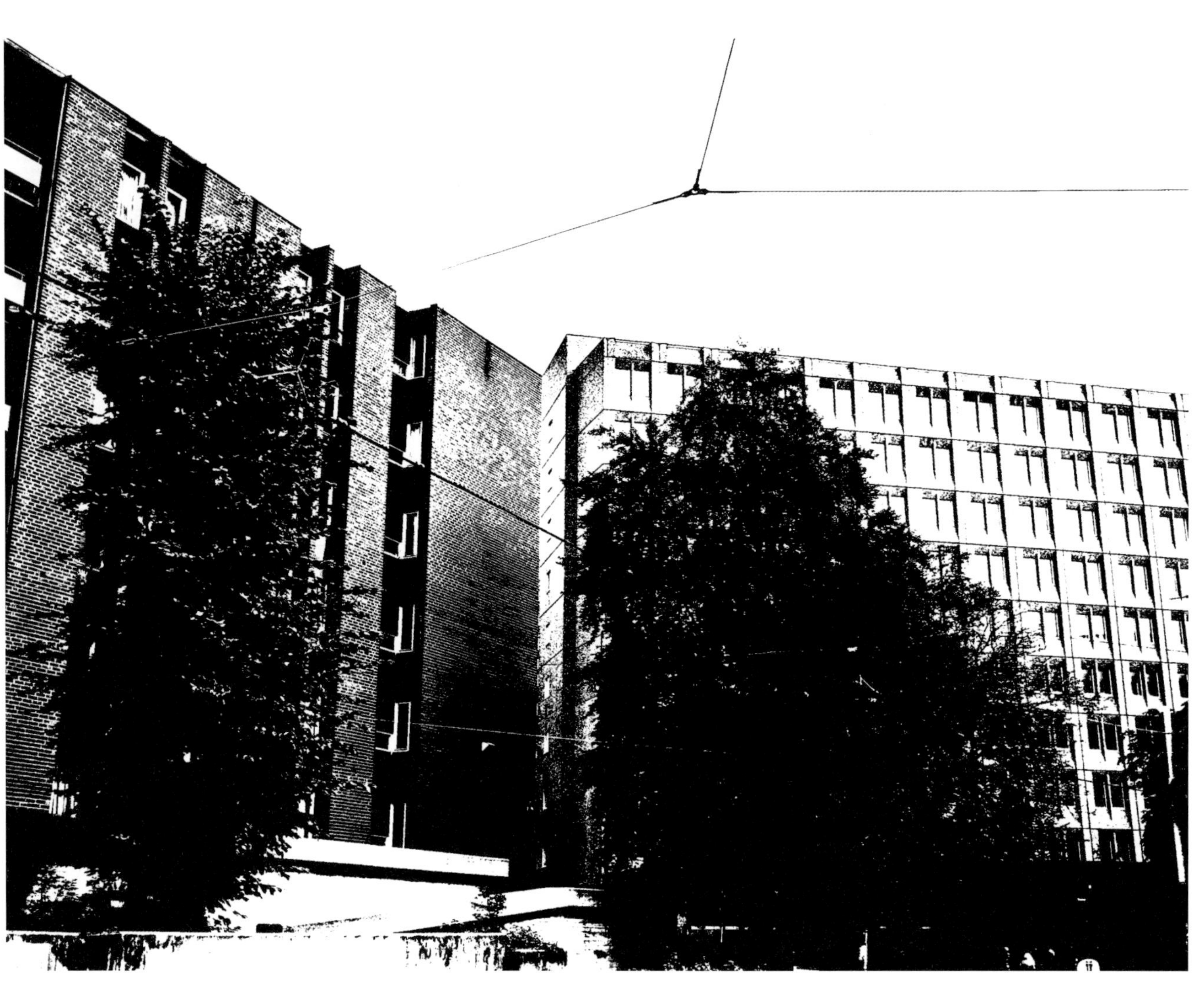

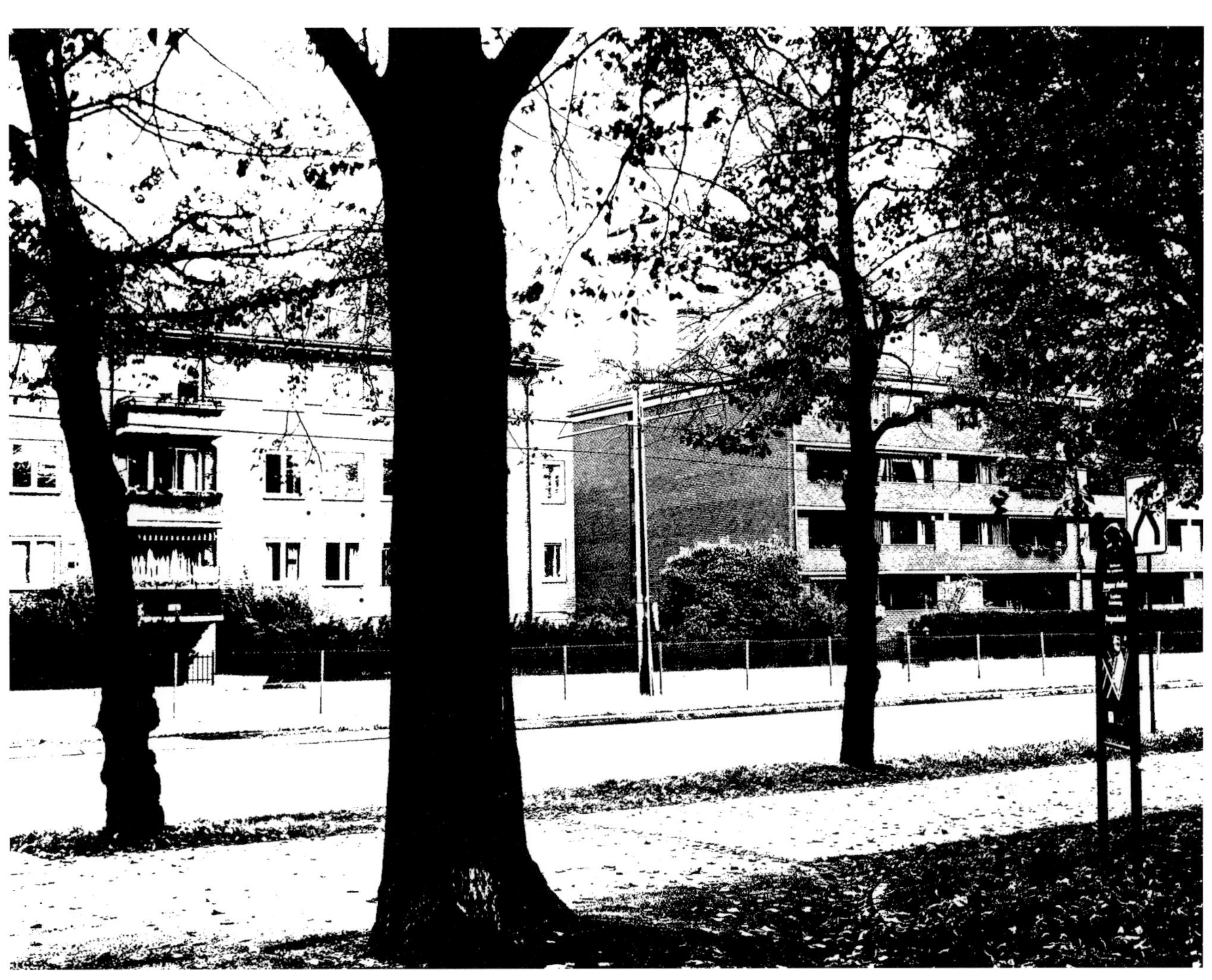

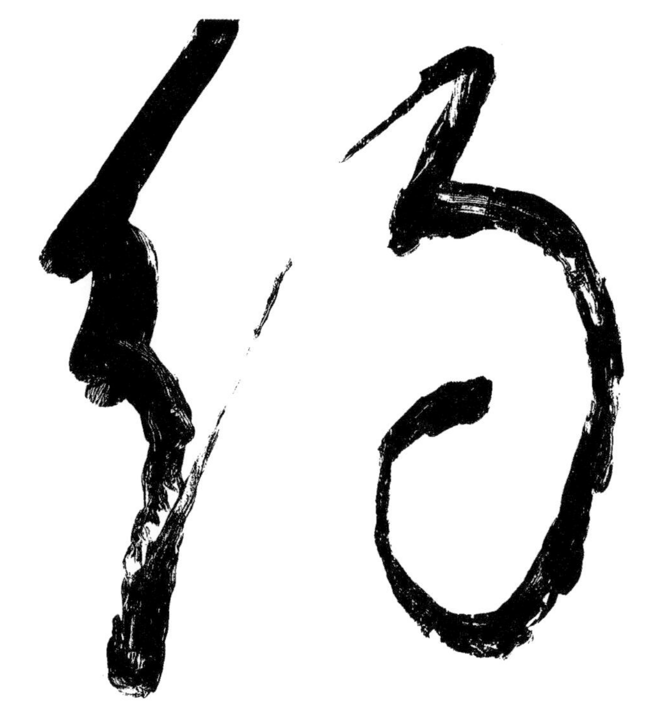

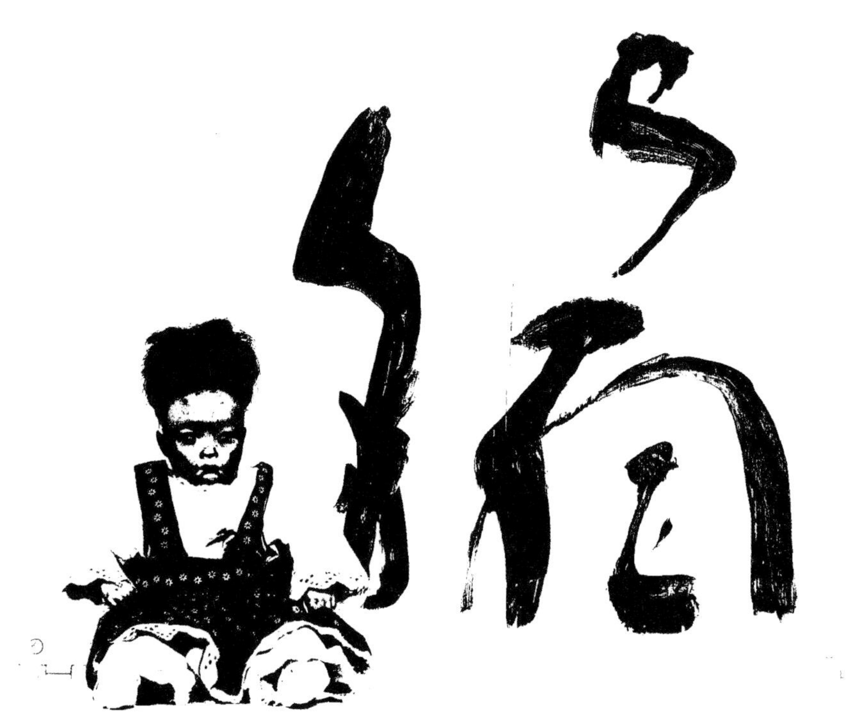

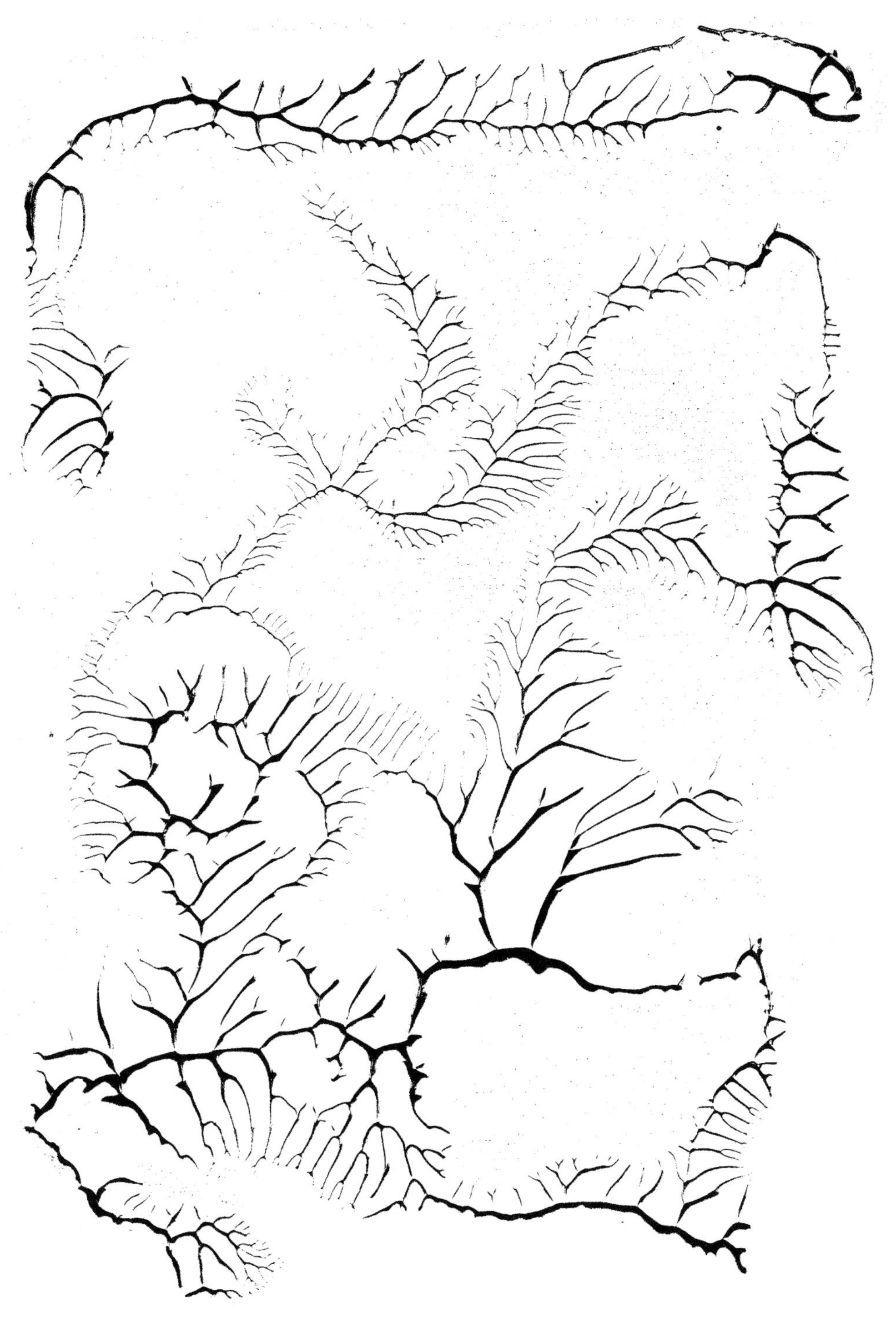

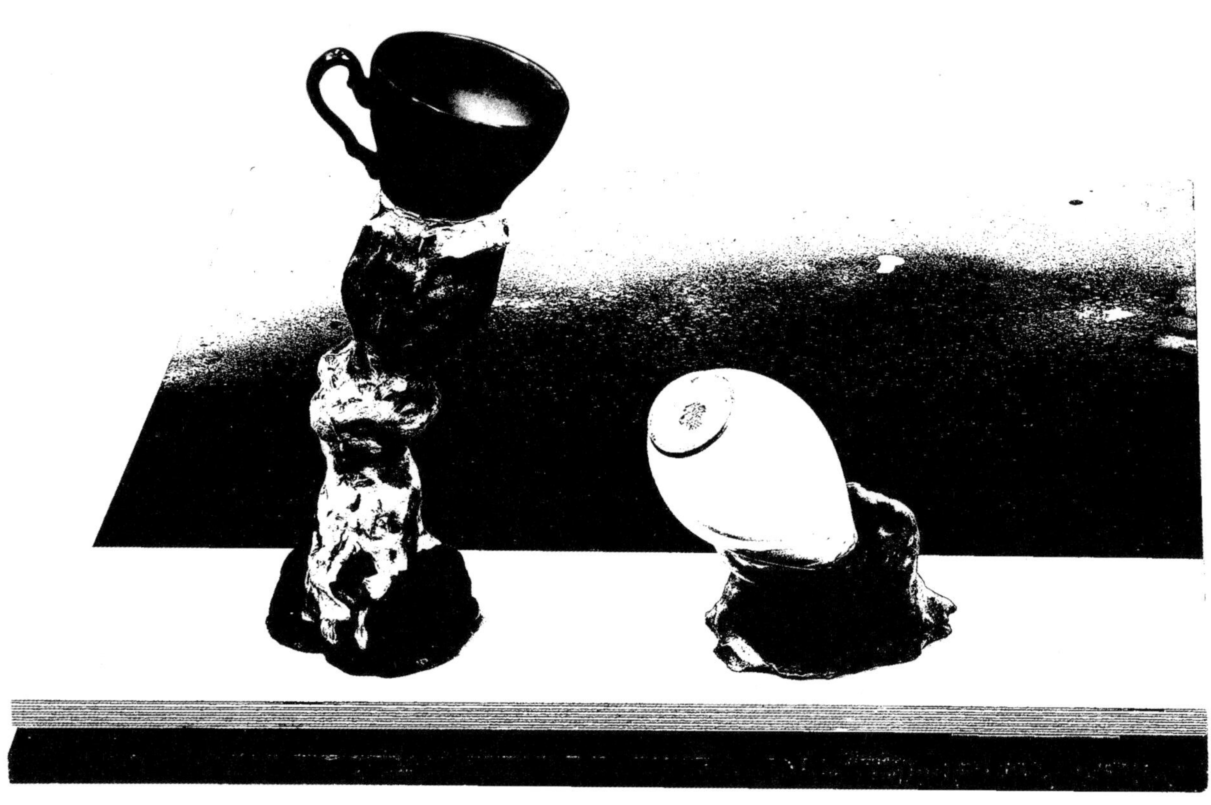

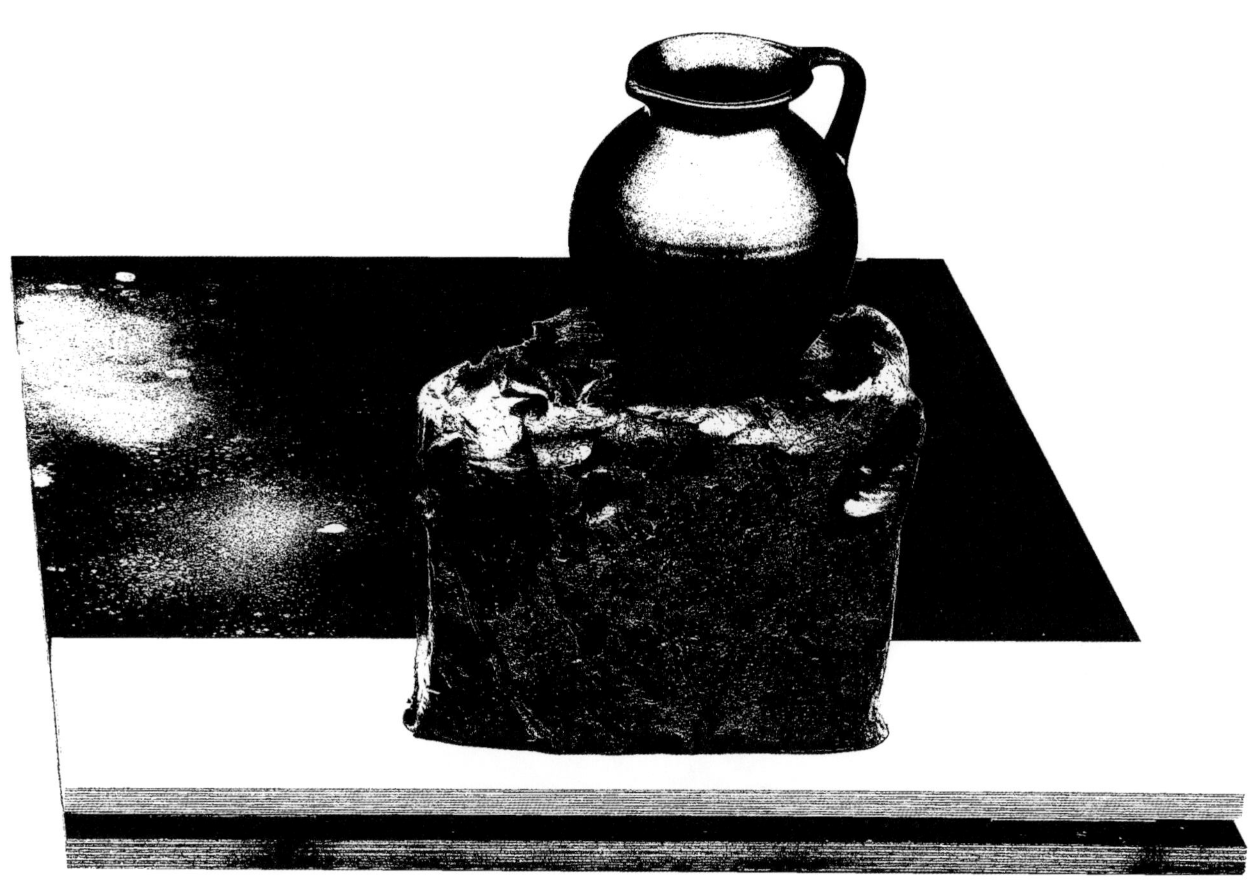

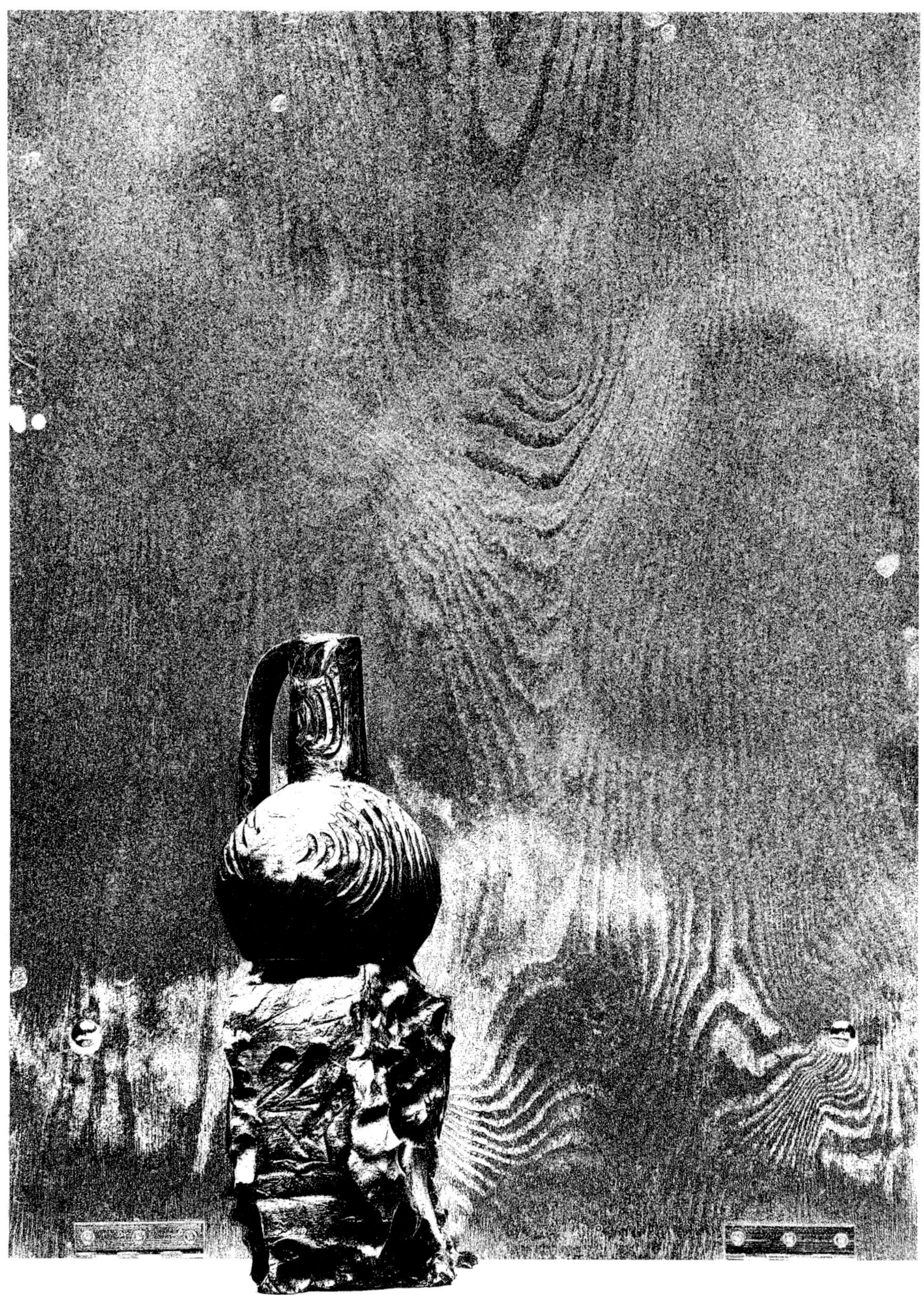

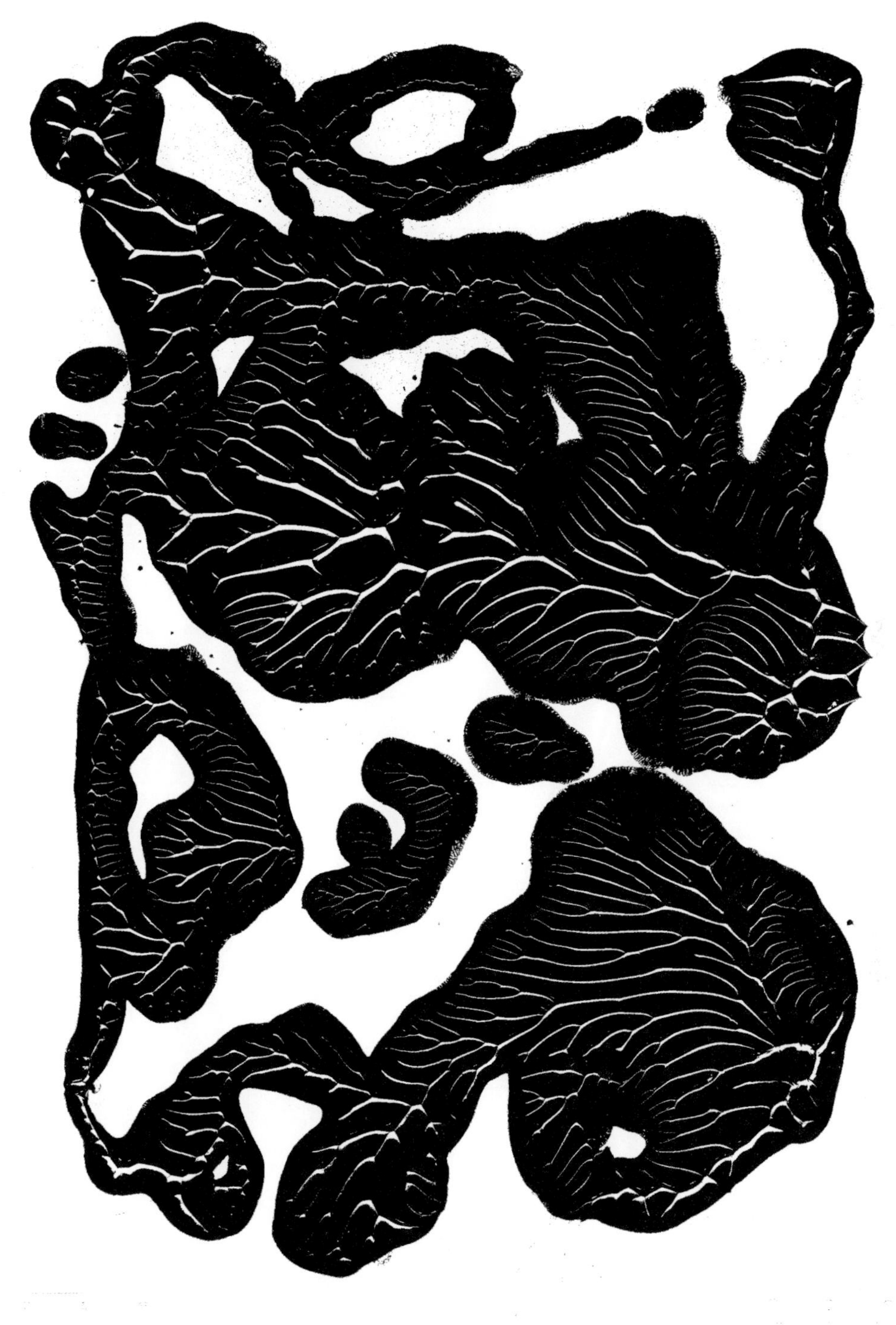

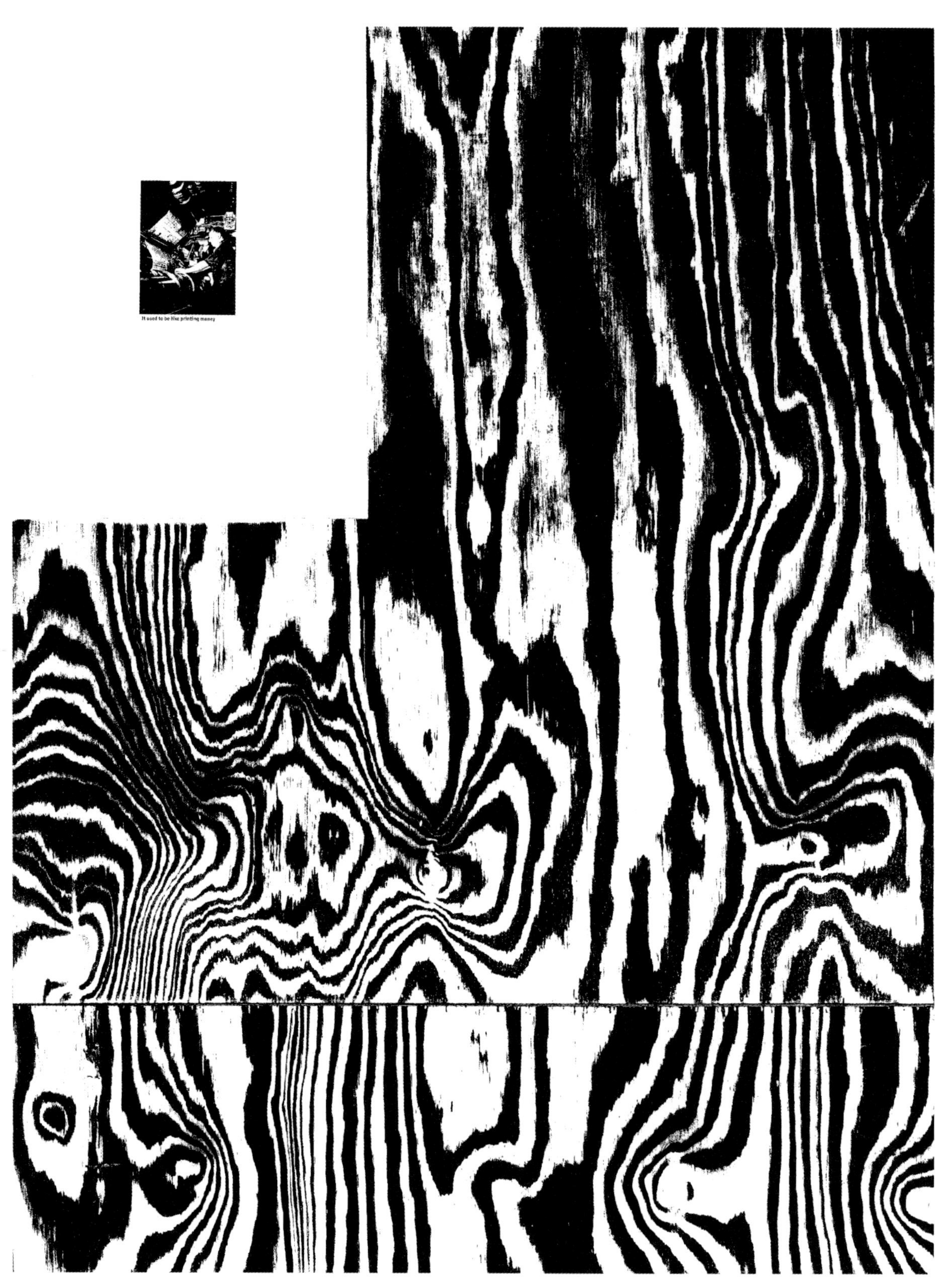

It used to be like printing money

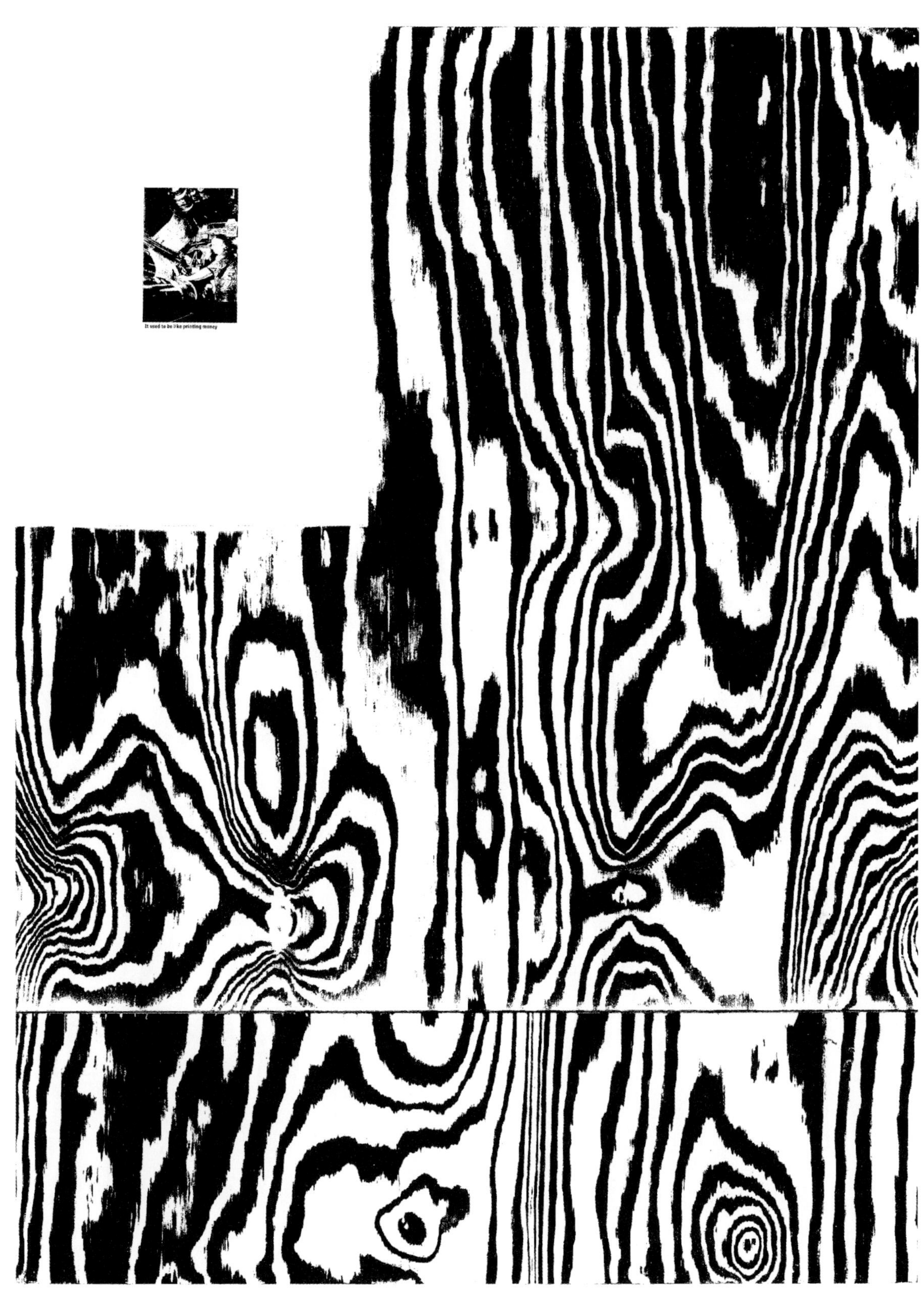
It used to be like printing money

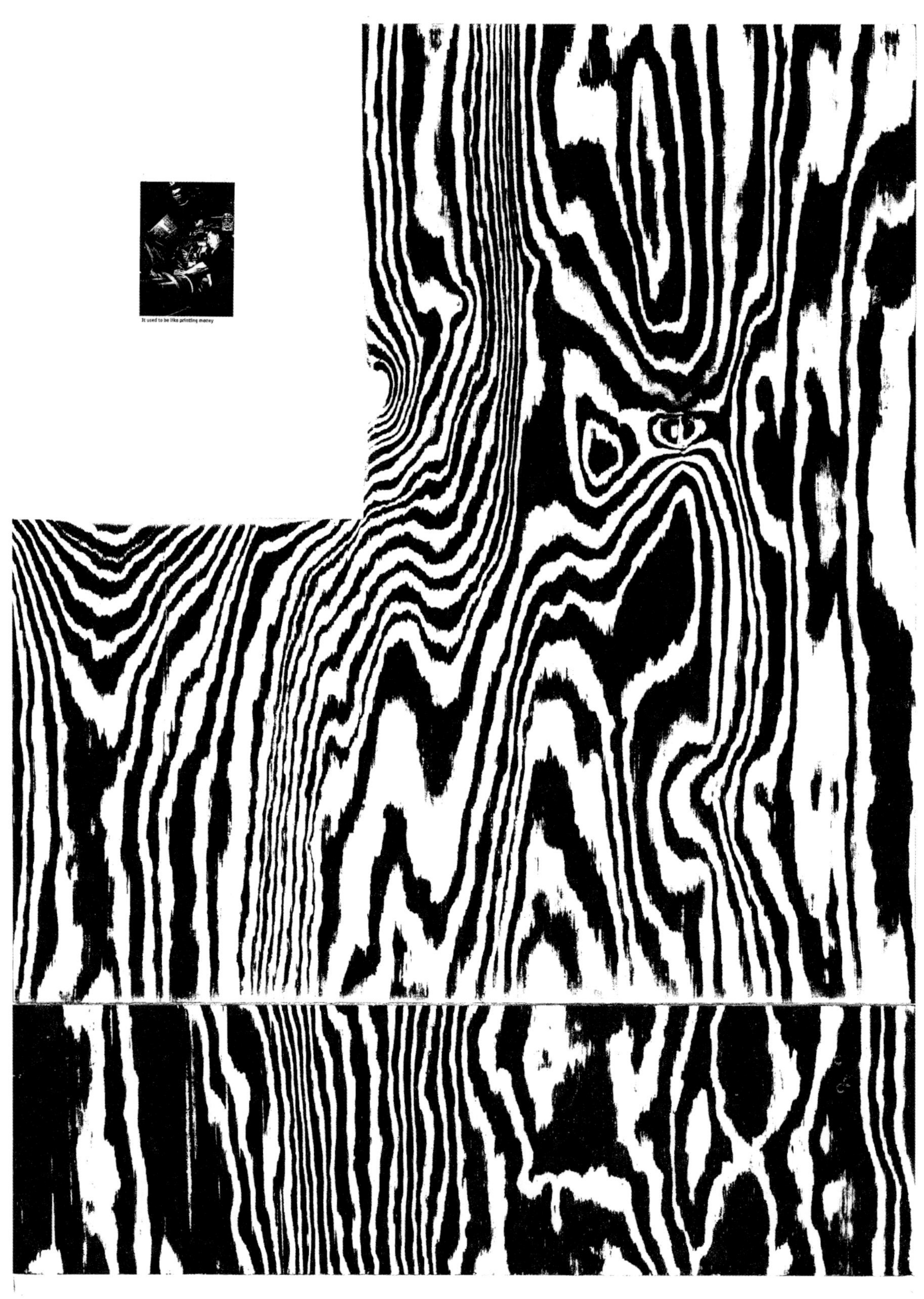
It used to be like printing money

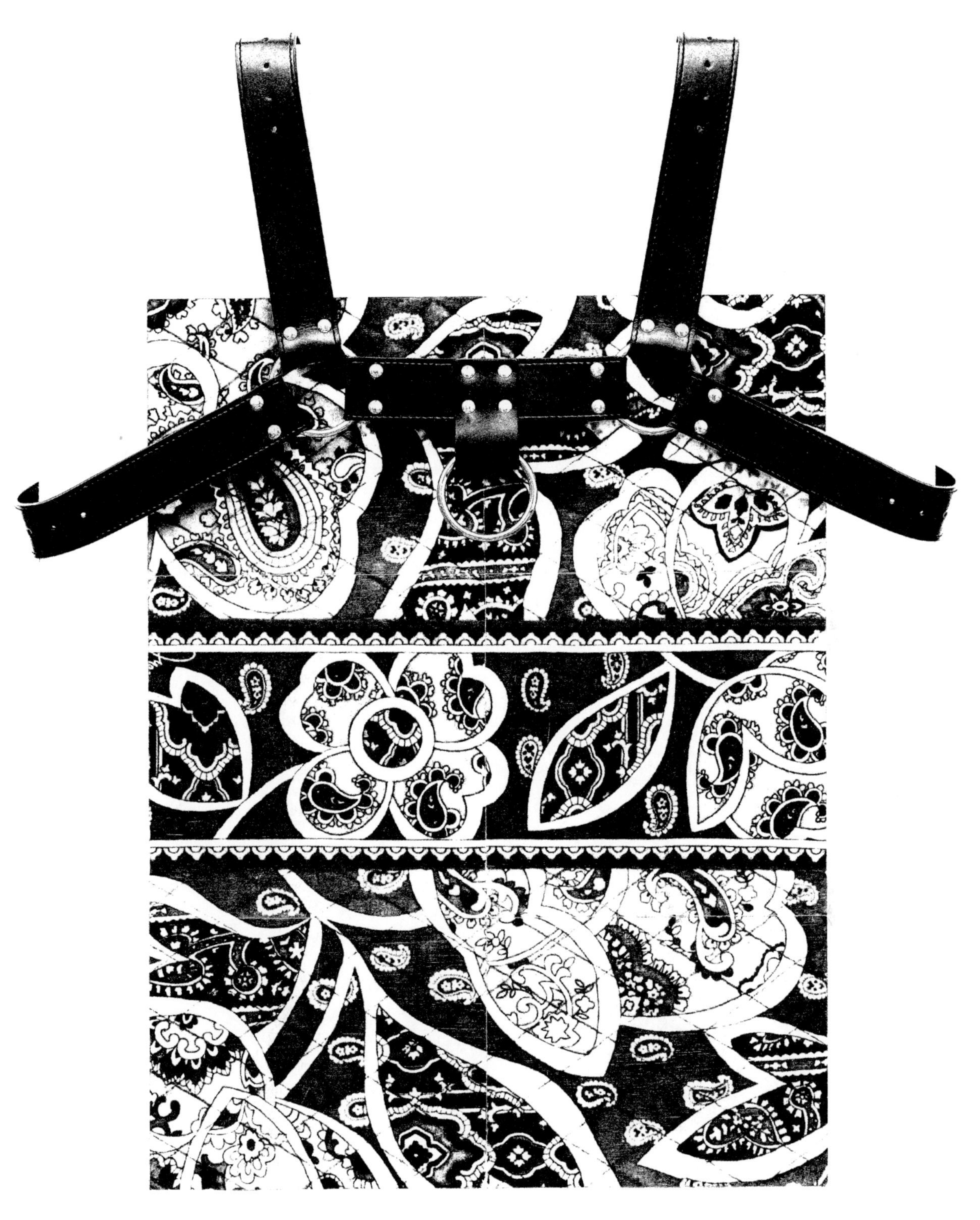

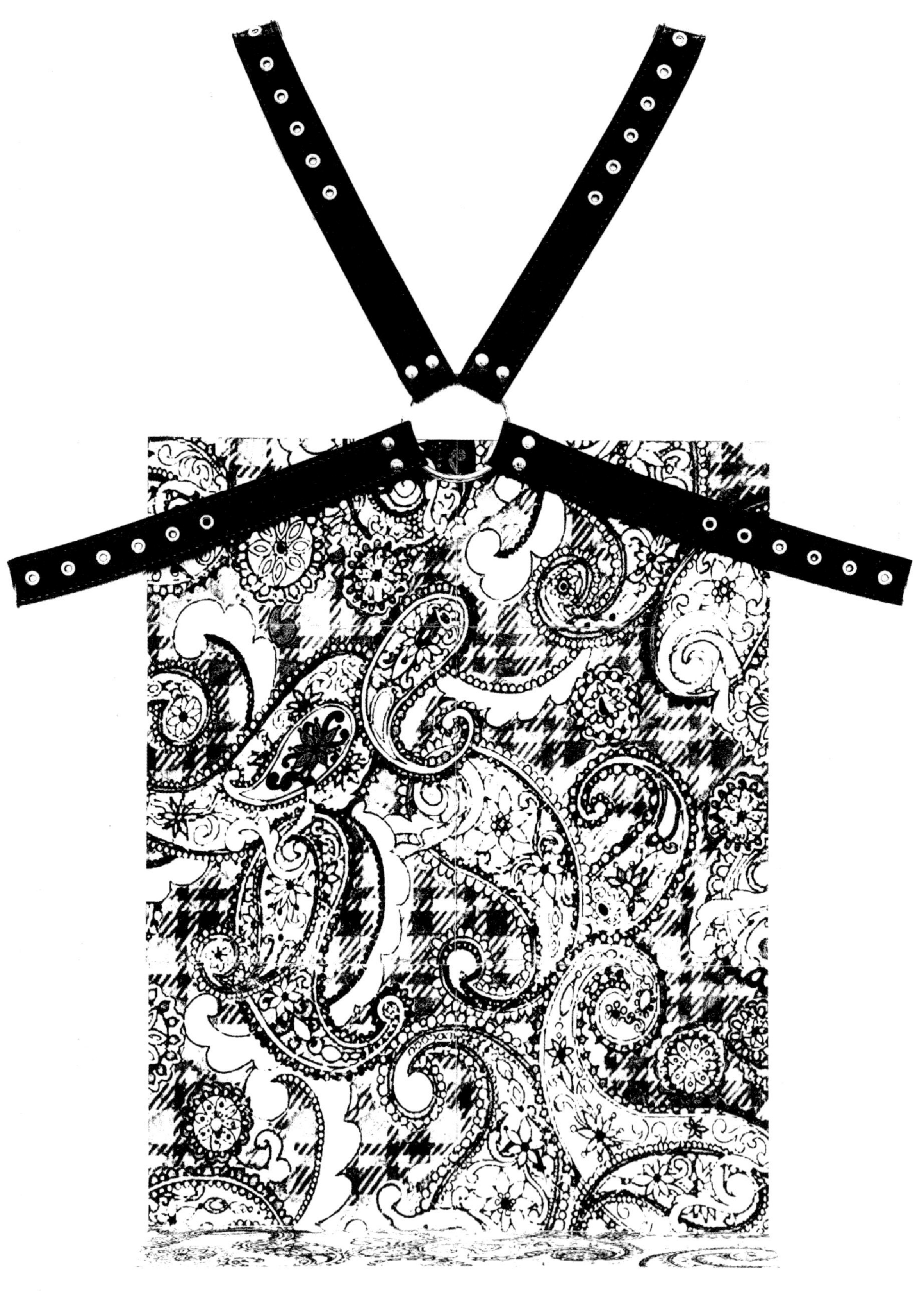

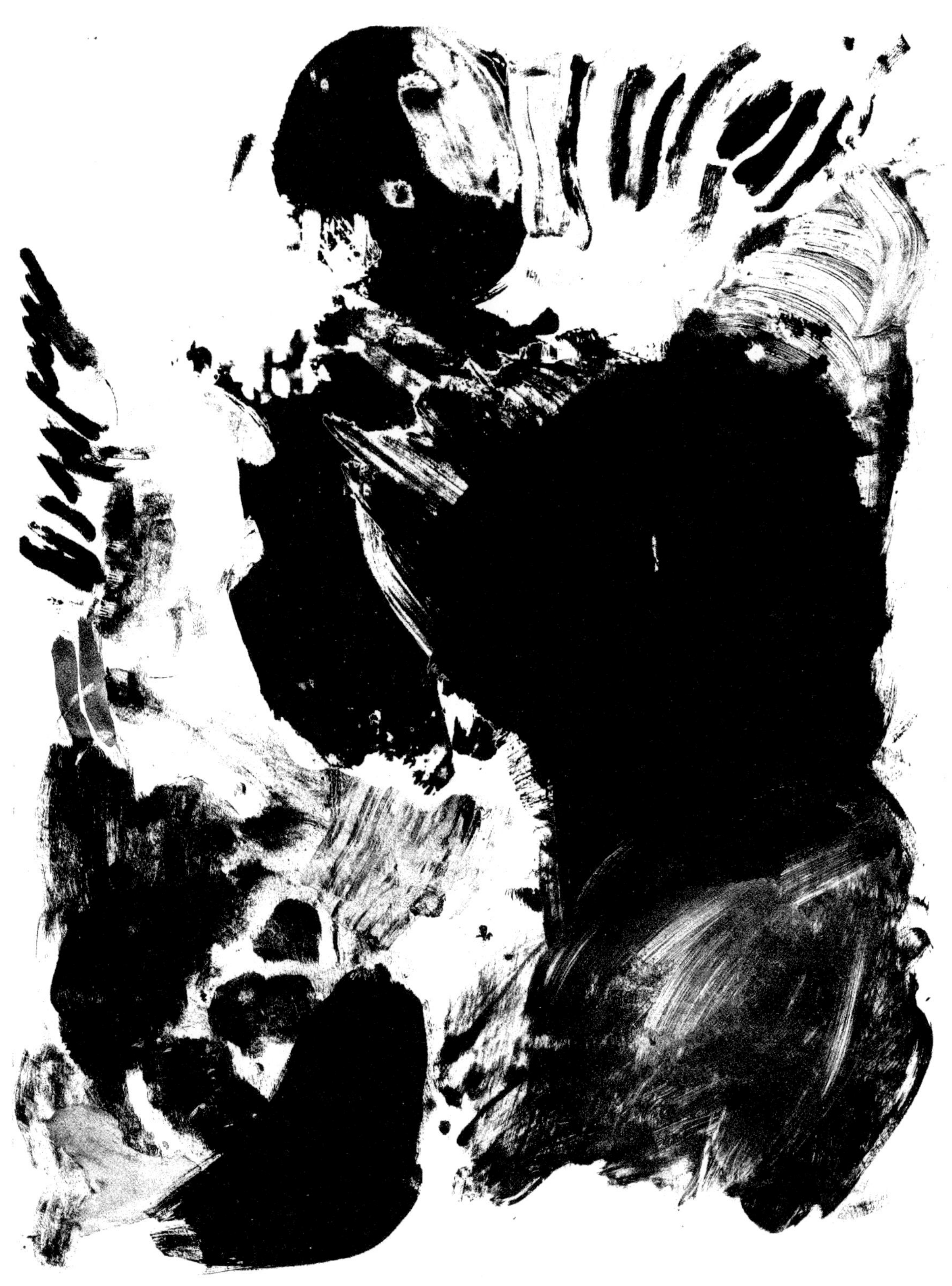

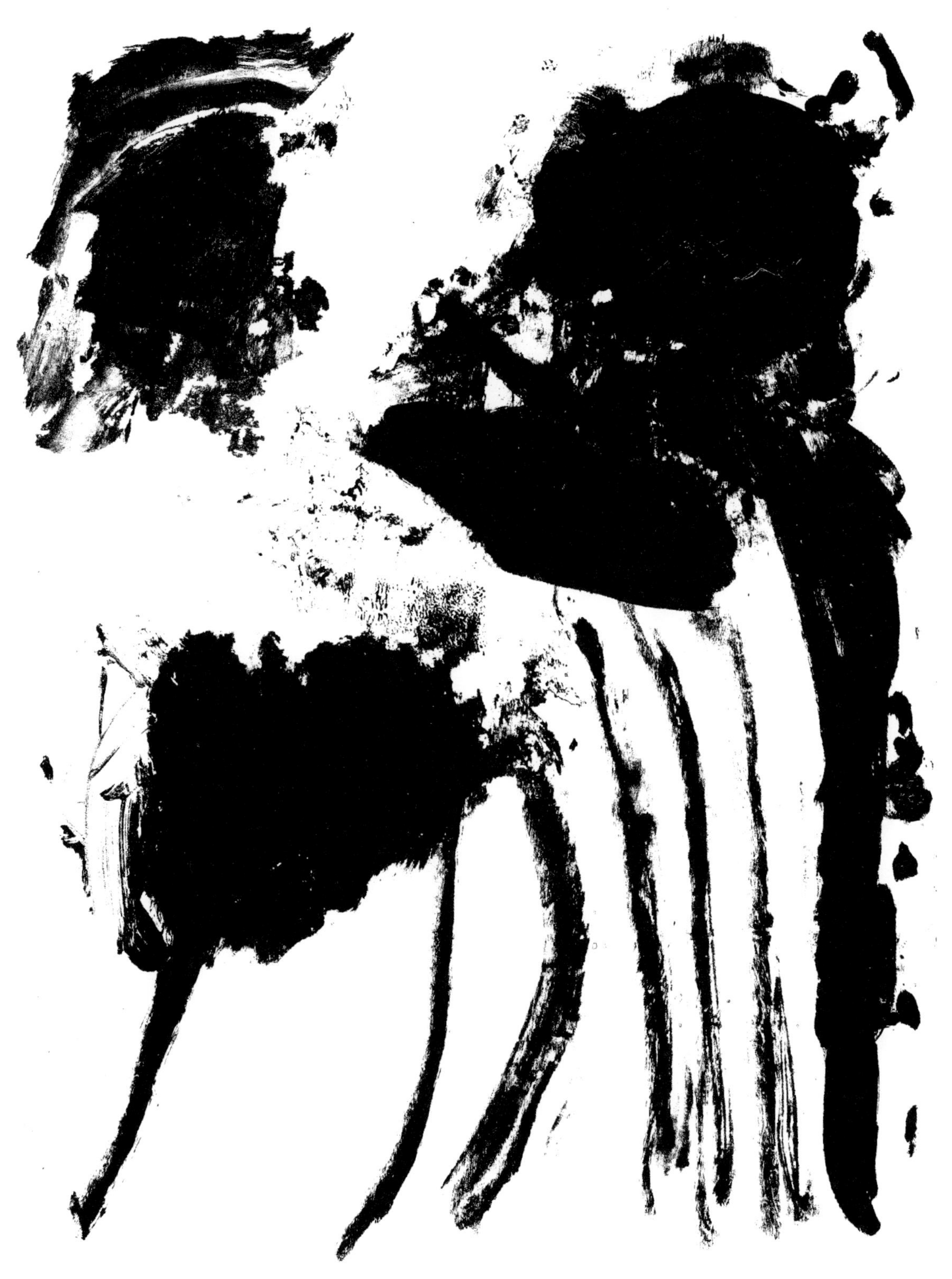

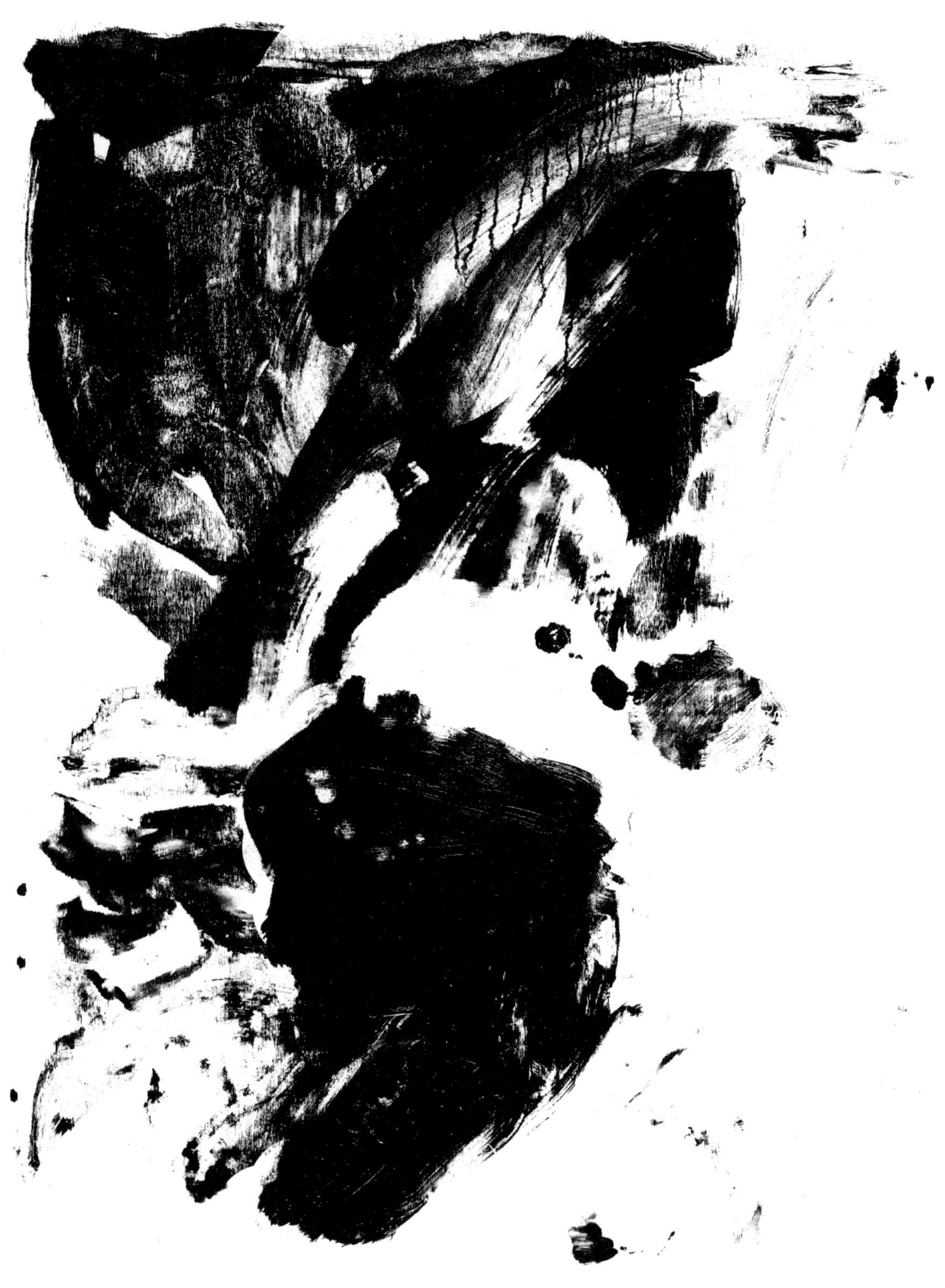

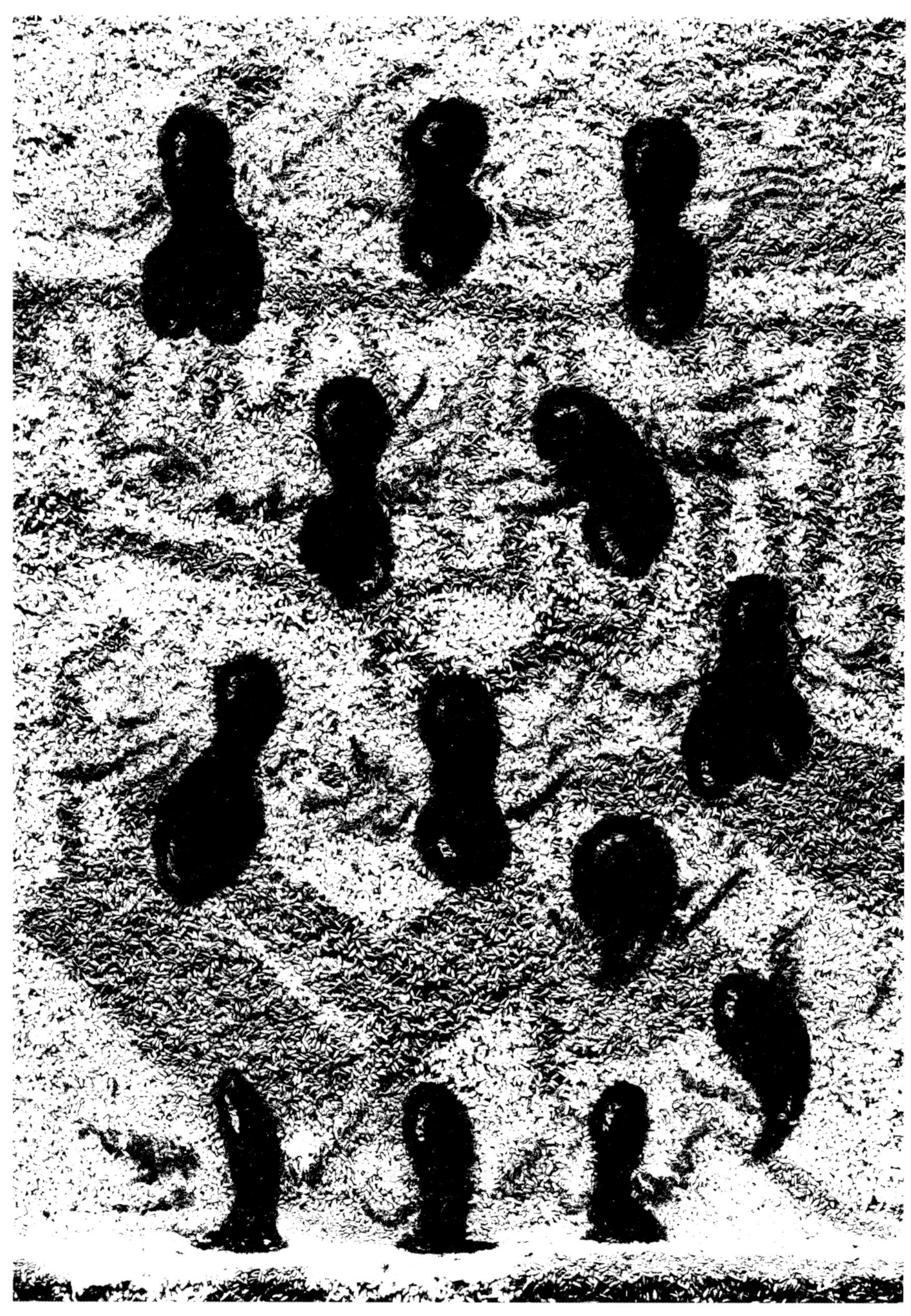

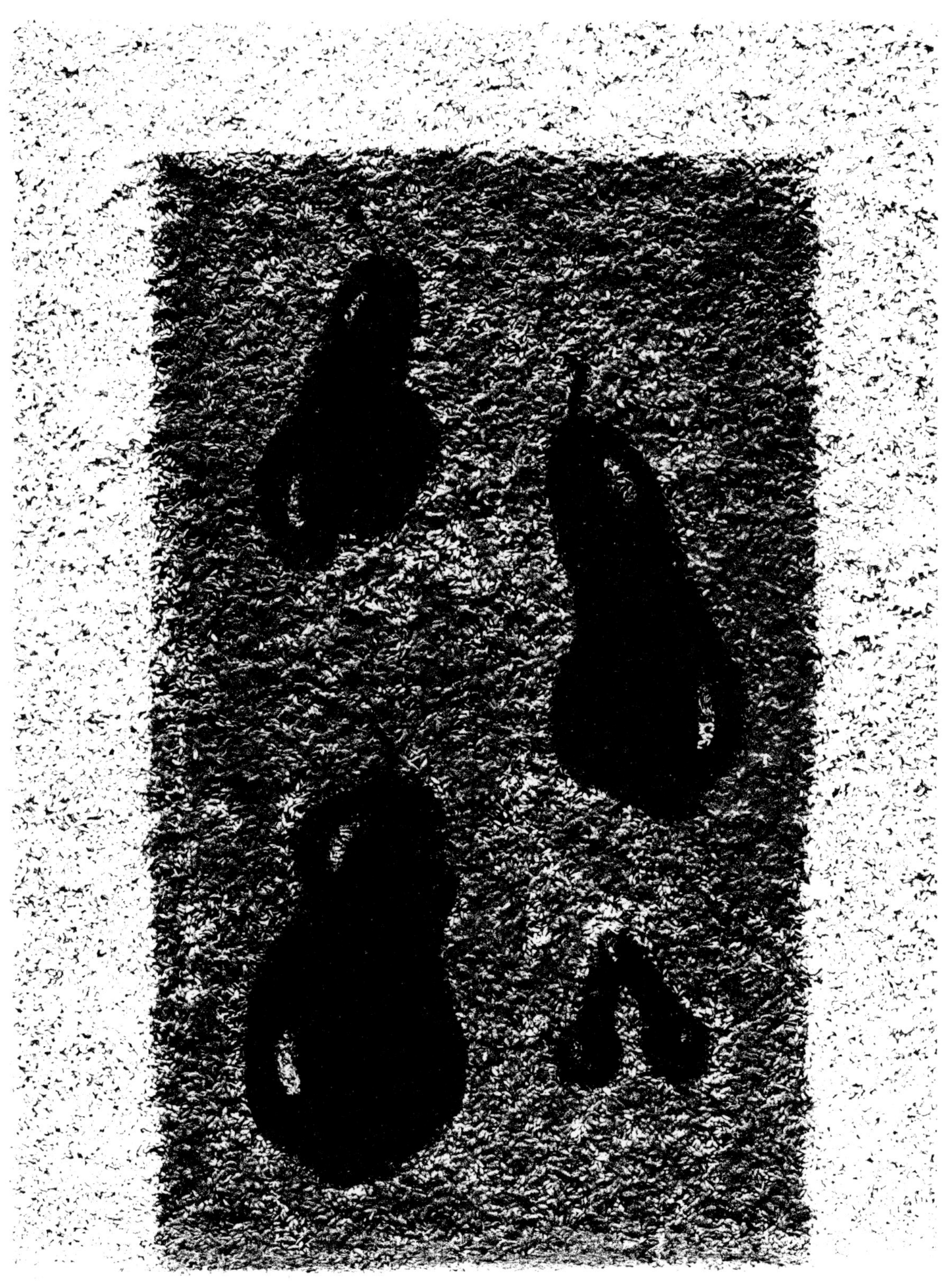

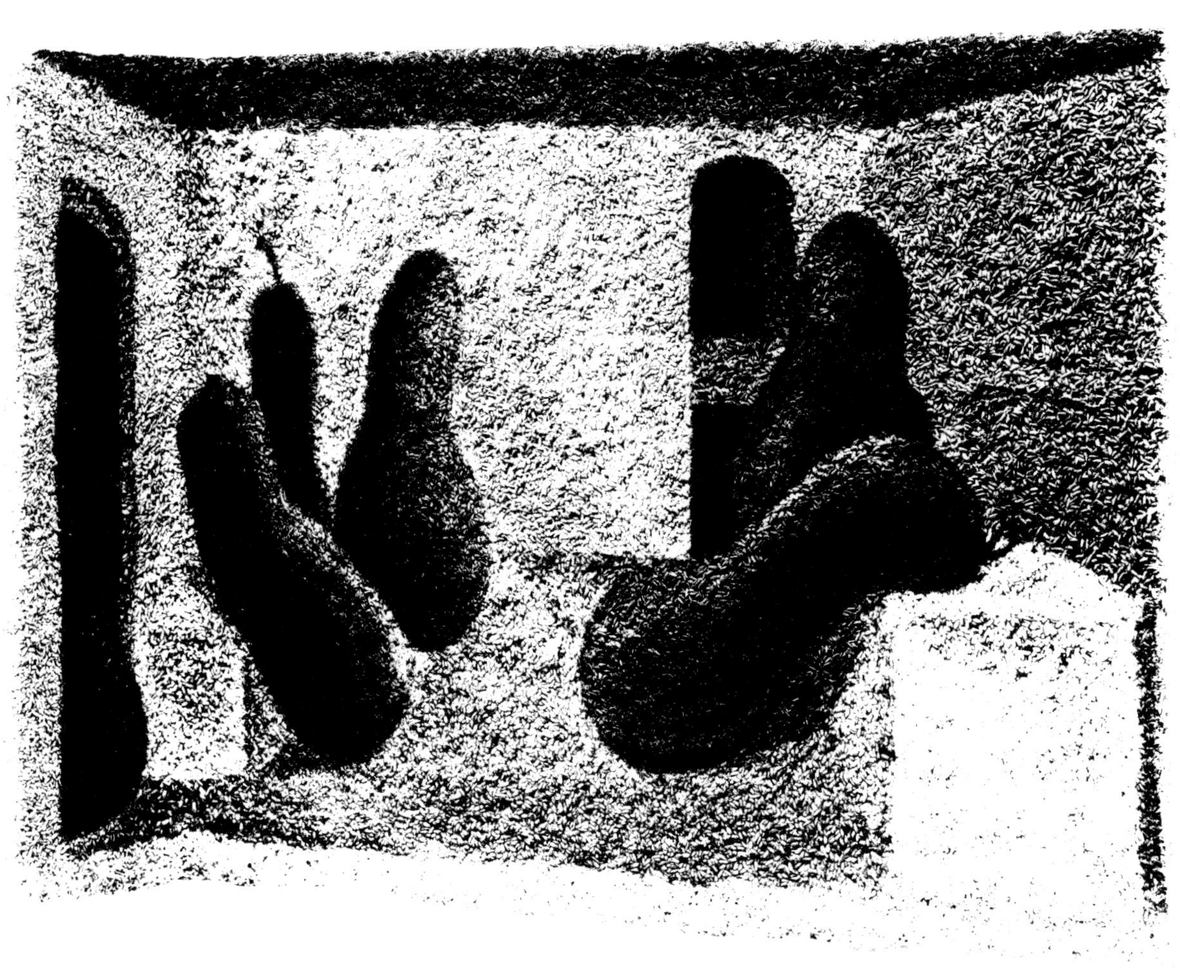

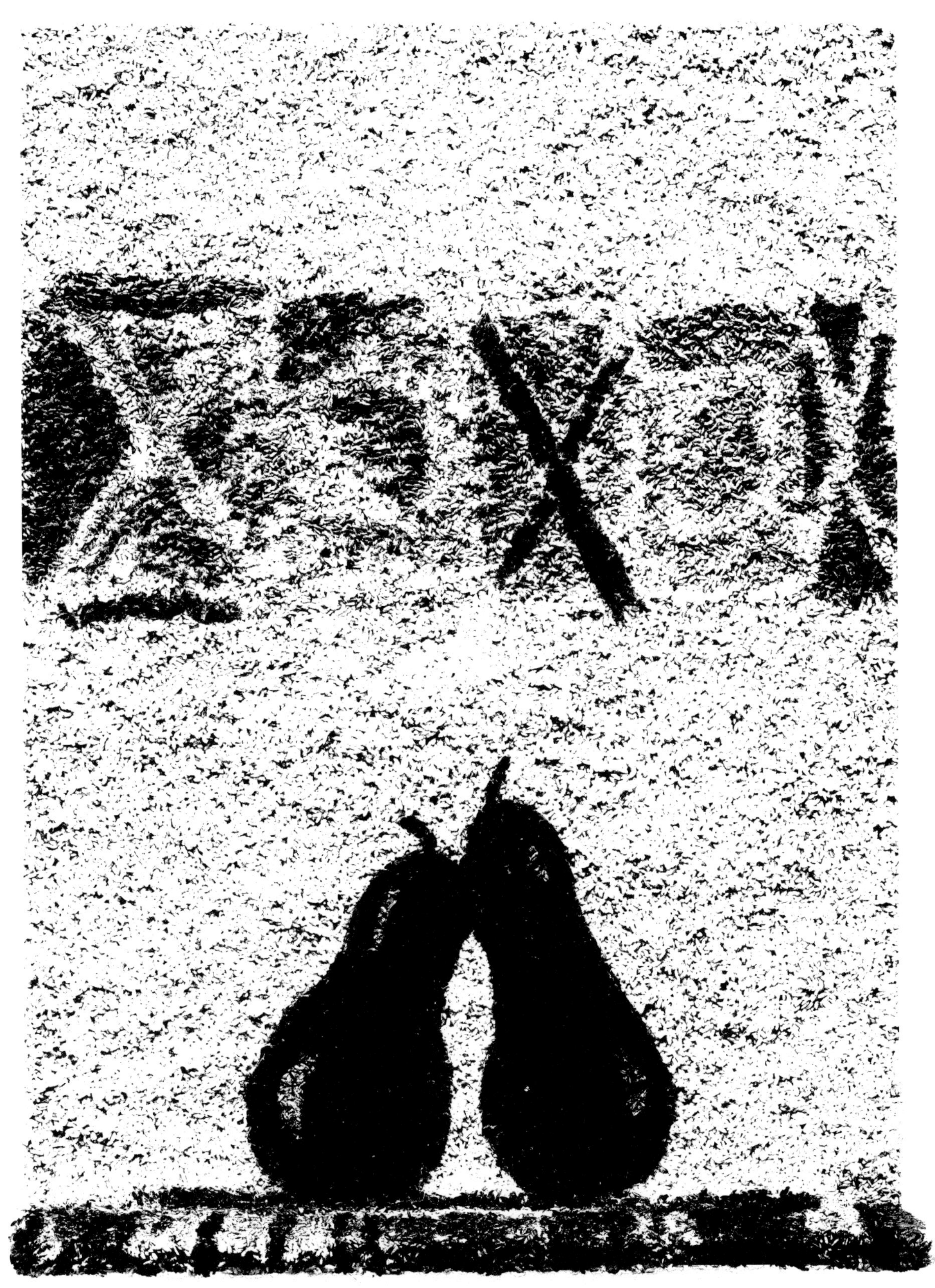

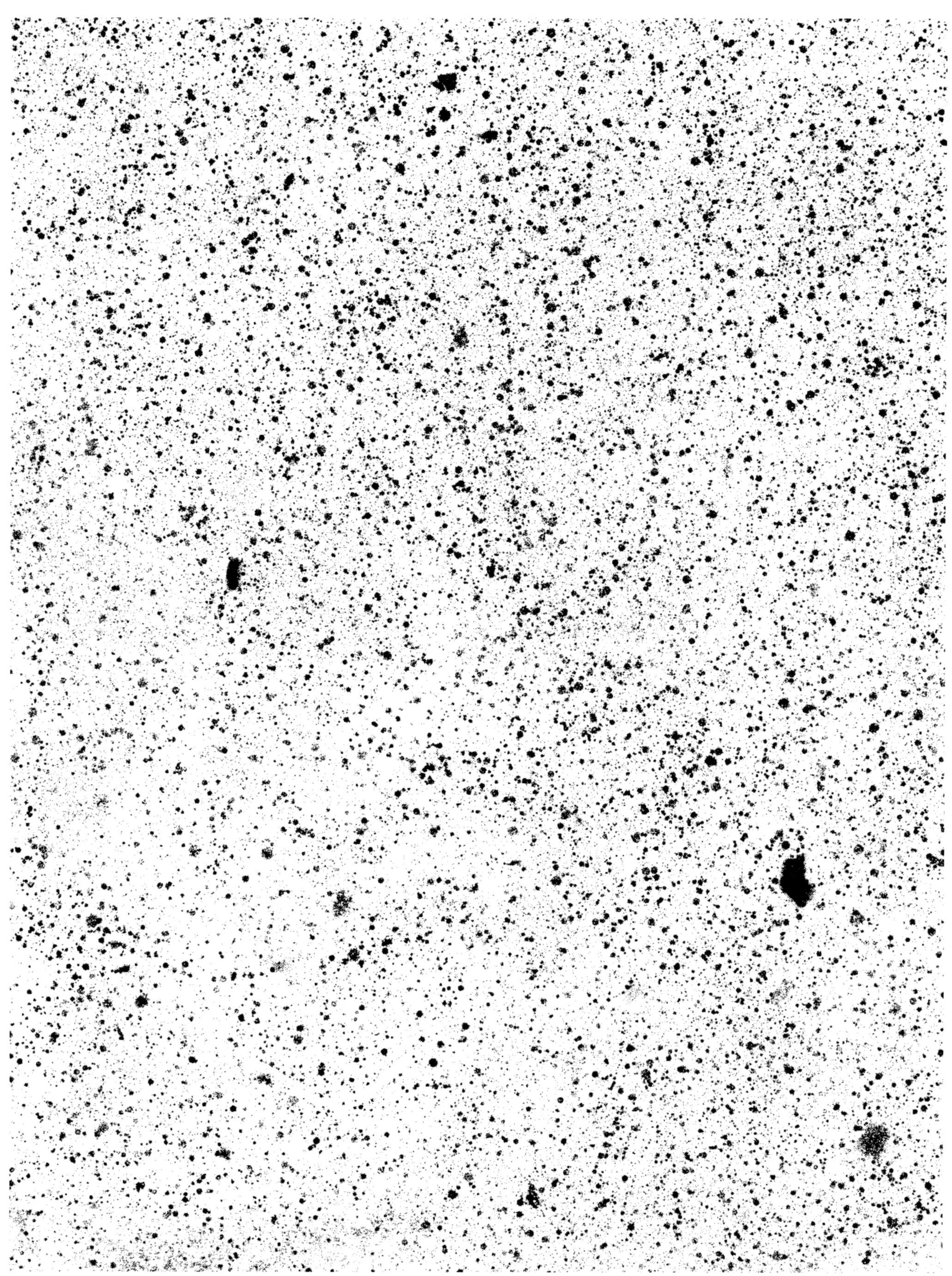

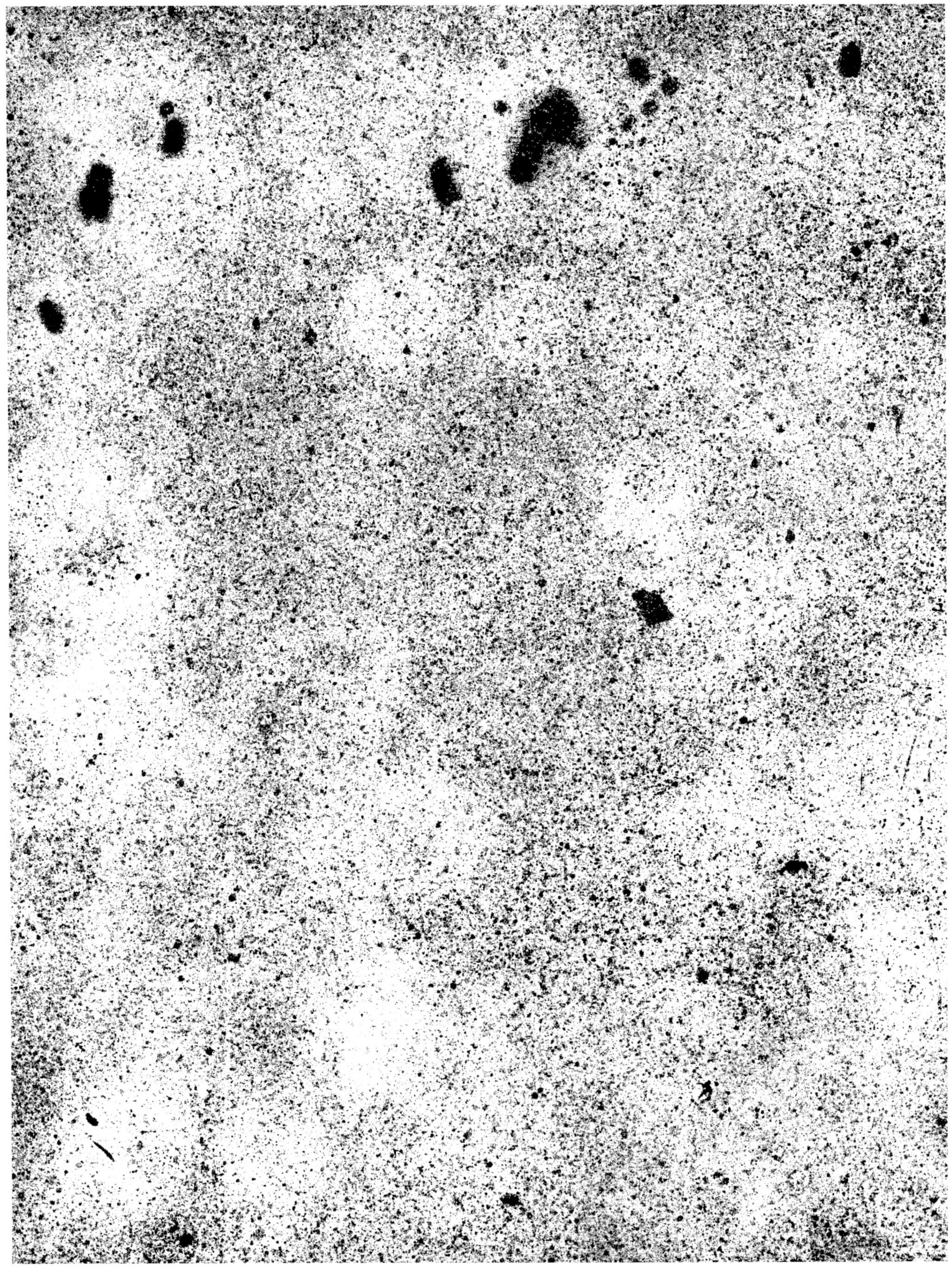

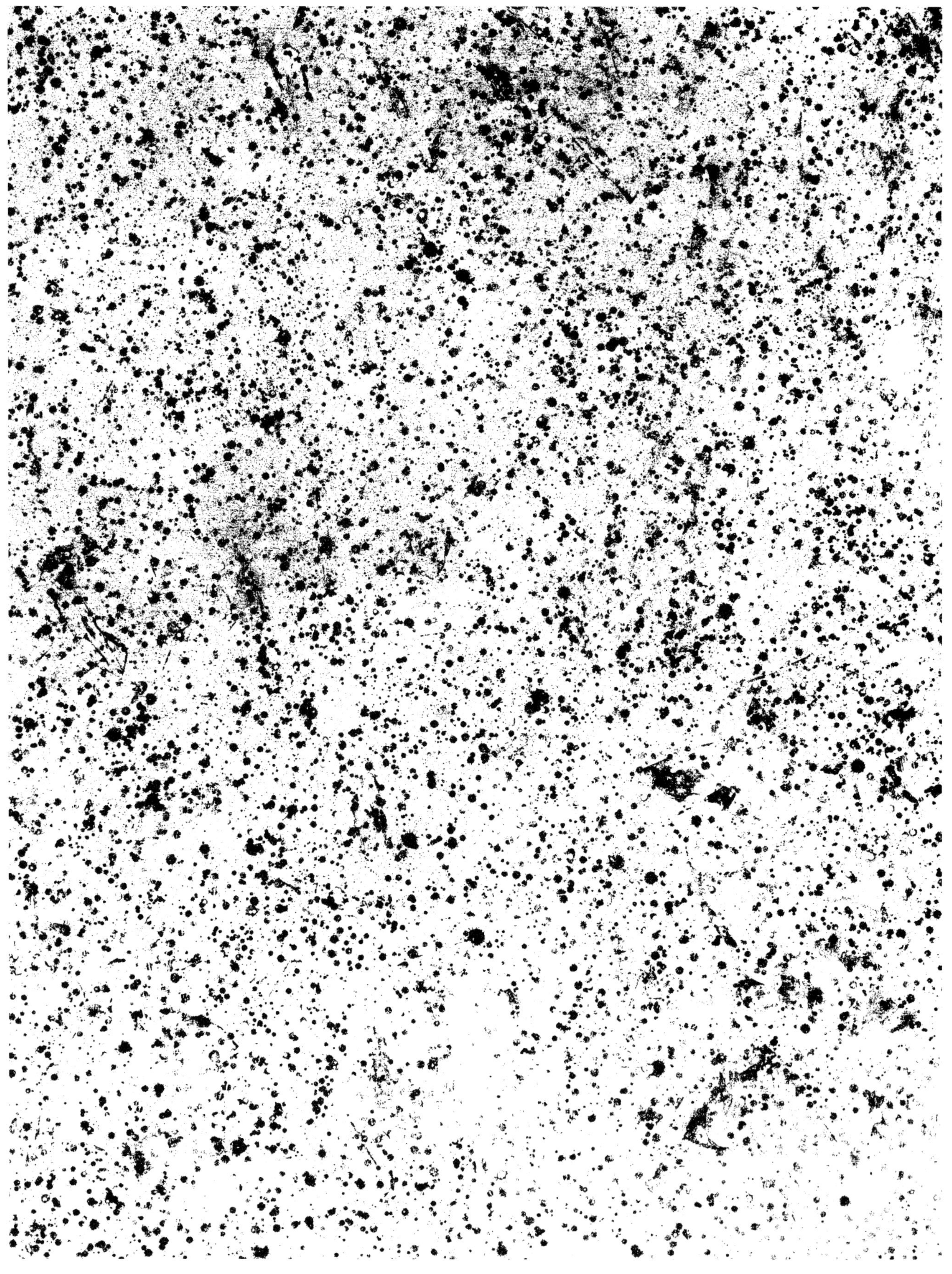

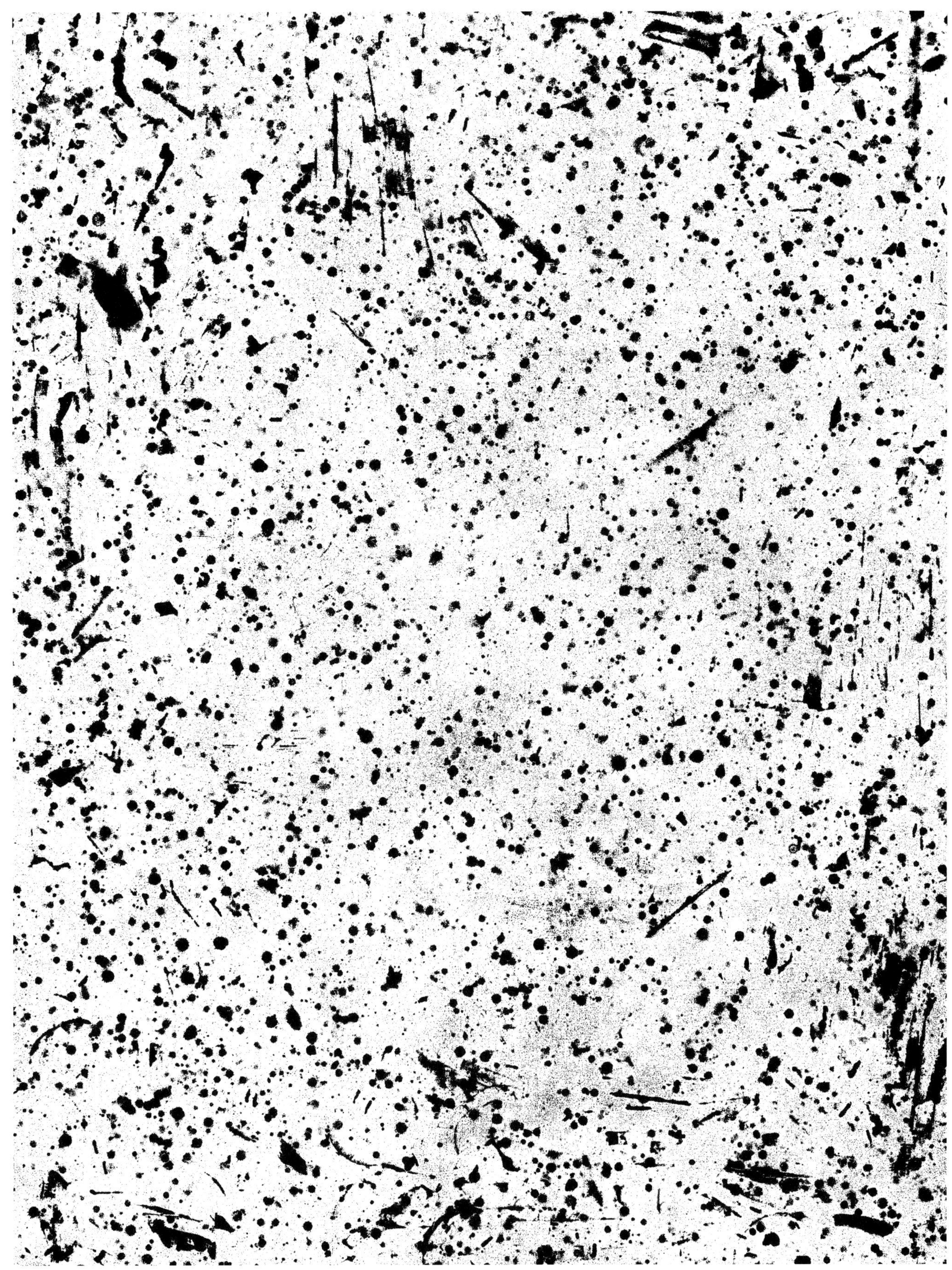

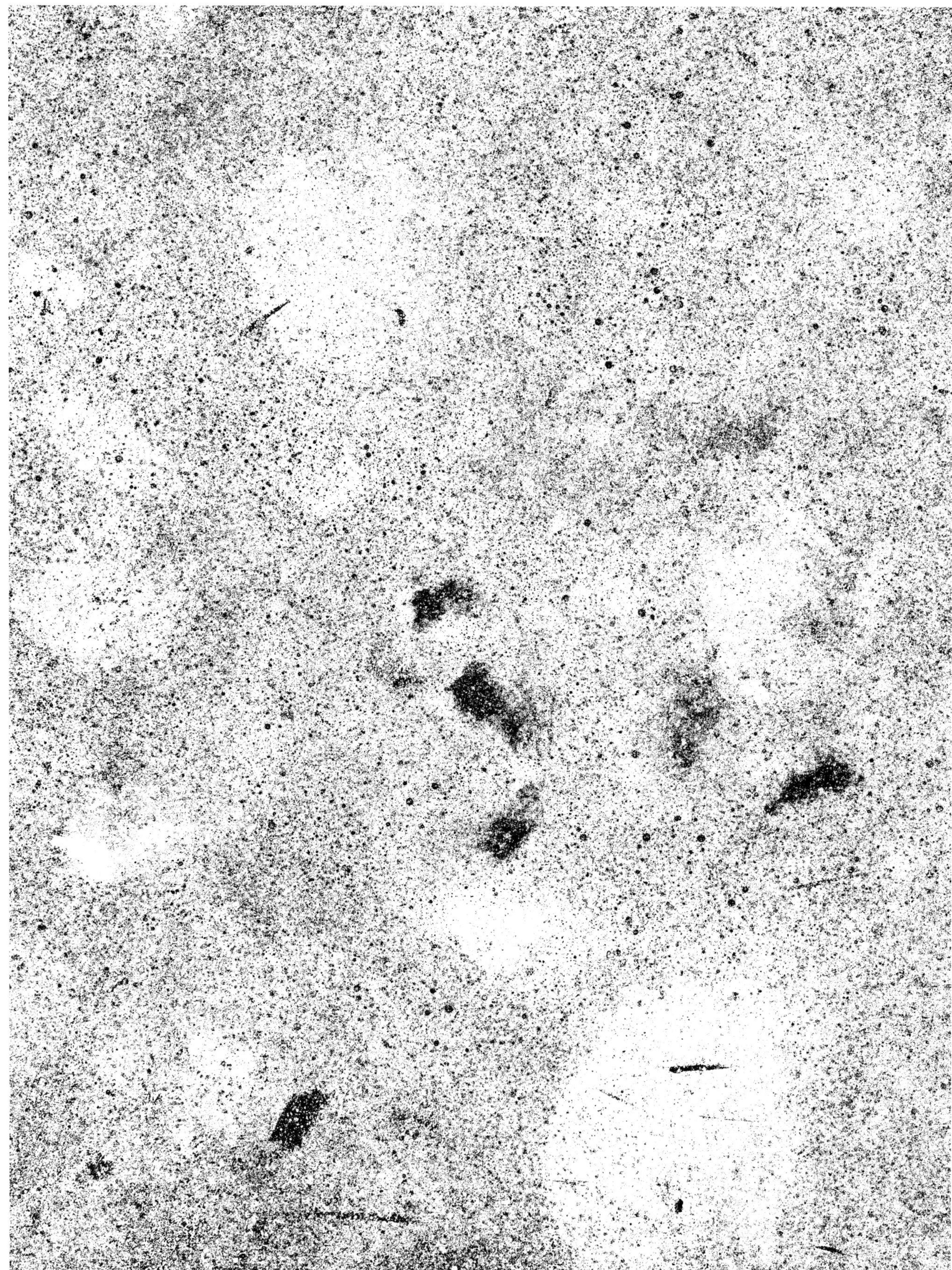

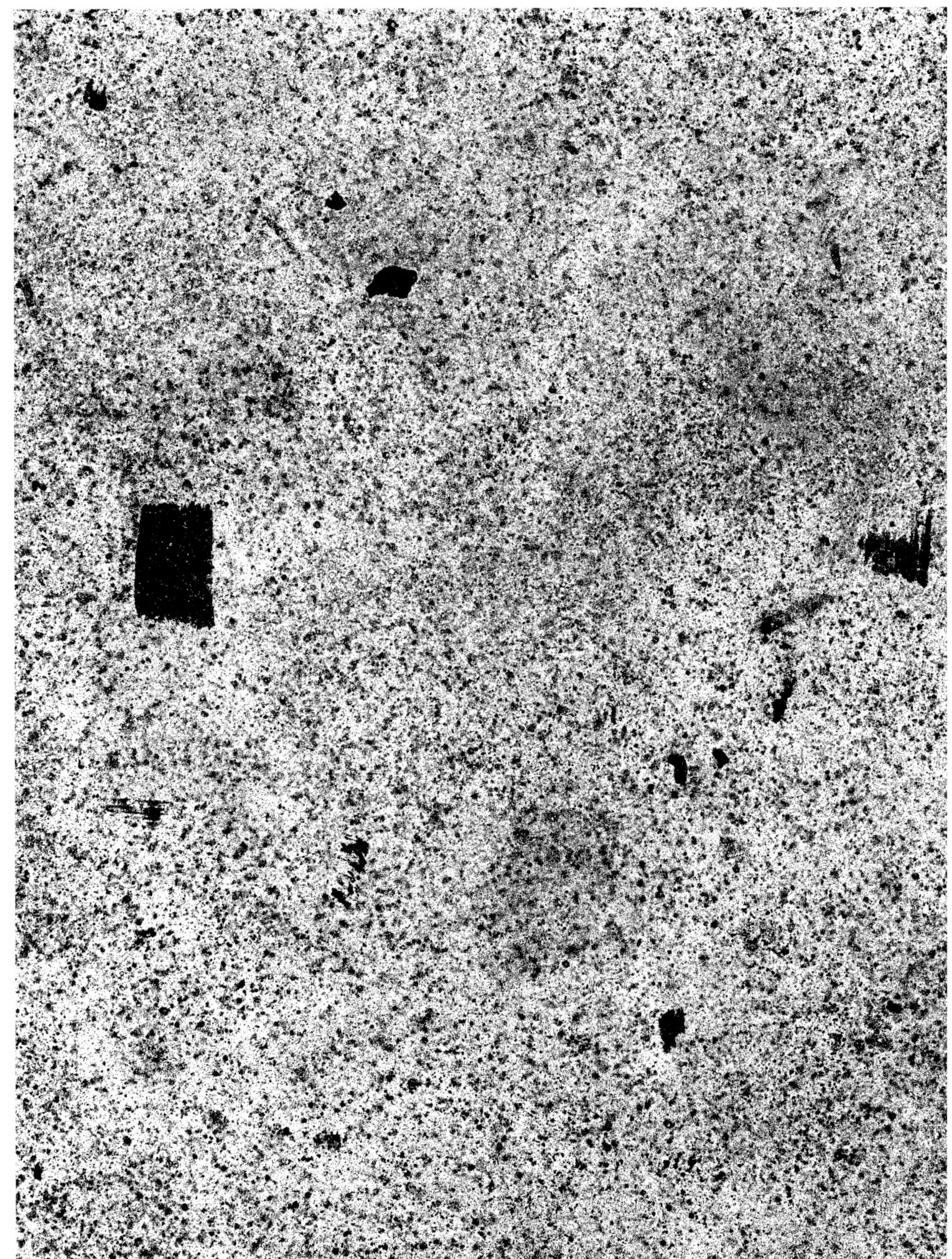

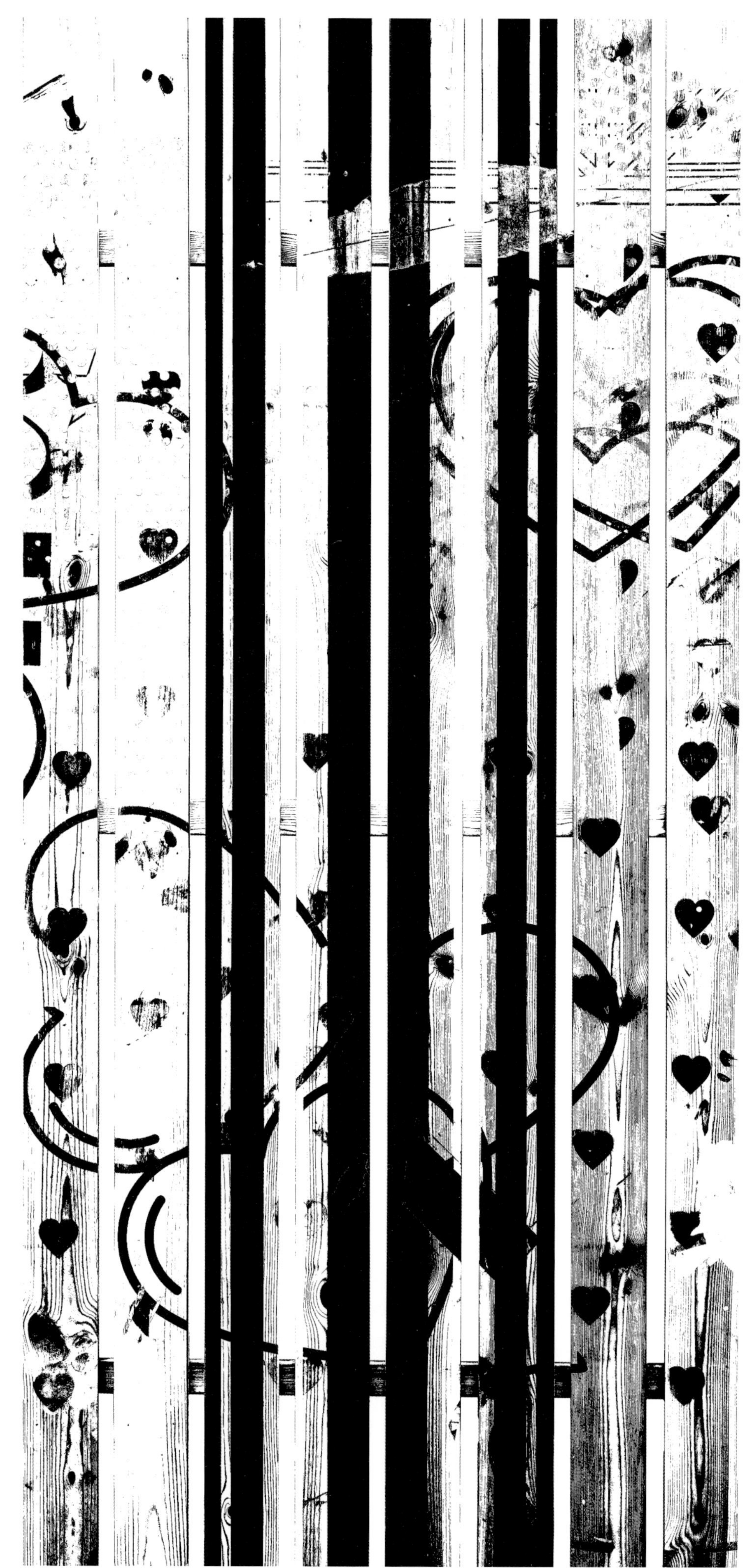

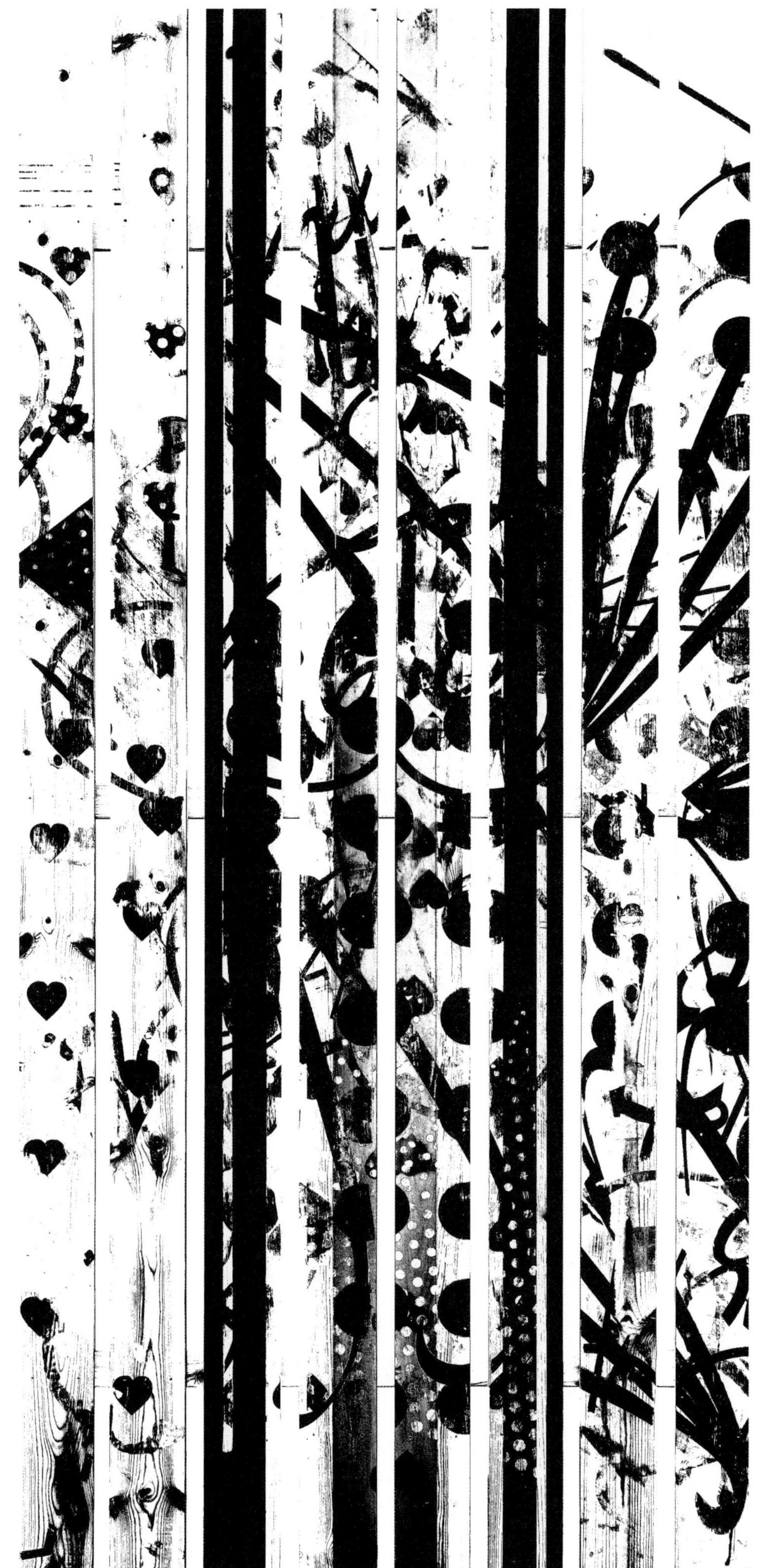

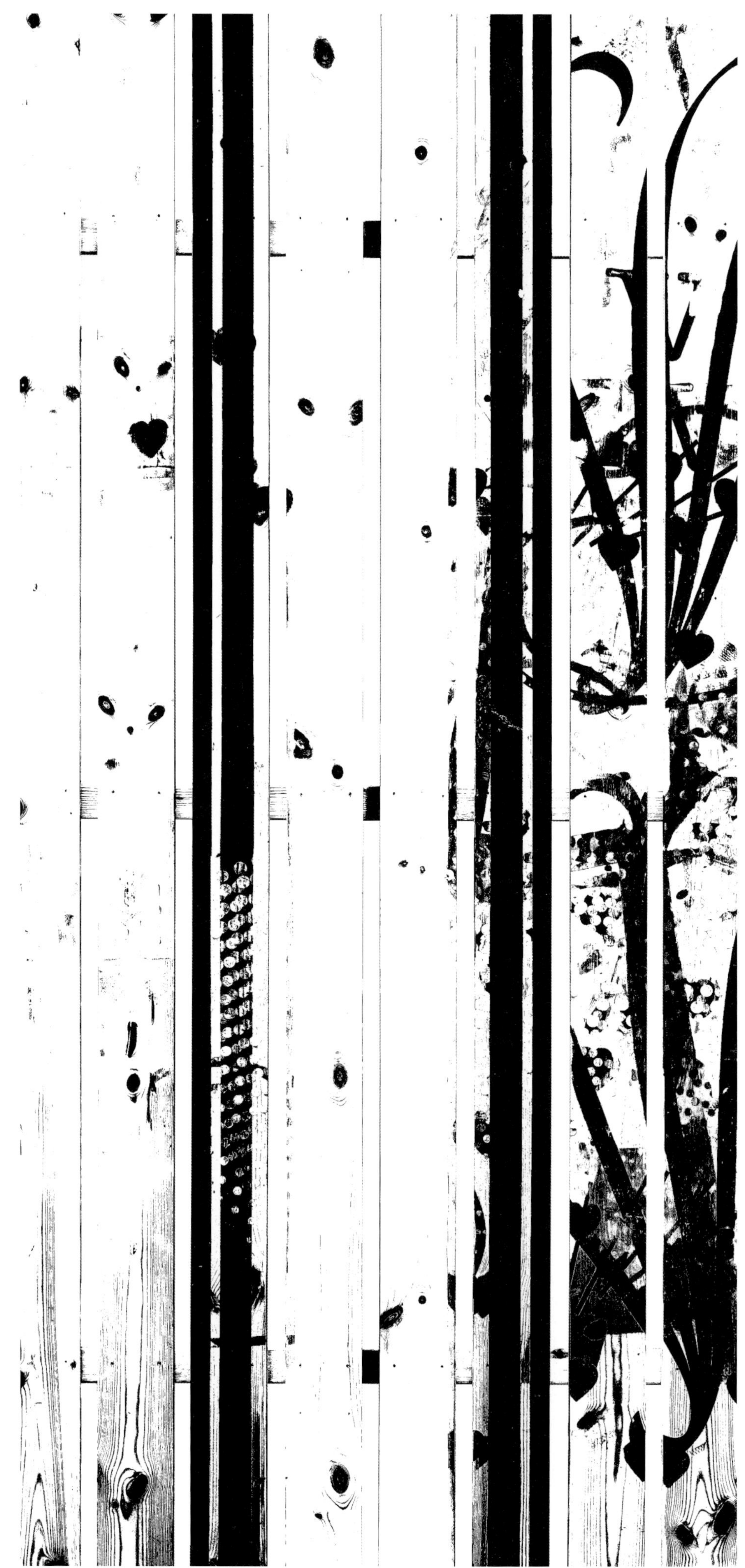

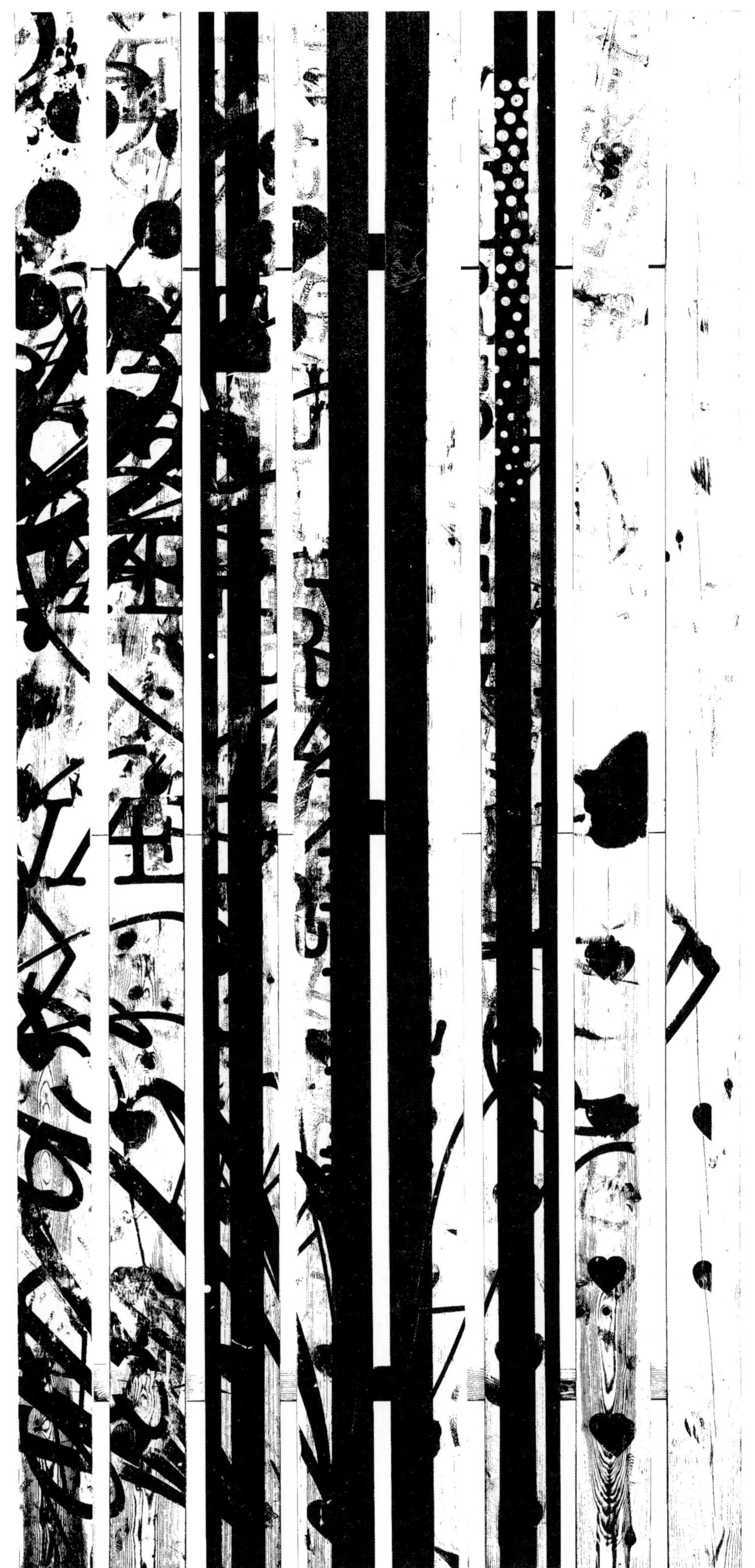

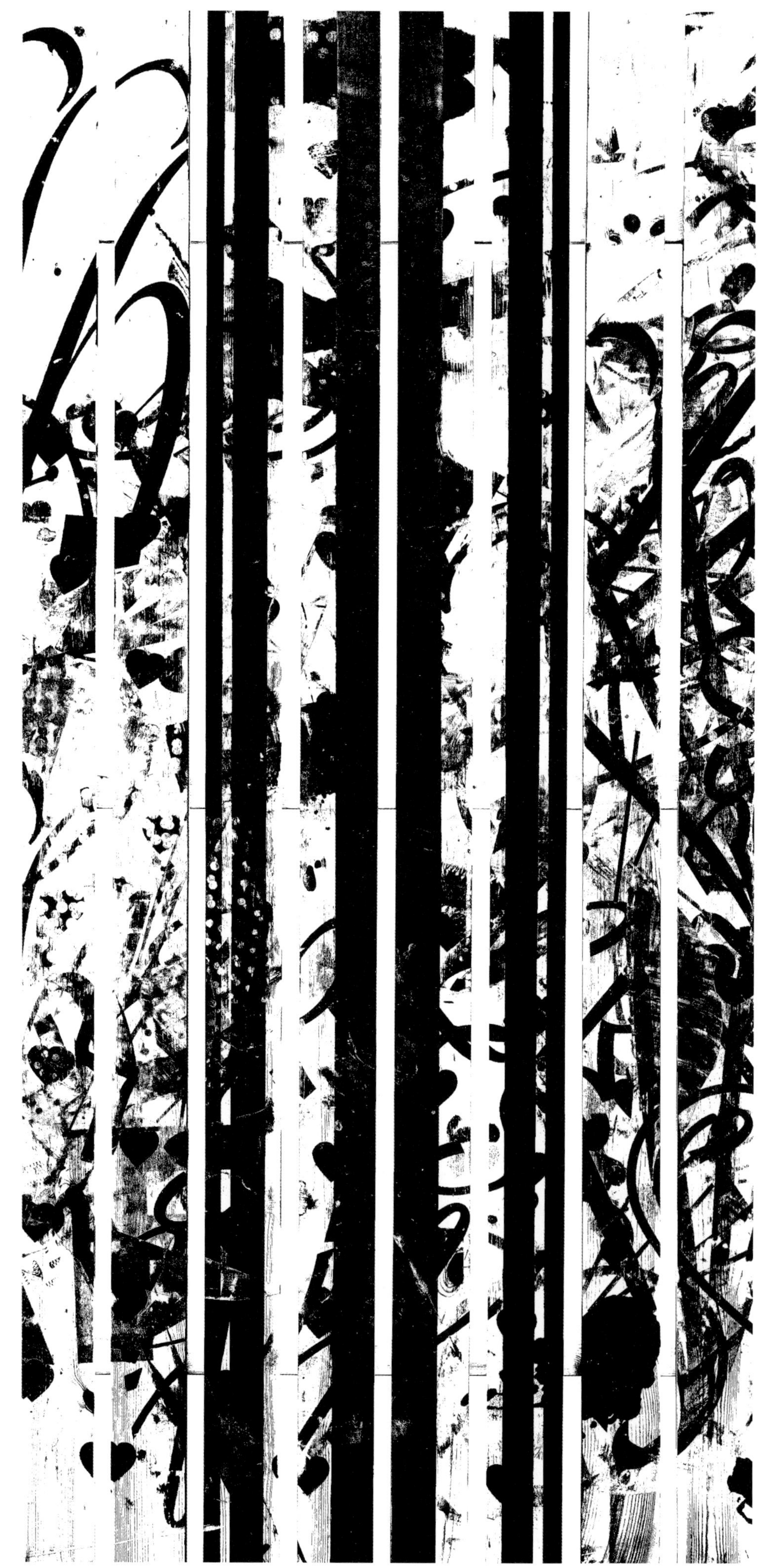

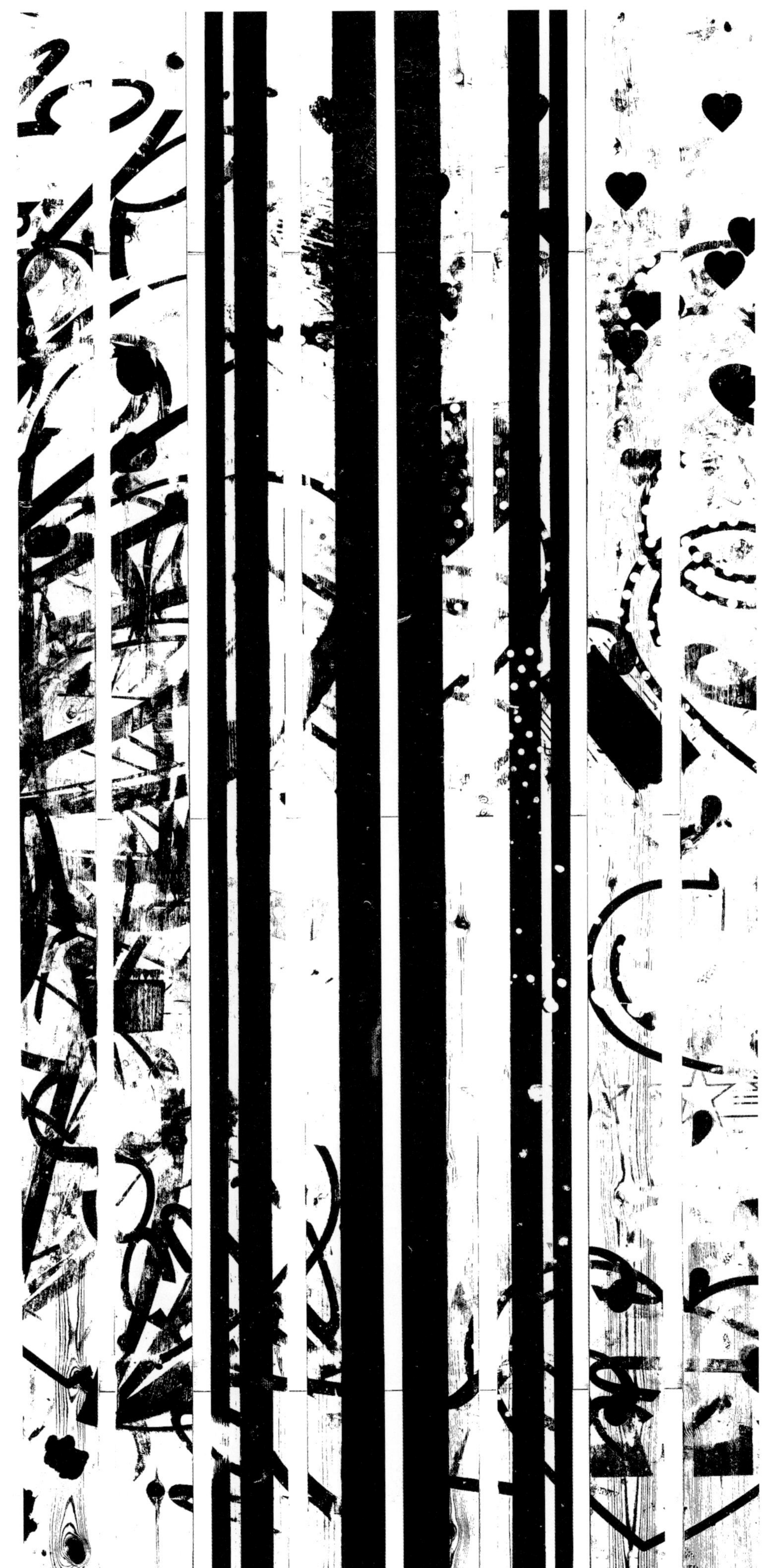

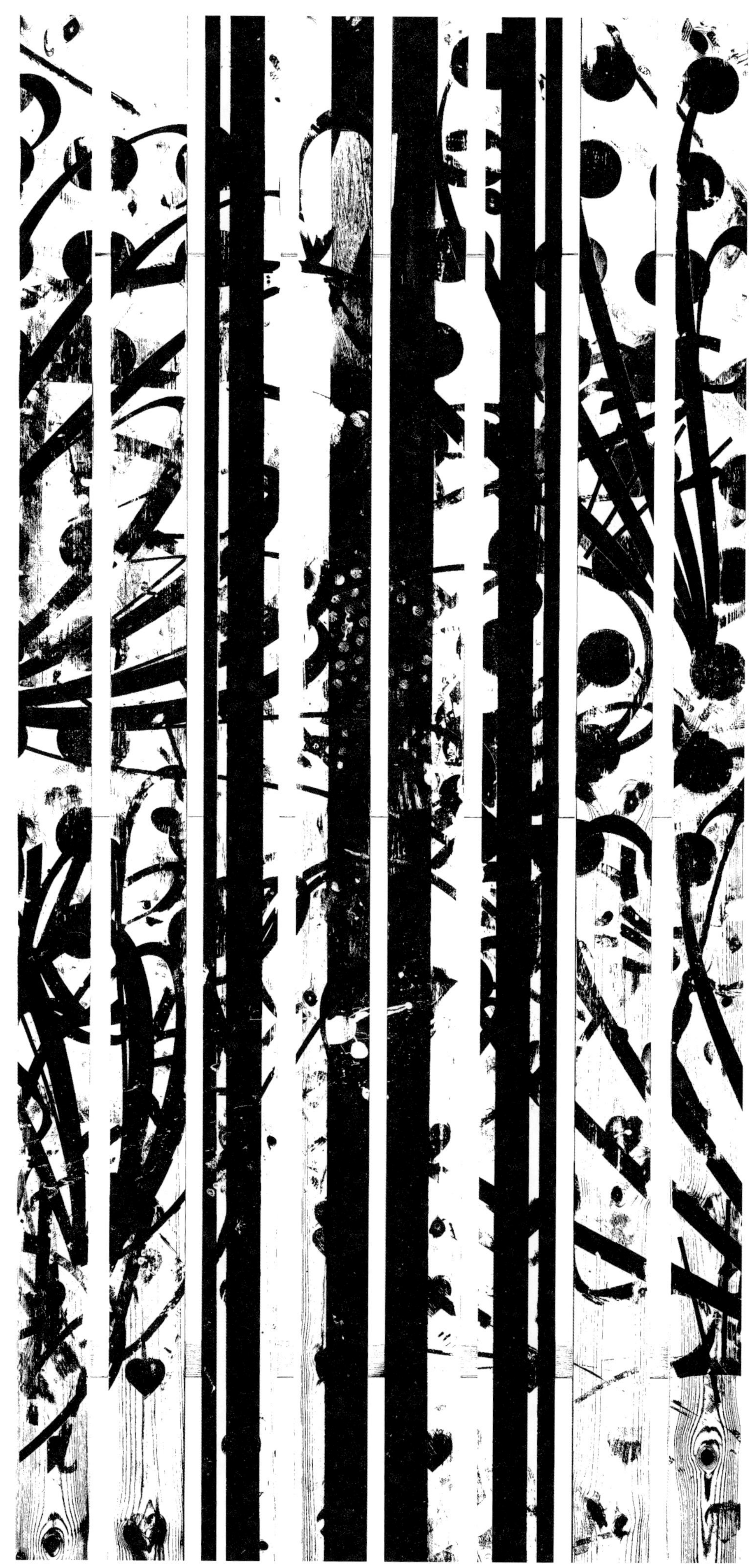

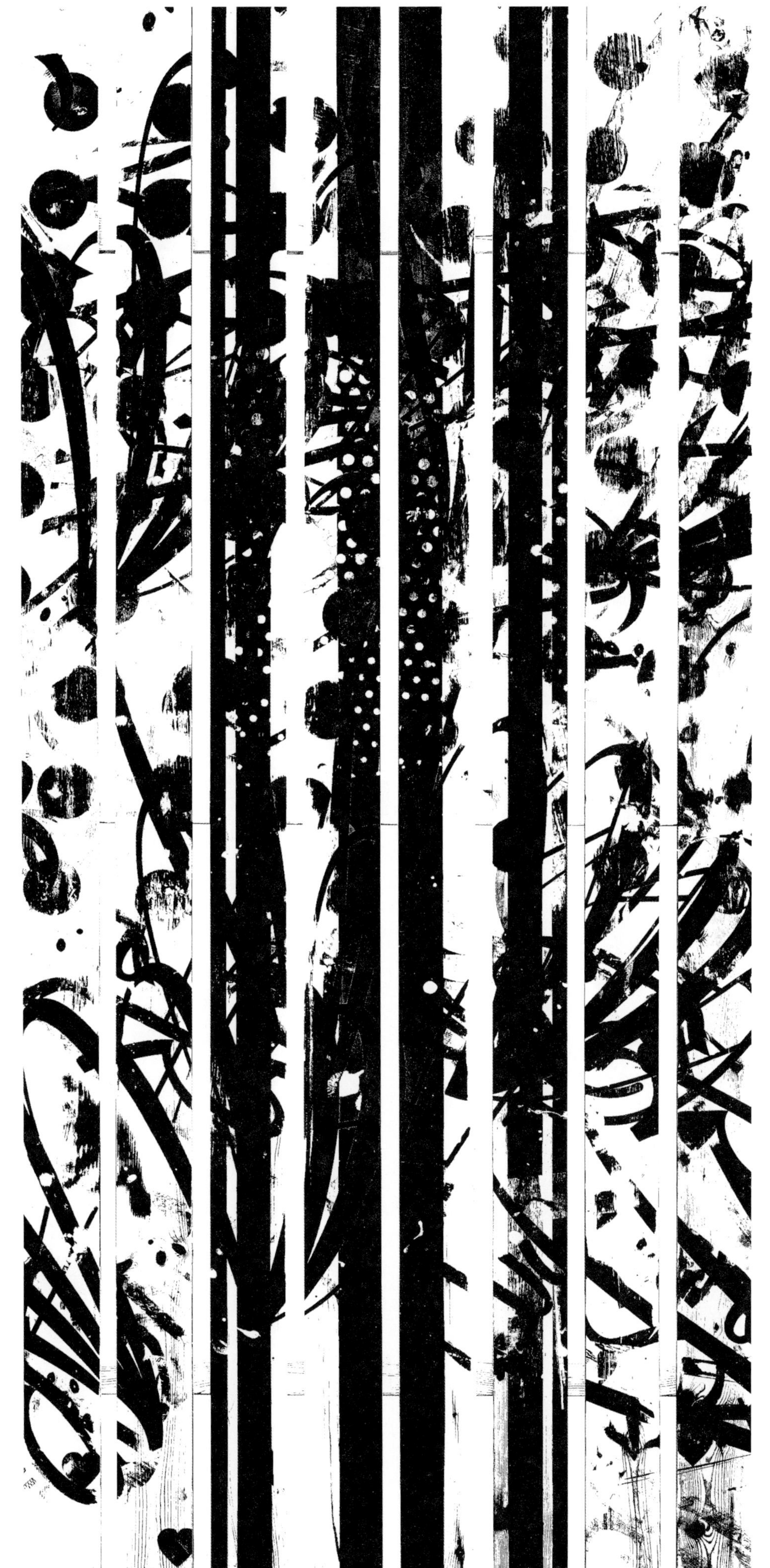

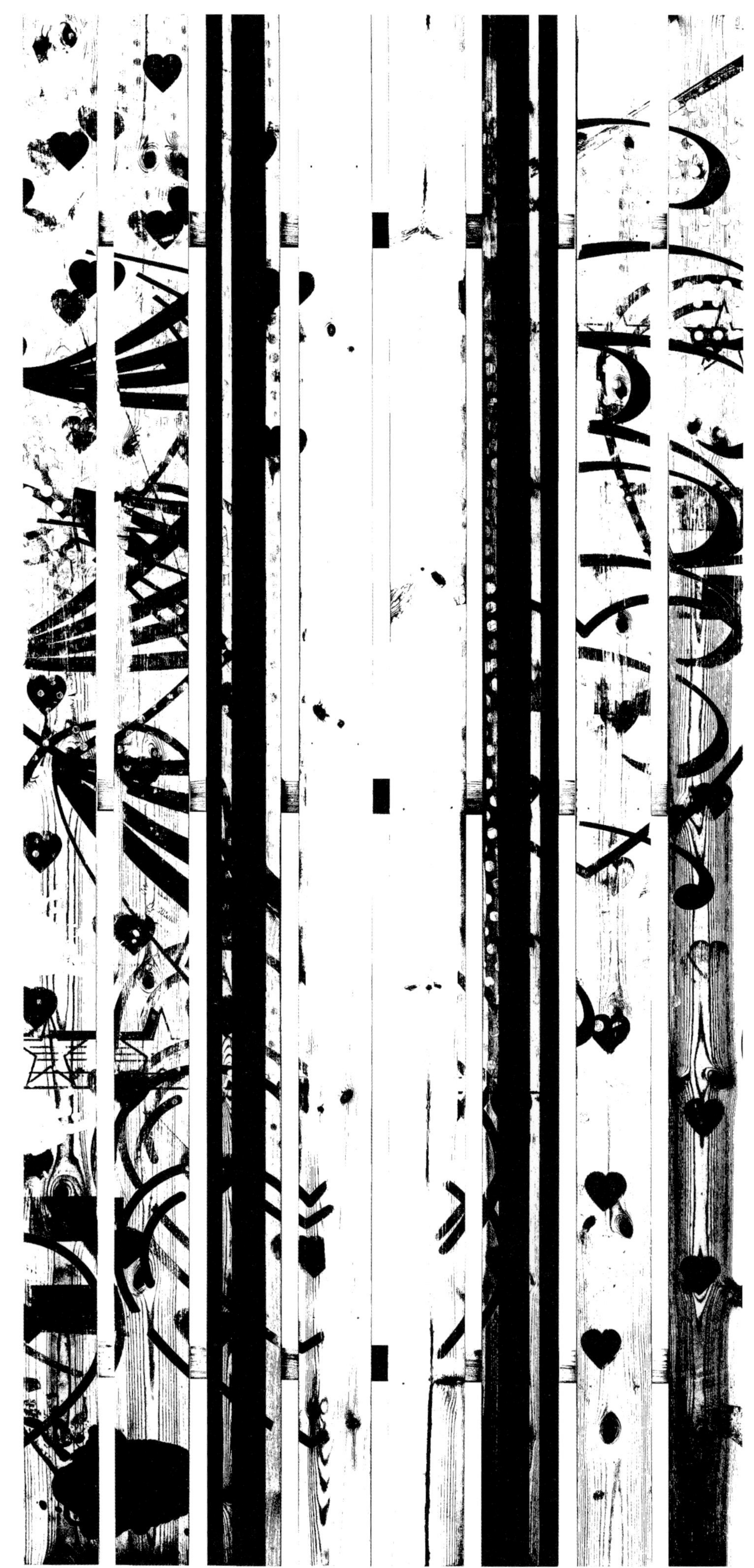

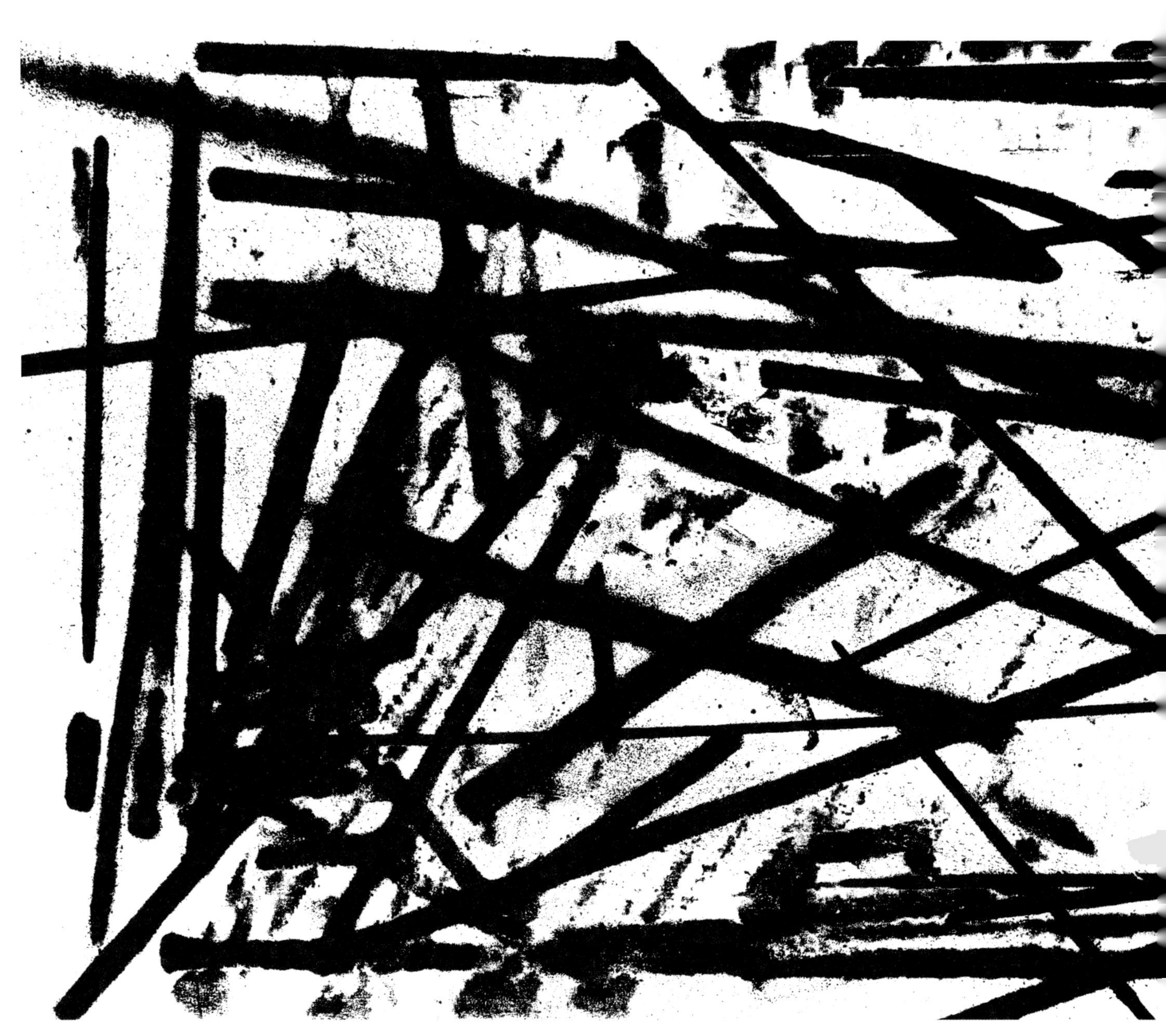

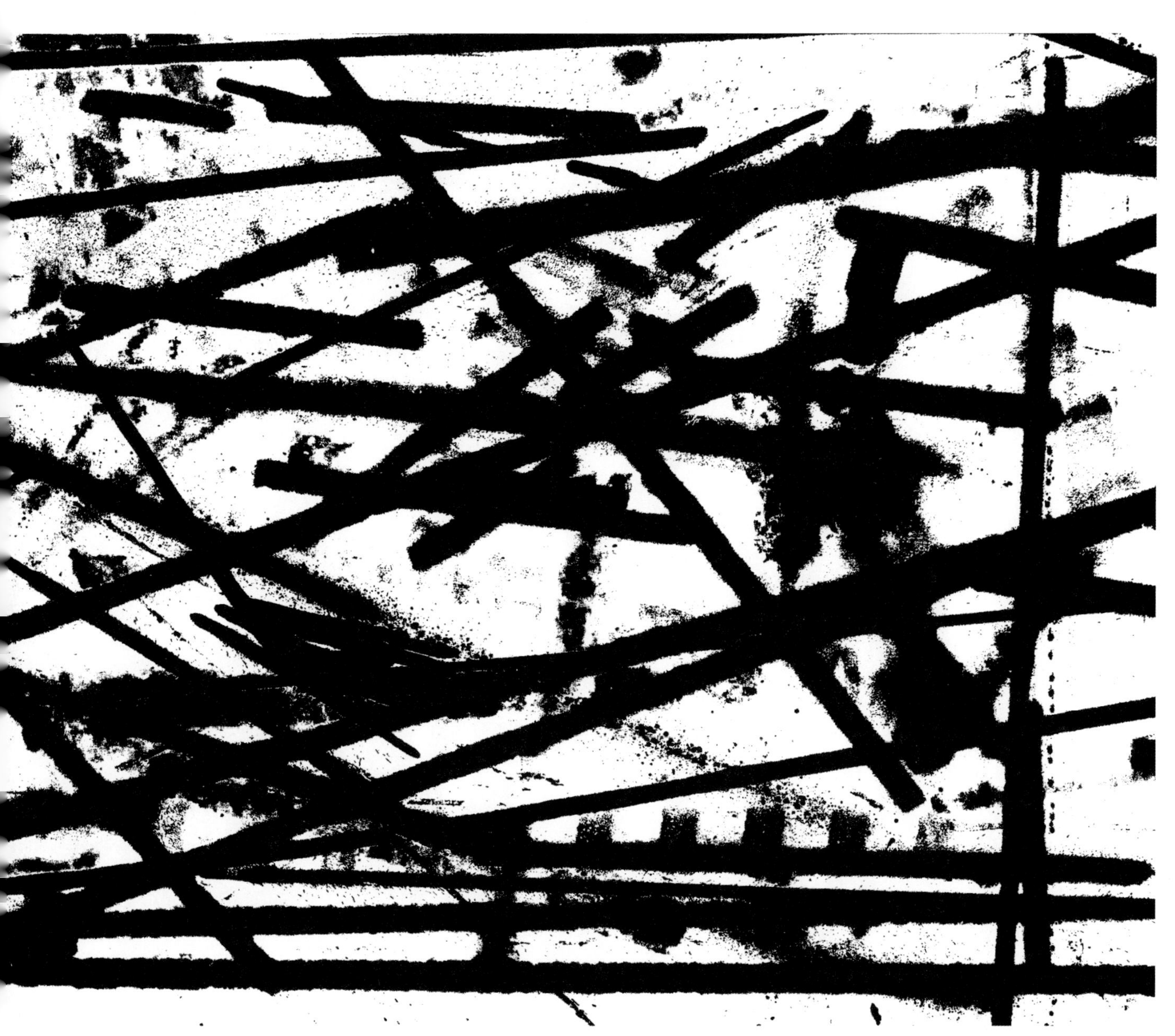

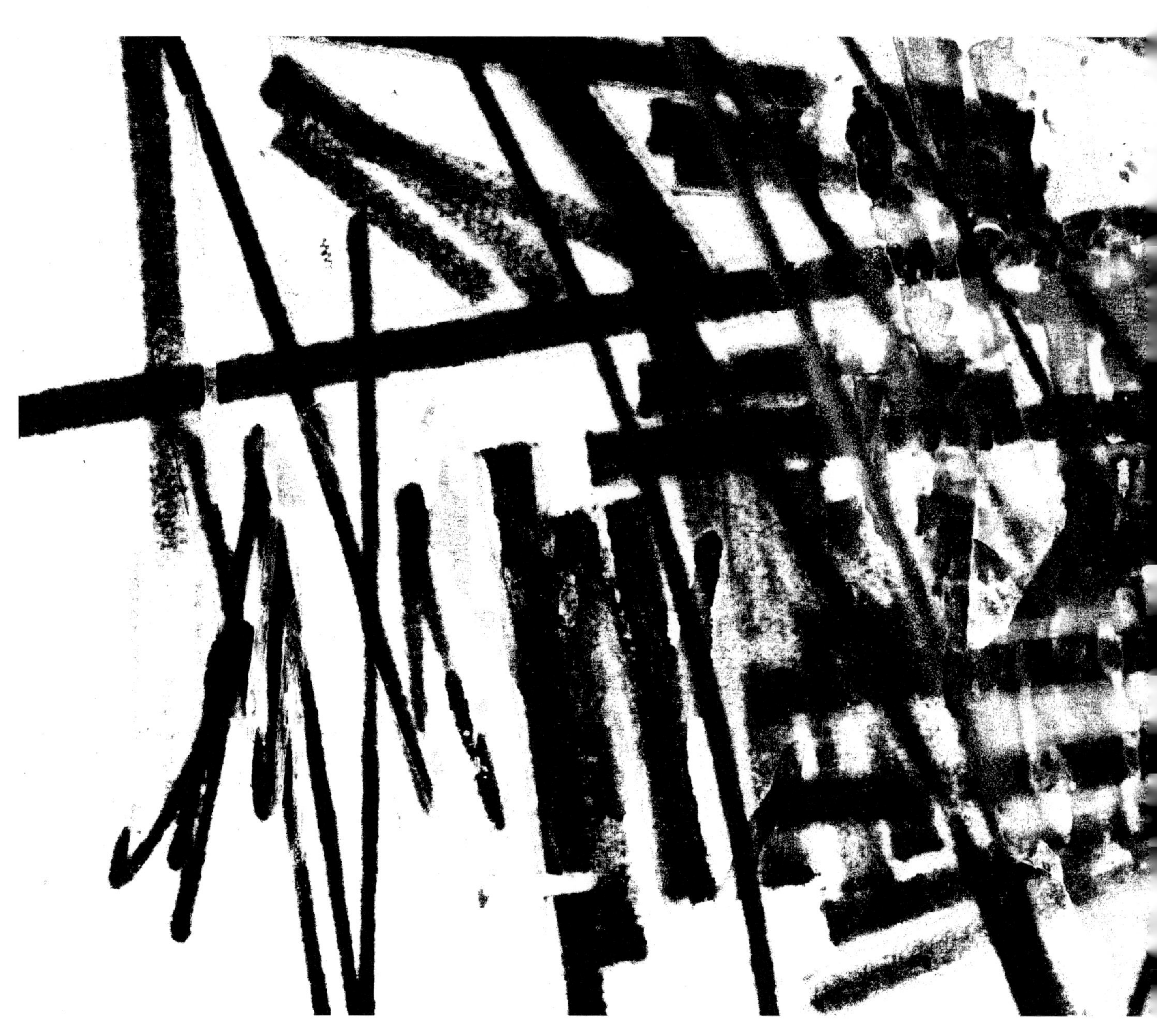

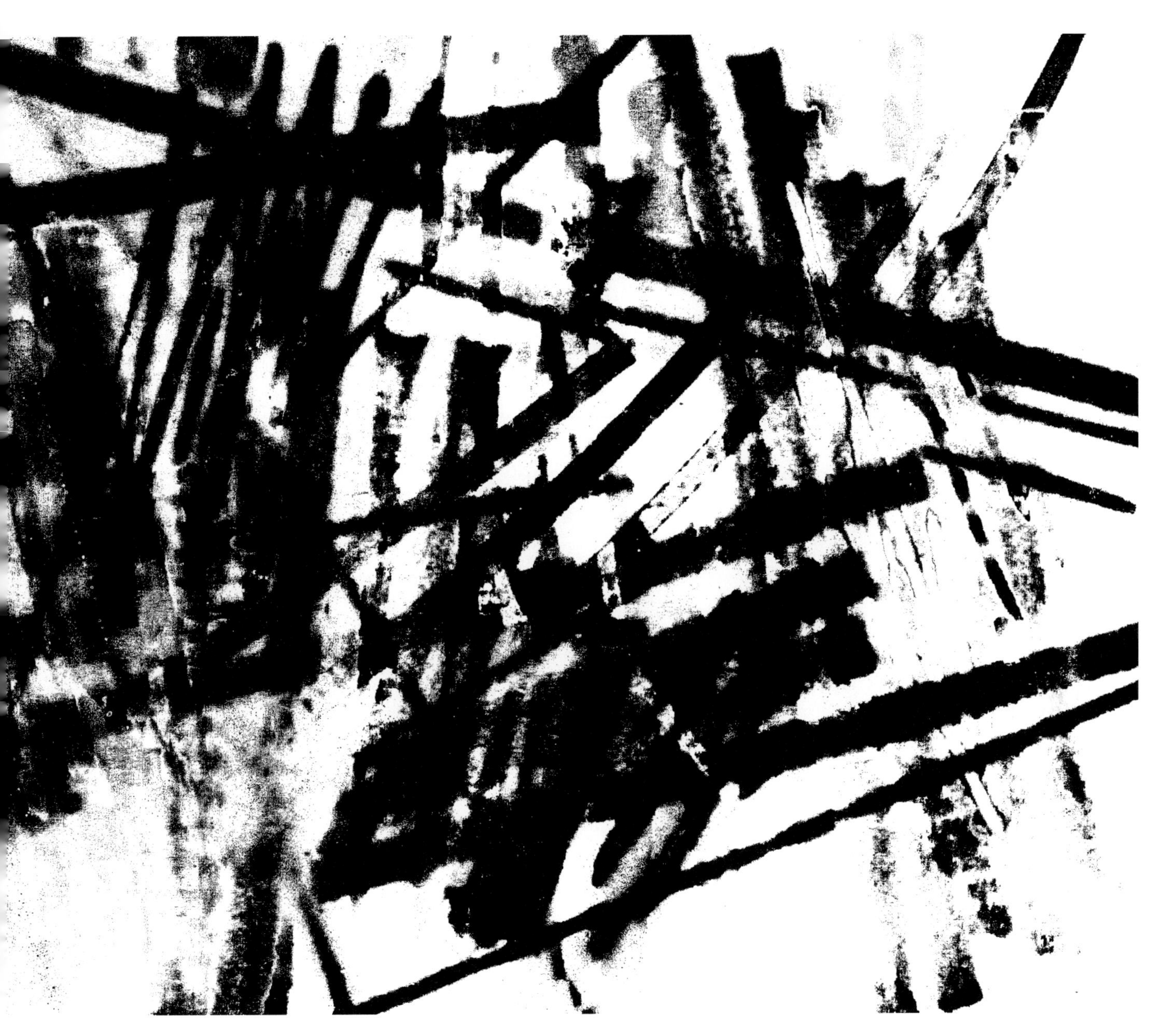

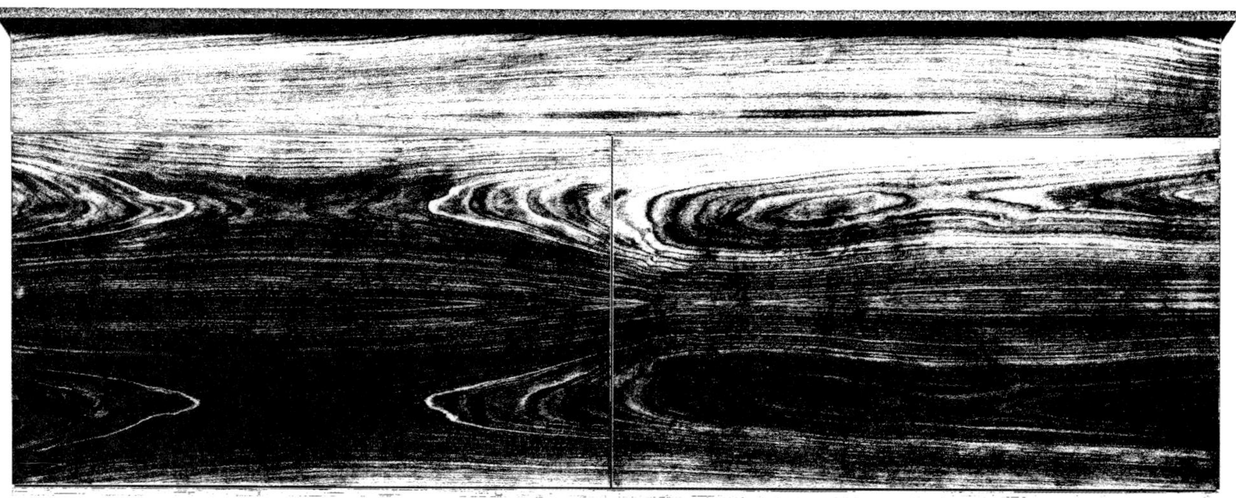

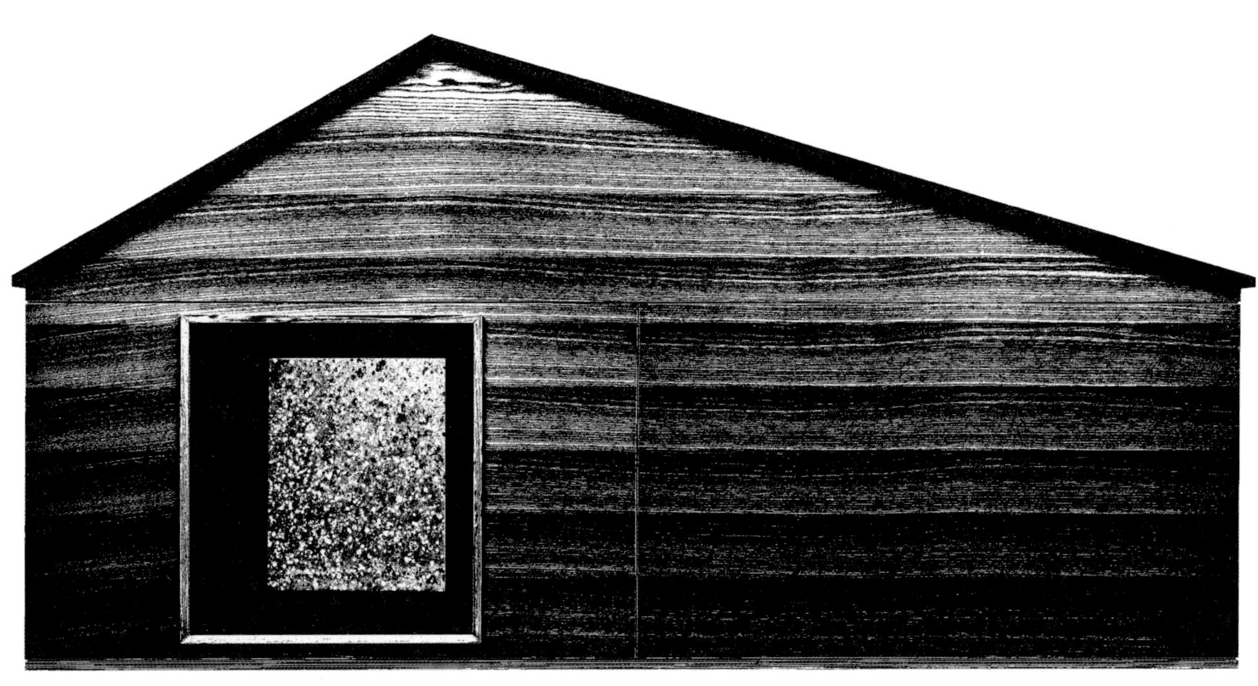

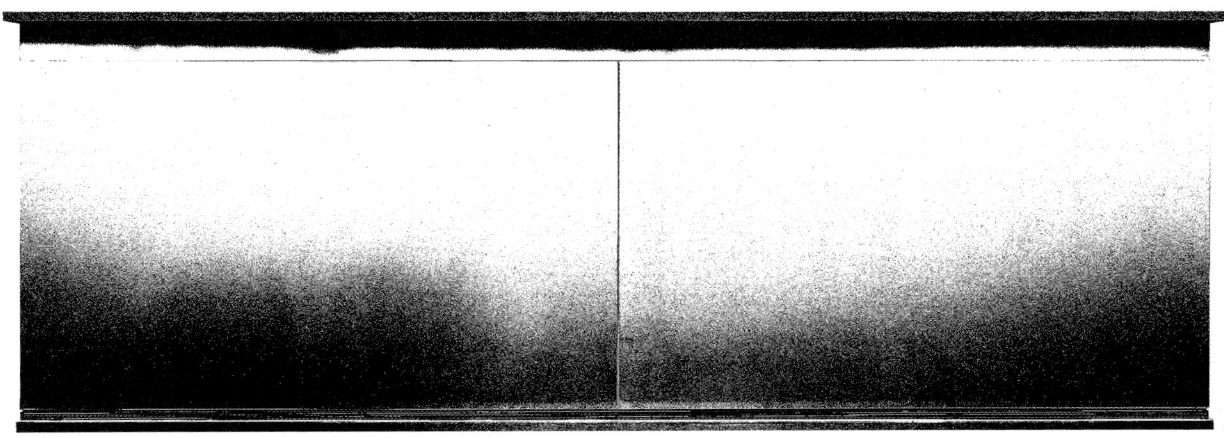

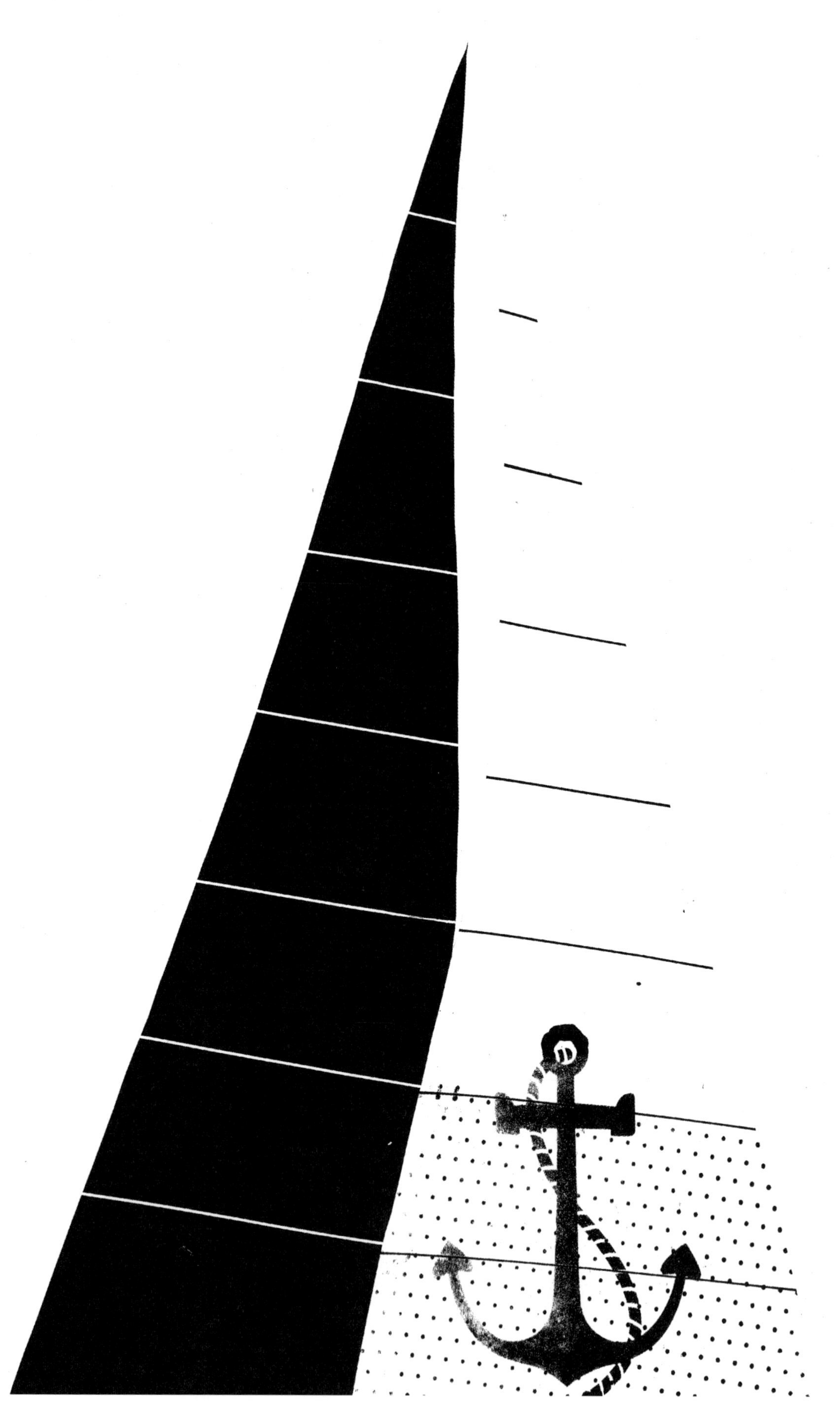

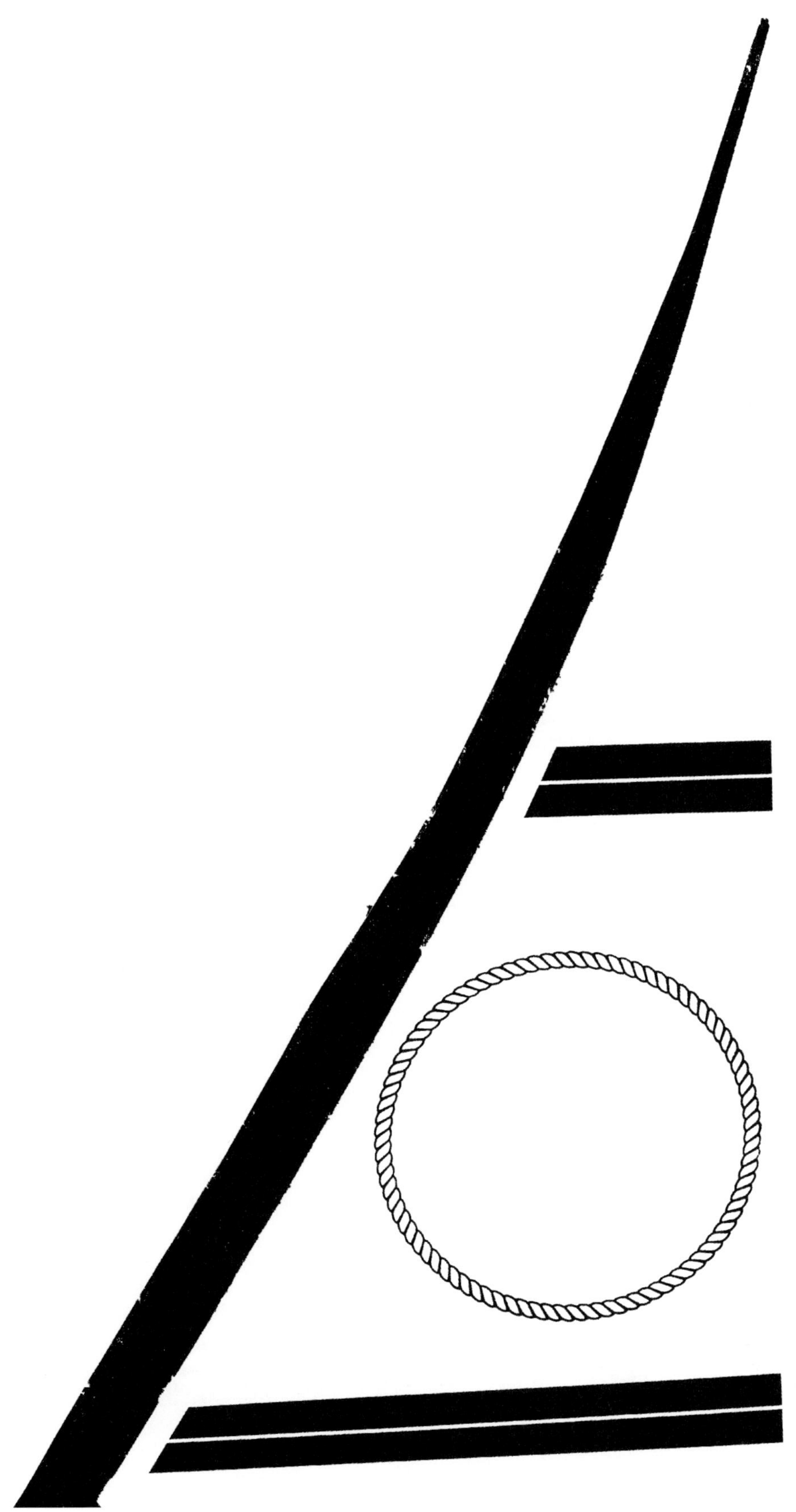

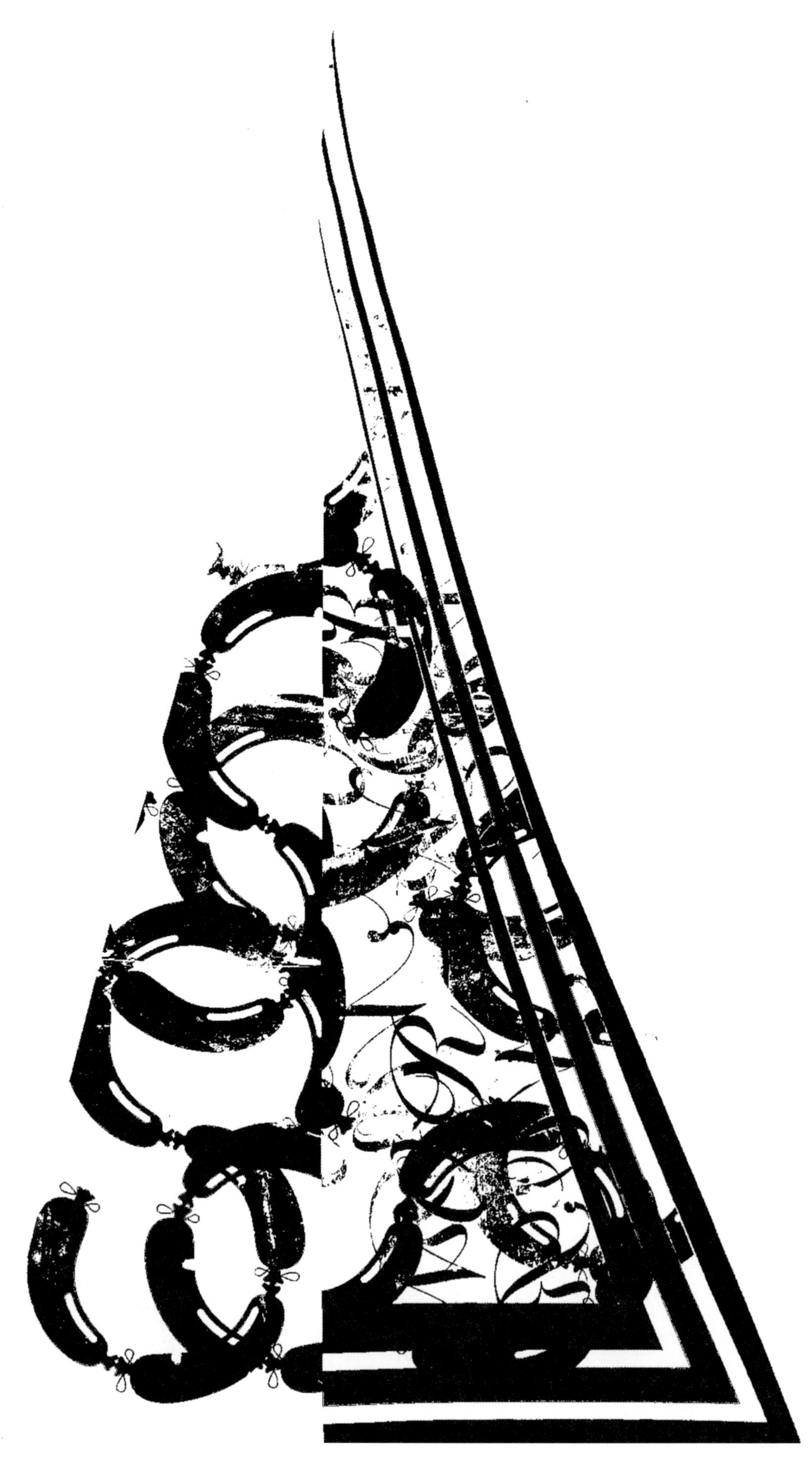

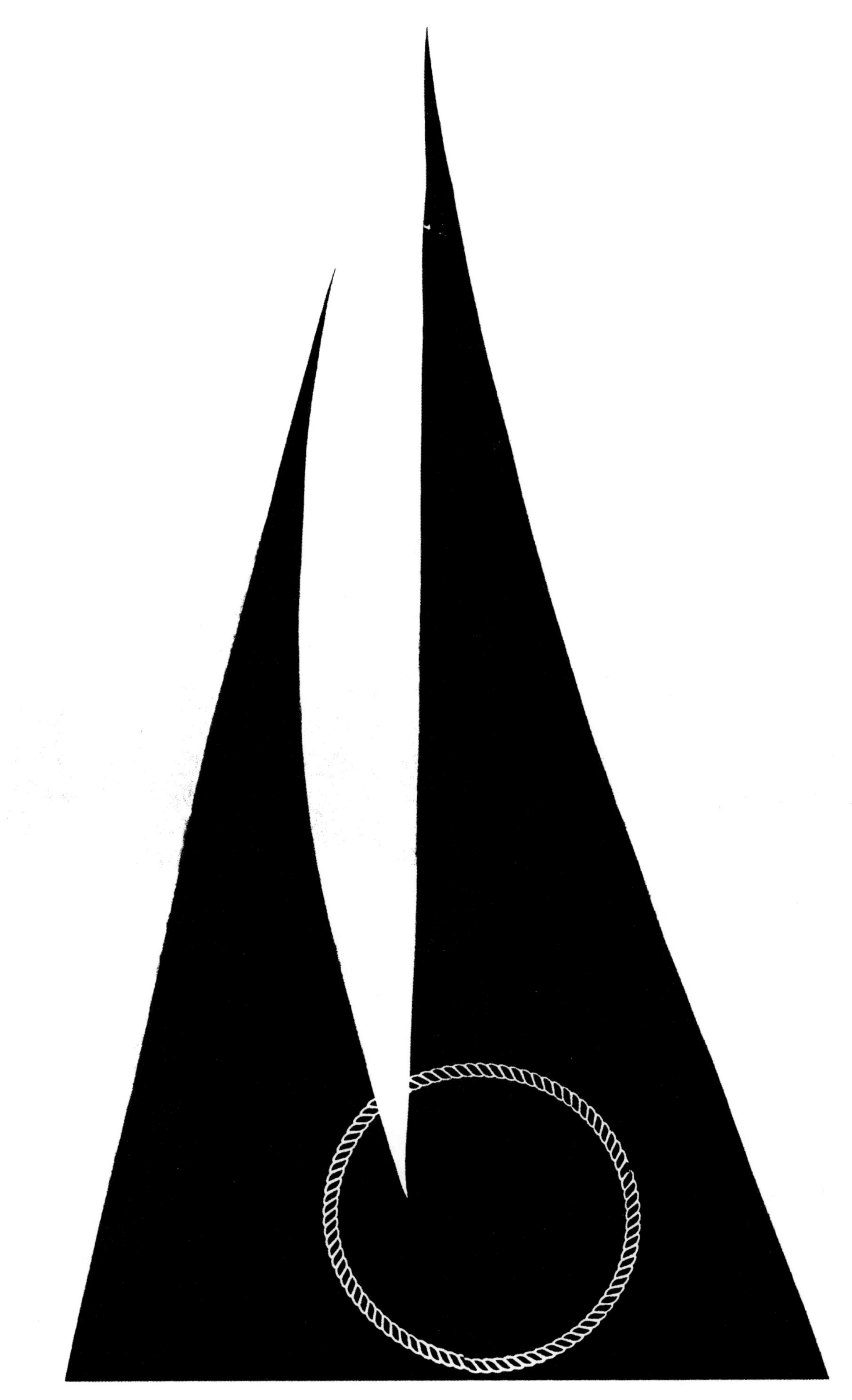

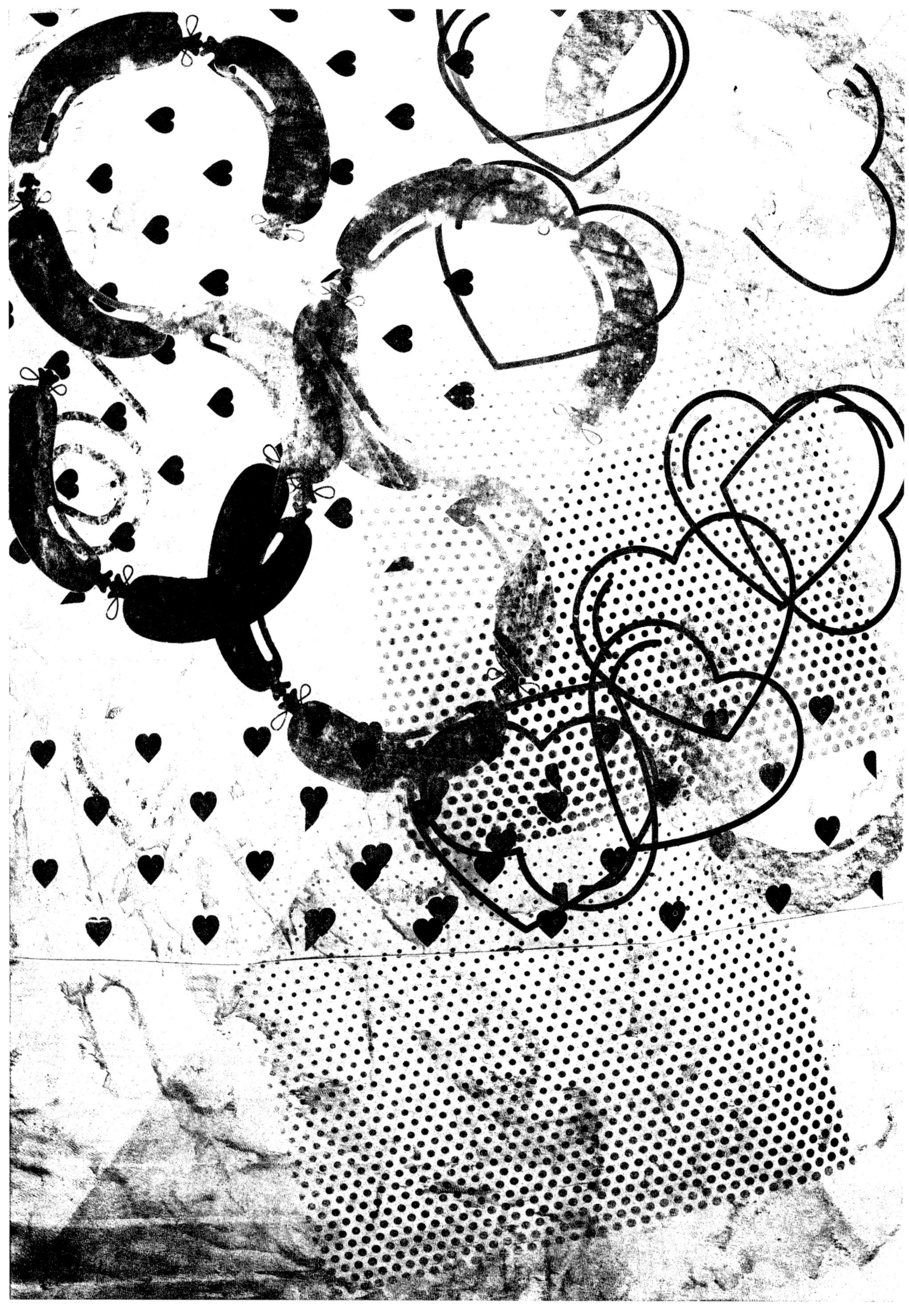

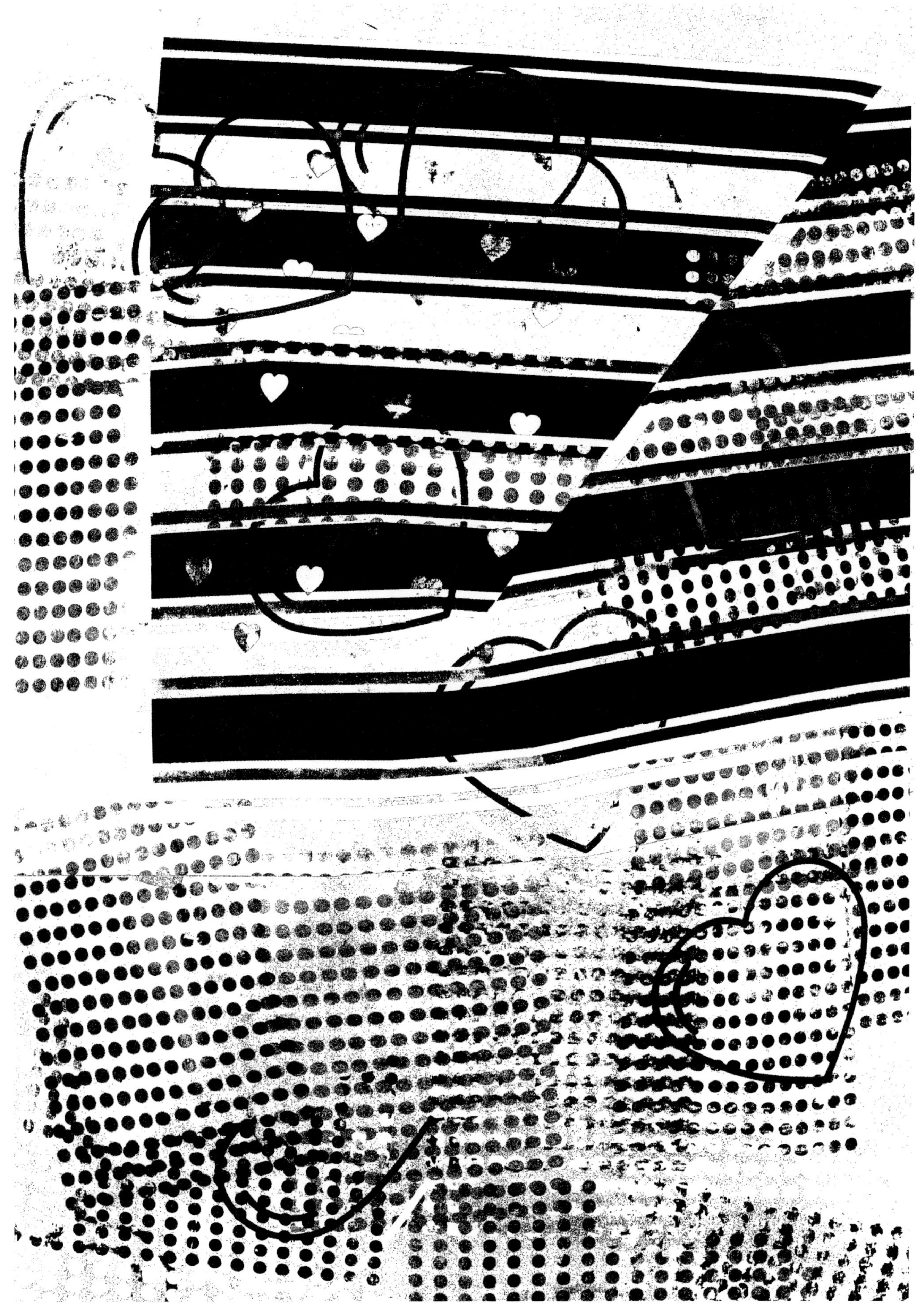

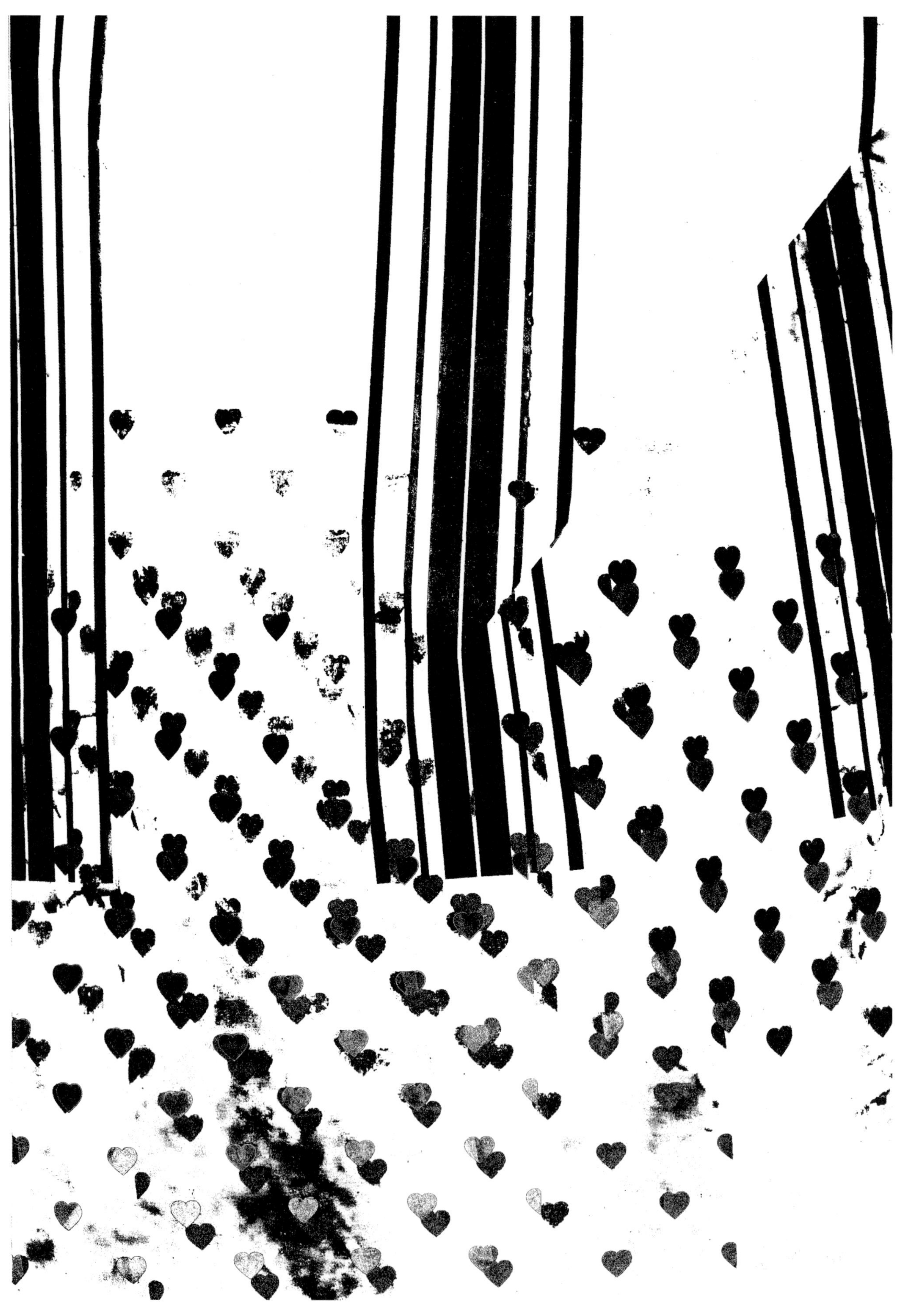

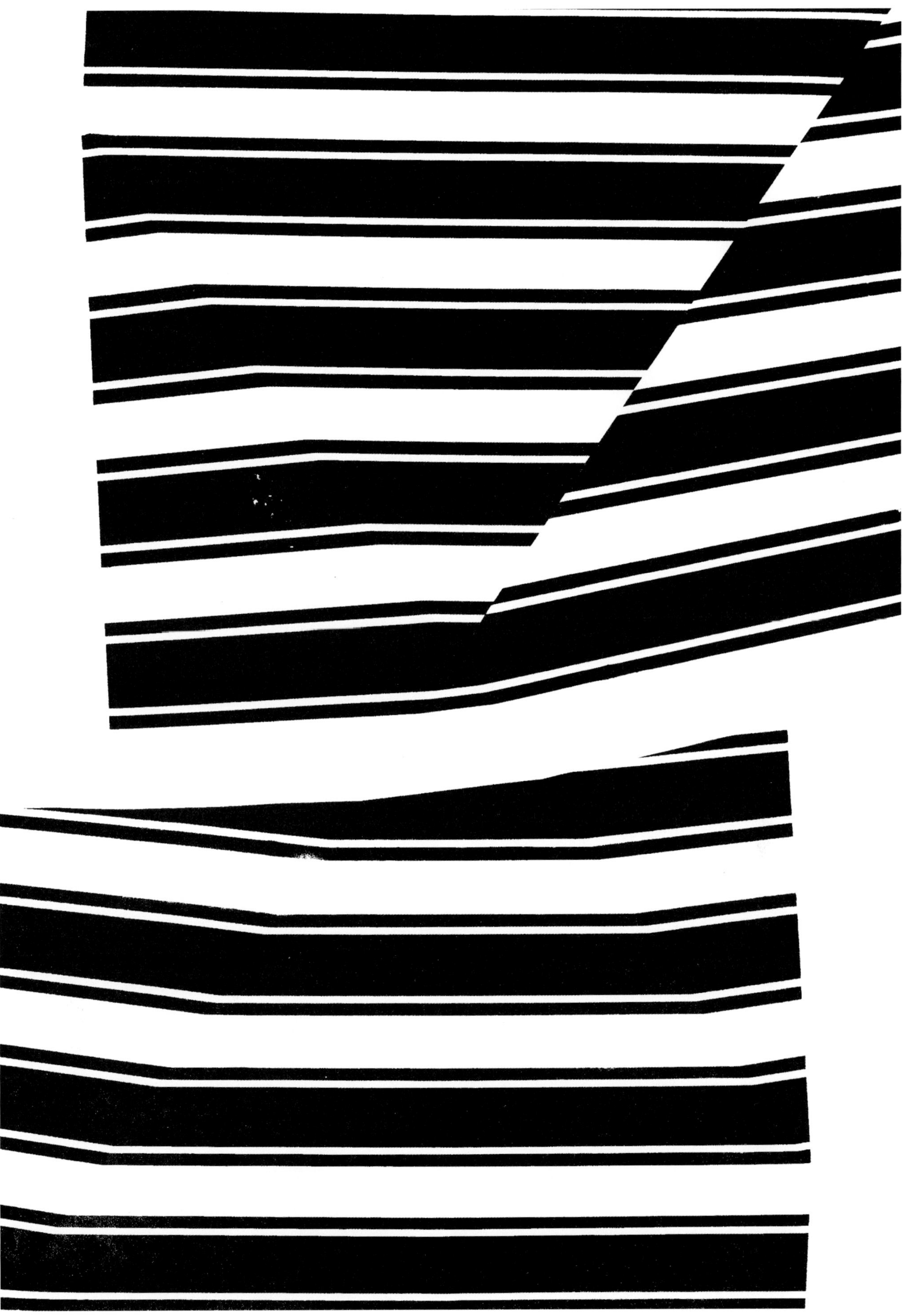

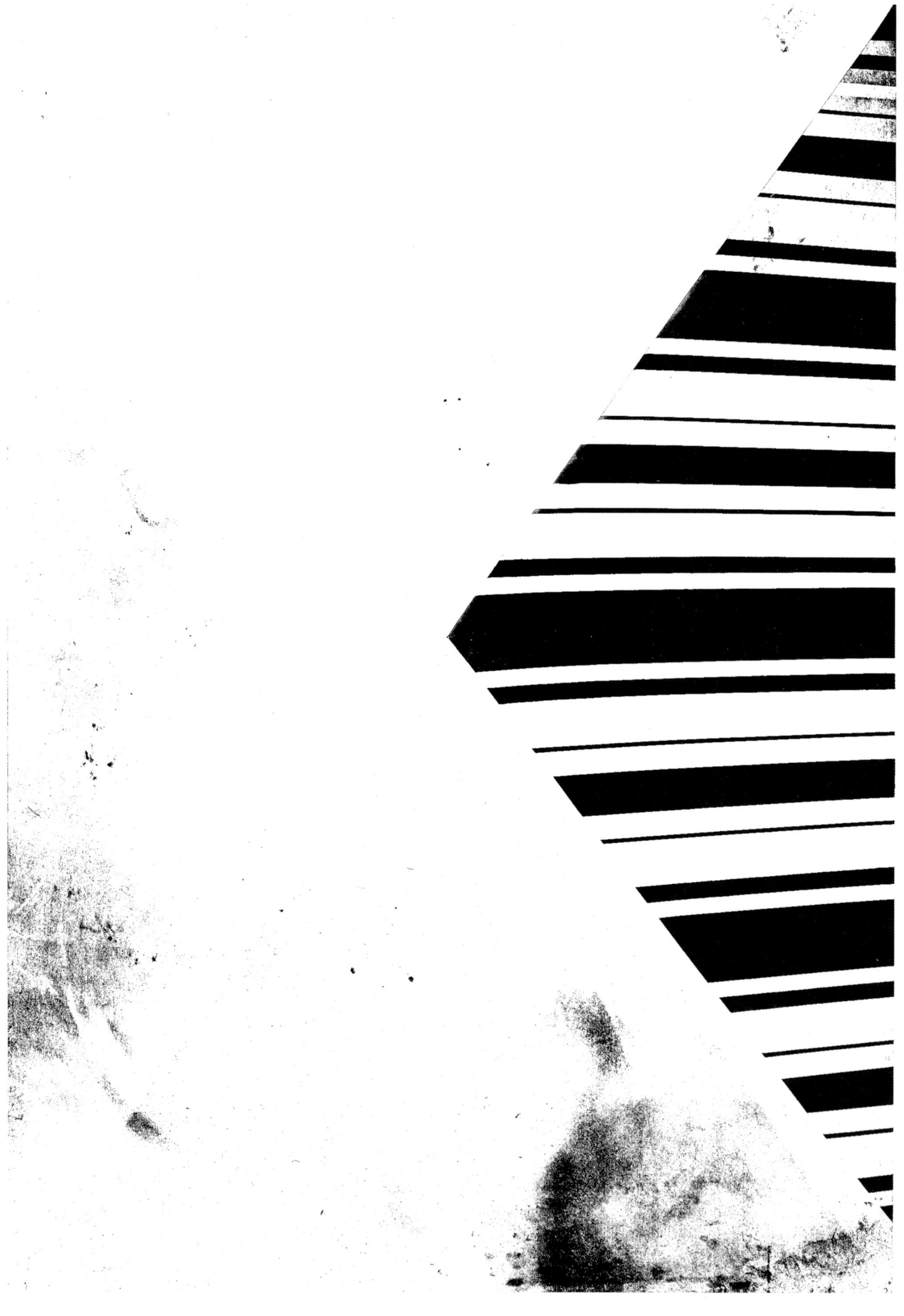

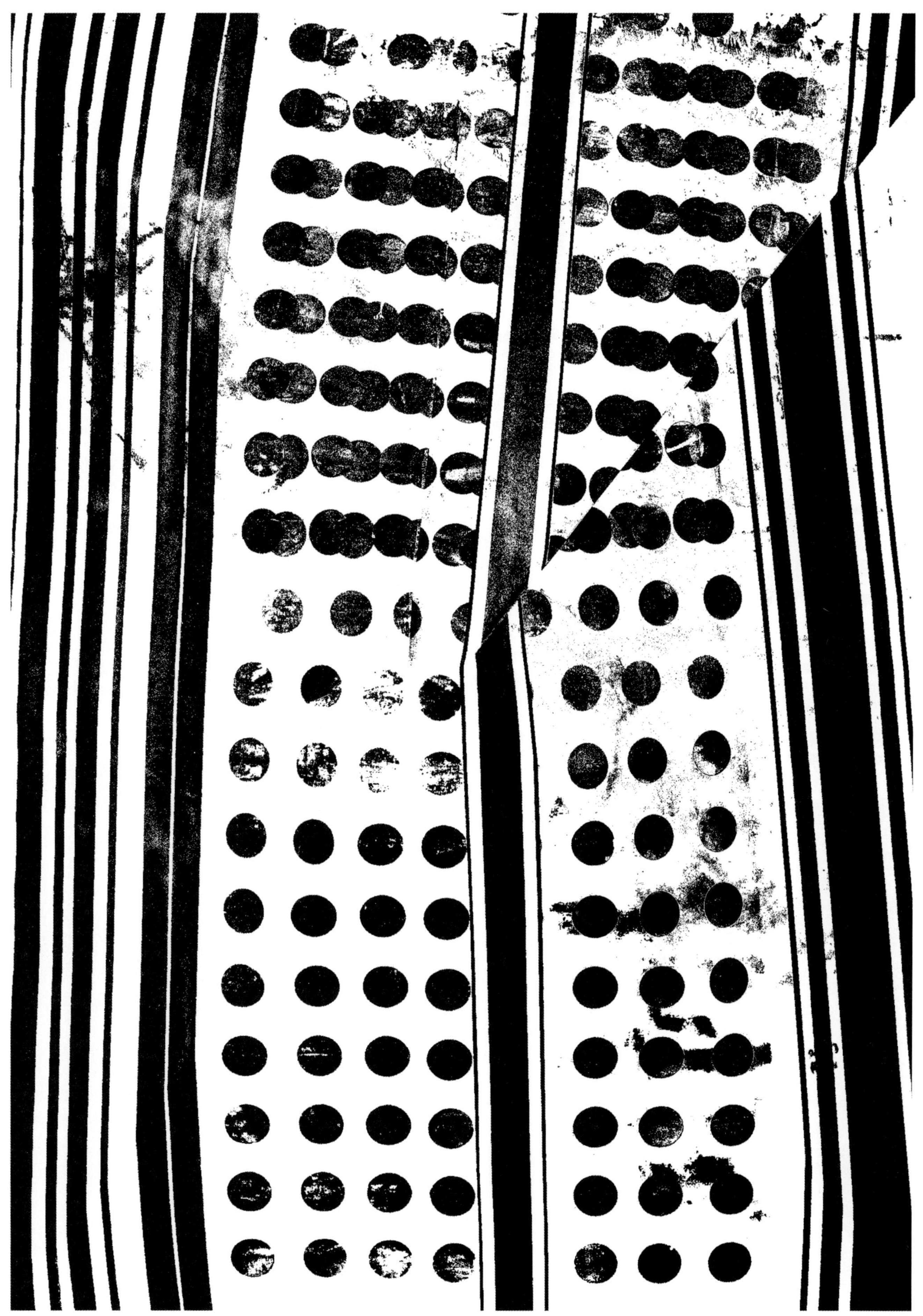

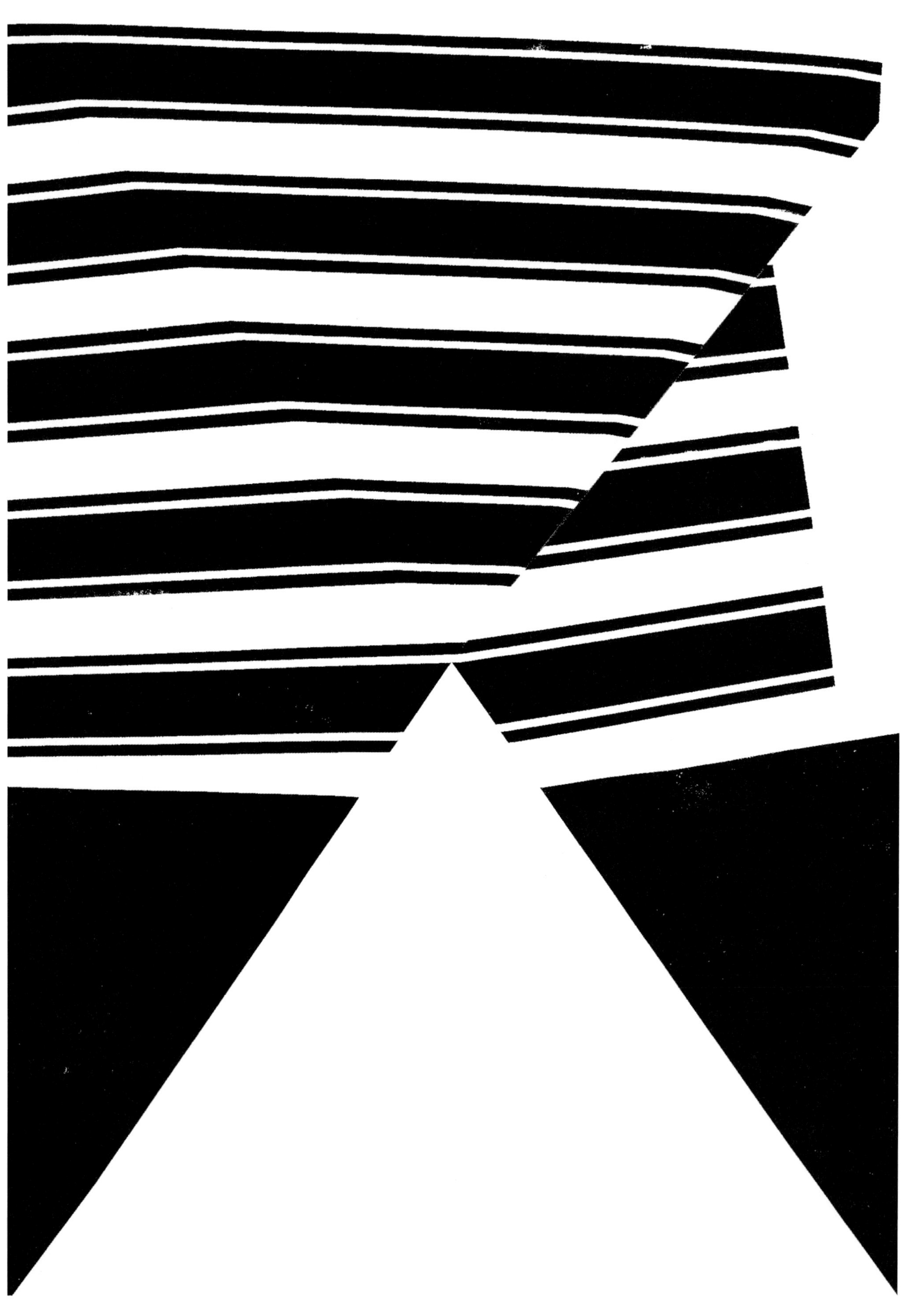

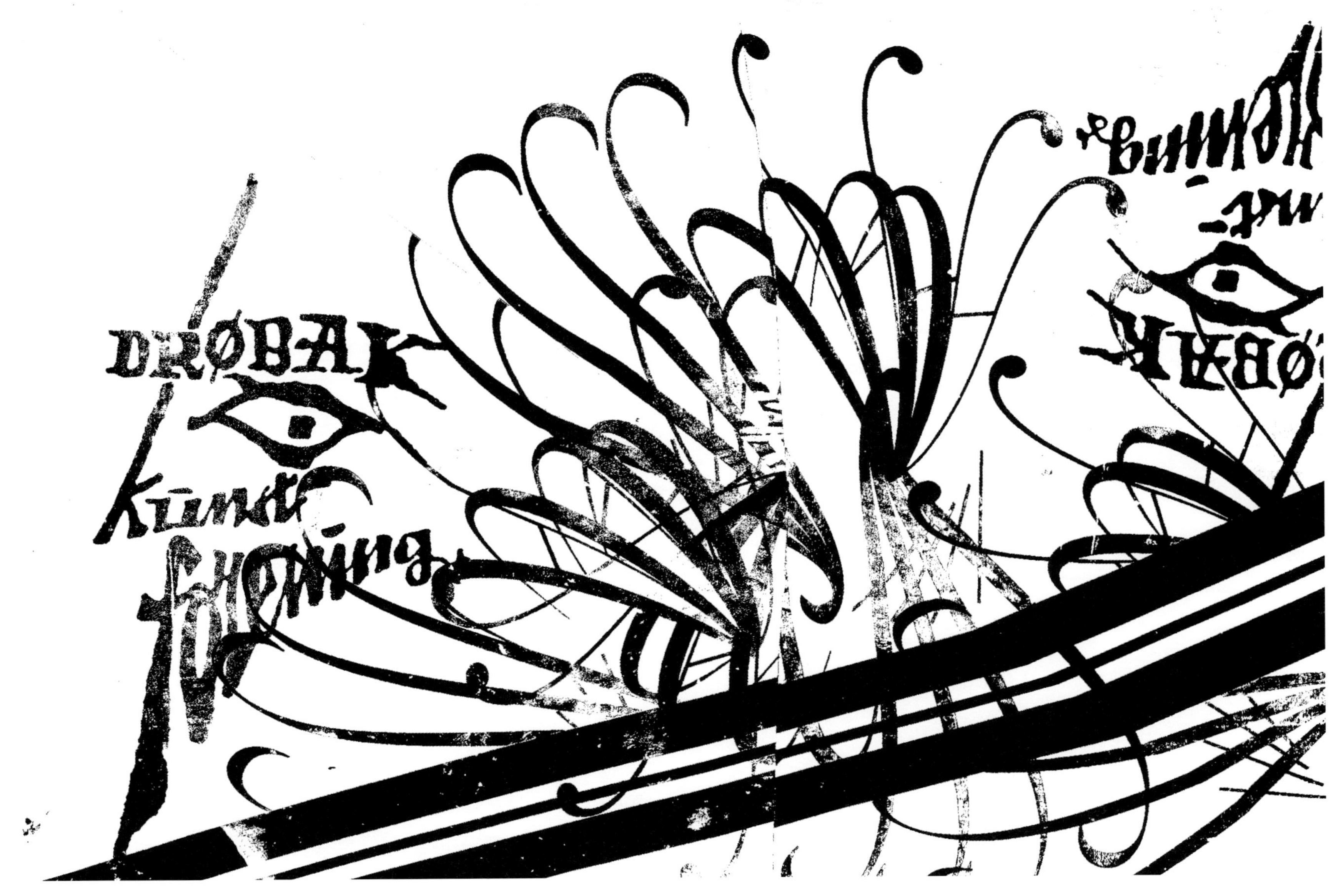

DRØBAK
kunst-
forening

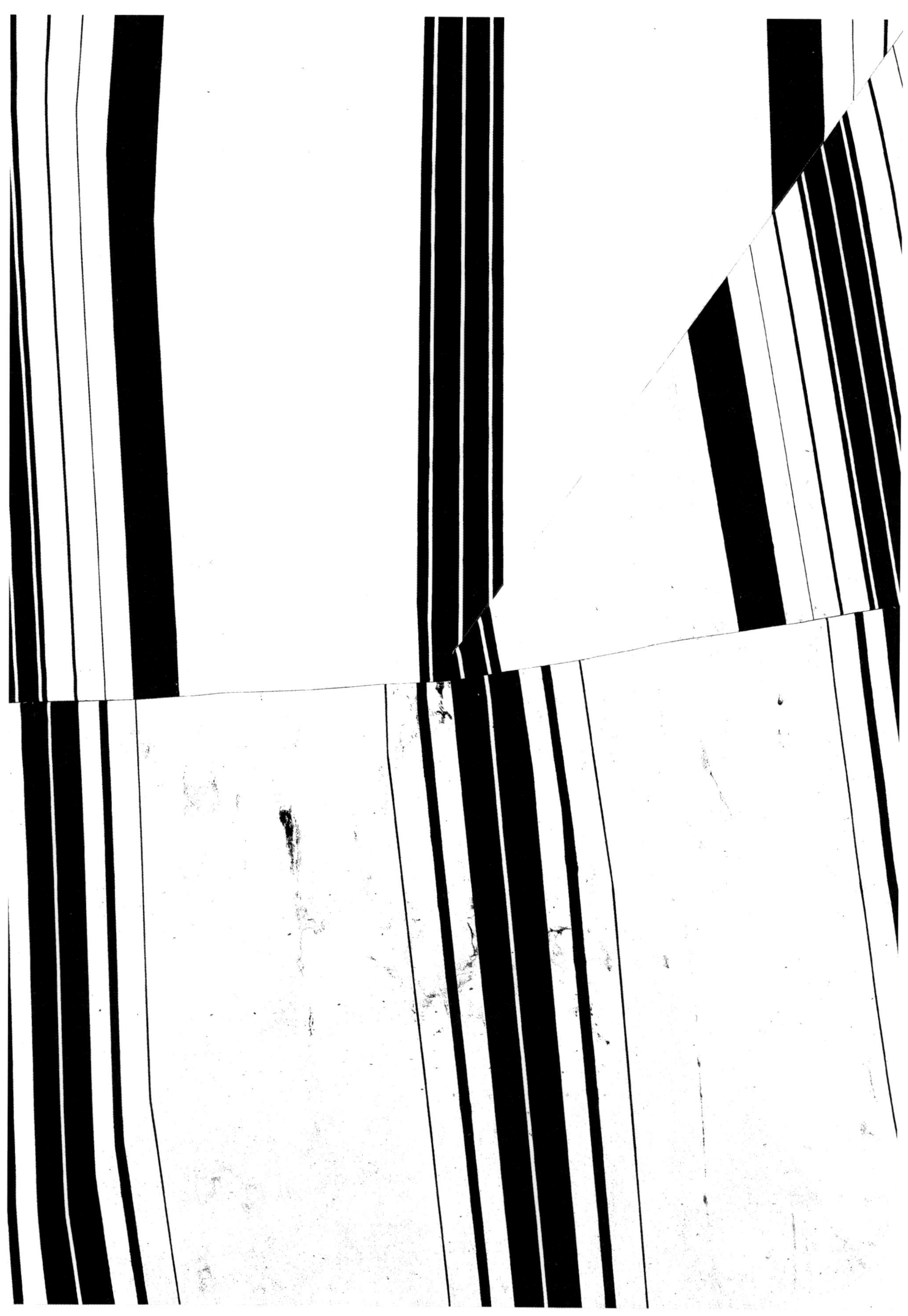

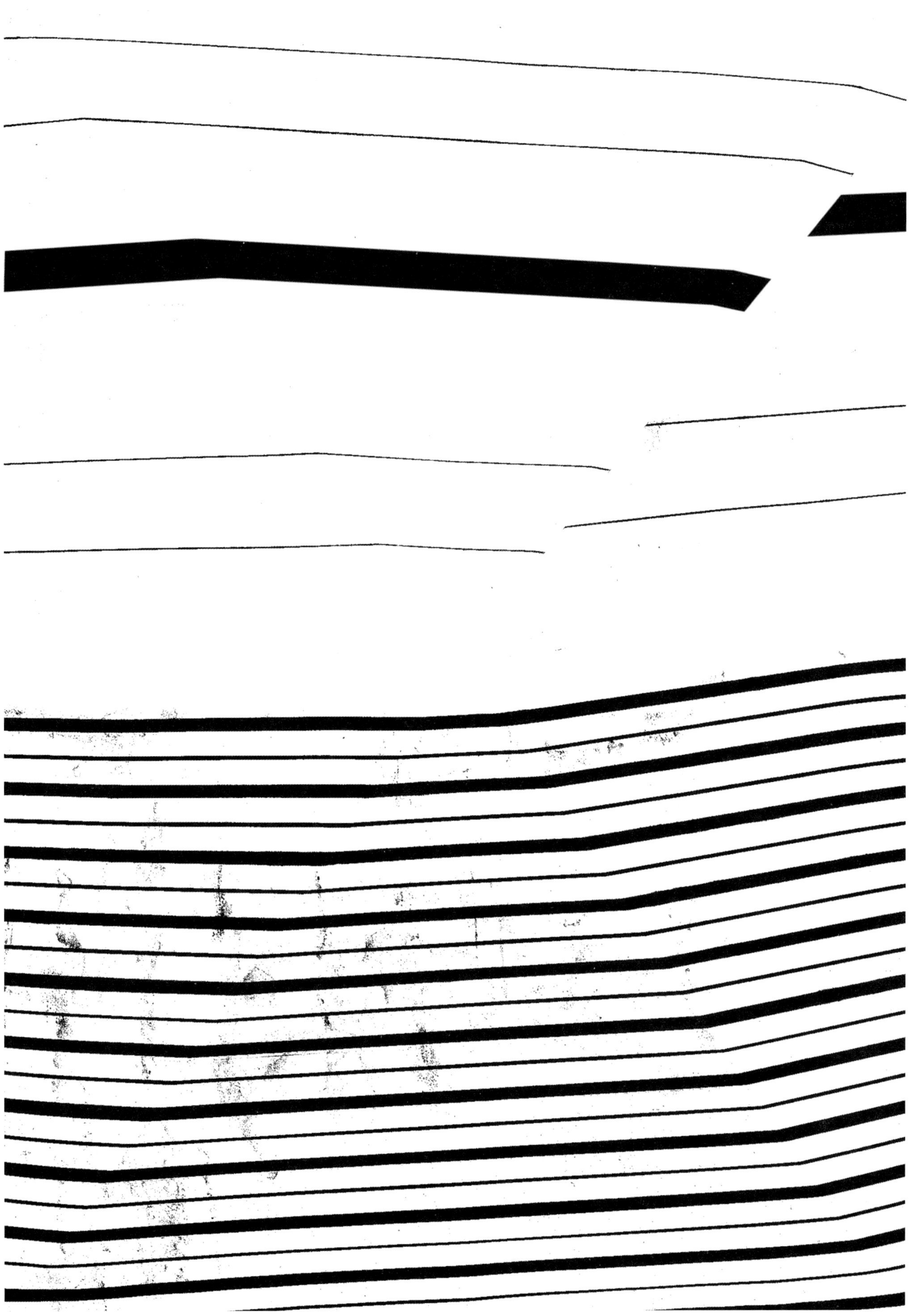

P. 1   Fredrik Værslev. *My Architecture (Malmoe #01)*, 2008–2011. Chromogenic print on fuji archival grey photo paper/Framed, 65 × 72 × 2.8 cm. Courtesy of the artist and STANDARD (OSLO), Oslo. Photo: Joe Clark

P. 2   Fredrik Værslev. *My Architecture (Malmoe #02)*, 2008–2011. Chromogenic print on fuji archival grey photo paper/Framed, 65 × 72 × 2.8 cm. Courtesy of the artist and STANDARD (OSLO), Oslo. Photo: Joe Clark

P. 3   Fredrik Værslev. *My Architecture (Oslo #12)*, 2008–2011. Chromogenic print on fuji archival grey photo paper/Framed, 65 × 72 × 2.8 cm. Courtesy of the artist and STANDARD (OSLO), Oslo. Photo: Joe Clark

P. 4   Fredrik Værslev. *My Architecture (Oslo #15)*, 2008–2011. Chromogenic print on fuji archival grey photo paper/Framed, 65 × 72 × 2.8 cm. Courtesy of the artist and STANDARD (OSLO), Oslo. Photo: Joe Clark

P. 5   Fredrik Værslev. *My Architecture (Oslo #11)*, 2008–2011. Chromogenic print on fuji archival grey photo paper/Framed, 65 × 72 × 2.8 cm. Courtesy of the artist and STANDARD (OSLO), Oslo. Photo: Joe Clark

P. 6   Fredrik Værslev. *My Architecture (Oslo #13)*, 2008–2011. Chromogenic print on fuji archival grey photo paper/Framed, 65 × 72 × 2.8 cm. Courtesy of the artist and STANDARD (OSLO), Oslo. Photo: Joe Clark

P. 7   Fredrik Værslev. *My Architecture (Oslo #14)*, 2008–2011. Chromogenic print on fuji archival grey photo paper/Framed. 65 × 72 × 2.8 cm. Courtesy of the artist and STANDARD (OSLO), Oslo. Photo: Joe Clark

P. 8   Nicolas Ceccaldi and Fredrik Værslev. *Shelf Painting (Butterfly)*, 2012. Spray paint, acrylic paint and matt transparent lacquer on pine plywood, brass hinges/antique doll, 76 × 55 × 17.5 cm. Private collection, Vestfossen.

Courtesy Studio of Fredrik Værslev/Nicolas Ceccaldi. Photo: Vegard Kleven

P. 9   Fredrik Værslev. *Shelf Paintings (Pottery in October #8)*, 2009. Mixed media sculpture: spray paint on plywood, birch shelf, brass screws and hinges/Acrylic squash print, 76 × 54 × 16 cm. Courtesy of the artist and STANDARD (OSLO), Oslo. Photo: Vegard Kleven

P. 10   Fredrik Værslev. *Shelf Paintings (Pottery in October #3)*, 2009. Mixed media sculpture: spray paint on plywood, birch shelf, brass screws and hinges/Ceramic objects, 76 × 54 × 16 cm. Collection of Nadia Bendriss and Pål Mitlid. Courtesy of the artist and STANDARD (OSLO), Oslo. Photo: Vegard Kleven

P. 11   Fredrik Værslev. *Shelf Paintings (Pottery in October #4)*, 2009. Mixed media sculpture: spray paint on plywood, birch shelf, brass screws and hinges/ Ceramic object, 76 × 54 × 16 cm. Courtesy of the artist and STANDARD (OSLO), Oslo. Photo: Vegard Kleven

P. 12   Fredrik Værslev. *Shelf Paintings (Pottery in October #5)*, 2009. Mixed media sculpture: spray paint on plywood, birch shelf, brass screws and hinges/Ceramic object, 76 × 54 × 16 cm. Private Collection, Oslo. Courtesy of STANDARD (OSLO), Oslo. Photo: Vegard Kleven

P. 13   Fredrik Værslev. *Shelf Paintings (Pottery in October #2)*, 2009. Mixed media sculpture: spray paint on plywood, birch shelf, brass screws and hinges/Acrylic squash print, 76 × 54 × 16 cm. Courtesy of the artists and STANDARD (OSLO), Oslo. Photo: Vegard Kleven

P. 14   Matias Faldbakken and Fredrik Værslev. *Shelf Paintings (Printing Money) #02*, 2012. Mixed media sculpture: Photo copy on 250g Daler-Rowney paper and staples on pine plywood, pine shelf, stainless steel screws and hinges, 76 × 54 × 18.4 cm. Courtesy of the artists and STANDARD (OSLO), Oslo. Photo: Vegard Kleven

P. 15   Matias Faldbakken and Fredrik Værslev. *Shelf Paintings (Printing Money) #05*, 2012. Mixed media sculpture: photo copy on 250g Daler-Rowney paper and staples on pine plywood, pine shelf, stainless steel screws and hinges, 76 × 54 × 18.4 cm. Courtesy of the artists and STANDARD (OSLO), Oslo. Photo: Vegard Kleven

P. 16   Matias Faldbakken and Fredrik Værslev. *Shelf Paintings (Printing Money) #04*, 2012. Mixed media sculpture: photo copy on 250g Daler-Rowney paper and staples on pine plywood, pine shelf, stainless steel screws and hinges, 76 × 54 × 18.4 cm. Private Collection, Vestfossen, Norway. Courtesy of STANDARD (OSLO), Oslo. Photo: Vegard Kleven

P. 17   Stewart Uoo and Fredrik Værslev. *Paisley Meets Plaid*, 2016. Plywood, acrylic decoupage, men's bicast leather harnesses, stainless steel, screws, 76 × 55 × 17.5 cm. Studio of Fredrik Værslev/Steward Uoo

P. 18   Stewart Uoo and Fredrik Værslev. *Rosy Posies*, 2016. Plywood, acrylic decoupage, men's bicast leather harnesses, stainless steel, screws, 76 × 55 × 17.5 cm. Studio of Fredrik Værslev/Steward Uoo

P. 19   Josh Smith and Fredrik Værslev. *Shelf Paintings (Untitled VIII)*, 2016. Mixed media sculpture: Oil paint on pine plywood, pine shelf, stainless steel screws and hinges, 76 × 54 × 18.4 cm. Courtesy of the artists and STANDARD (OSLO), Oslo. Photo: Vegard Kleven

P. 20   Josh Smith and Fredrik Værslev. *Shelf Paintings (Untitled V)*, 2016. Mixed media sculpture: Oil paint on pine plywood, pine shelf, stainless steel screws and hinges, 76 × 54 × 18.4 cm. Courtesy of the artists and STANDARD (OSLO), Oslo. Photo: Vegard Kleven

P. 21   Josh Smith and Fredrik Værslev. *Shelf Paintings (Untitled IV)*, 2016. Mixed media sculpture: Oil paint on pine plywood, pine shelf, stainless steel screws and hinges, 76 × 54 × 18.4 cm.

Courtesy of the artists and STANDARD (OSLO), Oslo. Photo: Vegard Kleven

P. 22   Josh Smith and Fredrik Værslev. *Shelf Paintings (Untitled III)*, 2016. Mixed media sculpture: Oil paint on pine plywood, pine shelf, stainless steel screws and hinges, 76 × 54 × 18.4 cm. Courtesy of the artists and STANDARD (OSLO), Oslo. Photo: Vegard Kleven

P. 23   Josh Smith and Fredrik Værslev. *Shelf Paintings (Untitled I)*, 2016. Mixed media sculpture: Oil paint on pine plywood, pine shelf, stainless steel screws and hinges, 76 × 54 × 18.4 cm. Courtesy of the artists and STANDARD (OSLO), Oslo. Photo: Vegard Kleven

P. 24   Allison Katz and Fredrik Værslev. *Shelf Painting 3 (Traffic, 2014)*, 2016. Rice, acrylic on wood, 76 × 55 × 17.5 cm. Studio of Fredrik Værslev/Allison Katz

P. 25   Allison Katz and Fredrik Værslev. *Shelf Painting 2 (Sand Painting, 2009–2013)*, 2016. Rice, acrylic, sand on wood, 76 × 55 × 17.5 cm. Studio of Fredrik Værslev/ Allison Katz

P. 26   Allison Katz and Fredrik Værslev. *Shelf Painting 4 (Pears in a room, 2012)*, 2016. Rice, acrylic on wood, 76 × 55 × 17.5 cm. Studio of Fredrik Værslev/Allison Katz

P. 27   Allison Katz and Fredrik Værslev. *Shelf Painting 1 (Black Pears, 2009)*, 2016. Rice, acrylic on wood, 76 × 55 × 17.5 cm. Studio of Fredrik Værslev/Allison Katz

P. 28   Fredrik Værslev. *Untitled*, 2010. Spray paint, house paint, acrylic paint, corrosion protective spray and White spirit on canvas/ wooden stretcher, 190 × 150 × 4 cm. Fekene collection, Tønsberg. Courtesy of the artist. Photo: Vegard Kleven

P. 29   Fredrik Værslev. *Untitled*, 2011. Spray paint, house paint, acrylic paint, corrosion protective spray and white spirit on canvas/ wooden stretcher, 195 × 145 × 4 cm. Private collection. Courtesy of the artist. Photo: Vegard Kleven

P. 30   Fredrik Værslev.
Untitled, 2011. Spray paint,
house paint, acrylic paint,
corrosion protective spray and
White spirit on canvas/wooden
stretcher, 195 × 145 × 4 cm.
Private collection. Courtesy of
the artist. Photo: Vegard Kleven

P. 31   Fredrik Værslev.
Untitled, 2011. Spray paint,
house paint, acrylic paint,
corrosion protective spray
and White spirit on
canvas/wooden stretcher,
195 × 145 × 3.5 cm. Private
collection. Courtesy of the
artist. Photo: Vegard Kleven

P. 32   Fredrik Værslev.
Untitled, 2011. Spray paint,
house paint, acrylic paint,
corrosion protective spray and
White spirit on canvas/wooden
stretcher, 195 × 145 × 4 cm.
Studio of Fredrik Værslev.
Courtesy of the artist.
Photo: Vegard Kleven

P. 33   Fredrik Værslev.
Untitled, 2011. Spray paint,
house paint, acrylic paint,
corrosion protective spray
and White spirit on
canvas/wooden stretcher,
195 × 145 × 4 cm.
Erling Kagge's collection.
Courtesy of the artist.
Photo: Vegard Kleven

P. 34   Fredrik Værslev.
Untitled, 2011. Spray paint,
house paint, acrylic paint,
corrosion protective spray
and White spirit on
canvas/wooden stretcher,
195 × 155.0 × 4 cm. Private
collection. Courtesy of the
artist. Photo: Vegard Kleven

P. 35   Fredrik Værslev.
Untitled, 2011. Spray paint,
house paint, acrylic paint,
corrosion protective spray and
White spirit on canvas/wooden
stretcher, 195 × 145 × 4 cm.
Private collection. Courtesy of
the artist. Photo: Vegard Kleven

P. 36   Fredrik Værslev.
Untitled, 2010. Spray paint,
house paint, acrylic paint,
corrosion protective spray and
White spirit on canvas/wooden
stretcher, 185 × 145 × 4 cm.
Private collection. Courtesy of
the artist. Photo: Vegard Kleven

P. 37   Fredrik Værslev.
Untitled, 2010. Spray paint,
house paint, acrylic paint,
corrosion protective spray
and White spirit on canvas/

wooden stretcher, 195 ×
145 × 4 cm. Eivind Aadland's
collection. Courtesy of the
artist. Photo: Vegard Kleven

P. 38   Fredrik Værslev.
Garden Painting AF #1, 2018.
Enamel paint, furniture oil
and spray paint on spruce/
steel support, 193 × 88 ×
26.5 cm. Studio of Fredrik
Værslev. Courtesy of the artist.
Photo: Vegard Kleven

P. 39   Fredrik Værslev.
Garden Painting AF #2, 2018.
Enamel paint, furniture oil
and spray paint on spruce/
steel support, 193 × 88 ×
26.5 cm. Studio of Fredrik
Værslev. Courtesy of the artist.
Photo: Vegard Kleven

P. 40   Fredrik Værslev.
Garden Painting AF #3, 2018.
Enamel paint, furniture oil and
spray paint on spruce/steel
support, 193 × 88 × 26.5 cm.
Studio of Fredrik Værslev.
Courtesy of the artist.
Photo: Vegard Kleven

P. 41   Fredrik Værslev.
Garden Painting AF #4, 2018.
Enamel paint, furniture oil and
spray paint on spruce/steel
support, 193 × 88 × 26.5 cm.
Studio of Fredrik Værslev.
Courtesy of the artist.
Photo: Vegard Kleven

P. 42   Fredrik Værslev.
Garden Painting AF #5, 2018.
Enamel paint, furniture oil and
spray paint on spruce/steel
support, 193 × 88 × 26.5 cm.
Studio of Fredrik Værslev.
Courtesy of the artist.
Photo: Vegard Kleven

P. 43   Fredrik Værslev.
Garden Painting AF #6, 2018.
Enamel paint, furniture oil and
spray paint on spruce/steel
support, 193 × 88 × 26.5 cm.
Studio of Fredrik Værslev.
Courtesy of the artist.
Photo: Vegard Kleven

P. 44   Fredrik Værslev.
Garden Painting AF #7, 2018.
Enamel paint, furniture oil
and spray paint on spruce/
steel support, 193 × 88 ×
26.5 cm. Studio of Fredrik
Værslev. Courtesy of the artist.
Photo: Vegard Kleven

P. 45   Fredrik Værslev.
Garden Painting AF #8, 2018.
Enamel paint, furniture oil
and spray paint on spruce/
steel support, 193 × 88 ×

26.5 cm. Studio of Fredrik
Værslev. Courtesy of the artist.
Photo: Vegard Kleven

P. 46   Fredrik Værslev.
Garden Painting AF #9, 2018.
Enamel paint, furniture oil and
spray paint on spruce/steel
support, 193 × 88 × 26.5 cm.
Studio of Fredrik Værslev.
Courtesy of the artist.
Photo: Vegard Kleven

P. 48   Fredrik Værslev.
Untitled, 2012–2018. Spray
paint, primer, and White spirit
on cotton canvas/wooden
stretcher, 230 × 200 × 3.5 cm.
Studio of Fredrik Værslev.
Courtesy of the artist.
Photo: Vegard Kleven

P. 49   Fredrik Værslev.
Untitled, 2012–2018. Spray
paint, primer, and White spirit
on cotton canvas/wooden
stretcher, 230 × 200 × 3.5 cm.
Studio of Fredrik Værslev.
Courtesy of the artist.
Photo: Vegard Kleven

P. 50   Fredrik Værslev.
Untitled, 2012–2018. Spray
paint, primer, and White spirit
on cotton canvas/wooden
stretcher, 230 × 200 × 3.5 cm.
Studio of Fredrik Værslev.
Courtesy of the artist
Photo: Vegard Kleven

P.51   Fredrik Værslev.
Untitled, 2012–2018. Spray
paint, primer, and White spirit
on cotton canvas/wooden
stretcher, 230 × 200 × 3.5 cm.
Studio of Fredrik Værslev.
Courtesy of the artist.
Photo: Vegard Kleven

P.52   Fredrik Værslev.
Untitled, 2012–2018. Spray
paint, primer, and White spirit
on cotton canvas/wooden
stretcher, 230 × 200 × 3.5 cm.
Studio of Fredrik Værslev.
Courtesy of the artist.
Photo: Vegard Kleven

P. 53   Fredrik Værslev.
Untitled, 2012–2018. Spray
paint, primer, and White spirit
on cotton canvas/wooden
stretcher, 230 × 200 × 3.5 cm.
Studio of Fredrik Værslev.
Courtesy of the artist.
Photo: Vegard Kleven

P. 54   Fredrik Værslev.
Untitled, 2012–2018. Spray
paint, primer, and White spirit
on cotton canvas/wooden
stretcher, 230 × 200 × 3.5 cm.
Studio of Fredrik Værslev.

Courtesy of the artist.
Photo: Vegard Kleven

P. 55   Fredrik Værslev.
Untitled, 2012–2018. Spray
paint, primer, and White spirit
on cotton canvas/wooden
stretcher, 230 × 200 × 3.5 cm.
Studio of Fredrik Værslev.
Courtesy of the artist.
Photo: Vegard Kleven

P. 56   Fredrik Værslev.
Untitled, 2012–2018. Spray
paint, primer, and White spirit
on cotton canvas/wooden
stretcher, 230 × 200 × 3.5 cm.
Studio of Fredrik Værslev.
Courtesy of the artist.
Photo: Vegard Kleven

P. 57   Fredrik Værslev.
Untitled, 2012–2018. Spray
paint, primer, and White spirit
on cotton canvas/wooden
stretcher, 230 × 200 × 3.5 cm.
Studio of Fredrik Værslev.
Courtesy of the artist.
Photo: Vegard Kleven

P. 58   Fredrik Værslev.
Untitled, 2012–2018. Spray
paint, primer, and White spirit
on cotton canvas/wooden
stretcher, 230 × 200 × 3.5 cm.
Studio of Fredrik Værslev.
Courtesy of the artist.
Photo: Vegard Kleven

P. 59   Fredrik Værslev.
Untitled, 2012–2018. Spray
paint, primer, and White spirit
on cotton canvas/wooden
stretcher, 230 × 200 × 3.5 cm.
Studio of Fredrik Værslev.
Courtesy of the artist.
Photo: Vegard Kleven

P. 60   Fredrik Værslev.
Untitled, 2012–2018. Spray
paint, primer, and White spirit
on cotton canvas/wooden
stretcher, 230 × 200 × 3.5 cm.
Studio of Fredrik Værslev.
Courtesy of the artist.
Photo: Vegard Kleven

P. 61   Fredrik Værslev.
Untitled, 2012–2018. Spray
paint, primer, and White spirit
on cotton canvas/wooden
stretcher, 230 × 200 × 3.5 cm.
Studio of Fredrik Værslev.
Courtesy of the artist.
Photo: Vegard Kleven

P. 62   Fredrik Værslev.
Untitled (Choppy Times),
2012–2013. Acrylic paint,
primer, and White spirit
on cotton canvas/wooden
stretcher, 220 × 198 × 4 cm.
Private collection, Brussels.

Courtesy of the artist.
Photo: Vegard Kleven

P. 63   Fredrik Værslev.
Untitled (Choppy Times),
2012–2013. Acrylic paint,
primer, and White spirit on
cotton canvas/wooden
stretcher, 220 × 198 × 4 cm.
Private collection. Courtesy of
the artist. Photo: Vegard Kleven

P. 64   Fredrik Værslev.
Untitled (Choppy Times),
2012–2013. Acrylic paint,
primer, and White spirit on
cotton canvas/wooden
stretcher, 220 × 198 × 4 cm.
Bjørholdt collection. Courtesy of
the artist. Photo: Vegard Kleven

P. 65   Fredrik Værslev.
Untitled (Choppy Times),
2012–2013. Acrylic paint,
primer, and White spirit on
cotton canvas/wooden
stretcher, 220 × 198 × 4 cm.
Private collection. Courtesy of
the artist. Photo: Vegard Kleven

P. 66   Fredrik Værslev.
Untitled (Choppy Times),
2012–2013. Acrylic paint,
primer, and White spirit on
cotton canvas/wooden stretcher,
220 × 198 × 4 cm. Courtesy
of the artist and Gio Marconi,
Milan. Photo: Vegard Kleven

P. 67   Fredrik Værslev.
Untitled (Choppy Times),
2012–2013. Acrylic paint,
primer, and White spirit on
cotton canvas/wooden
stretcher, 220 × 198 × 4 cm.
Private collection, Rome.
Courtesy of the artist.
Photo: Vegard Kleven

P. 68   Fredrik Værslev.
Untitled (Choppy Times),
2012–2013. Acrylic paint,
primer and White spirit on
cotton canvas/wooden
stretcher, 220 × 198 × 4 cm,
Jansen Collection, Berlin.
Courtesy of the artist.
Photo: Vegard Kleven

P. 70   Fredrik Værslev.
Untitled, 2014. Spray paint
on canvas, 201 × 478 × 4 cm.
Astrup Fearnley Collection.
Courtesy of the artist and
STANDARD (OSLO), Oslo.
Photo: Vegard Kleven

P. 72   Fredrik Værslev.
Untitled, 2018. Spray paint
on canvas, 201 × 464 × 4 cm.
Studio of Fredrik Værslev.
Courtesy of the artist.
Photo: Vegard Kleven

P. 74   Fredrik Værslev.
Untitled, 2016–2018. House:
MDF, veneer (plywood), pine,
acrylic paint, acrylic spray
paint, acrylic transparent
varnish with UV-filter and
galvanised screws. Paintings:
spray paint, turpentine on
cotton canvas/wooden
stretcher, 35 × 202 × 62 cm.
Studio of Fredrik Værslev.
Courtesy of the artist.
Photo: Vegard Kleven

P. 75   Fredrik Værslev.
Untitled, 2016–2018. House:
MDF, veneer (plywood), pine,
acrylic paint, acrylic spray
paint, acrylic transparent
varnish with UV-filter and
galvanised screws. Paintings:
spray paint, turpentine on
cotton canvas/wooden
stretcher, 35 × 202 × 62 cm.
Studio of Fredrik Værslev.
Courtesy of the artist.
Photo: Vegard Kleven

P. 76   Fredrik Værslev.
Untitled, 2016–2018. House:
MDF, veneer (plywood), pine,
acrylic paint, acrylic spray
paint, acrylic transparent
varnish with UV-filter and
galvanised screws. Paintings:
spray paint, turpentine
on cotton canvas/wooden
stretcher, 35 × 202 × 62 cm.
Studio of Fredrik Værslev.
Courtesy of the artist.
Photo: Vegard Kleven

P. 77   Fredrik Værslev.
Untitled, 2016–2018. House:
MDF, veneer (plywood), pine,
acrylic paint, acrylic spray
paint, acrylic transparent
varnish with UV-filter and
galvanised screws. Paintings:
spray paint, turpentine on
cotton canvas/wooden
stretcher, 35 × 202 × 62 cm.
Studio of Fredrik Værslev.
Courtesy of the artist.
Photo: Vegard Kleven

P. 78   Fredrik Værslev.
Untitled, 2016–2018. House:
MDF, veneer (plywood), pine,
acrylic paint, acrylic spray
paint, acrylic transparent
varnish with UV-filter and
galvanised screws. Paintings:
spray paint, turpentine
on cotton canvas/wooden
stretcher, 35 × 202 × 62 cm.
Private collection.
Courtesy of the artist.
Photo: Vegard Kleven

P. 80   Fredrik Værslev.
Untitled, 2016. Acrylic paint,
spray paint, primer, and White
spirit on cotton canvas/
wooden stretcher, 300 × 207 ×
3 cm. Cecilie Malm Bruntland
and Knut Brundtland's collection. Courtesy of the artist and
STANDARD (OSLO), Oslo.
Photo: Vegard Kleven

P. 81   Fredrik Værslev.
Untitled, 2016. Acrylic paint,
spray paint, primer and
White spirit on cotton canvas/
wooden stretcher, 288 × 205 ×
3 cm. Equinor art programme.
Courtesy of the artist and
STANDARD (OSLO), Oslo.
Photo: Vegard Kleven

P. 82   Fredrik Værslev.
Untitled, 2017. Primer, spray
paint, acrylic, White spirit,
cotton canvas on wooden
stretcher, 299 × 200 × 4 cm.
Astrup Fearnley Collection.
Courtesy of the artist and
STANDARD (OSLO), Oslo.
Photo: Dawn Blackman

P.83   Fredrik Værslev.
Untitled, 2016. Primer, spray
paint, acrylic, White spirit,
cotton canvas on wooden
stretcher, 298 × 205 × 3 cm.
Astrup Fearnley Collection.
Courtesy of the artist and
STANDARD (OSLO), Oslo.

P.84   Fredrik Værslev.
Untitled, 2018. Primer, spray
paint, silkscreen acrylic paint
and White spirit on cotton
canvas, steel construction/
wooden stretcher, 210 × 145 ×
38 cm. Private collection.
Courtesy of the artist.
Photo: Vegard Kleven

P. 85   Fredrik Værslev.
Untitled, 2018. Primer, spray
paint, silkscreen acrylic paint
and White spirit on cotton
canvas, steel construction/
wooden stretcher, 210 × 145 ×
38 cm. Studio of Fredrik
Værslev. Courtesy of the artist.
Photo: Vegard Kleven

P.86   Fredrik Værslev.
Untitled, 2018. Primer, spray
paint, silkscreen acrylic paint
and White spirit on cotton
canvas, steel construction/
wooden stretcher, 210 × 145 ×
38 cm. Studio of Fredrik
Værslev. Courtesy of the artist.
Photo: Vegard Kleven

P. 87   Fredrik Værslev.
Untitled, 2018. Primer, spray
paint, silkscreen acrylic paint
and White spirit on cotton
canvas, steel construction/
wooden stretcher, 210 × 145 ×

38 cm. Studio of Fredrik
Værslev. Courtesy of the artist.
Photo: Vegard Kleven

P. 88   Fredrik Værslev.
Untitled, 2018. Primer, spray
paint, silkscreen acrylic paint
and White spirit on cotton
canvas, steel construction/
wooden stretcher, 210 × 145 ×
38 cm. Studio of Fredrik
Værslev. Courtesy of the artist.
Photo: Vegard Kleven

P. 89   Fredrik Værslev
Untitled, 2018. Primer, spray
paint, silkscreen acrylic paint
and White spirit on cotton
canvas, steel construction/
wooden stretcher, 210 × 145 ×
38 cm. Studio of Fredrik
Værslev. Courtesy of the artist.
Photo: Vegard Kleven

P. 90   Fredrik Værslev.
Untitled, 2018. Primer, spray
paint, silkscreen acrylic paint
and White spirit on cotton
canvas, steel construction/
wooden stretcher, 210 × 145 ×
38 cm. Studio of Fredrik
Værslev. Courtesy of the artist.
Photo: Vegard Kleven

P. 91   Fredrik Værslev.
Untitled, 2018. Primer, spray
paint, silkscreen acrylic paint
and White spirit on cotton
canvas, steel construction/
wooden stretcher, 210 × 145 ×
38 cm. Studio of Fredrik
Værslev. Courtesy of the artist.
Photo: Vegard Kleven

P. 92   Fredrik Værslev.
Untitled, 2018. Primer, spray
paint, silkscreen acrylic paint
and White spirit on cotton
canvas, steel construction/
wooden stretcher, 210 × 145 ×
38 cm. Studio of Fredrik
Værslev. Courtesy of the artist.
Photo: Vegard Kleven

P. 93   Fredrik Værslev.
Untitled, 2018. Primer, spray
paint, silkscreen acrylic paint
and White spirit on cotton
canvas, steel construction/
wooden stretcher, 210 × 145 ×
38 cm. Studio of Fredrik
Værslev. Courtesy of the artist.
Photo: Vegard Kleven

P. 94   Fredrik Værslev.
Untitled, 2012. Spray paint,
primer, and White spirit on
cotton canvas/wooden
stretcher, 92 × 338 × 3.5 cm.
Studio of Fredrik Værslev.
Photo: Vegard Kleven

This catalogue is published in conjunction with the exhibition *Fredrik Værslev – Fredrik Værslev as I Imagine Him*, 21.09.2018 – 06.01.2019

EXHIBITION
Curators: Gunnar B. Kvaran and Therese Möllenhoff
Registrar and exhibition coordinator: Patricia Tveter
Exhibition manager: Jens-Morten Dahl

CATALOGUE
Editor: Gunnar B. Kvaran
Managing editors: Nina Magnus and Renate Thorbjørnsen
Translation: Peter Cripps (Thorkildsen), Shari Gerber Nilsen (Möllenhoff)
Design: Zak Group
Print: Printmanagement Plitt GmbH
Edition: 2000
Cat. no.: 111

Astrup Fearnley Museet
Strandpromenaden 2
POB 2074 Vika
N-0125 Oslo, Norway.
Tel: +47 2293 6060
afmuseet.no

The museum is generously supported by the Foundation Thomas Fearnley, Heddy and Nils Astrup and the Foundation Hans Rasmus Astrup. The museum also receives contributions from the Ministry of Culture.

DISTRIBUTED BY
JRP|Ringier
Limmatstrasse 270
CH–8005 Zurich
jrp-ringier.com

ISBN: 978-3-03764-534-5

JRP|Ringier publications are available internationally at selected bookstores and from the following distribution partners:

Switzerland:
AVA Verlagsauslieferung AG
ava.ch

Germany and Austria:
Vice Versa Distribution GmbH
viceversaartbooks.com

France:
Les presses du reel
lespressesdureel.com

UK and other European countries:
Cornerhouse Publications, HOME
cornerhousepublications.org

USA, Canada, Asia, and Australia:
ARTBOOK | D.A.P.
artbook.com

For a list of our partner bookshops or for any general questions, please contact JRP|Ringier directly at info@jrp-ringier.com, or visit our homepage jrp-ringier.com for further information about our program.

THE ARTIST AND THE MUSEUM WISH TO THANK
Annie Rana Aberle, Matt Aberle, Peter Amdam, Kjell Andersen, Hans Rasmus Astrup, Tauba Auerbach, Andy Avini, Gilda Axelroud, Aya & Agnes, John Beeson, Nadia Bendriss, Johan Berggren, Etienne Bernard, Giovanna Bertoni, Leonardo Bigazzi, Glen Bjørnholt, Ina Blom, Jürgen Bock, Theresa Bovi, Per Christian Brath, Maren Brauner, Stafford Broumand, Knut Brundtland, Cecilie Malm Brundtland, Brundtland & Krosby, Kristin Elisabeth Bråthen, Bonnie Camplin, Emanuela Campoli, Giovanni Carmine, Nicolas Ceccaldi, Rony Chandra, Bernadette Christensen, Martin Clark, Collection Frank and Nina Moore, Alice Conconi, Michelle Cotton, Jens-Morten Dahl, Clément Dirié, Xavier Douroux, Adrienne Drake, Gardar Eide Einarsson, Ida Møller Engebretsen, Equinor art programme, Øyvind Eriksen, Jacob Fabricius, Matias Faldbakken, Jan-Kåre Fekene, Kelsey Finn, Alex Fitzgerald, Flexiprint, Morten Fredriksen, Eivind Furnesvik, Kristine Furuholmen, Thor Johan Furuholmen, Anita Gadelius, Frank Gautherot, Floriana Gavriel, Edouard Genton, Andrea Geyer, Gió Marconi Gallery Milano, Giovanni Giuliani, Renato Gnutti, Jan Groth, Stian Grøgaard, Didier Guyot, Dominique Guyot, Geraldine Guyot, Ida Sannes Hansen, Geir Haraldseth, Ellen Johanne Hartmann, Jansen Collection Berlin, Johan Berggren Gallery Malmö, Karina Johnsen, Mathilde Emilie Johnsen, Gabriella Jorio, Erling Kagge, Timo Kappeller, Ruba Katrib, Allison Katz, Martha Kirszenbaum, Vegard Kleven, Hans Henrik Kloumann, Carl Kostyal, Katharine Kostyal, Michael Krebber, Andrew Kreps, Andrew Kreps Gallery, Andrea Kroksnes, Gunnar B. Kvaran, Megan Lang, Maria Loen, Nina Magnus, Gió Marconi, Kyla McDonald, Pål Midtlid, Frank Moore, Nina Moore, Liz Mulholland, Therese Möllenhoff, Joar Nedberg, Eivind Nesterud, Lisa Overduin, Kathy Paciello, Eirik Pettersen, Alden Pinnell, Jannelle Pinnell, Anne Pontegnie, Gil Presti, Pavel Pys, Esther Quiroga, Laura Ravelli, Annett Reckert, Dan Rees, Jørn Riiser, Carlomar Rios, Dieter Roelstraete, Willem de Rooij, Espen Ryvarden, Arve Rød, Bjørn Rønneberg, Irene Saevik, Elham Salame, Tony Salame, Alberto Salvadori, Gertrud Sanqvist, Herb Schorr, Lenore Schorr, Schorr Family Collection, Steinar Sekkingstad, Bruce Sherman, Asgeir Skotnes, Nora Sissel Skreien, Mari Slaattelid, Josh Smith, Caroline Soyez-Petithomme, Standard (Oslo), Simon Starling, Abe Steinberger, Rune Stokke, Véronique Svarstad, Rob Teeters, Agnes-Maarja Tero, Renate Thorbjørnsen, Åsmund Thorkildsen, Giulia Tiraboschi, Eric Troncy, Patricia Tveter, Stewart Uoo, Øystein Ustvedt, Vingen Bar, Kasper Viskum, Morten Viskum, Ståle Vold, Wenche Volle, Anne Britt Værslev, Ethan Wagner, Thea Westreich, Axel Wieder, Betty Woodman, Mary Grace Wright, Sacha Zerbib, Eivind Aadland, Emma Aars and to all those lenders who wish to remain anonymous.

MUSEUM SPONSORS

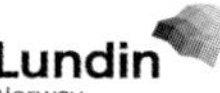 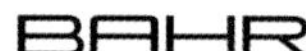

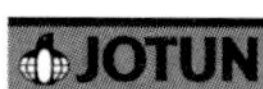

The exhibition and catalogue is sponsored by

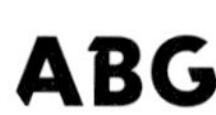 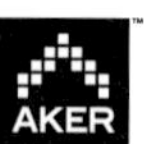